# AFGHANISTAN
# UNDER TALIBAN

# AFGHANISTAN UNDER TALIBAN

*Editor*

Vishal Chandra

MANOHAR PARRIKAR INSTITUTE FOR DEFENCE STUDIES AND ANALYSES

PENTAGON PRESS LLP

First published in 2025 by
PENTAGON PRESS LLP
206, Peacock Lane, Shahpur Jat
New Delhi-110049, India
Contact: 011-26490600

Typeset in Times New Roman, 11 Point
Printed by Aegean Offset Printers, Greater Noida

ISBN 978-81-988370-8-0

**Disclaimer:** The views expressed in the chapters of this book are those of the respective authors and do not necessarily reflect the views or opinions of the editors, the publisher, or the MP-IDSA, New Delhi associated with this publication. The editors and the MP-IDSA do not endorse or take responsibility for the accuracy, completeness, or legality of the content provided by the authors. Any errors, omissions, or misrepresentations in the individual papers are solely the responsibility of the author(s).

**www.pentagonpress.in**

# CONTENTS

# Acknowledgements

I am grateful to Amb Sujan R. Chinoy, Director General MP-IDSA; Gp Capt (Dr) Ajey Lele, Retd, Deputy Director General MP-IDSA; and my colleague Dr Ashok Behuria, Senior Fellow and Centre Coordinator South Asia, for their valuable support and guidance. I also owe gratitude to my senior colleague Dr Uttam Sinha for his warm encouragement during the finalisation of the volume.

I thank my colleague Mr Vivek Kaushik, Associate Editor MP-IDSA, for facilitating the copyediting and the publication process, and the Pentagon Press for publishing this volume in an efficient manner.

I must express my gratitude to the esteemed chapter contributors for their tremendous patience and cooperation without which it would not have been possible to finalise the edited volume for publication.

**Vishal Chandra**
*Editor*

# About the Contributors

**Dr Arian Sharifi** is an American-Afghan national security professional with two decades of high-level policy and academic experience. While serving in the former Afghan government, he advised the President and senior leaders on foreign and security affairs, led the development of over 20 national-level policies and strategies – including the National Security Policy and the Counter-terrorism Strategy – and implemented numerous operations, programmes, and projects in the security and intelligence sectors. Dr Sharifi has taught graduate school at Princeton University, conducted specialised research for major organisations, and advised leading institutions including the UN, NATO, the Global Initiative Against Transnational Organized Crime, Combating Terrorism Center at West Point, and others. He has published widely in academic and policy journals, and is a frequent commentator on strategic and security issues in Afghanistan, Pakistan, Iran and Central Asia.

**Mr Michael Kugelman** is a Washington-based South Asia analyst. He was Director of the South Asia Institute at the Wilson Center in Washington, DC from 2022 to 2025. He held the South Asia portfolio at the Wilson Center starting in 2007, and he managed its events, publications, and research on the region. He is also a columnist for *Foreign Policy* magazine and writes its *South Asia Brief*, a weekly newsletter of news and analysis on the region. His writing and views have also been featured by *The New York Times*, *The Washington Post*, *Wall Street Journal*, *Financial Times*, *CNN*, *BBC*, and major media outlets in India and around South Asia. His recent projects have focused on South Asia's shifting geopolitics, US–India tech cooperation, the future of US–Pakistan relations, and the role of strategy in the US-led war in Afghanistan.

**Mr Bruce Pannier** is the host of the Radio Free Europe/Radio Liberty's weekly *Majlis* podcast and author of *RFE/RL*'s weekly newsletter *Central Asia in Focus*. Prior to joining *RFE/RL* in 1997, Bruce worked at the Open

Media Research Institute in Prague. In 1992, he led a sociological project in Central Asia sponsored by the University of Manchester and the Soros Cultural Initiative Foundation. During that time he lived in villages in Kazakhstan, Kyrgyzstan, Turkmenistan and Uzbekistan. Mr Pannier studied at Tashkent State University in the summer of 1990 and studied at Columbia University under Professor Edward Allworth. He has also written for *The Economist*, *Janes Intelligence*, *Oxford Analytica*, Freedom House, *The Cairo Review*, *FSU Oil & Gas Monitor*, and *Energo Weekly*. Currently, Central Asia Fellow at the Foreign Policy Research Institute, member of the advisory board at the Caspian Policy Center, and member of the External Advisory Board, European Neighbourhood Council.

**Dr Akram Umarov** is Director, Institute for Advanced International Studies and Associate Professor, University of World Economy and Diplomacy (UWED), Tashkent. He has been a Fulbright Visiting Scholar at the Center for Governance and Markets, University of Pittsburgh. Previously, he was a Senior Research Fellow at the Institute for Strategic and Regional Studies and the Academy of Public Administration under the President of Uzbekistan. He has a PhD in International Relations from UWED, Tashkent and Master's in Governance, Development and Public Policy from the University of Sussex. Dr Umarov's research interests include security, conflict management and developments in Central Asia, Afghanistan, and the former Soviet space. He is the author of the monograph *Afghanistan and Regional Security of Central Asia: The Beginning of the XXI Century* (in Russian, 2017). His articles have appeared in *Asian Affairs*, *Central Asian Affairs*, *Asia and Africa*, *National Strategy Issues*, *Comparative Politics*, and other peer-reviewed journals.

**Dr Sherali Shukrullozoda Rizoyon**, PhD in Political Science, is a political analyst and independent researcher. He has worked at the Faculty of International Relations at the Tajik National University in Dushanbe (2019–2024) and at the Center for Strategic Studies under the President of the Republic of Tajikistan (2010–2019). He graduated in 2008 from the Faculty of Political Science and International Relations at the Tajik State University of Law, Business and Politics. Dr Rizoyon has over 150 publications to his credit, including two monographs. He has written extensively on Tajikistan's foreign policy, as well as on geopolitics and security in Central Asia and Afghanistan. His work has been published in both Tajik and foreign scientific and analytical publications.

**Mr Makhmud Faizulloevich Giyosov** serves on the Committee on Religion, Regulation of Traditions, Celebrations and Ceremonies under the Government of the Republic of Tajikistan. He earned his master's degree in

International Relations from the University of Tehran in 2004. He has published a monograph and over 30 articles in various Tajik and foreign scientific and analytical publications, He writes mainly on security and foreign policy issues, and developments in Afghanistan and the Middle East.

**Mr Mohsen Shariatinia** is an Assistant Professor of International Relations at the Shahid Beheshti University in Tehran. His research and teaching work are mainly focused on Iran's Asia policy and the evolving ties between East and West Asia. His research and analyses have appeared in peer-reviewed journals, as well as prestigious Persian and English outlets.

**Dr Hamed A. Kermani** has a PhD in International Relations. As an independent researcher, he mainly works on South-West Asia's relations and Iran's Asia policy. He has two books published in Persian, four peer-reviewed articles in Persian journals, as well as peer-reviewed book chapters for distinguished publishers such as *Routledge*.

**Dr Alexey Kupriyanov**, PhD in History, is Head of the Center of the Indo-Pacific Region, Primakov National Research Institute of World Economy and International Relations, Russian Academy of Sciences (IMEMO RAS). Born on 12 July 1979 in Moscow, Dr Kupriyanov studied Anglo-Saxon History at the Department of History of the Moscow City Teacher Training University and English Language and Literature in Ireland. He earned his Master's degree in International Relations (IR) after graduating from the Diplomatic Academy of the Ministry of Foreign Affairs of Russia. He has authored over 50 articles on international politics and military strategy. His research interests include the history and modernity of South, Southeast and East Asia; Indian external policy; Indo-Pacific region; Indo-Chinese relations; IR theory; and naval history and strategy.

**Prof Irina Zvyagelskaya**, Doctor of Science (History), is Head of the Center for the Middle East Studies at the Institute of World Economy and International Relations, Russian Academy of Sciences, Moscow. She is a corresponding member of the Russian Academy of Sciences. She was a Chief Research Fellow at the Institute of Oriental Studies. She had also been lecturing at the Moscow State Institute of International Relations under the Ministry of Foreign Affairs of Russia. Prof Zvyagelskaya's areas of expertise include contemporary history, conflicts, and international relations, and security issues in the Middle East and Central Asia. She has authored over 250 publications, including books, book chapters, and articles.

**Mr Ilya Zimin** is a Junior Fellow Researcher at Center for the Middle East Studies at the Primakov National Research Institute of World Economy and International Relations (IMEMO), Mosow. He graduated from the Institute of Asian and African Studies, Moscow State University. His research focuses on Afghanistan in international relations and its internal political processes.

**Amb Shamsher M. Chowdhury**, *Bir Bikram* is a former Bangladesh High Commissioner to Sri Lanka. He is a soldier turned diplomat and is a decorated freedom fighter. He was awarded the *Bir Bikram* by the state. A former Foreign Secretary, he has also served as ambassador to Germany, Vietnam, and the United States.

**Dr Mirwais Balkhi** is an adjunct professor in the Faculty of Political Science at James Madison University. He is also a non-resident scholar at Princeton University and the Wilson Center in Washington, DC. Previously, he was a visiting scholar at the School of Foreign Service, Georgetown University in Qatar. From 2018 to 2020, Dr Balkhi served as the Minister of Education in the Islamic Republic of Afghanistan, following his tenure as Deputy Ambassador to India. He has held academic positions at numerous institutions, including the American University of Afghanistan (AUAF), Kabul University, the Afghanistan Institute of Higher Education, and other Afghan universities. Between 2020 and 2022, he directed the Research Center at Afghanistan University. Dr Balkhi earned his PhD in International Relations from Jawaharlal Nehru University, New Delhi, specialising in West Asian politics. He is the author of several academic publications, in both English and Persian, and his scholarship bridges diplomacy, nation-state building, education policy, and regional studies.

**Ms Bilquees Daud** is an Assistant Professor at the Jindal School of International Affairs, OP Jindal Global University, India. She holds a graduate degree in social sciences from the American University of Afghanistan (AUAF), Kabul and a master's degree in public policy from the Willy Brandt School of Public Policy, University of Erfurt, Germany. She has worked extensively with local and international organisations, universities, and research centres in Afghanistan and abroad. Ms Daud has authored several research and analytical articles published by different sources, including Project for Democratic Union, *BBC Pashto*, ACKU Journal, and the *IIC Quarterly*. She has recently published a book on *Education for Peace: Rehabilitating Non-Violent Discourses in Afghanistan*. Her research interests include religious extremism, non-violent movements, the social impact of conflicts, peace education, politics of identity, and refugee crisis.

**Mr Shreyas D. Deshmukh** is a Research Associate with the National Security Programme of the Delhi Policy Group (DPG), a think tank based in New Delhi, India. Before joining DPG, he worked as a geopolitical risk analyst with MitKat Advisory Services and as a research assistant with the Centre for Land Warfare Studies (CLAWS), New Delhi. He holds a master's in Defence and Strategic Studies from the University of Pune, India. His work experience spans subjects, including geopolitical developments, traditional and non-traditional security, and socio-political stability in the South and Central Asian region.

**Mr Mahendra Ved** is a Delhi-based columnist and media educator. He is President Emeritus, Commonwealth Journalists Association (CJA), New Delhi. He worked for the *United News of India (UNI)*, *Hindustan Times* and *The Times of India* before turning freelance. In association with late Sreedhar of IDSA, he co-wrote three books on Afghanistan during 1997–2001. Of the three, *Afghan Buzkashi: Power Games and Gamesmen* (Wordsmiths, Delhi, 2001) was released by late K. Subrahmanyam with participation by late J.N. Dixit. He has also contributed chapters in books on Afghanistan and Pakistan edited by late Sreedharfor the Indian Council of World Affairs (ICWA) and for independent publishers. As war correspondent, Mr Ved reported the India–Pakistan conflict of 1971 from the Sindh–Rajasthan theatre. Posted to Bangladesh, he reported the events of August 1975. He was also columnist for the *New Straits Times* of Malaysia (2005–2018).

**Dr Ashok Behuria** is a Senior Fellow and Coordinator of the South Asia Centre at MP-IDSA. He has a PhD in International Relations from the Jawaharlal Nehru University (JNU), New Delhi. Before joining MP-IDSA he worked as Assistant Director at the International Centre for Peace Studies (ICPS), New Delhi. He has been the Editor of *International Studies*, the prestigious research journal from JNU. He has long been associated with the editorial boards of the *Journal of Peace Studies* (ICPS) and *Strategic Analysis*, the flagship journal of MP-IDSA. He has taught at the University of Delhi and Jamia Millia Islamia, New Delhi. Dr Behuria was awarded the prestigious K. Subrahmanyam Award for excellence in strategic studies for his work on Pakistan in 2009. He continues with his research on India's engagement with the neighbourhood, regional security, and inter-state cooperation. His latest book is on *Tehrik-e-Taliban Pakistan: Origin, Evolution & Future Portents*.

**Dr Ajay Darshan Behera** is a Professor at the MMAJ Academy of International Studies, Jamia Millia Islamia, New Delhi. His primary areas of research interest are IR theory, foreign policy and security issues in South Asia. He previously held the positions of Assistant Research Professor, Centre for Policy Research (CPR), New Delhi and Fellow, Institute for Defence Studies and Analyses (IDSA), New Delhi. He was the recipient of the 1996 Kodikara Fellowship awarded by Regional Centre for Strategic Studies, Colombo. He has also been a Visiting Fellow at the Brookings Institution, Washington, DC (October 2001–June 2002) and at the University of Illinois Urbana-Champaign (September 1997–January 1998). He is the author of the book *Violence, Terrorism and Human Security in South Asia* and the monograph *The Politics of Violence and Development in South Asia*. He has co-edited *Pakistan in a Changing Strategic Context*. He is currently the Domain Editor South Asia for the journal *Security Challenges* (Australia).

**Mr Vishal Chandra** studies Afghanistan at Manohar Parrikar IDSA, New Delhi. He joined MP-IDSA in 2003 and is currently a Research Fellow with the South Asia Centre of the Institute. He has travelled in Afghanistan and has participated in various national and international academic forums. He has delivered talks & lectures on Afghanistan at India's leading training academies and institutes. He is the author of the monograph, *Afghans in Need: Positing India's Continued Engagement with Afghanistan*, MP-IDSA, October 2024; and the book, *The Unfinished War in Afghanistan: 2001–2014*, IDSA, Pentagon Press, New Delhi, 2015. He has recently authored an Occasional Paper, *Taliban's "Contact Commission": Three Years Later*, MP-IDSA, July 2025; and a Special Feature, *The Why and What of Non-Inclusivity and Dissensus in the Taliban 'Emirate,'* MP-IDSA, November 2024. Mr Chandra also had a decade long editorial stint with the Institute's website, including as the Editor Website from 2019 to 2022.

# List of Abbreviations

| | |
|---|---|
| ADB | Asian Development Bank |
| AIHRC | Afghanistan Independent Human Rights Commission |
| ANASTU | Afghanistan National Agricultural Sciences and Technology University |
| AQIS | Al Qaeda in the Indian Sub-continent |
| BRI | Belt and Road Initiative |
| CAREC | Central Asia Regional Economic Cooperation |
| CASA | Central Asia–South Asia |
| CIS | Commonwealth of Independent States |
| CPEC | China–Pakistan Economic Corridor |
| CSTO | Collective Security Treaty Organization |
| EEU | Eurasian Economic Union |
| ETIM | East Turkestan Islamic Movement |
| ICCR | Indian Council for Cultural Relations |
| IGICH | Indira Gandhi Institute of Child Health, Kabul |
| IMT | Islamic Movement of Turkistan |
| IMU | Islamic Movement of Uzbekistan |
| INSTC | International North–South Transport Corridor |
| IPGL | India Ports Global Limited |
| ISI | Inter-Services Intelligence, Pakistan |
| ISIL | Islamic State in Iraq and Levant |
| IS–K | Islamic State–Khorasan |
| ISKP | Islamic State Khorasan Province |
| ITEC | Indian Technical and Economic Cooperation |
| JA | Jamaat Ansarullah |
| JeM | Jaish-e-Mohammad |
| LeT | Lashkar-e-Taiba |

| | |
|---|---|
| MEA | Ministry of External Affairs, India |
| MoE | Ministry of Education, Afghanistan |
| MoWA | Ministry of Women's Affairs, Afghanistan |
| NATO | North Atlantic Treaty Organization |
| NGOs | Non-Governmental Organisations |
| NRF | National Resistance Front |
| PTM | Pashtun Tahafuz Movement |
| SAARC | South Asian Association for Regional Cooperation |
| SCO | Shanghai Cooperation Organisation |
| SIV | Special Immigrant Visa |
| TAPI | Turkmenistan–Afghanistan–Pakistan–India |
| TIP | Turkestan Islamic Party |
| TTP | Tehrik-e-Taliban Pakistan |
| TTT | Tehrik-e Taliban Tajikistan |
| UAE | United Arab Emirates |
| UN | United Nations |
| UNSC | United Nations Security Council |
| US | United States |
| UTO | United Tajik Opposition |

# List of Tables, Maps, Graphs, and Images

# Introduction

It is an irony that Afghanistan is less violent after the Taliban returned to power in Kabul and yet peace and development continues to elude its people. The ultra-orthodox Islamic State–Khorasan Province (IS–KP) continues to pose a potent threat to regional security. Even as the Taliban fight the IS–KP to maintain order to prove that they are in control, their ability to run the statecraft in a wholesome manner is clearly in question. Women and ethnic minorities are visibly excluded from the structures of governance. The economy is fragile and one of worst humanitarian crises is staring the country in the face as over two million Afghans have returned from Pakistan, Iran, and other countries. Even as the neighbours of Afghanistan increasingly engage the Taliban regime—politically and economically—they remain as worried as they were earlier about the possible spread of Islamist radicalism in the central-southern Asian region.

The ongoing humanitarian crisis in Afghanistan has forced the international community to stay engaged with the Taliban regime even as they flout their own commitments on inclusive governance and women and minority rights. The Taliban cabinet is remarkably all-Taliban and overwhelmingly Pashtun, while the non-Pashtuns remain unrepresented at the highest level. There is neither any promise nor any show of urgency by the Taliban to correct the anomaly. Women have been flushed out of the administrative structure and girls' education is in a state of suspended animation. However, the Taliban appear to be less ruthless in their behaviour while executing their policies on minorities and women than they were during their earlier avatar. The Taliban have learnt how to pursue their conservative agenda, without provoking the conscience of the international community by operating below its tolerance threshold.

The Taliban remain deeply critical of the US and the West for not funding the process of reconstruction and hold them responsible for the deepening humanitarian crisis. The Ukraine War has had its debilitating effect on food supply and its adverse impact on global economy has come down to haunt states with poor financial structures like Afghanistan most severely.

In these circumstances, the broader international community have found it problematic to upscale their funding to enable the Taliban to meet the crisis at hand. There is a genuine fear that this might strengthen the hands of the Taliban and lead to further hardening of their stance on issues that have direct repercussions on women and minority rights. For them, quite demonstrably so, the Taliban are known for making false promises and helping them tide over the economic crisis would only add to their stature and stubbornness.

MP-IDSA's South Asia Centre has been closely following the developing situation in Afghanistan. It had organised a conference in virtual mode as early as in December 2021 to discuss the possible implications of the return of the Taliban to power Afghanistan. Some of the scholars and analysts who were invited to the virtual conference to share their perspectives on the theme later agreed to contribute papers for an edited volume on Afghanistan under Taliban. To expand the scope of the volume, more scholars and experts from the wider region were subsequently approached. The papers received have gone through several reiterations in the course of time and have been updated by most of the authors until early 2025. It is important to state that amidst the recent developments in West Asia (or the Middle East), the edited volume retains the focus on the situation in Afghanistan.

The edited volume comprises 16 chapters contributed by Afghan, Central Asian, Iranian, Russian, Western, and Indian scholars and analysts. The chapters not only dwell on country perspectives but also key issues of concern to the people of Afghanistan and the wider region. It includes terrorism, transnational crime, drug production and distribution, the governance system and the state of education in Afghanistan. The contributions in the volume paint an unflattering view of the ground reality in Afghanistan, and a connecting thread of pessimism runs through various analyses.

The primary backers of the Taliban had not recognised the Taliban regime in Kabul until early this year. Russia finally broke the ranks in July to accord recognition to the Taliban government. There is an overwhelming consensus nevertheless that the Taliban would have to at least demonstrate their sincerity about fulfilling their international commitments without which their government would not be considered for wider formal recognition.

Unfortunately, the Taliban have gone ahead with their plans to impose an ultra-orthodox version of Islamic laws, per their interpretation, that militates against gender rights, modern education, and have excluded the minority ethnicities from the governing structures. Four years into power, the Taliban governing structures remain notably Taliban-only and overwhelmingly Pashtun-centric. Such inflexibility on their part coupled with the ambivalence of the international community to invest in Afghan re-reconstruction, which could bolster up the morale of the Taliban hardliners, characterise the unfolding strategic scenario in Afghanistan.

This edited volume will help the interested readers in deciphering the evolving regional dynamics and the strategic games that will be played in Afghanistan in the coming times.

**Vishal Chandra**
*Editor*

# 1

# Afghanistan at a Crossroads: Inclusive Government or Endless Turmoil?

*Arian Sharifi*

## Introduction

Almost four years into Taliban rule, Afghanistan faces an increasingly uncertain future. The Taliban continue to enforce a rigid theocracy, silencing opposition, restricting civil liberties, and denying women access to education and public life. Meanwhile, the economy is shrinking, unemployment is soaring, poverty is worsening, and the country remains in total diplomatic isolation. Struggling with growing internal divisions, the Taliban seem oblivious to the presence of foreign terrorist organisations, expanding organised crime networks, and emerging military opposition groups that could pose a serious future challenge. Despite these challenges, however, there are some positive developments that could mark the first steps toward steering Afghanistan in the right direction: the war has ended, the security situation has significantly improved, and opium cultivation has dropped by an unprecedented 90 percent. Most warlords have been subdued, corruption has declined, and state control has been reestablished over the entire country for the first time in nearly half a century.

The Taliban face a critical choice: they can build on recent positive developments to guide Afghanistan toward lasting peace, stability, and prosperity, or they can persist with their current approach, pushing the country into a new phase of war, bloodshed, and foreign interference, leading not only to a potential disintegration of Afghanistan, but also posing a serious threat to the region and beyond. What is certain is that the *status quo* is unsustainable. To avert further crisis, the Taliban must act swiftly to implement sweeping reforms, leading to the establishment of a constitutional government that ensures meaningful political inclusion and guarantees the fundamental rights of all Afghan men and women. Such reforms would bolster domestic legitimacy, open the door to international recognition, and lay the groundwork for economic recovery and development. If they fail to seize this opportunity, Afghanistan risks descending into another cycle of violence and becoming an epicenter for global terrorism and transnational organised crime.

This chapter explores four key trends that, if left unaddressed, could push Afghanistan into renewed conflict and instability with grave implications for the security and stability of the region and beyond. These include: internal divisions within the Taliban, presence of regional and global terrorist groups, rise of anti-Taliban resistance, and expansion of illicit economy and drug smuggling. A brief threat assessment follows the analysis of each of these factors. The chapter concludes with a brief discussion on the steps needed to avert these risks and give Afghanistan a chance to recover and rejuvenate, setting it on a path toward lasting stability.

## A. INTERNAL DIVISIONS WITHIN THE TALIBAN

At present, four major fault lines exist within the Taliban, which continue to widen rifts within the movement:

1. *Tribal Division*: The historical power politics between the two main Pashtun tribes—Durrani and Ghilzai—is manifesting within the Taliban, creating a serious rift in the movement.[1] While the rivalry between the Durrani and Ghilzai Taliban existed from the outset, the contest was substantially exacerbated after their return to power.[2] Sources in Kabul report that problems on this grid have become severe and have caused political discontent and some violent skirmishes between the two.[3] Given its historical roots, the Durrani–Ghilzai rivalries within the Taliban feed into other rifts, fueling political incoherence, potential structural disintegration, and even violent conflict.
2. *Factional Fragmentation*: Related to the tribal rivalry within the Taliban is the structural rift between the Quetta Shura and the Haqqani Network—the two main factions within the movement. The Haqqani Network predates the Taliban movement by at least two decades, and while it joined the Taliban in the early months of the movement's conception in the mid-1990s, the Haqqanis maintained their *de facto* autonomy and their main power base in eastern Afghanistan.[4] Now in the seat of power, both the factions are attempting to gain key positions in the government. The Quetta

Shura Taliban, being the founders and the majority, hold the largest share of power,[5] while the Haqqanis claim they deserve more, given they had led some of the most daring attacks against Western and Afghan forces, including some of the most gruesome suicide missions during the two-decade war.[6]

3. *Ideological Fragmentation*: The stark disagreements between the hardliners and more pragmatic Taliban leaders further intensify the rifts within the Taliban movement. Figures such as supreme leader Mullah Haibatullah Akhundzada, Mullah Mohammad Hassan, Qayoom Zakir, Sadr Ibrahim, Mullah Tajmir Jawad, and others are hardliners. They believe that the Taliban must maintain their loyalty to their strict ideological roots, excluding all non-Taliban political figures from the government, and implement puritanical laws and regulations.[7] On the other hand, individuals like Mullah Abdul Ghani Baradar, Sirajuddin Haqqani, Mullah Amir Khan Muttaqi, Sher Mohammad Abbas Stanikzai, and some others within the leadership, take a more pragmatic approach.[8] They advocate for inclusion in the government structure and moderation in policy, arguing that both would help in gaining domestic legitimacy and foreign recognition. This difference of opinion has created a major rift within the Taliban leadership.
4. *Structural Fragmentation:* The final crack within the Taliban movement is due to the differences of opinion between the leadership and some mid-level commanders. For years, the nucleus of the Taliban's war machine has been the *Delgais*—units of 70 to 90 fighters led by a *Delgai Meshr* or commander.[9] While under the overall command of the top leadership, the *Delgai Meshrs* have always enjoyed great autonomy in combat decisions at the operational and tactical levels and have had direct operational relations with foreign terrorist groups.[10] Since the Taliban took power over three years ago, there has emerged a rift between the commanders and the movement's leadership. The commanders claim that they have borne the real burden of the war for years, that the leadership is spoiled with luxurious lifestyles, and that the leadership is abandoning the mission of a "global jihad" since they took power in Afghanistan.[11] This has resulted in occasional disobedience of orders and directives issued by the top leadership. To bring the *Delgais* under control, the Taliban leaders tried to dismantle the movement's structure and integrate the *Delgais* into the formal structures of the ministries of defence and interior affairs. To their dismay, however, the *Delgai* commanders are said to have

openly refused such integration and vowed to remain intact in their old structures.[12]

**Threat Assessment:** The implications of the Taliban's fragmentation can be manifold for Afghanistan and the wider region. At least four potential threats can be assessed as a result of the Taliban's weakening cohesion:

(a) *Political Instability*: Fragmentation within the Taliban movement can lead to further political instability within Afghanistan, creating a more conducive environment for radicalism, terrorism, and organised crime. Given the trans-border nature of these activities, spillover effects into the region and beyond can be confidently predicted.

(b) *Armed Conflict*: Disintegration entails strong potential for armed clashes within the different factions, which can in turn exacerbate socio-economic problems, leading to both increased outward migration and spillover of violence into the region and beyond. Further, violent conflict might cause widespread killing and the death of innocent people, war crimes, and large-scale human rights violations, which could eventually compel the international community to intervene.

(c) *Unclear Lines of Communication*: While no country has recognised the Taliban as the government of Afghanistan, many currently communicate with them as the *de facto* authorities. Maintaining such communication is important for carrying out humanitarian operations and dealing with emergency political and security issues. Fragmentation within the Taliban eliminates a single address with which the international community can communicate, leading to confusion, uncertainty, and unpredictability. In such a situation, the international community would not be able to hold anyone accountable for any action, virtually causing a situation of chaos and instability.

(d) *Favourable Environment for Foreign Terrorists*: Fragmentation within the Taliban makes the environment more conducive for foreign terrorist groups, as they can play one faction against another to their benefit. Factions could have special relations with foreign terrorist groups without other factions' knowledge and without the possibility of being held accountable by the international community. The presence and killing of al-Qaeda leader Ayman al-Zawahiri is one example of this, as some observers, including Zalmay Khalilzad, the former US Special Envoy for Afghanistan, suggest that only some Taliban may have known about Zawahiri's presence in Kabul.[13]

## B. PRESENCE OF REGIONAL AND GLOBAL TERRORIST GROUPS

According to sources, many groups, including Pakistani, Central Asian, Chinese, and Arabare present in Afghanistan.[14] According to the UN Security Council, the largest group is believed to be the Tehrik-e-Taliban Pakistan (TTP) with upwards of 6,500 fighters in the country, allegedly using Afghanistan's territory to plan, stage, and conduct attacks in Pakistan.[15] Besides TTP, other groups, including the Chinese Turkistan Islamic Party (TIP), Islamic Movement of Uzbekistan (IMU), Tajikistani Jamaat-e-Ansarullah, and Khatiba-e-Imam Bukhari, are believed to be present in Afghanistan. While their numbers are hard to pinpoint, these groups aim to use the Afghan territory to train and then infiltrate Central Asia, China, and Russia to conduct attacks.[16]

Al-Qaida seems to remain consistently present in Afghanistan, primarily focusing on advising, training, and relation-building with other terrorist groups.[17] Despite keeping a low profile, the group is believed to continue to disseminate propaganda to bolster recruitment and gradually rebuild its operational capacity. While its ability to conduct large-scale attacks remains limited, but its intent remains strong, reinforced by the capabilities of its affiliates to carry out external operations. The Taliban deny al-Qaeda's existence in Afghanistan, stating that there might be a handful of old al-Qaeda members in the country who live normal lives and are under strict surveillance and control by the Taliban.[18]

The Islamic State Khorasan Province (ISKP), meanwhile, continues to show resilience in the face of heightened Taliban offensives. Since coming to power about four years ago, the Taliban have managed to significantly weaken ISKP, clearing all territory, including its strongholds in eastern Afghanistan.[19] As such, ISKP's leadership, including its leader Sanaullah Ghaffari, is believed to have moved to the Baluchistan area of Pakistan while the group operates underground cells in Afghanistan.[20] Using these cells, ISKP has managed conduct high profile attacks against the Taliban, including the killing of the Acting Minister of Refugees, Khalil Haqqani, in December 2024.[21] In 2024, ISKP also conducted many attacks in the broader region, including the Kerman double suicide bombing in Iran, as well as the Crocus City Hall attack in Moscow, both of which were believed to have links to ISKP's presence in Afghanistan.[22]

**Threat Assessment:** The composition of the foreign terrorist groups in Afghanistan signifies the wide range of threats they pose to the country, the region and beyond. These groups have intended to conduct terrorist attacks on the world stage and are now assembling people to use the Afghan territory as a haven. Given the geographical proximity, countries in the region, including the Central Asian states, China, Russia, and India, could become the first destinations for targets, followed by Europe and North America. Threats could be posed in at least five ways:

(a) *Coordinated Member Attacks*: Terrorist groups could plan, stage, coordinate, and conduct attacks across the world, using the Afghan territory as a haven, and utilising all resources that are now at their disposal—training grounds, volunteers, financial resources, access to weapons and explosives, means of communication, and others. These attacks would be carried out by group members, planned and facilitated by groups from inside Afghanistan and their cells worldwide.

(b) *Lone Conspirator Attacks*: Terrorist groups from inside Afghanistan could facilitate the preparation of attacks carried out single-handedly by lone individuals affiliated with the groups worldwide. Facilitation of the precursor activities—preparation of needed funds, weapons and explosives, selection and surveillance of targets, know-how and knowledge of attacks, and others—is a critical component of terrorism. Without safe havens and resources from terrorist groups at terrorist groups' disposal, conducting these activities is extremely difficult for lone actors.

(c) *Affiliated Loner Attacks*: Terrorist groups with footing in Afghanistan can send their affiliated members to various target destinations with general ideas of attacks, and who would then plan, stage, and conduct operations on their own without receiving any further assistance from the groups. Such attacks are difficult to predict and prevent, since individual attackers often act on their own without much or any communication with their groups. Again, the existence of groups in safe havens is critical for these lone actors' identification, recruitment, radicalisation, and motivation.

(d) *Lone Wolf Attacks*: Terrorist groups in Afghanistan can inspire individuals who, without any affiliation or communication with any terrorist group, would plan, stage, and conduct terrorist attacks worldwide.

## C. RISE OF ANTI-TALIBAN RESISTANCE

Armed resistance against the Taliban is on the rise, albeit in nascent state. So far, at least 14 armed groups, including the National Resistance Front, Afghanistan Freedom Front, Supreme Resistance Council, Freedom Uprising, and others, have sprung up, with many of them claim to conduct military operations against the Taliban in various parts of the country.[23] While these groups are small now, they could conceivably morph into a large, serious resistance movement against the Taliban. This is because all the ingredients needed for the emergence of a formidable resistance against the Taliban are present: grievances are rising, given the Taliban's disregard for people's rights and values; individuals willing to fight are in abundance; the country is overrun with weapons and ammunitions, and sponsorships for proxies have never been in shortage in Afghanistan.

**Threat Assessment:** While the emergence of anti-Taliban armed resistance could be used as a pressure point against the Taliban to soften their stances on political and social rights, the exacerbation of armed conflict in Afghanistan does not serve the interest of the region and the world. It would lead to further instability and violence in Afghanistan, which would not only lead to the killing of innocent people and further destruction of Afghanistan, but it could also have spillover effects in the region, trigger even larger waves of migration, and further facilitate the transnational organised criminal activities, particularly boosting the drug industry.

## D. EXPANSION OF ILLICIT ECONOMY AND DRUG SMUGGLING

There has traditionally been a symbiotic relationship between transnational terrorism and transnational organised crime, each feeding the other. At least seven types of transnational organised criminal activity are present in Afghanistan, threatening the security of the country, the region, and the world. These include the narcotics trade, cannabis trade, arms smuggling, illicit mining, human trafficking, human smuggling, flora crimes, and fauna crimes.[24] Sources interviewed by the author confirmed that narcotics, illicit mining, and illicit logging are instrumental in providing financial resources for many of the terrorist groups in Afghanistan, including ISKP.[25] While the Taliban's ban on opium cultivation has drastically decreased production, a decrease in supply has led to a seven-fold increase in prices, driving the profit from the industry to unprecedented highs.[26] Illicit mining and logging are also said to have greatly increased since the Taliban's takeover, as 'they have abandoned the lengthy bidding and contracting procedures of the previous government, and handle the sale of these resources as if they personally owned them'.[27]

The Taliban vowed to disrupt all illicit economic activities, including the drug industry[28] and illegal mining and logging, to project the image of a strong national government domestically and a responsible state internationally. However, these activities provide livelihood for a large number of the rural Afghan population, as well as powerful strongmen whose support the Taliban urgently needs. Any move to disrupt these activities would anger large swaths of the population, offend powerful tribal leaders, undercut major support for the Taliban government, and deny the Taliban the badly needed sources of income. As a result, the Taliban seem to have allowed and taxed the opium production and trade in the south, joined forces with warlords that run the illicit mineral extraction in the north, and turned a blind eye to illicit logging by tribes in the east.[29] Some of the proceeds from these illicit economies return to Afghanistan, but most outflows into the region and the world, particularly Pakistan, Turkey, and the United Arab Emirates, for investment.[30]

**Threat Assessment:** Given the transnational nature of organised criminal activities and their close ties to transnational terrorism, their spread and persistence have a global impact. Drug flows from Afghanistan into Pakistan, Iran, Central Asian states, China, Russia, Turkey, and Europe are on the rise, including heroin, opium, methamphetamine, and cannabis, among others. In addition to these drugs, other illicit activities such as illegal mining, logging, and the smuggling of small arms and light weapons continue to thrive in the unstable environment in Afghanistan. Since illicit goods often require wealthy consumers, Central Asia, the Gulf, and Europe have become primary destinations for many of these products, with European markets particularly sought after due to their large consumer base with disposable income. While Europe has been a significant destination for such goods for decades, the sharp increase in production and the ease of smuggling following the Taliban's return to power have exacerbated this trend. The negative consequences for the region are far-reaching, ranging from public health and security issues to crime, instability, erosion of legal order, and widespread human rights violations.

## Conclusion

An Afghanistan ruled exclusively by the Taliban under a rigid theocracy not only risks plunging the country into a new phase of violence and instability but also poses a significant threat to regional and global security. This danger is already materialising, as foreign terrorist groups and transnational criminal organisations with networks spanning the region, Europe, and North America concentrate within Afghanistan. While countering some of these groups' activities beyond Afghanistan's borders may provide short-term relief, a lasting solution requires the establishment of an inclusive government—one that reflects the will of the Afghan people, engages with the international community, denies safe havens and resources to terrorist groups, disrupts illicit economic activities, and remains accountable to global standards.

However, achieving such a transformation is no simple task. The Taliban, having seized power following the collapse of the Republic, feel entitled to their rule. Hardline factions within the movement believe they can sustain their exclusionary governance, enforce puritanical policies, and continue harbouring extremist groups committed to global jihad. In contrast, more pragmatic elements within the Taliban leadership recognise that maintaining the status quo may neither be feasible nor desirable. They acknowledge the need for change and the establishment of a more inclusive political framework.

The international community has a critical role in shaping the outcome in favour of moderation and inclusivity. To ensure that pragmatic voices within the Taliban prevail, global and regional actors must engage with and empower Taliban leaders who advocate for reform, apply diplomatic pressure on hardliners, and support responsible, educated Afghan political figures in exile. By facilitating the formation of a strong political platform, these efforts can help bridge the gap between the Taliban and the international community, paving the way for the creation of a legitimate, inclusive government in Afghanistan.

## NOTES

1. For a more in-depth discussion, see Bernt Glatzer, 'The Pashtun Tribal System', in Georg Pfeffer and Deepak Kumar Behera (eds.), *The Concept of Tribal Society*, Contemporary Society: Tribal Studies, Vol. 5, Concept Publishing Company, New Delhi, 2002, pp. 265–282, at https://www.nps.edu/documents/105988371/107571254/glatzer_ pashtun_tribal_ system.pdf/b0004d32-a1c2-4ade-94b5-a0d54d1b08b9 (Accessed 6 March 2025).
2. Ron Synovitz, 'Will the Taliban Stay United to Govern, or Splinter into Regional Fiefdoms?', *Radio Free Europe/Radio Liberty*, 25 August 2021, at https://www.rferl.org/a/taliban-govern-regional-factions/31428069.html (Accessed 6 March 2025).
3. Virtual interview with a former Senior Advisor at the Office of National Security Council, 25 July 2022.
4. Jeff M. Smith, 'The Haqqani Network: The New Kingmakers in Kabul', *War on the Rocks*, 12 November 2021, at https://warontherocks.com/2021/11/the-haqqani-network-afghanistans-new-power-players/ (Accessed 6 March 2025).
5. Virtual interview with a former Senior Advisor at the Office of National Security Council, 25 July 2022.
6. Marvin G. Weinbaum and Meher Babbar, 'The Tenacious, Toxic Haqqani Network', MEI Policy Focus, 2016-23, Middle East Institute, September 2016, at https://www.mei.edu/sites/default/files/publications/PF23_WeinbaumBabbar_Haqqani_web_0.pdf (Accessed 6 March 2025).

7. Virtual interviews with a former Deputy Minister of Interior Affairs, a former Director General at the Ministry of Interior Affairs, and a former National Directorate of Security operative, on 26 July 2022, 1 August 2022, and 5 August 2022, respectively.
8. Ibid.
9. Virtual interview with General Helaluddeen Helal, former Deputy Minister of Interior Affairs and former Deputy Minister of Defence, 24 August 2022.
10. Ibid.
11. Ibid.
12. Ibid.
13. 'Ambassador Zalmay Khalilzad on Ayman al-Zawahiri', NPR, 2 August 2022, at https://www.npr.org/2022/08/02/1115266990/ambassador-zalmay-khalilzad-on-ayman-al-zawahiri (Accessed 7 March 2025).
14. Virtual interviews with a former Deputy Minister of Interior Affairs, a former Director General at the Ministry of Interior Affairs, and a former National Directorate of Security operative, on 26 July 2022, 1 August 2022, and 5 August 2022, respectively.
15. 'Fifteenth Report of the Analytical Support and Sanctions Monitoring Team Submitted Pursuant to Resolution 2716 (2023) Concerning the Taliban and Other Associated Individuals and Entities Constituting a Threat to the Peace, Stability and Securityof Afghanistan', United Nations, 18 July 2024, at https://docs.un.org/en/S/2024/499 (Accessed 8 March 2025).
16. Ibid.
17. Virtual interview with a former National Directorate of Security operative, 28 July 2024.
18. Virtual interview with a member of the Taliban, 20 February 2025.
19. Virtual interview with a former National Directorate of Security operative, 20 February 2025.
20. Ibid.
21. Simon Fraser and Caroline Davies, 'Suicide Bomb Kills Taliban Minister in Kabul', *BBC News*, 12 December 2024, at https://www.bbc.com/news/articles/cvg952q81x8o (Accessed 8 March 2025).
22. Amira Jadoon, Abdul Sayed, et al., 'From Tajikistan to Moscow and Iran: Mapping the Local and Transnational Threat of Islamic State Khorasan', *CTC Sentinel*, Combating Terrorism Center at West Point, Vol. 17, Issue 5, May 2024, at https://ctc.westpoint.edu/from-tajikistan-to-moscow-and-iran-mapping-the-local-and-transnational-threat-of-islamic-state-khorasan/ (Accessed 8 March 2025).
23. 'انفوگرافیکگروههایضدطالباندرافغانستان' [Infographic: Anti-Taliban Groups in Afghanistan], *Islamic World News*, 14 July 2022, at https://iswnews.com/68640/اینفوگرافیک-گروههای-□د-طالبان-در-اف/ (Accessed 8 March 2025). In Persian.
24. Mark Shaw and Marcena Hunter, *Illicit Economies in Afghanistan and Pakistan: Shifting Political Economies and Regional Dynamics*, Royal United Services Institute Europe, October 2021, at https://illicitflows.eu/illicit-economies-in-afghanistan-and-pakistan-shifting-political-economies-and-regional-dynamics/ (Accessed 26August 2022).
25. Virtual interviews with a former Deputy Minister of Interior Affairs and a former Director General at the Ministry of Interior Affairs, on 1 August 2022 and 5 August 2022, respectively.

26. United Nations Office on Drugs and Crime, *Afghanistan Drug Insights Volume 1: Opium Poppy Cultivation 2024*, November 2024, at https://www.unodc.org/documents/crop-monitoring/Afghanistan/Afghanistan_Drug_Insights_V1.pdf (Accessed 8 March 2025).
27. Virtual interview with a former Director General at the Ministry of Finance, 2 September 2022.
28. Niko Vorobyov, 'The Taliban Plans to Ban Drugs in Afghanistan. That Could Change the World for the Worse', *Independent*, 19 August 2021, at https://www.independent.co.uk/voices/taliban-afghanistan-drugs-heroin-ban-b1905589.html (Accessed 9 March 2025).
29. Virtual interviews with a former Deputy Minister of Interior Affairs and a former Director General at the Ministry of Interior Affairs, on 1 August 2022 and 5 August 2022, respectively.
30. Jessica Davis, 'Illicit Financing in Afghanistan: Methods, Mechanisms, and Threat-agnostic Disruption Opportunities', SOC ACE Research Paper No. 11, University of Birmingham, May 2022, pp. 25–26, at https://www.birmingham.ac.uk/documents/college-social-sciences/government-society/publications/illicit-financing-in-afghanistan-paper.pdf (Accessed 9 March 2025).

# 2

# The Future of US Policy in Afghanistan

*Michael Kugelman*

The US withdrawal from Afghanistan in August 2021 was a watershed moment for American foreign policy. In the immediate term, because of the chaotic nature of the final phase of the withdrawal, US credibility came into question and Washington incurred some reputational costs.[1] More broadly, the withdrawal reflected the Joe Biden administration's broader goal of downsizing the US military presence overseas, in order to focus more fully on its Indo-Pacific policy and competition with China.

The withdrawal also raised questions about the future of US interests in Afghanistan, and in broader South Asia. Critics of the withdrawal argued that a reduced US presence in the region would embolden China, Iran, Pakistan, and Russia—all key regional players who happen to be bitter rivals or difficult partners of Washington—and prompt them to fill the vacuum in Afghanistan left by the United States.[2] Such predictions have so far largely proven false: Much of the region has been cautious about deepening its footprint in Afghanistan, preferring to wait and watch and see how the Taliban address concerns about women's rights and—even more—terrorism.[3]

Still, the US withdrawal has produced major shifts for the geopolitics of Afghanistan and its neighbours. Most Central and South Asian states—including India—have taken steps to deepen engagement with the Taliban regime, albeit without formally recognising it.[4] In early 2023, a Chinese firm inked an oil exploration deal with the Taliban—the first known energy extraction agreement between an international actor and the Taliban since the group retook power in 2021. In October 2023, Beijing invited the Taliban to attend a forum marking 10 years of China's Belt and Road Initiative. And in

January 2024, China accepted the credentials of a Taliban-appointed representative to serve as ambassador in Beijing—a gesture that came close to extending formal recognition to the Taliban regime. While Beijing has conducted some of the most visible outreach to the Taliban, many governments—including Washington and New Delhi—have held meetings with Taliban leaders since they retook power. With the Taliban facing no viable opposition, the region appears to have concluded that it has little choice but to engage.

And yet, questions endure about the future of US engagement with Afghanistan, post-withdrawal. America has a lot of clout because of its long-time presence in Afghanistan. It still retains influence in Afghanistan post-withdrawal due to its sanctions on many Taliban leaders. There are billions of Afghan Central Bank assets frozen in US financial institutions. The US has also been a top supplier of humanitarian assistance. How Washington crafts its future policy toward Afghanistan matters greatly for Afghanistan and its neighbours because of all these factors.

This paper offers reflections on the future of US policy in Afghanistan. The focus is on US objectives and interests in Afghanistan post-withdrawal, with attention given to the immediate term, intermediate term, and longer term. The paper's main argument is that, moving forward, the US policy will be narrowly focused and modest in scope. In the short term, it will largely revolve around issues like securing the release of Americans held captive and monitoring terrorist threats, while further down the road it may focus more on developing a deeper counterterrorism capacity to be wielded from outside Afghanistan. Beyond the short term, US policy with Afghanistan will depend on factors such as policy bandwidth, the nature of the terrorist threat in Afghanistan, relations with Pakistan, and the key question of who holds power in Kabul.

## Historical Context: A Longstanding Desire to Depart

The US withdrawal from Afghanistan has resulted in a more limited and modest American policy. It bears mentioning, however, that US officials had long telegraphed a preference for downsizing policy in Afghanistan.[5] For many years, Washington had had its eyes on the exits, and going back even further, US officials were willing to reduce America's role in the country even with troops still on the ground. In March 2003, at the very moment when the Taliban—overthrown by US forces just over a year earlier—were starting to plan for the launch of an insurgency against American forces and the allied Afghan Government, the George W. Bush administration launched an invasion of Iraq, causing it to take its eye off the ball in Afghanistan.

Later, in 2009, President Barack Obama announced a troop surge but at the same time stated that within 18 months a phased withdrawal of troops would begin. In 2014, the US formally ended its combat war and transitioned to training and advising mission in Afghanistan.

Obama's successor, Donald Trump, was never comfortable staying in Afghanistan. He announced a policy in 2017 that entailed staying the course and even adding more troops, but he soon decided to execute a full withdrawal, resulting in negotiations with the Taliban that in 2020 would result in an agreement calling for all US troops to leave by May 2021. So, when President Biden announced in April 2021 that he would uphold Trump's decision to withdraw, he was echoing the sentiments of several predecessors. In fact, Biden himself had long been opposed to a long-term presence in Afghanistan. As Obama's vice president, he was one of the most vocal opponents of the 2009 surge, his boss's decision to make large increases in troop deployments to Afghanistan.

In effect, US policy had been gradually moving toward a withdrawal decision for quite some time.

**Future US Policy: Immediate Priorities**

Future US policy in the near term is simple. The second Trump administration will have two chief goals: Press for the release of any Americans still being held by the Taliban, and track down terrorists that have threatened or targeted Americans.

The Biden administration successfully negotiated the release of two Americans, though several others remain in captivity. Shortly after Trump's inauguration, Secretary of State Marco Rubio indicated that the Taliban are holding more American hostages than previously reported, though he didn't indicate how many[6] Trump, whose foreign policy blends transactionalism and nationalism, will likely push his administration to use whatever leverage it has to secure the freedom of America's remaining hostages in Afghanistan—and elsewhere in the world.

While counterterrorism more broadly is likely to be a more medium-term objective, as described later in this paper, the Trump administration will look to identify opportunities where it can in the immediate term apprehend terrorists that are threats to the US. An example during the early days of the second Trump administration is instructive. In March 2025, in a joint address to Congress, Trump revealed that the US, in cooperation with Pakistan, had tracked down Mohammad Sharifullah, a terrorist with Islamic State-Khorasan (IS-K, the Afghanistan/Pakistan affiliate of Islamic State) who played a major role in an attack outside the Kabul airport during the US withdrawal, which killed 13 American soldiers and about 170 Afghan civilians.[7] US intelligence officials shared information about Sharifullah's location with Pakistani counterparts, and Pakistani security forces found him near the border with Afghanistan and detained him before extraditing him to the US. Trump and other key senior officials, especially National Security Advisor Michael Waltz, an Afghanistan war veteran who warned about the dangers of terrorist groups like Islamic State in the days before the administration took power, will feel strongly about the immediate-term need to maintain this focus on counterterrorism.

The Biden administration had pursued two immediate-term goals: One was to help get out of Afghanistan those Afghan citizens who worked with the US military or government and held the Special Immigrant Visa (SIV) status. The other was to try to help ease the humanitarian crisis in Afghanistan. Neither of those objectives were achieved. In the case of the former, Washington slowed its pursuit of the goal, even though attaining it remained elusive. And in the case of the latter, the scale of the challenge militated against success. The second Trump administration, judging by policy decisions made early in its term related to refugees and foreign aid (which included suspending all US foreign aid and taking steps to eliminate the US Agency for International Development), is unlikely to pursue either of these goals.

Many of the Afghans that the Biden administration had pledged to help get out of the country remain there. There are no exact figures on the number of SIV-status Afghans still in the country, but anecdotally this author—and others with contacts in Afghanistan—can confidently state that there are still quite a few Afghans in the country who worked with the US and want to leave, but cannot. It has fallen to US veterans' groups and civil society organisations to spearhead efforts to evacuate those SIV-status Afghans still wanting to leave. But some of those leading these evacuation efforts have said from the start that they need help from the US Government in order to succeed.[8]

The Biden administration allocated the majority of its Afghanistan-focused policy space to the humanitarian crisis, but with limited success—not for lack of trying, but rather because of the sheer scale of the crisis. The US has been one of the biggest bilateral suppliers of humanitarian aid to Afghanistan post-Taliban takeover.[9] But those contributions have had limited effect on a crisis that has included more than 20 million people experiencing acute hunger and a near total collapse of the country's healthcare sector, due to lack of funds. To make matters worse, in the years since the Taliban takeover, Afghanistan has been hit by a tragic variety of humanitarian disasters—droughts, floods, and, during a period of less than two weeks in October 2023, four major earthquakes in and near the city of Herat.

To make matters even worse, Afghanistan also faces an acute economic crisis, marked in particular by severe shortages of liquidity. The economic crisis was triggered in great part by the sharp reduction in foreign development assistance to Afghanistan after the Taliban, which faces US sanctions, took over. The Biden administration was aware that humanitarian assistance—such as food shipments and emergency medical supplies—would not do enough to address Afghanistan's broader economic crisis. But its options for tackling the economic crisis were limited because this would entail putting money into the hands of the Taliban regime—one that Washington did not and has not recognised. Washington's hands were tied for legal reasons: Funding the Taliban regime would violate the US sanctions regime.

The Biden administration's hands were also tied for political reasons. Given the Taliban's well-chronicled close ties to multiple terrorist groups, including al-Qaeda, as well as its harsh crackdowns on women's rights—which have arguably been more draconian than any world governments, including that of Saudi Arabia—the Biden administration would have faced a major political backlash at home if it sent financial assistance to Kabul. Furthermore, sending money to the Taliban would have amplified just how much US objectives failed in Afghanistan: The US would have been financing a regime that it had long vowed to degrade and defeat. That would have had deleterious political consequences for the Biden administration, and especially as it approached elections in November 2024.

Accordingly, the Biden administration largely refrained from providing assistance to the Taliban regime. It did continue to provide humanitarian assistance to the Afghan people—support that is channelled through the United Nations (UN) and other international charitable agencies on the ground. However, even routing funding through trusted international aid agencies became difficult, given that several international aid groups suspended operations in Afghanistan after the Taliban in December 2022 announced a new ban on women working for nongovernmental organisations.

Additionally, the Biden administration did look into possible ways of carving out some exemptions from the US sanctions regime that would have allowed limited inflows of non-humanitarian economic assistance to Afghanistan to assist the general public.[10] US officials, however, admitted that it was a hard sell to convince ultra-risk-averse banks and other financial institutions that any funds they send to Afghanistan will not run afoul of the American sanctions regime.[11] The Biden administration did explore options for getting $3.5 billion in Afghan central bank assets and frozen in US banks back to the Afghan central bank. An executive order announced in February 2022 ensures that these funds would be protected from litigation by some families of 9/11 attack victims that were trying to gain access to them.[12] Administration officials recognised that the sanctions regime greatly complicated any attempts to unfreeze those funds, though they still looked into options.[13] In September 2022, Washington announced that it would transfer $3.5 billion in Afghan central bank reserves to a new trust fund based in Switzerland but without any Taliban role in drawing on or disbursing the fund. The Taliban swiftly rejected this US move. There were no other notable developments with the central bank reserves during the Biden era.

The Biden administration did consider a series of middle ground options proposed by scholars and analysts that went further than simply providing humanitarian aid but fell short of ending sanctions and unfreezing frozen assets. These included calls for releasing some funds in order to bring relief to critical areas that would not benefit the Taliban directly. Examples included providing funds to reputable Afghan banks to ease the liquidity crisis; to public servants to pay their salaries, especially in the health and education sectors; and to critical infrastructure like roads and bridges that facilitate basic service delivery.[14] There was little indication, however, of forward movement on policy levels with any of these ideas.

The Biden administration had open communication channels with the Taliban, meaning that formal recognition was not needed for access to the group. Senior Biden administration officials met with and negotiated with Taliban leaders multiple times after the Taliban takeover. Additionally, US immediate-term goals in Afghanistan post-withdrawal were narrowly focused, meaning the Biden administration didn't have to be ambitious in its relations with the Taliban. Furthermore, it designated Qatar, a close US partner, as the country to represent US interests in Taliban-led Afghanistan. This move was another indication that Washington had little interest, not to mention—given the sanctions regime—ability to recognise the Taliban regime.

This dynamic will likely remain in place with the Trump administration over the immediate term. It will engage with the Taliban when it needs to pursue its interests—such as on the matter of pressing for the release of captive Americans. It likely also won't hesitate to convey its concerns to the Taliban about terrorism in Afghanistan. Additionally, while the Trump administration, as of its first few months in power, had not signaled whether it will honor the Biden decision to have Qatar represent US interests in Afghanistan, it will likely be perfectly comfortable deferring to trusted partners on matters like Afghanistan, which won't be a strategic priority for the administration.

Though the Trump administration is unlikely to prioritise humanitarian assistance and other support to the Taliban, it may use the possibility of such aid as leverage. Trump, for example, has demanded that the Taliban return US-made weaponry that it seized from collapsing Afghan security forces. He may hold out the prospect of assistance—such as humanitarian aid, or the release of Afghan central bank funds—to try to get the Taliban to agree to send back weaponry. While this would be a hard sell—the Taliban are highly unlikely to return arms they regard as their own—the Taliban's political leadership in Kabul badly seeks more international assistance to address significant economic stress.[15]

The Trump administration, however, will confront a key challenge on immediate-term Afghanistan policy that its predecessor did not: There is a sharp difference of view within the administration on how to approach the Taliban. Trump, who oversaw the talks with the Taliban that led to the 2020 Doha accord, appears willing to engage with the Taliban. He would be comfortable authorising his administration to negotiate with the group over the release of captive Americans, and possibly even to discuss counterterrorism concerns—IS-K is a shared US–Taliban threat. Biden administration officials grudgingly acknowledged that the Taliban, through its ground offensives against IS-K, has indirectly been helpful to the US. Trump may also be willing to make this acknowledgement, and to be content with deferring to Taliban efforts to manage the IS-K threat inside Afghanistan.

However, Waltz, Trump's national security advisor, is a Taliban hawk. He opposed the US withdrawal from Afghanistan and wanted American forces to stay there to fight terrorists.[16] He is a harsh critic of the Taliban, and has described its rule as a caliphate that enables IS-K, al-Qaeda, and other groups. He may be less comfortable than his boss would be about engaging with the Taliban. This difference in views—unless it is bridged—could have implications for the administration's immediate-term Afghanistan policy on various levels, from its approach to talks with the Taliban over captive Americans to any considerations about sending assistance to Afghanistan to how the US tackles its terrorism concerns.

### Future US Policy: The Medium Term

As we move closer to 2026, the aforementioned short-term goals will likely continue to be in place. It is difficult to predict what new objectives may emerge, but one strong possibility relates to counterterrorism.

The Biden administration vowed to build an "over-the-horizon" counterterrorism capacity, which would enable America to monitor and if need be target terrorist threats in Afghanistan—all from outside the country.

For the first year after the US withdrawal, this goal took a back seat. It does not appear to have been a major issue of focus at the Pentagon.[17] And yet, in July 2022, nearly a year after US forces left Afghanistan, President Biden announced that a US drone strike had taken out al-Qaeda leader Ayman al-Zawahiri in Kabul. It was the first confirmed US drone strike or any type of kinetic American counterterrorism operation in Afghanistan since the US withdrawal.

The hit on Zawahiri hinted at the possibility that the Biden administration may well redirect attention to the issue of terrorism. Counterterrorism has long been the main lens through which US officials in multiple administrations have looked at Afghanistan. Counterterrorism was why US forces entered Afghanistan to start with. All four wartime US presidents identified it as a key objective. Biden, who made the formal decision to withdraw, justified that decision by saying the US had achieved its original counterterrorism goals—but he also vowed to track down the perpetrators of the deadly IS-K attack near the Kabul airport during the final days of the withdrawal.

In a speech announcing the operation against Zawahiri, Biden made clear his intention to maintain a post-withdrawal focus on counterterrorism:

> When I ended our military mission in Afghanistan almost a year ago, I made a decision that after 20 years of war, the United States no longer needed thousands of boots on the ground in Afghanistan to protect America from terrorists who seek to do us harm. I made a promise to the American people that we'd continue to conduct effective counterterrorism operations in Afghanistan and beyond. We've done just that.[18]

As illustrated by the operation to take out Zawahiri, US security interests benefit in a big way from the existence of an over-the-horizon capacity. The default plan, which likely was deployed in the Zawahiri raid, has been to use existing US military bases in the Arab Gulf region as staging grounds for counterterrorism activities. But these bases are far from Afghanistan. Counterterrorism operations cannot be very effective when assets are so far from the target area. Even worse, US military assets, particularly aircraft, would need to fly around Iran, where the US does not have overflight rights, to get over to Afghanistan.

The Biden administration's attempts to ease tensions with Tehran failed. The horrific terrorist attack by the Palestinian militant group Hamas—which is sponsored by Tehran—on Israel in October 2023, along with Iranian support for Hamas, Hezbollah, and Houthi rebels amid increasing destabilisation in the Middle East in 2023 and 2024, effectively ended any hope of a less hostile US–Iran relationship.

This means that Iran is highly unlikely to consider providing any airspace rights to Washington—even though the two countries did quietly cooperate on Afghanistan issues during the early years of the war there.[19] The implication here is that despite the successful mission to take out Zawahiri, US over-the-horizon capacity could stand to improve in a big way. US officials and counterterrorism experts admitted as much in the days after the operation, noting that going after a single top target is, in the words of former Central Intelligence Agency (CIA) analyst Beth Sanner, 'a whole different ball of wax' compared to a more complex and broader effort to prevent Afghanistan from once again becoming a sanctuary for transnational terrorist groups.[20] To that end, in March 2023, General Michael Kurilla, head of U.S. Central Command (CENTCOM) estimated that IS-K could stage 'an external operation against U.S. or Western interests abroad in under six months.'[21] Indeed, in 2023 and 2024, IS-K, from its base in Afghanistan, demonstrated a growing capacity to project a threat to the West, including the US. Several IS-K plots were reportedly foiled in the West, including in the US.[22]

US diplomatic attempts to address these challenges produced limited results in the Biden era. There were no known new deals with any of Afghanistan's neighbours, post-US withdrawal, which would have allowed America to base troops on their soil or to have intelligence-sharing mechanisms in place. The one exception may be Pakistan. In October 2021, Washington and Islamabad were reportedly negotiating a new accord that would give America permission to use Pakistani airspace.[23] US aircraft often used Pakistani airspace during the war in Afghanistan. But even if it retains this benefit in the post-withdrawal era, Washington would need more to have a truly robust over-the-horizon capacity.[24] The operation that took out IS-K member Sharifullah in March 2025 demonstrated that the US can still cooperate on counterterrorism with Pakistan in the post-withdrawal era. But the operation didn't require over-the-horizon capacity: Sharifullah was reportedly based in, and apprehended on, the Pakistan side of the Afghanistan–Pakistan border.

Under the circumstances currently in place, it is quite difficult for the US to monitor and manage terrorism threats in Afghanistan. Ultimately, however, the extent to which the Trump administration eventually focuses on developing an over-the-horizon capacity for Afghanistan will depend on three key factors.

First is bandwidth. The Trump administration hopes to reduce the US's global footprint. Its main areas of foreign policy focus will be trying to end the wars in Ukraine and the Middle East and engaging in its competition with China. The administration will have limited bandwidth to focus on Afghanistan. That said, if the wars in Ukraine and the Middle East end or deescalate in a big way, or if competition with Beijing were to recede, the administration may choose to allocate more policy space to Afghanistan.

Second is the evolution of the terrorism threat in Afghanistan. Washington worries most about terrorism that poses a threat to US interests, not to mention the US homeland. In effect, the administration will be particularly inclined to pursue over-the-horizon capacity if it believes that terrorist groups in Afghanistan are developing, or could soon develop, the ability to carry out attacks far beyond Afghanistan. Currently, al-Qaeda is much weaker than it was in the pre-9/11 era, but IS-K has demonstrated a growing capacity to project a threat to US interests, both abroad and to the US homeland itself. The Trump administration would not seek to build a counter-terrorism capacity simply to reduce terrorist attacks in Afghanistan, or even cross-border terror attacks in Pakistan or Central Asia. The core goal is to ensure that terrorists do not have the capacity to carry out longer-range attacks that can strike US interests or soil far beyond Afghanistan.

Accordingly, if US officials believe that either al-Qaeda or IS-K is strengthening their capacities and could pose a broader transnational threat, then American policymakers will have a stronger incentive to focus more on building up Washington's counterterrorism capability. One indication that could show that al-Qaeda and IS-K are successfully developing the capacity to threaten US interests, nationals, and territory is increasing financial, manpower, and weapons support from the various other terrorist groups that operate in Afghanistan—most of which are allied with al-Qaeda. Another indication would be inflows of foreign fighters into Afghanistan that are from, or have prior experience operating in, areas far beyond Afghanistan—especially Europe or even the United States.

In a television interview in January 2025, soon before the second Trump administration took office, Waltz suggested that terrorism concerns in Afghanistan will be coming into sharp focus in the months ahead. Waltz emphasised the need to 'keep a lid on ISIS and al-Qaeda,' including in Afghanistan. He also called for a new counterterrorism strategy, noting that the Taliban 'have a caliphate again in Afghanistan, where ISIS and al-Qaeda are brewing…We have to do a complete day one relook.'[25]

A third key factor that will impact the likelihood of Washington focusing on building up over-the-horizon capacities is the US relationship with Pakistan, Afghanistan's eastern neighbour. Despite a fraught relationship, Pakistan did provide counterterrorism assistance to Washington during the war in Afghanistan that enabled the US to pursue some of its security interests in Afghanistan. These include intelligence support, airspace rights, ground and air transit privileges, and basing arrangements for the launching of US drones. If Washington were able to gain back some of these privileges, thereby lessening its reliance on faraway resources in the Middle East, then building out its over-the-horizon capacity would be a more doable prospect.

During the early years of the war in Afghanistan, the US did benefit from similar support from several Central Asian states. During the Biden administration, the Russian invasion of Ukraine and the hostile state of relations between Washington and Moscow made the possibility of Russia's backyard providing military support to the United States quite unlikely.[26] However, the return of President Trump, who takes a more restrained view of Moscow than did his predecessor, might create an opening for some form of US–Russia cooperation on terrorism in Afghanistan (or some degree of buy-in from Moscow on the US partnering with Central Asian states), and especially if the war in Ukraine were to end and provide Moscow with more policy space. Afghanistan-based terrorism is a major concern to Moscow, and especially after IS-K—which has long recruited jihadists from Central Asia—claimed a devastating attack on a Moscow nightclub in 2024 that killed 145 people.

Still, because of geography and its past history of counterterrorism partnership with Washington, Pakistan would be the key player in any US considerations about engagements with external players to assist Washington's over-the-horizon approaches. And yet, the future of US–Pakistan relations is uncertain.[27] A new Pakistani government took office in April 2022 following the ouster via no confidence vote of Prime Minister Imran Khan. The new government called for strong relations with Washington but it was a weak government that struggled to ease a severe economic crisis. The same government returned to power after national elections in January 2024, though it is also unpopular because many Pakistanis believe it benefited from a rigged election.

With some exceptions, most of the high-level bilateral engagements with Pakistan in the Biden era focused on non-security issues. US security assistance to Pakistan remained suspended, after Trump froze it back in 2018. This made forward movement on security cooperation quite elusive.[28] Two developments during the early days of the second Trump administration—US–Pakistan cooperation on the Sharifullah operation, and Washington's release of nearly $400 million to finance maintenance of Pakistan's fleet of F-16 fighter jets—suggested some receptivity within the administration to engage with Pakistan on security issues. Still, the presence of harsh critics of

Pakistan within the administration (including Trump himself), the Trump administration's strong commitment to security partnership with India, and Pakistan's deep defence alliance with China, among factors, impose limits on the possibilities of a renewed bilateral security partnership in the second Trump administration.

Even if there were to be new US commitments to Afghanistan-focused US–Pakistan security cooperation, there would be major obstacles. If the US were to resume operational and kinetic forms of cooperation with Pakistan, this could prompt terrorists to target Americans or American interests in Pakistan. With the exception of IS-K, terrorist groups active in Pakistan—including the most potent one, Tehreek-e-Taliban (TTP)—do not currently target or even threaten American nationals. The Trump administration would not want to pursue any policy that could put American nationals more at risk.

Additionally, while both Washington and Islamabad view IS-K as a threat, Pakistan is much more concerned about the Afghanistan-based TTP, which has dramatically scaled up attacks in Pakistan since the Taliban re-took power. While Washington worries about the TTP as well, its main focus of any over-the-horizon plans would be IS-K (and what remains of al-Qaeda), not TTP (which in Washington's view does not presently pose a direct threat to the US). This disconnect in terrorist threat perceptions could militate against any future US–Pakistan counterterrorism cooperation in Afghanistan.

Despite these challenges, Pakistan's powerful military, which has long driven security relations with Washington, will seek some form of counterterrorism partnership with Washington. It began this pitch during the Biden era. It exploited growing concerns in Washington about Afghanistan-based terrorism, emphasising how it is a shared US–Pakistan anxiety. The military likely also sought to leverage its own importance in US–Pakistan relations; most US administrations have viewed Pakistani military and intelligence officials as critical interlocutors. Officer-to-officer ties have generally been warm, even when bilateral relations more broadly are shaky. This may explain why US assistance for Pakistani military education and training programmes has tended to be exempted from freezes on American security aid.

These Pakistani pitches will likely intensify in the second Trump era. The military will be aware of Waltz's strongly worded expressions of concern about terrorism in Afghanistan, and it knows that Trump shares these concerns. The military will also hope that its willingness to act expeditiously to track down Sharifullah will sharpen Washington's interest in a new partnership.

The main reason why Pakistan's military seeks a new security partnership with the US—besides its need for more aid and weaponry—is its inability on its own to curb a worsening TTP threat. The Taliban in Afghanistan, close allies with TTP, have been unwilling to target the group's bases and fighters in that country. During the Biden era, the Taliban did mediate talks between TTP leaders and Pakistani officials, but those talks went nowhere, and Pakistani forces would subsequently stage several cross-border strikes on what they claimed were TTP bases. Such activities did little to address the problem, and likely prompted the Taliban to double down in its refusal to help Pakistan curb the TTP threat in Afghanistan.

The Biden administration, while open to exploring some forms of counterterrorism cooperation with Islamabad, and willing to participate in several rounds of counterterrorism dialogue, was generally unreceptive to a new formal security partnership. This was not just because it did not view TTP as a threat to the US, but also because it was focused on priorities elsewhere.[29] In 2023, US officials acknowledged that the Taliban's own efforts to curb the threat posed by IS-K—the only terror group in Afghanistan with which the Taliban is not allied—had produced some successes.[30] That same year, the Taliban claimed it had killed the mastermind of the Kabul airport attack, and US officials reportedly agreed with the Taliban's contention.[31] This US view that the Taliban was helpful on the IS-K front likely became another factor that militated against deeper US–Pakistan counterterrorism cooperation. In effect, Washington likely reasoned that with the Taliban indirectly helping pursue US counterterrorist goals in Afghanistan, the US had little need to work with Pakistan.

The Trump administration is likely to take a similarly cautious approach. It will have little desire to partner with Pakistan on a goal—such as taking on TTP—that doesnot directly address US interests. It will be willing to cooperate with Pakistan on the IS-K issue, but likely on a limited and episodic basis: Instead of seeking a deep partnership, it will look to Pakistan to help when the US gets actionable information about the location of a sought-after terrorist. But such cooperation would likely be limited to threats in Pakistan. Though Pakistan has carried out periodic strikes in Afghanistan against TTP targets, it is unlikely—given the risks of such operations, and given that they strain tensions with the Taliban—to use such cross-border activities to go after IS-K targets, unless those targets had previously hit Pakistan or are believed to pose a clear and present danger to Pakistan.

## Future US Policy: The Long Game

Predicting longer-term US policy is difficult, but two considerations can help provide some context for how to think about what to expect in the coming months and years.

First, the Biden Administration made clear that its biggest priorities were elsewhere, outside of Afghanistan. Biden himself, in speeches announcing and justifying his decision to withdraw, indicated that he decided to leave in great part to be able to focus on what he believed to be more important issues—climate change, competition with China, and a terrorism threat that in his view evolved far beyond Afghanistan.[32] Later on, the wars in Ukraine and the Middle East became Washington's biggest foreign policy priority, strengthening Biden's earlier contention that Afghanistan simply is not a top US priority anymore. Tellingly, in December 2022, US National Security Adviser Jake Sullivan said that having US troops out of Afghanistan enhanced Washington's options to help the Ukraine military.[33] It also bears noting that Biden once famously sought to diminish Afghanistan's strategic importance by telling then Afghan President Hamid Karzai that Pakistan is '50 times more important' than Afghanistan.[34] The Trump administration, with its desire to play less of a role globally, and with its plans to deploy the bulk of its foreign policy capital elsewhere, is likely to feel similarly—though it will keep Afghanistan on the policy radar, mainly due to terrorism concerns.

This suggests that in the longer term, one could see US engagement in Afghanistan start to diminish. A critical factor determining the extent of longer-term US engagement with Kabul is the future of the Taliban. So long as the Taliban remain in power, US engagement will be necessarily limited due to American sanctions on the group. If the Taliban were to lose power, or if a viable anti-Taliban resistance emerges that is able to chip away at Taliban control and results in some form of civil war or other armed conflict, then the dynamic of US engagement could change. To be sure, in such a scenario, unlike in the immediate post-9/11 era, Washington would not step in to back anti-Taliban groups in Afghanistan. But US officials would have to consider questions about how to orient limited US policies toward Afghanistan, particularly in terms of pursuing a counterterrorism capacity and helping ease humanitarian and economic stress. An Afghanistan that is once again at war would have significant implications for US policy.

Second, considerations about great power rivalry and other strategic factors are unlikely to prompt Washington to step up engagement in Afghanistan. While the Ukraine and Middle East conflicts will be among the top US foreign policy concerns so long as they continue to rage, the biggest such concern in the long-term will remain competition with China. This means that US policymakers will look at the world through the lens of US–China rivalry. This has prompted some commentators to argue that leaving Afghanistan was a bad idea because China will step into the vacuum left by the US and become a prime actor in Afghanistan.

However, as noted at the beginning of this paper, that narrative is flawed. China has actually been relatively cautious about Afghanistan post-US withdrawal and has held back from moving in. China has long been willing to tolerate security risks in the volatile areas it invests in abroad, from Pakistan to parts of Southeast Asia and Sub-Saharan Africa. And yet, it was a cautious actor in Afghanistan throughout the US-led war. It has some economic assets there, but it limited its on-ground presence because of security concerns. China has been and will continue to look for more security assurances before it aims to scale up its influence and footprint in Taliban-led Afghanistan.

To be sure, a Chinese firm did sign an oil exploration deal with the Taliban in early 2023. But that was only one deal, and it was announced only after the Taliban carried out an offensive that apprehended IS-K terrorists involved in a recent attack on Chinese nationals. Beijing will continue to closely monitor how the Taliban deal with terrorists on Afghan soil that threaten China. Consequently, that oil deal should not necessarily be seen as an opening salvo of a Chinese investment spree. Indeed, so far, the Taliban have not indicated an ability or willingness to target the groups that worry China the most—IS-K, The East Turkistan Islamic Movement/Turkistan Islamic Party (comprised mainly of Uighur militants), and the TTP, which has targeted Chinese interests in Pakistan.

Additionally, Afghanistan is arguably not a major battleground for US–China rivalry. Washington and Beijing have cooperated in Afghanistan more than they have competed in it. They were both members of the Troika Plus, a key Afghanistan-focused regional diplomatic entity. On multiple levels, the two see eye to eye on Afghanistan: They want more stability, they want less terrorism, and they are wary of the Taliban but they are willing to engage with it. In effect, the China factor will not tempt Washington to increase engagement in Afghanistan in the longer run because US competition with China is simply not a major issue in Afghanistan.

Furthermore, during the early days of his second term, President Trump signaled a desire to ease tensions with Beijing.[35] While US economic competition with Beijing will likely continue if not intensify during his second administration, Trump's desire not to get dragged into a conflict with China could prompt him to pursue an understanding with Beijing that would make the relationship a bit less contentious. This makes it even less likely that China's modest activities in Afghanistan, which wasn't a prime battleground for US–China rivalry even when the broader US–China competition was raging furiously, would prompt Washington to want to engage more with Afghanistan to counter Beijing.

**Conclusion**

This paper argues that future US policy in Afghanistan will be limited in scope and goals. In the immediate term, the main focus will be on securing the release of Americans still held there and monitoring terrorist threats to the US. Washington may engage with the Taliban as part of its efforts to pursue these goals but it will not recognise the regime.

Beyond the immediate term, and in the aftermath of the successful mission to target al-Qaeda's Zawahiri, Washington may be inclined to intensify its focus on building an over-the-horizon counterterrorism capacity in Afghanistan, though the likelihood of it doing so will depend on considerations like policy bandwidth, the evolution of the terrorism threat in Afghanistan, and US relations with Pakistan.

In the longer term, one can expect US officials to reduce their engagement with Afghanistan, though the question of who is in power in Afghanistan will impact the way Washington chooses to align its policy in Afghanistan. If the Taliban regime were to collapse and there is a resurgence of civil war, Washington would be unlikely to play a role in backing anti-Taliban factions—or any factions. This is because the US would have no compelling interests to do so, unlike in the immediate 9/11 era, when the Taliban's hosting of the al-Qaeda leadership prompted the Bush administration to back the anti-Taliban Northern Alliance.

The takeaway from these observations about future US policy in Afghanistan is that, as more time goes on, Washington will likely put more distance between itself and Afghanistan, with the country in Washington's rear view mirror and then conceivably disappearing from it altogether. We are likely to see US increasingly less engaged in Afghanistan in the long term, with counterterrorism concerns the main factor potentially keeping US officials focused on the country. That said, increased terror attacks in Afghanistan will not necessarily prompt stepped-up US attention to counterterrorism. But if terror groups are perceived to be developing the ability to project a threat far beyond Afghanistan, so that US interests, citizens, and soil are impacted, this could trigger more US attention to counterterrorism.

This, then, gets to a key question many have asked about future US policy, post-withdrawal: Could America ever return to Afghanistan, in the form of a redeployment of US military assets and forces? This is highly unlikely. The only possible exception is if the United States were to conclude that there is credible evidence and intelligence suggesting that terrorists are actively using Afghanistan to plot an attack on the US. For Washington, however, the goal would be to act pre-emptively to reduce or eliminate that threat so that there is no need to put US boots back on the ground in Afghanistan later on. The strong preference in Washington would be to rely on the over-the-horizon capacity to nip transnational terrorist threats in the bud, in order to prevent the need to redeploy troops to Afghanistan.

While some prominent voices in Washington (including the current national security advisor) never wanted US forces to leave Afghanistan, the last two men to occupy the White House—one, Trump, a Republican, the other, Biden, a Democrat—made clear that they did not favour a US military presence in Afghanistan. This suggests that there is bipartisan support in Washington for the view that future US policy in Afghanistan, however it pans out, will be limited in scope and modest in ambition. It's a position that Trump, during his second administration, is likely to embrace as well.

## NOTES

1. Jack Stone Truitt, 'Top US General Says Afghanistan Withdrawal has Damaged Credibility', *Nikkei Asian Review*, 29 September 2021, at https://asia.nikkei.com/Politics/International-relations/Afghanistan-turmoil/Top-US-general-says-Afghanistan-withdrawal-has-damaged-credibility.
2. Ron Synovitz, 'Regional Powers Seek to Fill Vacuum Left by West's Retreat from Afghanistan', *Radio Free Europe/Radio Liberty*, 25 December 2021, at https://www.rferl.org/a/afghanistan-power-vacuum-russia-iran-china-pakistan/31624955.html.
3. Joshua Keating, 'No One Wants To Be the First Country to Recognize the Taliban', *Slate*, 18 August 2021, at https://slate.com/news-and-politics/2021/08/afghanistan-taliban-international-recognition-united-nations.html; and Michael Kugelman, 'The Politics of Taliban Recognition', *South Asian Voices*, 10 November 2021, at https://southasianvoices.org/the-politics-of-taliban-recognition/.
4. Perhaps most surprising is that India—no friend of the Taliban—decided to partially reopen its embassy in Kabul less than a year after the Taliban takeover. See Suhasini Haidar, 'India Reopens Embassy in Kabul', *The Hindu*, 24 June 2022, at https://www.thehindu.com/news/national/india-reopens-embassy-in-kabul/article65558557.ece.
5. For additional information on how US officials so often telegraphed a desire to leave Afghanistan, see 'Collapse of the Afghan National Defense and Security Forces: An Assessment of the Factors That Led to its Demise', Special Inspector General For Afghanistan Reconstruction (SIGAR), Interim Report, May 2022, at https://www.sigar.mil/pdf/evaluations/SIGAR-22-22-IP.pdf; and Michael Kugelman, 'Mission Creep on Repeat: Deconstructing US Strategy in Afghanistan', in Adib Farhadi and Anthony Masys (eds.), *The Great Power Competition Volume 24: Lessons Learned inAfghanistan: America's Longest War*, Springer, New York, 2023, pp. 249–270, at https://link.springer.com/book/10.1007/978-3-031-22934-3.
6. Kanishka Singh, 'US May Put "Very Big Bounty" on Taliban Leaders, Secretary of State Rubio Says', *Reuters*, 25 January 2025, at https://www.reuters.com/world/us-may-put-very-big-bounty-taliban-leaders-secretary-state-rubio-says-2025-01-25/.

7. 'Remarks by President Trump in Joint Address to Congress', The White House, 4 March, 2025, at https://www.whitehouse.gov/remarks/2025/03/remarks-by-president-trump-in-joint-address-to-congress/.
8. Roger Cohen, 'These US Veterans Won't Rest Until They've Kept a Wartime Promise', *The New York Times*, 19 October 2021, at https://www.nytimes.com/2021/10/19/world/us-veterans-afghan-evacuation.html; and Phil McCausland, 'Veterans Leading Afghan Evacuations Demand Help from Biden and Congress', *NBC News*, 1 December 2021, at https://www.nbcnews.com/news/us-news/veterans-leading-afghan-evacuations-demand-biden-congress-help-rcna3525.
9. 'The United States Announces More than $144 Million in Additional Humanitarian Assistance for Afghanistan', USAID, Office of Press Relations, 28 October 2021, at https://www.usaid.gov/news-information/press-releases/oct-28-2021-united-states-announces-more-144-million-additional-humanitarian.
10. One encouraging step came in February 2022, when the US Treasury Department issued new licenses that allowed more authorisations for some forms of economic activity in Afghanistan, in an effort to facilitate more economic assistance that does not run afoul of US sanctions. See 'US Treasury Issues General License to Facilitate Economic Activity in Afghanistan', US Department of the Treasury, 25 February 2022, at https://home.treasury.gov/news/press-releases/jy0609.
11. This observation is based on the author's private discussions with US officials.
12. 'Executive Order to Preserve Certain Afghanistan Central Bank Assets for the People of Afghanistan', The White House, 11 February 2022, at https://home.treasury.gov/news/press-releases/jy0609.
13. In July 2022, the Biden administration and the Taliban leaders exchanged proposals on how to return Afghan Central Bank assets to Afghanistan, though the sides would remain far apart. See Charlotte Greenfield and Jonathan Landay, 'Exclusive: US and Taliban Make Progress on Afghan Reserves, But Big Gaps Remain', *Reuters*, 26 July 2022, at https://www.reuters.com/world/exclusive-us-taliban-make-progress-afghan-reserves-big-gaps-remain-2022-07-26/.
14. See 'Beyond Emergency Relief: Averting Afghanistan's Humanitarian Catastrophe', International Crisis Group, Report No. 317, 6 December 2021, at https://www.crisisgroup.org/asia/south-asia/afghanistan/317-beyond-emergency-relief-averting-afghanistans-humanitarian-catastrophe.
15. Michael Kugelman, 'Trump's Approach to Afghanistan is Already Limited', *Foreign Policy*, 26 February 2025, at https://foreignpolicy.com/2025/02/26/afghanistan-trump-taliban-military-weapons/.
16. Craig Whitlock, 'For Trump's National Security Advisor, Afghanistan Still Looms Large', *The Washington Post*, 18 January 2025, at https://www.washingtonpost.com/investigations/2025/01/17/trump-cabinet-national-security-afghanistan/.
17. This observation is based on the author's private discussions with US officials.
18. 'Al-Qaeda Leader Ayman Al-Zawahiri Killed in Drone Strike, Biden Says', *CBS News*, 1 August 2022, at https://www.cbsnews.com/live-updates/biden-successful-counterterrorism-operation-watch-live-stream-today-2022-08-01/.
19. Barbara Slavin, *Bitter Friends, Bosom Enemies: Iran, the U.S., and the Twisted Path to Confrontation*, St. Martin's Griffin, New York, 2007; and James Dobbins, 'Negotiating with Iran: Reflections from Personal Experience', *The Washington Quarterly*, Vol. 33, Issue 1, 2010, pp. 149–162.
20. Katie Bo Lillis, 'Despite al-Zawahiri Strike, US Officials Are Concerned about Tracking Terrorism Threats in Afghanistan', *CNN*, 5 August 2022, at https://www.cnn.com/2022/08/05/politics/us-counterrorism-afghanistan/index.html.
21. 'Senate Armed Services Committee Hearing on Posture of USCENTCOM and USAFRICOM in Review of the Defense Authorization Request for FY24 and the Future

Years Defense Program,' US Central Command, DOD Transcripts, March 17, 2023, https://www.centcom.mil/MEDIA/Transcripts/Article/3332606/senate-armed-services-committee-hearing-on-posture-of-uscentcom-and-usafricom-i/.

22. Aaron Zelin, 'IS-K Goes Global: External Operations from Afghanistan', Washington Institute for Near East Policy, 11 September, 2023, at https://www.washington institute.org/policy-analysis/iskp-goes-global-external-operations-afghanistan; and Tricia Bacon, 'The Islamic State in Khorasan Province: Exploiting a Counterterrorism Gap', Center for Strategic and International Studies, 11 April 2024, at https://www.csis.org/analysis/islamic-state-khorasan-province-exploiting-counterterrorism-gap.
23. Natasha Bertrand, Oren Liebermann, Zachary Cohen and Ellie Kaufman, 'US Nearing a Formal Agreement to Use Pakistan's Airspace to Carry Out Military Operations in Afghanistan', CNN, 23 October 2021, at https://www.cnn.com/2021/10/22/politics/us-pakistan-afghanistan-airspace/index.html.
24. For more details on Washington's earlier options for an over-the-horizon capacity under current circumstances, see Jonathan Schroden, 'New Ideas for Over-the-Horizon Counterterrorism in Afghanistan', *Lawfare*, 8 May 2022, at https://www.lawfareblog.com/new-ideas-over-horizon-counterterrorism-afghanistan.
25. 'Rep. Waltz: This Was Not a Coincidence', Incoming national security advisor Mike Waltz joins 'Fox & Friends' to discuss the terror attack in New Orleans and President-elect Trump's plan to address terror threats, *YouTube*, 3 January 2025, at https://www.youtube.com/watch?v=Apk-4WxD8pU.
26. Temur Umarov, 'Is There a Place for a US Military Base in Central Asia?', Carnegie Endowment for International Peace, 4 June 2021, at https://carnegiemoscow.org/commentary/84685.
27. Michael Kugelman, 'Political Crisis Heightens US-Pakistan Tensions', *Foreign Policy*, 7 April 2022, at https://foreignpolicy.com/2022/04/07/pakistan-political-crisis-imran-khan-us/; and Madiha Afzal, 'An Uneasy Limbo for US-Pakistan Relations Amidst the Withdrawal from Afghanistan', Brookings, 6 August 2021, at https://www.brookings.edu/blog/order-from-chaos/2021/08/06/an-uneasy-limbo-for-us-pakistan-relations-amid st-the-withdrawal-from-afghanistan/.
28. US–Pakistan security cooperation in Afghanistan post-withdrawal became politicised when Prime Minister Imran Khan vowed that Pakistan would never allow US forces to use Pakistani military bases. However, David Hale, a former senior State Department official and ambassador to Pakistan, later indicated that he did not believe that the Biden administration had ever requested basing facilities in Pakistan post-Afghanistan withdrawal. See 'Beyond Afghanistan: US Perspectives on the Future of US-Pakistan Relations', Wilson Center Webcast, 19 July 2021, at https://www.wilsoncenter.org/event/beyond-afghanistan-us-perspectives-future-us-pakistan-relations.
29. These observations are based on private discussions with US and Pakistani officials.
30. See for example, 'US Policy Toward Afghanistan: A Conversation with Tom West', Stimson Center, Event Transcript, 12 September 2023, at https://www.stimson.org/wp-content/uploads/2023/08/U.S.-Policy-Toward-Afghanistan-A-Conversation-with-Tom-West_Event-Transcript.pdf.
31. Nadine Yousif, 'Taliban Kill IS Leader Behind Kabul Airport Bombing', BBC, 25 April 2023, at https://www.bbc.com/news/world-us-canada-65382277.
32. See 'Remarks by President Biden on the Way Forward in Afghanistan', The White House, 14 April 2021, at https://www.whitehouse.gov/briefing-room/speeches-remarks/2021/04/14/remarks-by-president-biden-on-the-way-forward-in-afghanistan; and 'Remarks by President Biden on the Drawdown of US Forces in Afghanistan', The White House, 8 July 2021, at https://www.whitehouse.gov/briefing-room/speeches-remarks/2021/07/08/remarks-by-president-biden-on-the-drawdown-of-u-s-forces-in-afghanistan/.

33. 'The Biden Foreign Policy at Two Years: A Conversation with National Security Adviser Jake Sullivan', Carnegie Endowment for International Peace, 16 December 2022, at https://carnegieendowment.org/2022/12/16/biden-foreign-policy-at-two-years-event-8006.
34. Steve Coll, *Directorate S: The CIA and America's Secret Wars in Afghanistan and Pakistan*, Penguin Press, New York, 2018, p. 352.
35. Didi Tang and Ken Moritsugu, 'Trump Appears to Relax Stance on China after Talking Tough During Campaign', *Associated Press*, 29 January 2025, at https://apnews.com/article/trump-xi-china-tiktok-tariffs-228c21dc088a22f5c816d3e827a 97860.

# 3

# Central Asia's Approach Towards Taliban-controlled Afghanistan

*Bruce Pannier*

Central Asia shares a nearly 2,300-kilometre border with Afghanistan and since the five Central Asian countries—Kazakhstan, Kyrgyzstan, Tajikistan, Turkmenistan, and Uzbekistan—became independent in late 1991, when the Soviet Union collapsed, concerns about Afghanistan have been ever present for these countries north of the Afghan border. The period when the United States-led foreign forces were in Afghanistan provided some respite for the Central Asian states but by 2013, fighting was returning to areas of northern Afghanistan. By that time, the United States (US) and its foreign allies had started the gradual withdrawal of their forces from Afghanistan.

The last US troops were not even gone from Afghanistan when the Taliban entered Kabul on 15 August 2021. But the reaction in Central Asia was very different than it had been in late September 1996 when the Taliban first seized Kabul. Much has changed in the way most of the Central Asian states viewed Afghanistan, and even in the way they viewed the Taliban. Likely, none of the Central Asian governments is pleased that the Taliban are their neighbours again, but the situation is different now than it was some 25 years ago.

## The Late 1990s

When the Taliban took control of Kabul on 26 September 1996, there was panic in most of Central Asia. On 4 October 1996, a hastily arranged meeting of the Kazakh, Kyrgyz, Tajik, and Uzbek presidents, along with Russian Prime Minister Viktor Chernomyrdin took place in the then capital of

Kazakhstan, Almaty. The group discussed what to do about the advancing Taliban forces in Afghanistan. Memories of the Soviet Union's 1979–1989 war in Afghanistan were fresh and there were disagreements over what response, if any, the Central Asian states or Russia should make.

Hanging over the meeting was the shadow of Tajikistan's civil war which had been raging for more than four years when the Taliban entered Kabul. Tajik government forces were battling with the United Tajik Opposition (UTO), a curious coalition of democratic and regional forces dominated by the Islamic Renaissance Party of Tajikistan (IRPT). Afghanistan's civil war started in 1992 just before the outbreak of the civil war in Tajikistan and there had been concerns since then that the two conflicts could merge, and fighting could spread to other Central Asian countries. In September 1996, there was a stalemate in the civil war in Tajikistan and leaders in neighbouring states were greatly worried about the prospect of Taliban fighters reaching the Tajik border.

The Central Asian countries had only been independent for about five years. The leaders of the countries were former members of the Communist Party of the Soviet Union (CPSU). They had little knowledge of Islam but Islamic groups were suddenly the greatest threat to their security. Russian Prime Minister Chernomyrdin's attendance at the October 1996 meeting in Almaty provided small comfort as Russia had just concluded a ceasefire agreement in Chechnya in August and withdrawn its forces after battling an Islamic guerrilla force for 20 months.

Uzbek President Islam Karimov was the only one at the Almaty meeting who wanted to provide support to the enemies of the Taliban, albeit to Karimov's choice of anti-Taliban forces in Afghanistan, ethnic Uzbek field commander Abdul Rasheed Dostum who guarded the gateway to Uzbekistan in his stronghold in Mazar-i-Sharif. The meeting ended without any joint decision and Karimov went on to provide aid to Dostum, and Russia, with the help of Tajik President Emomali Rahmon (then called Rakhmonov), gave assistance to the forces of ethnic Tajik field commander Ahmad Shah Masoud, the legendary Lion of Panjshir who had so effectively battled Soviet forces from his lair in the Panjshir Valley.

Tajikistan and Uzbekistan are two of the three countries directly bordering Afghanistan. The third country, Turkmenistan, adopted a different policy towards events unfolding in Afghanistan. Turkmen authorities made clear right after the Taliban seized Kabul that it would not enter into any military alliances and was willing to talk with whoever was in power in Afghanistan. Turkmenistan had just received the UN-recognised status as a neutral country in December 1995, so the government in Ashgabat was uniquely positioned to deal with all the parties in Afghanistan.

Turkmenistan's interests in Afghanistan were in any case solely economic. Turkmenistan is a sparsely inhabited country with a weak military but possesses the world's fourth largest reserves of natural gas. However, as a legacy of its time as a republic of the Soviet Union, Turkmenistan's only gas pipelines connected it to the Russian gas pipeline network. When the Taliban entered Kabul in September 1996, there were already plans for building the Turkmenistan–Afghanistan–Pakistan–India (TAPI) natural gas pipeline to bring some 33 billion cubic metres (bcm) of gas through Afghanistan, which would receive 5 bcm, to Pakistan and India, who would each receive 14 bcm.

More than 25 years later, TAPI is still a priority project for Ashgabat, but, outside of Turkmenistan, hardly any progress has been made on realising the pipeline. In the mid-1990s, there was still great optimism that TAPI could be built and Taliban control over Afghanistan seemed, if anything, efficacious towards reaching that goal. Turkmenistan did not recognise the Taliban government but allowed the Taliban to establish a representative office in Ashgabat. And Turkmenistan hosted Afghan peace talks in March 1999. Though the Turkmen Government had its own interests for engaging with the Taliban, the relationship Ashgabat developed with the militant group would be a model for other Central Asian governments more than 20 years later.

In the late 1990s, Turkmenistan was an outlier in its position toward the Taliban. While the Tajikistan and Uzbek governments supported ethnic Tajik and Uzbek forces inside Afghanistan, they also fortified their borders, easier to do for Uzbekistan, with a 158-kilometre border with Afghanistan, than for Tajikistan, with a 1,344-kilometre border with Afghanistan most of which zigzags back-and-forth through the Pamir Mountains. Tajik government forces were still battling the UTO, so the Tajik border with Afghanistan was mainly guarded by Russian border guards with the help, after September 1992, of troops from Kazakhstan, Kyrgyzstan, and Uzbekistan, though Kazakhstan greatly reduced its contingent after 17 of its soldiers were killed in clashes along the Tajik–Afghan border in April 1995 and Kyrgyzstan followed by recalling almost all its troops.

The Tajik National Peace Accord was signed on 27 June 1997 and many felt the UN, and the countries helping, and often urging a deal, Iran and Russia, were anxious for an end to the Tajik civil war before the Taliban arrived at Tajikistan's border.

The Taliban knew the Uzbek and Tajik governments were helping Dostum and Masoud, respectively, and they warned both the governments not to meddle in Afghanistan's internal affairs. The Taliban chased Dostum from Mazar-i-Sharif at the start of August 1998. Taliban fighters were at that time within 20 kilometres of the Tajik border in some areas of northeastern Afghanistan. Masoud's forces continued their resistance and both Masoud and former Afghan President Burhanuddin Rabbani were regularly in Tajikistan as the battle against the Taliban continued.

The Taliban could not attack either Tajikistan or Uzbekistan directly, but they found a way to distract the attention of their two hostile northern neighbours. There were foreign fighters in the ranks of Tajikistan's opposition during the Tajik civil war, including citizens of Uzbekistan. These Uzbeks were welcomed by the Tajik opposition during the war but when peace came there was suddenly no place for them in Tajikistan. The Tajik peace deal was just that, a Tajik peace deal, and with no war, there was no longer any need for foreign fighters.

With the final stage of disarmament of Tajik opposition fighters set for early August 1999, some of the Uzbek groups in Tajikistan chose to go into southern Kyrgyzstan where they took a village hostage and then also took hostage several Kyrgyz officials who were sent there to negotiate. By the end of August there were several hundred Uzbek militants in the mountains of southern Kyrgyzstan, and they declared publicly that they were the Islamic Movement of Uzbekistan (IMU), and their goal was to overthrow Uzbek President Karimov and his government.

The IMU was led by long-time opponents of Karimov, some of whom had already been tried in absentia back in Uzbekistan and convicted of terrorism. From remote hiding places in the rugged Pamir Mountains, the IMU fought a low intensity campaign in Kyrgyzstan until October 1999 when winter finally arrived. Then under a deal worked out with Kyrgyz and Tajik authorities, they were allowed free passage to northern Afghanistan and helicopters belonging to the Russian border guards in Tajikistan ferried them there. The Kyrgyz, Tajik, and Uzbek governments hoped they had seen the last of the IMU.

The IMU already had contacts with the Taliban. The Uzbek and Tajik governments still opposed the Taliban rule in Afghanistan and were still helping, to the best of their abilities, those fighting against the Taliban. So, the Taliban allowed the IMU to regroup and re-arm in northern Afghanistan. Then in the summer of 2000, the IMU returned to southern Kyrgyzstan and this time also to south-eastern Uzbekistan. The effect was that the governments of Kyrgyzstan, Uzbekistan and Tajikistan were forced to divert their attention to their own internal security problems with far less attention being paid to what was happening in Afghanistan. This experience helps to explain why the Central Asian governments are willing to talk to the Taliban now.

The situation completely changed after 11 September 2001. When summer 2001 came, the governments in Kyrgyzstan, Tajikistan, and Uzbekistan were watching and waiting for the reappearance of the IMU. In late July, the IMU militants attacked a Kyrgyz border post along the Kyrgyz–Tajik frontier and were repelled. This time, they did not return.

Instead, the IMU fighters remained to assist the Taliban in trying to finish off Masoud's forces, which by that time were the last significant obstacle to total Taliban domination of Afghanistan. The IMU were deployed across northern Afghanistan's Takhar and Kunduz provinces when the US bombing campaign of Afghanistan started. The IMU was decimated in US bombing strikes in November 2001, the group's leader was killed, and the remnants of the IMU were forced to flee to the tribal areas of Pakistan where most of them remained for more than 10 years. For the first time since the Central Asian states became independent, there was calm along the Afghan border.

### Connecting Central Asia and Afghanistan

International organisations and individual countries rushed to provide aid to Afghanistan and work to build up its primitive infrastructure. The Asian Development Bank (ADB) launched its Central Asia Regional Economic Cooperation (CAREC) programme in 2001 that included a prominent role for Central Asia in developing Afghanistan. Since independence in 1991, and during the time the Taliban had been in power, it was easy for Central Asia to limit contact with Afghanistan because there was not much of what today is called connectivity.

The only border crossing of significance was the Dustlik (Friendship) Bridge that traversed the river Amu Darya from Uzbekistan to Afghanistan and had a railroad track down the middle. The railway line ended at the town of Hairaton, just a few kilometres after it entered Afghanistan. The last Soviet troops to leave Afghanistan did so crossing the Dustlik Bridge. The bridge was closed after Dostum's forces were chased from Mazar-i-Sharif and the Taliban took control of the area along the Uzbek border in August 1998.There was also another railway dating back to the Tsarist era that connected Kushka (now called Serhetabat) in Turkmenistan to Torghundi in Afghanistan.

Connectivity between Afghanistan and Central Asia is one of the success stories of the 20 years when US-led foreign forces were in Afghanistan. The railway line across the Dustlik Bridge was extended to Mazar-i-Sharif, the largest city in northern Afghanistan. The Serhetabat–Torghundi railway was repaired, and another railway was built that connected Imamnazar in Turkmenistan to Aqina in Afghanistan.

Four bridges for commercial traffic were built along the Tajik–Afghan border; one between Vanj in Tajikistan and Jamarj-e Bala in Afghanistan that was completed in 2011; a second between Pyanj Poyon in Tajikistan and Sher Bandar in Afghanistan that was completed in 2007; another at Qalai Khumb in Tajikistan connecting to Afghanistan's Darvoz District that opened in 2004; the fourth bridge at Temin Khorog, the regional capital of eastern Tajikistan Gorno-Badakhshan Autonomous Oblast, that crosses to Demogan in Afghanistan that opened in 2002.

Power transmissions lines were built to bring electricity from Tajikistan, Turkmenistan, and Uzbekistan to Afghanistan and eventually these three Central Asian countries provided some 78 per cent of Afghanistan's electricity imports.[1] The Central Asia–South Asia power transmission project, better known as CASA–1000, aims to bring 1300 Megawatts (MW) from hydropower plants in Kyrgyzstan and Tajikistan to Afghanistan (300 MW) and Pakistan (1000 MW). In May 2016, the Kyrgyz and Tajik presidents and the Afghan and Pakistani prime ministers met in the Tajik capital Dushanbe to officially launch the construction of CASA–1000.[2] It was scheduled to be completed in 2023 but increased fighting in areas along the route through Afghanistan, then the return of the Taliban to power in August 2021, have left the project only partially completed. In February 2024, the World Bank announced it was resuming support for CASA–1000[3] and Kyrgyzstan's Energy Ministry said at the end of July that year that exports of Kyrgyz electricity via CASA–1000 should start in the summer of 2025.[4]

The current border of Central Asia and Afghanistan was drawn at the end of the nineteenth century when it divided the Russian and British empires, and later the same border divided the Soviet Union from Afghanistan. For more than 100 years, the emphasis had always been on separating the two regions, but between 2001 and 2021, there was a focus on connecting the two regions and projects such as CAREC viewed Afghanistan and Central Asia as inseparable parts of an Inner Asia that could be a crossroads again of East–West and North–South trade, as it had been in the days of the ancient Silk Road.

When the Taliban returned to power in Afghanistan in August 2021, this new level of connectivity between Central Asia and Afghanistan made it more complicated for the three Central Asian states with an Afghan frontier to close their borders as they had worked to do in the late 1990s. And there were economic reasons for the Central Asian countries to want to keep the border open and reconsider their policies toward the Taliban.

### The Old Neighbour Returns

On 15 August 2021, the Taliban moved into Kabul, taking control of the Afghan capital. There was no panic north of the border in Central Asia as there had been 25 years earlier, even though Afghan refugees fleeing the advancing Taliban in northern Afghanistan had crossed into Tajikistan and Uzbekistan, and 46 Afghan government aircraft carrying a total of 585 Afghan government military personnel flew to Termez in Uzbekistan and other Afghan government military aircraft had flown to Tajikistan.

Tajikistan's State Committee for Emergency Situations initially said three military planes and two helicopters with 143 people aboard had landed in the southern Tajik town of Bokhtar,[5] but the Afghan Embassy in Tajikistan later clarified that two passenger and 16 military planes had flown to Tajikistan.[6] Afghan President Ashraf Ghani reportedly attempted to flee to Tajikistan,[7] but his plane was denied permission to land and he went instead to the United Arab Emirates (UAE).

Despite the Afghan spill over along the Central Asian border, the governments in Central Asia remained calm. The day the Taliban seized control of Kabul, Uzbekistan's foreign ministry announced that the Uzbek Embassy in the Afghan capital and the consulate in Mazar-i-Sharif were still operating.[8] Kazakhstan and Kyrgyzstan confirmed shortly after that their embassies were operating as well, which was another sign of the closer connections Central Asia had with Afghanistan. In 1996 when the Taliban first captured Kabul, Tajikistan was the only Central Asian country with an embassy in Afghanistan and which closed immediately after the Taliban arrived in the Afghan capital.

Much had changed since 1996 when the Taliban first took Kabul. At that time, the Taliban had swept through Afghanistan, advancing rapidly after making their initial forays into the south-eastern parts of the country in 1994. They were a new group, virtually unknown to the Central Asian governments, and were viewed as the most radical Islamic group, arguably, in the world. As mentioned, Tajik government forces were fighting an opposition that was mainly comprised of an Islamic group, the IRPT, and Russian forces had just been fighting what the Kremlin called Islamic extremists in Chechnya.

US President Barack Obama had announced plans to start reducing US forces in Afghanistan in 2010 and by 2014, most NATO troops had already left. Though the process of withdrawing all US and other foreign forces was delayed, it was clear to the Central Asian governments that the day was approaching when the situation in Afghanistan would deteriorate quickly. Already in 2013 there was fighting between the Taliban and Afghan government forces in the northwestern Afghan provinces of Herat and Faryab that bordered Turkmenistan. Every year after 2013, the Taliban made gains in northern Afghanistan and eventually controlled nearly all the districts bordering Turkmenistan and several districts bordering Tajikistan, while the meagre Afghan government forces in northern Afghanistan shuttled from one hot spot to another trying to dislodge Taliban fighters from areas they had captured.

Uzbek Foreign Minister Abdulaziz Kamilov met with the Taliban representatives in March 2019 in Doha to discuss prospects of Uzbekistan as a possible venue for talks between the Taliban and representatives of the Afghan Government.[9] In August that year, a Taliban delegation visited Uzbekistan to meet Uzbek foreign ministry officials.[10] Kamilov and other representatives of Uzbekistan's foreign ministry continued to meet with the Taliban representatives and after the Taliban regained control of Afghanistan, Kamilov was the first Central Asian foreign minister to visit Kabul when he made the trip in early October 2021.[11]

Taliban representatives had visited Turkmenistan in February and July 2021, and on 11 August, just days before Kabul fell, Turkmen foreign ministry officials met with the Taliban representatives in Doha.

The Turkmen and Uzbek governments were hedging their bets by engaging with the Taliban while President Ghani was still in power. But both governments had watched as the Taliban extended their control over areas of northern Afghanistan and both must have considered that after the total withdrawal of foreign forces from Afghanistan, the Taliban were likely to retain control over large swaths of territory on or near the Central Asian border.

And the Taliban were no longer the threat they appeared to be in the late 1990s. Groups such as the so-called Islamic State of Iraq and Syria (ISIS) and their offshoot in Afghanistan, the Islamic State of Khorasan (ISK), were more vicious, as they were stateless actors looking to seize footholds anywhere in the world they could.

The ISK had already appeared in several small pockets in northern Afghanistan, notably in Jawzjan Province that bordered Turkmenistan where a disgruntled former Taliban commander named Qari Hikmatullah had gathered local forces and raised the black flag of ISIS in 2017. For months, Hikmatullah's force had caused pandemonium in Jawzjan and the neighbouring Faryab Province as they attacked both Taliban and Afghan government forces until Hikmatullah was killed in a drone strike in Faryab in April 2018.[12]

Among their first acts on returning to power, the Taliban called on the Central Asian states to maintain friendly ties. Similar calls in September and October 1996 had fallen on deaf ears across the northern border, but in 2021, most of the Central Asian governments were willing to listen and talk with the Taliban about future cooperation.

### A New Arrangement

The Taliban had something to offer to the Central Asian governments, certainly the Uzbek and Tajik governments.

There were still hundreds, at least, of citizens of Uzbekistan and Tajikistan who had been in Afghanistan for many years as part of the Taliban or as part of groups such as the IMU or Jamaat Ansarullah that were allied with the Taliban in battling foreign and Afghan government forces. Jamaat Ansarullah was once the Tajik wing of the IMU, but after the IMU was mauled in US bombing in late 2001, Jamaat Ansarullah gradually emerged as a separate group. Jamaat Ansarullah later absorbed many IMU fighters who were chased from the Pakistani tribal areas by the Pakistani military operation that came after the IMU carried out an attack on the Jinnah International Airport in Karachi in June 2014.Ghani's government often referred to this group as Jundallah.

After returning to power, the Taliban pledged they would keep these foreign fighters under control and that none would use the Afghan territory to plan or carry out attacks on Afghanistan's neighbours. How much the Central Asian governments believed the Taliban is not known, but the Taliban's promise was better than nothing and it did pave the way for the establishment of a business relationship between Central Asia and the new rulers of Afghanistan.

In the late 1990s, Uzbekistan was the most anti-Taliban of all the Central Asian countries, but since the Taliban's return to power, no Central Asian country has engaged the Taliban more actively than Uzbekistan. The Dustlik Bridge was closed as the Taliban were moving on to Mazar-i-Sharif in the middle of August 2021. After the Taliban took control of Kabul, Uzbekistan's foreign ministry released a statement saying it was in close contact with the Taliban and that 'any attempts to violate the state border will be strictly suppressed,'[13] by which the Uzbek Government meant Afghan refugees or government troops.

On 17 August 2021, Nodirbek Jalilov, the head of the Termez Cargo Centre, located some two kilometres from the Afghan border, said the centre was waiting for the resumption of trade with Afghanistan.[14] The Termez Cargo Centre opened in 2016 and was intended to handle what Uzbekistan hoped would be increased trade with Afghanistan through Uzbekistan's rail and roadways.

Uzbekistan also has other economic reasons for developing ties with the Taliban. Uzbekistan has been hoping for a greatly expanded trade to the south, through Afghanistan, to the Arabian Sea and Indian Ocean. Small examples of the potential have been seen already in 2022. A private company in India successfully shipped some 140 tonnes of goods, mainly sugar, through Pakistan and Afghanistan to Uzbekistan in March[15] and a shipment of Uzbek goods headed to India left the Pakistani port at Karachi at the end of May.[16] Kazakhstan also conducted a trial run of the route through Afghanistan to Pakistan in July 2023, sending several trucks on the journey to Pakistan and back.[17]

The railway that crosses the Dustlik Bridge was extended with ADB financing from Hairaton to Mazar-i-Sharif and started operation in 2011. NATO used this railway line as part of its Northern Distribution Network (NDN) to ferry cargo to and from Afghanistan after 2008 and China incorporated the railway line into its Belt and Road Initiative (BRI). The first train from China arrived in Afghanistan in September 2016.

Uzbekistan signed a deal with Pakistan in February 2021 to build a 573-kilometre railway connecting Mazar-i-Sharif to Peshawar where it would connect with the Pakistani railway network leading to Pakistan's Arabian Sea ports.[18] Uzbek President Shavkat Mirziyoyev met the then Pakistani Prime Minister Imran Khan ahead of a Central Asia–South Asia connectivity forum in Tashkent in July 2021 to discuss the project and in September 2021 the two met again on the sidelines of the Shanghai Cooperation Organisation (SCO) summit in Dushanbe with the railway at the top of their agenda. Uzbek officials have mentioned the Mazar-i-Sharif–Kabul–Peshawar railway many times since the Taliban returned to power.

The project continued after the Taliban's return to power in Afghanistan in August 2021. In late March 2022, Uzbek media outlet *UzDaily* reported that Pakistan, Uzbekistan, and Afghanistan had agreed on the route[19] and on 12 April 2022, Taliban railway officials visited the Uzbek border city of Termez for talks with their Uzbek counterparts on extending the railway line from Mazar-i-Sharif to Kabul and Peshawar.[20] The survey work of the proposed route started in July 2022,[21] and in July 2023, Pakistani, Uzbek, and Taliban officials met in Islamabad to approve the route[22] and begin discussions on financing and technical aspects of the project.[23] Uzbek authorities said in October 2023 that they were discussing financing of the railway with Qatar.[24] In February 2024, representatives of the Afghan National Railway Administration, Uzbekistan, and the United Arab Emirates signed a memorandum of understanding for a feasibility study of the Trans-Afghan railway.[25] Uzbekistan's Transport Minister Ilhom Makhkamov said in February 2025 that he expected work on the Trans-Afghan railway would start in 2025.[26]

Turkmenistan never forgot about TAPI. Former President Gurbanguly Berdymukhammedov focused on the project since he came to power at the end of 2006. But despite many meetings with officials from Afghanistan, India, and Pakistan over the course of more than a decade, including a ground-breaking ceremony in Herat, Afghanistan on 23 February 2018, that Berdymukhammedov, Afghan President Ghani, Indian Minister of State for External Affairs M.J. Akbar, and Pakistani Prime Minister Shahid Khaqan Abbasi attended,[27] there was no progress on the project outside of Turkmenistan. The Taliban had pledged for several years before their return to power in Afghanistan that they would not disrupt work on TAPI as it benefitted the Afghan people and had even offered to help provide security for workers building the pipeline.

Turkmen Foreign Minister Rashid Meredov visited Kabul at the end of October 2021,[28] Turkmen Deputy Foreign Minister Wepa Hajiyev led a delegation to Kabul in January 2022,[29] and the Taliban's Acting Foreign Minister Amir Khan Muttaqi visited Ashgabat right after Hajiyev's visit[30] to discuss the construction of TAPI. Berdymukhammedov's son Serdar was elected Turkmenistan's president on 12 March 2022, but the father remains a powerful figure as chairman of the *Halk Maslahaty* (People's Council), the upper house of parliament, and undoubtedly the realisation of the TAPI project will remain a priority for Turkmenistan so long as Berdymukhammedov, who turned 67 years in late June 2024, is alive.

Turkmen and Afghan officials held another ceremony on 11 September 2024, marking the start of construction of the TAPI pipeline on Afghan side of the border.[31] Taliban acting Prime Minister Muhammad Hassan Akhund and Gurbanguly Berdymukhammedov attended the event. Herat Governor Maulana Islam Jar's press office said on 27 January 2025, that six kilometres of the pipeline had already been laid in Afghanistan.[32]

Tajikistan, Turkmenistan, and Uzbekistan continue to supply Afghanistan with electricity despite the Taliban admitting they cannot pay all of it at this time. By May 2022, Afghanistan owed more than $100 million to just Tajikistan and Uzbekistan,[33] but as of February 2024, the Taliban had made payments totaling some $627 million for electricity imports from its three immediate Central Asian neighbours[34] and owed Uzbekistan only some $1.2 million.[35] Prior to Taliban's return to power in 2021, more than 60 per cent of Kazakhstan's flour exports, along with exports of wheat and other grains went to Afghanistan. Kazakh authorities initially announced they were suspending these exports after the Taliban seized Kabul,[36] but by April 2022, Kazakhstan's ambassador to Afghanistan said his country was increasing its wheat exports to Afghanistan to previous levels.[37] Kazakh Trade Minister Serik Zhumangarin led a delegation to Kabul in April 2023, ostensibly to deliver humanitarian aid,[38] but during his visit Zhumangarin discussed trade with Taliban officials. Months later, in early August, Kazakhstan hosted a Kazakh–Afghan business forum with representatives of 150 companies, including some 70 from Afghanistan, taking part.[39] Kazakhstan's media reported at the time that Kazakh-Afghan trade for 2022 totaled some $987.9 million, and Zhumangarin told delegates at the forum the two countries aimed to increase this to $3 billion annually.[40] Uzbekistan has set a similar goal of $3 billion for trade with Afghanistan and in 2024 their bilateral trade reached $1.1 billion.[41]

During Zhumangarin's April 2023 visit to Kabul, Taliban's Acting Deputy Prime Minister Abdul Ghani Baradar announced that Taliban representatives would soon take up posts at the Afghan Embassy in Kazakhstan.[42] By that time, the Taliban already had accredited diplomats at the Afghan embassies in Kyrgyzstan, Turkmenistan, and Uzbekistan,[43] and the Taliban sent a delegation to Tajikistan in late March 2023, to discuss access to the Afghan consulate in Khorugh, the regional capital of Tajikistan's eastern Gorno-Badakhshan Autonomous Oblast,[44] though the embassy in Dushanbe was still occupied by representatives of the former government as 2024 came to an end.

Zhumangarin visited Afghanistan again in April 2024, and said Kazakhstan was interested in taking part in construction of the Trans-Afghan railway between Termez, Uzbekistan and Peshawar, Pakistan, and also the proposed Herat–Kandahar–Spin-Boldak railway project.[45] Baradar visited Uzbekistan in February 2025 and said Uzbekistan agreed to work on a railway from the Afghan river town of Hairaton, on the other side of the Amu-Darya from Termez to Herat in western Afghanistan.[46] This railway branch could link up to a recently opened line between Herat and Khaf in Iran that goes further west into Turkey.

## The Same Old Problems

Most of the Central Asian countries have adopted Turkmenistan's policy of the late 1990s towards the Taliban-controlled Afghanistan—that business interests and non-interference in internal affairs should be the basis for engagement with the Taliban. But not all Central Asian countries have established contact with the Taliban. Tajikistan's government was clearly displeased with the Taliban returning to power. In a meeting with visiting Pakistani Foreign Minister Shah Mahmood Qureshi on 25 August 2021, Tajik President Rahmon said Tajikistan would not recognise any such government in Afghanistan that excludes non-Pushtuns, and specifically mentioned that the Afghan Tajiks must have a place in any government the Taliban form.

Among the current leaders of the countries neighboring Afghanistan, Rahmon is the only one who was in power when the Taliban last controlled Afghanistan in the late 1990s. He did not want the Taliban as neighbours then and does not want them as Tajikistan's neighbour even now.

Additionally, the IRPT received positions in the Tajik Government as part of the 1997 peace agreement. It was the only registered Islamic party not only in Tajikistan, but anywhere in Central Asia. It was a genuine opposition party with its own proposals for the development of Tajikistan. It was also the second largest political party in Tajikistan after President Rahmon's ruling People's Democratic Party of Tajikistan. Rahmon, subsequently, moved to eliminate the IRPT.

The IRPT's share of positions in the government dwindled over the years. It lost its last two seats in the parliament in the elections held in March 2015. By August that year, the party's activities had been suspended by the Tajik courts and in September, the IRPT was accused of involvement in a plot led by Tajikistan's deputy defence minister to overthrow the government in early September. The IRPT was declared an extremist organisation at the end of September 2015 and officially banned. The government has continued to portray the IRPT as an extremist group, but the IRPT is far more moderate than the Taliban, a group the IRPT condemned shortly after the 11 September 2001 attacks in the US. It would be difficult for the Tajik authorities to continue vilifying the IRPT and at the same time engage in talks with the more radical Taliban.

The Tajik Government has allowed the Afghan ambassador appointed by the former Ghani Government, Mohammad Zahir Agbar, to remain on his post. For the first few months after the Taliban retook control over Afghanistan, Agbar was something of a spokesman for the National Resistance Front (NRF), a group of mainly ethnic Tajiks under the command of Ahmad Shah Masoud's son that was based in their traditional stronghold in Afghanistan's Panjshir Valley.

Tajikistan conducted a series of military exercises, including joint manoeuvres with Russian and Uzbek forces, in the weeks after the Taliban returned to power in Afghanistan. The Taliban responded by stationing fighters from their foreign allies, Jamaat Ansarullah, to guard parts of the border with Tajikistan. In July 2022, there was a report that the Taliban had established a new observation post in the Darvoz District close to the border with Tajikistan and manned it with fighters from Jamaat Ansarullah.[47]

There are reports that the leadership of the NRF is often in Tajikistan and that Tajikistan might be either providing or funneling aid to the NRF inside Afghanistan. Afghan politician and former mujahidin leader Gulbuddin Hekmatyar had stated in May 2022 that Tajikistan was 'sheltering the Afghan armed opposition,' which he regarded as a 'declaration of war against Afghanistan.'[48] As noted earlier, Tajikistan is the only Central Asian country where the Afghan embassy is still staffed by representatives of the former Ghani Government. On 13 September 2023, the Afghan Embassy in Dushanbe held a memorial service for the slain ethnic Tajik Afghan commander Ahmad Shah Masoud, who was assassinated by al-Qaeda suicide bombers posing as journalists on 9 September 2001.[49]

Another problem facing not only Tajikistan but Uzbekistan as well is the activity of ISK in northern Afghanistan. ISK claimed responsibility for the March 2022 bombings of Shia mosques in Mazar-i-Sharif that killed 34 people and injuring some 80 others, and in Kunduz city that killed four people and wounded 18 others.

ISK has twice fired rockets at Uzbekistan from the Afghan border town of Hairaton, once on 18 April 2022 when none of the 10 rockets fired made it across the Amu Darya into the Uzbek territory,[50] and again on 5 July 2022 when five rockets fired from Hairaton landed in a Termez neighbourhood but none exploded.[51]

ISK also launched rockets at a border guard post in Tajikistan from an Afghan border village in the Khojagor region of the Takhar Province on 7 May 2022.[52] Tajik border guards reportedly fired back destroying the vehicle the ISK militants used, but the militants themselves managed to flee the scene.[53] Tajik authorities downplayed the incident saying some stray bullets from Afghanistan had "accidentally" landed on Tajikistan's territory.[54] Tajik authorities blame ISK for the bombing of a car belonging to the leader of the Kulob branch of the ruling Democratic Party of Tajikistan Salim Sayvalizoda on 5 January 2024.[55] Sayvalizoda was wounded in the attack and later Tajik officials said they had detained nine people who were accused of being ISK members.[56]

In 2022, ISK increasingly targeted its propaganda at ethnic minority groups in northern Afghanistan, Tajiks, Turkmen, and Uzbeks, portraying the Taliban as heretics and Pushtuns that would never respect or satisfy the needs of the indigenous peoples of northern Afghanistan. There have been problems between Pushtun members of the Taliban sent to northern Afghanistan and locals with claims that the Pushtuns had evicted Turkmen and Tajik farmers and seized their lands. A prominent local ethnic Uzbek Taliban commander, Makhdoom Alam, was arrested in January 2022 and taken to Kabul, sparking protests and fighting that left four people dead in Faryab's provincial capital Maimana that saw local Uzbeks disarm the Taliban fighters and march them outside the city limits.[57] ISK has claimed in some of its propaganda videos that the Taliban have been killing ethnic Tajiks and Uzbeks in Afghanistan.[58] ISK has also aimed its propaganda at the governments of Uzbekistan and particularly Tajikistan,[59] calling on citizens of those two countries to join ISK and help oust their governments.

The intent of the ISK campaign seems aimed at preventing the Central Asian states and the Taliban from developing a closer relationship that could make it more difficult for ISK to achieve its own goals in Afghanistan. The ISK's choice of Termez as a target for rocket attacks was significant. It was clearly intended to demonstrate that the key crossing at the Dustlik Bridge was not safe for trade and the Taliban cannot make good on their promises that the Afghan territory would not be used by any group to carry out attacks on the neighbouring countries.

However, events outside Central Asia show ISK propaganda appears to have succeeded in luring some Tajik citizens outside Tajikistan into staging attacks. In late December 2023, police in Germany detained seven people suspected of plotting terrorist attacks,[60] identified as Tajiks and Uzbeks,[61] allegedly connected to ISK. At that same time, police in Austria detained three people linked to one of the Tajik nationals detained in Germany. In all, 11 people were detained in Germany and Austria and most were Tajik nationals. At the start of 2024, two ISK suicide bombers who killed more than 90 people in Kerman, Iran at a commemorative service for deceased Iranian General Qasem Soleimani. Iranian authorities said one of the bombers was a citizen of Tajikistan.[62]

On 22 March 2024, terrorists attacked Moscow's Crocus City Hall, killing more than 140 people. ISK took responsibility for the attack. Russian authorities arrested more than dozen people, most of whom were Tajik nationals working in Russia.

### A New Problem

The issue that is proving most contentious between the Taliban-ruled Afghanistan and the Central Asian states bordering Afghanistan is the use of water from Amu Darya. The effects of climate change are already manifesting in Central Asia with decreased annual rainfall, rapidly melting glaciers in the eastern mountains, and three straight summers (2021–23) of record high temperatures and drought. Downstream communities in Uzbekistan and Turkmenistan are already noticing effects of climate change. Residents of Turkmenistan's eastern Lebap Province said in June 2023 that the level of water in Amu Darya was one-third of its normal level for that time of the year.[63]

In March 2022, Taliban authorities announced the start of work on the Qosh Tepa canal that will be 100 metres wide, 8.5 metres deep, and extend some 285 kilometres through Afghanistan's northern Balkh, Jawzjan, and Faryab provinces. Taliban officials promise that the canal will irrigate some 500,000 hectares of agricultural land and provide some 250,000 people with work.[64] The project was estimated to be completed in 2028, but it is ahead of schedule.

The water for the canal comes from the Amu Darya and there are estimates that when the canal is completed, it will siphon off some 15 per cent of the water that currently reaches downstream communities in Uzbekistan and Turkmenistan.[65]

Since the Taliban were unable to attract any foreign interest for participating in the construction or in financing of the US$ 684 million project, the canal is being built by an Afghan state company. There are concerns about the quality of the construction. One report said, 'The construction methods employed appear remarkably rudimentary, with a mere "digging" approach devoid of proper reinforcement or lining for the canal's bottom and banks,' which the report said 'poses a grave risk, as significant water losses may occur due to seepage into the dry, sandy soil.'[66]

There are no agreements on water use between Afghanistan and any of the Central Asian states. Under international law, Afghanistan is entitled to its share of the water from the Amu Darya. The Afghan media outlet *The Khaama Press* wrote in March 2023 that 'due to the two decades of conflict [Afghanistan] has yet to be able to use its water resources,' and added, 'As a result, most neighbouring countries took advantage of the situation and utilized the water without consulting Afghanistan.'[67]

Taliban officials have repeatedly mentioned that they will take into account the interests of their northern neighbours as Afghanistan draws water into the Qosh Tepa canal. Eighteen months after construction started, the canal was already 108-kilometres long. At a ceremony in Balkh Province on 11 October 2023, marking the completion of the first phase of the canal's construction, Taliban's Acting Second Deputy Prime Minister Abdul Salam Hanafi said, 'There should be no worries for our neighbours here.' Similarly,

Acting Deputy Foreign Minister Stanikzai said, 'If our neighbours have worries in this regard, we are ready to contact them through diplomatic channels.'[68] The Taliban officials have indicated they will not be swayed from completing the canal.

At a meeting on the Aral Sea in Dushanbe in September 2023, Uzbek President Mirziyoyev expressed concerns about the canal stating that it 'could fundamentally change the water regime and balance in Central Asia'.[69] The Acting Taliban Minister for Hydropower Abdul Latif Mansur replied, 'We did not accept any obligations. There is no agreement. Therefore, we do what we consider necessary.'[70] The Taliban have already demonstrated in May that they will fight over water issues if required.

Iran has been pressing Afghanistan to release more water from its reservoirs into the Helmand River that flows into Iran's Sistan and Baluchistan Province, but the Taliban said drought had left the reservoirs low on water. Former Iranian President Ebrahim Raisi visited the eastern Iranian province on 18 May 2023, and on seeing the effects of the drought warned the 'rulers of Afghanistan, that they should immediately give water rights to the people of Sistan and Baluchistan'.[71] The Taliban replied that Iranian officials should 'present their requests with appropriate language' and also sent military reinforcements to the border with Iran. On 27 May 2023, Taliban militants and Iranian border guards exchanged machine gun and mortar fire that left at least two Iranian border guards and one Taliban militant dead.[72]

Construction of the Qosh Tepa canal will likely be the end for many downstream agricultural communities in Uzbekistan and Turkmenistan. Uzbekistan's *kun.uz* news outlet reported in February 2023 that the Qosh Tepa canal 'could have serious consequences for [Uzbekistan's] Khorezm, Bukhara, Surhandarya and Navoi provinces, as well as the Republic of Karakalpakstan…'[73] Tens of thousands of people in the two Central Asian countries will need to be relocated if the sources of water dry up.

**Summing Up**

The Central Asian states' approach toward the Taliban in the late 1990s raised tensions with Afghanistan and helped create domestic militant organisations such as the IMU and Jamaat Ansarullah. The current approach by the Central Asian governments, with the exception of Tajikistan, has resulted in a peaceful though fragile coexistence that focuses on mutually beneficial trade projects. However, the problem of water is already putting a strain on Afghanistan's ties with Uzbekistan and Turkmenistan.

The presence of Central Asian militants in Afghanistan, whether allied with, or fighting the Taliban, will always be a cause for concern for the

Central Asian governments. Any attack on Central Asian soil that can be credibly attributed to one of these Central Asian militant groups currently located in Afghanistan has the potential to upset Central Asia's ties with the current Afghan authorities. Perhaps, most importantly, Central Asian governments are secular. Their leaders make a public display of attending mosques and making the Hajj, but most were raised on the atheistic Soviet communist system. Their views of governance and society differ significantly from the Taliban and this factor will be an obstacle to closer ties between Central Asia and Afghanistan.

## NOTES

1. 'Afghanistan: Sector Assessment (Summary): Energy', Asian Development Bank, North–South Power Transmission Enhancement Project (RRP AFG 46392), at https://www.adb.org/sites/default/files/linked-documents/46392-001-ssa.pdf.
2. 'В Таджикистанезапущенпроект CASA–1000' [CASA–1000 project launched in Tajikistan], Radio Free Europe Radio Liberty Tajik Service, 12 May 2016, at https://rus.ozodi.org/a/27729618.html.
3. 'World Bank agrees Afghanistan CASA-1000 power project restart amid neighbouring nations' "stranded asset" fears', *bne Intellinews*, 25 February 2024, at https://www.intellinews.com/world-bank-agrees-afghanistan-casa-1000-power-project-restart-amid-neighbouring-nations-stranded-asset-fears-313984/.
4. 'Kyrgyzstan and Tajikistan to supply electricity to Pakistan under CASA-1000', *Daryo.uz*, 31 May 2024, at https://daryo.uz/en/2024/05/31/kyrgyzstan-and-tajikistan-to-supply-electricity-to-pakistan-under-casa-1000.
5. 'В Таджикистанприлетелиболее 140 военныхизАфганистана – власти' [More than 140 military personnel from Afghanistan flew to Tajikistan – authorities], *Radio Free Europe Radio Liberty Tajik Service*, 16 August 2021, at https://rus.ozodi.org/a/31412530.html.
6. 'Tajik MFA: We Receive a SOS Signal from Afghanistan', *Asia-Plus Tajikistan*, 17 August 2021, at https://asiaplustj.info/en/news/tajikistan/politics/20210817/tajik-mfa-we-receive-a-sos-signal-from-afghanistan.
7. 'Afghan Pres Ghani Leaves for Tajikistan–Interior Ministry Official', *Reuters*, 15 August 2021, at https://www.reuters.com/world/asia-pacific/afghan-pres-ghani-leaves-tajikistan-interior-ministry-official-2021-08-15/.
8. 'Посольство Узбекистана в Кабуле и консульство в Мазари-Шарифепродолжаютработать' [Embassy of Uzbekistan in Kabul and consulate in Mazar-i-Sharif continue to work], *gazeta.uz*, 15 August 2021, at https://www.gazeta.uz/ru/2021/08/15/bridge/.
9. 'Uzbek Foreign Minister Meets Taliban Officials in Qatar', *Tashkent Times*, 4 March 2019, at http://tashkenttimes.uz/world/3605-uzbek-foreign-minister-meets-taliban-officials-in-qatar.

10. 'Встреча с представителями движения «Талибан»' [Meeting with representatives of the Taliban movement], *UzDaily.uz*, 8 August 2019, at https://www.uzdaily.uz/ru/post/45426.
11. Riyaz ul Khaliq, 'Uzbekistan's Foreign Minister Meets Afghan Counterpart in Kabul', *Anadolu Agency*, 7 October 2021, at https://www.aa.com.tr/en/asia-pacific/uzbekistans-foreign-minister-meets-afghan-counterpart-in-kabul/2385882.
12. Bill Roggio, 'US Military Kills Senior Islamic State Commander in Afghan North', *FDD's Long War Journal*, 9 April 2018, at https://www.longwarjournal.org/archives/2018/04/us-military-kills-senior-islamic-state-commander-in-afghan-north.php.
13. 'Заявление Министерстваиностранныхдел РеспубликиУзбекистан' [Statement of the Ministry of Foreign Affairs of the Republic of Uzbekistan], Ministry of Foreign Affairs of the Republic of Uzbekistan, 17 August 2021, at https://mfa.uz/ru/press/news/2021/zayavlenie-ministerstva-inostrannyh-del-respubliki-uzbekistan---30142.
14. 'В Узбекистанеждутвосстановленияторговли с Афганистаном' [Uzbekistan expects restoration of trade with Afghanistan]', *TASS*, 17 August 2021, at https://tass.ru/ekonomika/12153183.
15. Ayaz Gul, 'For First Time, Indian Cargo Travels Via Pakistan, Afghanistan to Uzbekistan', *Voice Of America*, 16 March 2022, at https://www.voanews.com/a/for-first-time-indian-cargo-travels-via-pakistan-afghanistan-to-uzbekistan/6488459.html.
16. 'ICTSI Pakistan HandlesFirst Uzbek Export', *Hellenic Shipping News*, 31 May 2022, at https://www.hellenicshippingnews.com/ictsi-pakistan-handles-first-uzbek-export/.
17. Saniya Sakenova, 'Kazakhstan Sends First Trucks on New Trade Route to Pakistan', *The Astana Times*, 1 August 2023, at https://astanatimes.com/2023/08/kazakhstan-sends-first-trucks-on-new-trade-route-to-pakistan.
18. Cuenca Olivia, 'Strategic PlanSigned for 573km Trans-Afghan Railway', *International Railway Journal*, 9 February 2021, at https://www.railjournal.com/infrastructure/strategic-plan-signed-for-573km-trans-afghan-railway/.
19. 'Uzbekistan Starts the Creation of the Trans-Afghan Railway', *UzDaily.uz*, 29 March 2022, at https://uzdaily.uz/en/post/72091.
20. 'Афганскаясторонавыразилаполнуюудовлетворенностьработойпоэксплуатациижелезнодорожнойлинии «Хайратон – Мазари-Шариф' [Afghan side expresses complete satisfaction with the work on the operation of the Hairaton–Mazar-i-Sharif railway line], *UzDaily.uz*, 17 April 2022, at https://www.uzdaily.uz/ru/post/68344.
21. 'НачаласьреализацияпроектаТрансафганскойжелезнойдороги' [Implementation of the Trans-Afghan Railway project has started], *gazeta.uz*, 20 July 2022, at https://www.gazeta.uz/ru/2022/07/20/railway/.
22. Fidel Rahmati, 'Afghanistan, Pakistan, Uzbekistan Sign Tripartite Railway Project', *The Khaama Press*, 19 July 2023, at https://www.khaama.com/afghanistan-pakistan-uzbekistan-sign-tripartite-railway-project/.
23. 'НачалсязаключительныйэтаппереговоровпоТрансафганскойжелезнойдороге' [The final stage of negotiations on the Trans-Afghan Railway has begun], *gazeta.uz*, 18 July 2023, at https://www.gazeta.uz/ru/2023/07/18/trans-afghan-railway-project/.
24. 'УзбекистанрешилпривлечьКатар к строительствуТрансафганскойжелезнойдороги' [Uzbekistan decided to involve Qatar in the construction of the Trans-Afghan railway], *Fergana Media*, 25 October 2023, at https://fergana.media/news/131793/.

25. 'Memorandum signed for feasibility study of Trans-Afghan railway project', *Amu TV*, 20 February 2024, at https://amu.tv/84164/.
26. 'Узбекистан рассчитывает начать строительство Трансафганской железной дороги в 2025 году' [Uzbekistan expects to begin construction of the Trans-Afghan Railway in 2025], *Gazeta.uz*, 4 February 2025, at https://www.gazeta.uz/ru/2025/02/04/trans-afghan-railway/.
27. Bruce Pannier, 'Afghan TAPI Construction Kicks Off, But Pipeline Questions Still Unresolved', *Qishloq Ovozi*, RFERL, 23 February 2018, at https://www.rferl.org/a/qishloq-ovozi-tapi-pipeine-afghanistan-launch/29059433.html.
28. 'Afghanistan Taliban PM Akhund Meets Turkmen FM Discussed TAPI Project', *ANI*, 30 October 2021, at https://www.aninews.in/news/world/asia/afghanistan-taliban-pm-akhund-meets-turkmen-fm-discusses-tapi-project20211030214904/.
29. Najibullah Lalzoy, 'Turkmenistan DelegationVisiting Kabul to Assess TAPI', *The Khaama Press*, 9 January 2022, at https://www.khaama.com/turkmenistan-delegation-visiting-kabul-to-assess-tapi-876875/.
30. 'Taliban and Turkmenistan Discussed the TAPI Pipeline Project', Special Eurasia, 17 January 2022, at https://www.specialeurasia.com/2022/01/17/taliban-turkmenistan-tapi/.
31. 'Construction of Afghanistan section of TAPI gas pipeline launched', *Ariana News*, 11 September 2024, at https://www.ariananews.af/construction-of-afghanistan-section-of-tapi-gas-pipeline-launched/.
32. 'TAPI project making 'rapid' progress: Herat governor', *Ariana News*, 27 January 2025, at https://www.ariananews.af/tapi-project-making-rapid-progress-herat-governor/.
33. 'Афганистан задолжал свыше $100 млн за электроэнергию Узбекистану и Таджикистану' [Afghanistan owes over $100 million for electricity to Uzbekistan and Tajikistan], *Gazeta.uz*, 19 May 2022, at https://www.gazeta.uz/ru/2022/05/19/electricity/.
34. 'Талибан» погасил долг перед Узбекистаном за электроэнергию' [Taliban repays debt to Uzbekistan for electricity], *RFERL Uzbek Service*, 8 February 2024, at https://rus.ozodlik.org/a/32810642.html.
35. 'Афганистан почти полностью погасил долг перед Узбекистаном за поставки электроэнергии' [Afghanistan has almost completely repaid its debt to Uzbekistan for electricity supplies], *Gazeta.uz*, 8 February 2024, at https://www.gazeta.uz/ru/2024/02/08/dabs/.
36. Almaz Kumenov, 'Kazakhstan Wheat RedirectedAway from Afghanistan', *Eurasianet*, 26 August 2022, at https://eurasianet.org/kazakhstan-wheat-redirected-away-from-afghanistan.
37. 'Kazakhstan Hikes Wheat Exports to Afghanistan', *Bakhtar News Agency*, 17 April 2022, at https://bakhtarnews.af/en/kazakhstan-hikes-wheat-exports-to-afghanistan/.
38. 'Kazakh Delegation Hands Humanitarian Aid to Afghanistan', *Kazinform*, 17 April 2023, at https://en.inform.kz/news/kazakh-delegation-hands-humanitarian-aid-to-afghanistan_a4057506/.
39. 'Казахстанско-афганскийделовойфорумпройдет в Астане 3-5 августа' [The Kazakh–Afghan business forum will be held in Astana on August 3–5], *TASS*, 28 July 2023, at https://tass.ru/ekonomika/18393503/amp.

40. 'Kazakhstan, Afghanistan Pledge to Bolster Trade, Investment Partnership', *Astana Times*, 4 August 2023, at https://astanatimes.com/2023/08/kazakhstan-afghanistan-pledge-to-bolster-trade-investment-partnership/.
41. 'Uzbekistan-Afghanistan Trade Reaches $1.1 Billion', *Tolo News*, 7 February 2025, at https://tolonews.com/business-192958.
42. Fidel Rahmati, 'Kazakhstan is Ready to Welcome Afghan Diplomats, Says Baradar', *The Khaama Press*, 17 April 2023, at https://www.khaama.com/kazakhstan-is-ready-to-welcome-afghan-diplomats-says-baradar/.
43. Dmitri Mazorenko, 'Казахстансогласилсяаккредитоватьдипломатов, предложенныхновымивластямиАфганистана' [Kazakhstan agreed to accredit diplomats proposed by the new Afghan authorities], *Vlast.kz*, 17 April 2023, at https://vlast.kz/novosti/54801-kazahstan-soglasilsa-akkreditovat-diplomatov-predlozennyh-novymi-vlastami-afganistana.html.
44. 'The Ebb and Flow of the Taliban's Relations with Central Asia', *RFERL Majlis Podcast*, 2 April 2023, at https://www.rferl.org/a/majlis-podcast-taliban-relations-central-asia/32345891.html.
45. Nikita Drobny, 'Казахстанготовстроитьжелезныедорогидляталибов в Афганистане' [Kazakhstan is ready to build railways for the Taliban in Afghanistan], *Orda.kz*, 25 April 2024, at https://orda.kz/kazahstan-gotov-stroit-zheleznye-dorogi-dlja-talibov-v-afganistane-385614/.
46. 'Узбекистан и Афганистандостиглисоглашения о строительствежелезнойдороги Хайратон-Герат' [Uzbekistan and Afghanistan reached an agreement on the construction of the Hairatan-Herat railway], *RFERL Uzbek Service*, 24 February 2025, at https://rus.azattyk.org/a/uzbekistan-i-afganistan-dostigli-soglasheniya-o-stroitelstve-zheleznoy-dorogi-hayraton-gerat/33325479.html.
47. Mumin Ahmadi, Sirojiddin Islam and Nigora Fazliddin, 'Надписьнаскале – провокацияпротив Таджикистана? «Талибан» строитновый КПП наафганско-таджикскойгранице' [Is the inscription on the rock a provocation against Tajikistan? Taliban build new checkpoint on Afghan–Tajik border], *RFERL Tajik Service*, 8 July 2022, at https://rus.ozodi.org/a/31934770.html.
48. 'By Providing Asylum to Afghan Opposition, Tajikistan Declares War Against Afghanistan, Says Hekmatyar', *Asia-Plus Tajikistan*, 10 May 2022, at https://asiaplustj.info/en/node/311668.
49. Amir Isaev, 'В Душанбепрошелденьпамяти Ахмада Шаха Масуда' [Day of Remembrance of Ahmad Shah Massoud was held in Dushanbe], *RFERL Tajik Service*, 13 September 2023, at https://rus.ozodi.org/a/32591548.html.
50. Ayaz Gul, 'Islamic State Khorasan Claims Rocket Attack on Uzbekistan', *Voice of America*, 18 April 2022, at https://www.voanews.com/a/islamic-state-khorasan-claims-rocket-attack-on-uzbekistan-/6534866.html.
51. 'На территорию Узбекистанаупалипятьснарядовпредположительноо стороны Афганистана' [Five shells allegedly from Afghanistan fell on the territory of Uzbekistan], *gazeta.uz*, 5 July 2022, at https://www.gazeta.uz/ru/2022/07/05/afghanistan/.
52. 'ИСТОЧНИКИ: С ТЕРРИТОРИИ АФГАНИСТАНА БЫЛО ВЫПУЩЕНО НЕСКОЛЬКО РАКЕТ В СТОРОНУ ТАДЖИКИСТАНА' [Sources: Several Rockets Were Fired From Afghanistan Towards Tajikistan], bomdodrus.com, 7 May 2022, at

https://bomdodrus.com/2022/05/08/strong-istochniki-s-territorii-afganistana-bylo-vypushheno-neskolko-raket-v-storonu-tadzhikistana-strong/.

53. 'БОЕВИКИ ИГИЛ – "ХОРАСАН" ВЗЯЛИ НА СЕБЯ ОТВЕТСТВЕННОСТЬ ЗА РАКЕТНЫЙ ОБСТРЕЛ ГРАНИЦ ТАДЖИКИСТАНА' [ISIS fighters – "Khorasan" Takes Responsibility for Rocket Fire on the Borders of Tajikistan], bomdodrus.com, 8 May 2022, at https://bomdodrus.com/2022/05/08/boeviki-igil-horasan-vzjali-na-sebja-otvetstvennost-za-raketnyj-obstrel-granic-tadzhikistana-video/.
54. 'ГКНБ: «Пулислучайнопопалинатерриторию Таджикистанасостороныафганскогорайона Ходжагор»' [State Committee for National Security: 'Bullets accidentally hit the territory of Tajikistan from the Afghan region of Khojagor'], *RFERL Tajik Service*, 8 May 2022, at https://rus.ozodi.org/a/31839739.html.
55. 'След "ИГИЛ-Хорасана"? Глава МВД назвал взрыв в Кулябе терактом' [Trace of "ISIS-Khorasan"? The head of the Ministry of Internal Affairs called the explosion in Kulyab a terrorist attack], *RFERL Tajik Service*, 15 February 2024, at https://rus.ozodi.org/a/32820677.html.
56. '"Сшила флаг ИГИЛ". Подробности дела о теракте в Кулябе' ["I sewed an ISIS flag." Details of the case of the terrorist attack in Kulyab], *RFERL Tajik Service*, 23 July 2024, at https://rus.ozodi.org/a/sshila-flag-igil-podrobnosti-dela-o-terakte-v-kulyabe/33047754.html.
57. Mrityunjoy Kumar Jha, 'Taliban Deploys Suicide Bombers to Quell Uprising in Afghanistan's Faryab Province', *India Narrative*, 18 January 2022, at https://www.indiannarrative.com/world-news/taliban-deploys-suicide-bombers-to-quell-uprising-in-afghanistan-s-faryab-province-143621.html.
58. Lucas Webber and Riccardo Valle, 'Islamic State in Afghanistan Looks to Recruit Regional Tajiks, Inflict Violence Against Tajikistan', *The Diplomat*, 29 April 2022, at https://thediplomat.com/2022/04/islamic-state-in-afghanistan-looks-to-recruit-regional-tajiks-inflict-violence-against-tajikistan.
59. Lucas Webber, 'Islamic State-Supporting Tajik Media Outlet Turns Gaze From Middle East Toward Afghanistan', *Militant Wire*, 23 May 2022, at https://www.militantwire.com/p/islamic-state-supporting-tajik-media.
60. 'German police say they are holding a man in connection with a threat to Cologne Cathedral', *Associated Press*, 27 December 2023, at https://apnews.com/article/germany-cologne-cathedral-threat-detention-866e23097855b15294e716d1c4deb1b2.
61. 'Немецкие СМИ о подробностях задержаний граждан Таджикистана, подозреваемых в подготовке к терактам' [German media about details of the detentions of Tajik citizens suspected of preparing for terrorist attacks], *RFERL Tajik Service*, 8 January 2024, at https://rus.ozodi.org/a/32765454.html.
62. 'Iran Claims One of Kerman Suicide Bombers Was a Tajik', *Iran International*, 5 January 2024, at https://www.iranintl.com/en/202401056540.
63. 'Уровеньводы в Амударьеснизился в несколькораз' [The water level in the Amu Darya has dropped several times], *RFERL Turkmen Service*, 4 June 2023, at https://rus.azathabar.com/a/32443779.html.
64. '«Талибан» объявил о завершенииистроительствапервогоучасткаканалаКоштепа' [The Taliban announced the completion of the first section of the Koshtepa Canal], *RFERL Uzbek Service*, 13 October 2023, at https://rus.ozodlik.org/a/32635600.html.

65. 'Taliban Threaten Water Resources of Uzbekistan, Turkmenistan and Tajikistan', *bne Intellinews*, 17 March 2023, at https://bne.eu/bnegreen-taliban-threaten-water-resources-of-uzbekistan-turkmenistan-and-tajikistan-273219/.
66. Kunduz Adylbekova, 'Water Crisis Looming: Uzbekistan and Turkmenistan's Imperative for the Grand Afghan Canal', *Central Asia Bureau for Analytical Reporting*, 22 July 2023, at https://cabar.asia/en/water-crisis-looming-uzbekistan-and-turkmenistan-s-imperative-for-the-grand-afghan-canal.
67. Fidel Rahmati, 'Afghanistan to Build Large Canal on Amu River; Turkmenistan, Uzbekistan Worried: Experts', *The Khaama Press*, 16 March 2023, at https://www.khaama.com/afghanistan-to-build-large-canal-on-amu-river-turkmenistan-uzbekistan-worried/.
68. ZikrullahYaazdani, 'Work on Second Phase of Qosh Tepa Canal Starts', *Tolo News*, 11 October 2023, at https://tolonews.com/afghanistan-185493.
69. 'МирзиёевпредложилпривлечьАфганистан к переговорам о водныхресурсах' [Mirziyoyev proposed involving Afghanistan in negotiations on water resources], *TASS*, 15 September 2023, at https://tass.ru/mezhdunarodnaya-panorama/18757411.
70. 'Воднаяполитикапревращается в геополитику: чемгрозит Узбекистанустроительствоканала Коштепа в Афганистане' [Water politics turns into geopolitics: what does the construction of the Koshtepa canal in Afghanistanthreaten Uzbekistan with], *nuz.uz*, 11 October 2023, at https://nuz.uz/politika/1287241-vodnaya-politika-prevrashhaetsya-v-geopolitiku-chem-grozit-uzbekistanu-stroitelstvo-kanala-koshtepa-v-afganistane.html.
71. 'Taliban Rejects Iran's Warning over Helmand River Water Rights, Iranian FM Hits Back', *Kabul Now*, 19 May 2023, at https://kabulnow.com/2023/05/taliban-rejects-irans-warning-over-helmand-river/.
72. 'At Least Three Killed in Clash on Iran-Afghan Border', *Reuters*, 27 May 2023, at https://www.reuters.com/world/two-killed-clash-iran-afghan-border-taliban-official-says-2023-05-27/.
73. 'Уровеньводы в Амударьеможетрезкоуменьшиться. Чтопредставляетсобойканал, которыйстроятталибы?' [The water level in the Amu Darya may decrease sharply. What is the canal that the Taliban are building?], *kun.uz*, 17 February 2023, at https://kun.uz/ru/news/2023/02/17/uroven-vody-v-amudare-mojyet-rezko-umenshitsya-chto-predstavlyayet-soboy-kanal-kotoryy-stroyat-taliby.

# 4

# Central Asia and Taliban-led Afghanistan

*Akram Umarov*

The Taliban movement's takeover in August 2021 did not come as a surprise to the countries of Central Asia. However, the speed with which Ashraf Ghani's government collapsed and the international force withdrew raised eyebrows in the region. Given the pace of developments in Afghanistan before 2021, the Central Asian states had been preparing for a potential change of power and reconfiguration of the political system in Kabul. Central Asia, given its deep cultural, humanitarian, trade and economic ties with neighbouring Afghanistan, is not fully supportive of the idea of completely isolating the Taliban regime until it fulfils certain conditions. A pragmatic approach dictates that regional states maintain contacts with the Taliban in order to help avert the possible collapse of the entire country, mitigate the humanitarian crisis, and the potential spill-over of instability into the neighbouring territories.

In order to understand the position of the Central Asian states, especially Uzbekistan, Tajikistan and Turkmenistan that have a common border with Afghanistan, with regard to the fundamental change in the situation in Afghanistan, it is important to see how the Taliban have carried out governance over the past years, the importance of the Central Asian states in the international community's efforts to stabilise Afghanistan, as well as key elements of the foreign policy of Uzbekistan and Tajikistan towards the Taliban government.

## Taliban Three Years After

The ease with which the Taliban was able to remove the government of Ashraf Ghani from power created an illusion about the power and readiness of the group to take full control of the country. The international community expected the Taliban to stabilise the situation in Afghanistan and eliminate security challenges that terrorism and drug trafficking posed to the neighbouring states. However, the US hit against al-Qaeda chief Ayman al-Zawahri raised questions about the credibility and honesty of the Taliban movement.[1] Over the past three-and-a-half years since coming to power, the Taliban has been facing a number of serious internal problems, such as increased factional clashes over interaction with foreign partners, rise of Pashtun nationalism, and the exit of ethnic minorities from the movement, as well as the inability to stabilise the state administration.

First, almost since the seizure of power in Afghanistan, there have been systematic clashes within the Taliban for leadership and for setting the movement's agenda for cooperation with the international community. A serious confrontation took place between the Taliban factions on the issue of distribution of power and position in the government. Mullah Abdul Ghani Baradar, who successfully led the negotiations with the US in Doha, was relegated to the post of acting deputy prime minister for economic affairs, and Abdul Kabir, who was appointed as the acting deputy prime minister for political affairs, enjoyed greater authority and confidence of the Taliban's supreme leader.[2]

The growing presence and influence of radical factions in the Taliban power structures has made it difficult for Kabul to make any ideological compromises, particularly on the issue of women's rights. The conservative group within the Taliban is helmed by the leader of the movement, Sheikh Hibatullah Akhundzada. Other prominent representatives of the conservative group are Prime Minister Mullah Hassan Akhund, Chief Justice of the Supreme Court Mawlawi Abdul Hakim Haqqani, and Acting Minister of Higher Education Mawlawi Nida Mohammad Nadeem. The ranks of moderate representatives of the Taliban include the Acting Deputy Prime Minister Mullah Baradar, former Acting Mining and Petroleum Minister and now Acting President of Afghan Red Crescent Society Sheikh Shahabuddin Delawar, and Acting Deputy Foreign Minister Sher Mohammad Abbas Stanekzai. At the same time, certain influential Taliban figures such as Acting Interior Minister Sirajuddin Haqqani and Acting Defence Minister Mullah Mohammad Yaqoob have been trying to manoeuvre between these opposing camps without joining either.[3]

Second, there has been a clear trend within the Taliban towards strengthening and significantly expanding the role of the Pashtun nationality.[4] While the Taliban have previously been able to recruit Uzbeks, Tajiks and Hazaras in the north and elsewhere to further their goals,[5] the movement's leadership is still dominated by the same old radical Pashtun leaders who ruled Afghanistan in the 1990s and opposed any compromise with the regime's ideology or change in power balance. If the Taliban can find a formula to unite various factions, it will only strengthen the regime. Otherwise, it will weaken the group's hold on the country and strengthen certain non-Pashtun groups opposed to its rule.

One of the most important factors in the success of the Taliban in the summer of 2021 was the role of Uzbek and Tajik groups that joined the movement in northern Afghanistan and effectively neutralised resistance from the local warlords and the government forces.[6] However, in early 2022, an Uzbek Taliban commander, Makhdoom Alam, was persecuted.7 Haji Mali Khan,an uncle of Sirajuddin Haqqani, was assigned in March 2022 as the deputy chief of army staff to closely monitor the activities of the chief of army staff, Fasihuddin Fitrat, who is a Tajik.[8] There has also been an increase in tensions between the Taliban and the Hazara ethnic minority in Afghanistan.[9] In addition to a series of terrorist attacks directed against them, some Hazaras collaborating with the Taliban have been subjected to unjustified persecution. If the Taliban leadership cannot find a way to solve ethnic problems internally, a substantial number of non-Pashtun members of the Taliban armed forces could join the ranks of the resistance groups or terrorist organisations based in Afghanistan.

Third, despite being in power for more than three years now, the Taliban movement has yet to demonstrate the ability to govern the country effectively. The Taliban, being a movement with a predominantly horizontal hierarchy, has always had a decentralised system of rule. The Taliban forces on the ground acted within the framework of a single strategy approved by the leadership of the group. However, at the same time, they had considerable autonomy in choosing tactics to achieve their goals and independently determine their operational tasks. Such an approach attracted a wide range of militants, opposed to the government of Ashraf Ghani, to the ranks of the Taliban.

Since seizing power in August 2021, the Taliban has built a highly centralised system of government, with officials at the local level directly appointed by Kabul.[10] The government is predominantly Pashtun in composition, and is based on a rigid vertical hierarchy. It has impacted the balance of power between the local commanders and the top leadership. The redistribution of sources of income that accompanies such changes, transfer of commanders to the remote parts of the country, and the filling of vacant positions by appointing mostly Pashtuns has radically changed the balance of power within the movement and significantly weakened the Taliban ability to control the situation in the provinces.

There has been a serious split at various levels within the Taliban. The growing confrontation between different factions on issues of development strategy and ideology of the group, cooperation with the outside world, and on the inclusion of representatives of the non-Pashtun ethnic groups in the highest authority significantly weakens the power of the Taliban and makes a split in their ranks highly possible. The Taliban government has yet to demonstrate the ability to overcome these systemic problems.

Such discord is expected to intensify the power struggle between the various factions of the Taliban movement. If the influential external actors become disappointed with the inability of the Taliban to resolve the situation in the country, the support for the activities of the opposition forces may increase significantly. Accordingly, this will lead to a new round of a full-scale civil war in Afghanistan based on inter-ethnic confrontations. The Taliban with its radical ideology and uncompromising position has been gradually moving towards international isolation and the label of "rogue state" cannot be excluded from this trajectory. Credible and open dialogue with the outside world, security guarantees to the neighbouring countries, trustworthy cooperation on eliminating all terrorist groups from the Afghan territory, and enhancement of external trade relations can help the Taliban overcome its challenges and become a full-fledged member of the international community.

## Central Asia: A Crucial Partner in Establishing a Peaceful Afghanistan

The international community is facing enormous challenges in dealing with the new reality in Afghanistan. The withdrawal of international military forces and the evacuation of only a small number of Afghans who previously collaborated with them generated considerable reputational damage to the credibility of the United States (US), the North Atlantic Treaty Organization (NATO), and their allies. The chaos and casualty caused during the evacuation left the people shocked around the world. The return of the Taliban to power has not brought any long lasting peace or sustainable development and prosperity to Afghanistan.

However, the Taliban cannot be blamed for all the current problems of the country, for they inherited an underdeveloped state with high levels of poverty, overdependence on foreign aid and inefficient administration. The Taliban have been able to improve the security situation in the country, but are encountering substantial problems in other aspects of governance.[11] The lack of an inclusive government and the lack of respect for the rights and freedoms of women are primary issues of disagreement between the movement and the international community, particularly when it comes to recognising the Taliban as the legitimate regime representing Afghanistan.

Reflecting on their past military and political experience in Afghanistan, Western countries can draw the following primary lessons:

First, nation building should be a truly internal process without much foreign intervention. Afghanistan has proved once more that a blueprint approach never works and externally orchestrated reforms might be tenuous. There are no ready recipes for conflict resolution and post-conflict reconstruction. There can be some principles and approaches for supporting countries after the end of a conflict; however, each case requires substantial attention in designing a unique model. It should be done internally by the local communities. Devil is always in the details.

Second, the attempt to build a highly centralised governance system under the leadership of a strongman has not brought the expected outcomes. A country with a historical tradition of decentralised administrations would not accept the establishment of a personalist regime.[12] Oddly, the US and its allies decided to neglect their own principles and commitment to democratic procedures. Both Karzai and Ghani governments were legitimised under the direct coordination and interference of external actors.[13] Despite their efforts to consolidate power, they were predominantly perceived as West manipulated leaders without necessary internal support and ability to deliver key results on conflict resolution and national development. This political experiment clearly demonstrated that an over-centralised and super-presidential model is not a guarantee for building a secure and stable Afghanistan.

Third, ignoring regional countries, when designing strategies on peace-making and post-conflict rebuilding, has not delivered successful results in Afghanistan. The future of Afghanistan cannot be considered and decided without the significant support of its neighbours. Due to various reasons, US avoided or minimised its cooperation with several regional countries on the Afghan issue. Some of the regional countries were mainly used as transit routes and hosts of the US and Western military infrastructure essential for their operations in Afghanistan.[14] All major international gatherings on Afghanistan were hosted in Europe, US, or Japan; all were very far from the region and had limited understanding of the local traditions, contexts, and the history. Concerns and proposals of the states next to Afghanistan were barely listened to and considered as policy options for the US and its allies.

No wonder that the Joseph Biden administration was willing to forget such breakdown and further engage with Afghanistan in a limited manner.

There are still many questions on how to deal with the Taliban and its tough ideological approach to certain public policy issues. There is an ongoing process for the recognition of the Taliban by the international community. Nonetheless, the Taliban government has been facing difficulties as it still lacks the political credibility required to seek formal cooperation with foreign states. So, the question is what the current administration can do to improve the security situation in Afghanistan. Below are a few policy recommendations:

First, there is a strong lack of trust between the Taliban and the US. Conducting bilateral negotiations between the two sides under such circumstances will not be effective, especially as the Taliban continue to host various extremist groups, particularly al-Qaeda, in Afghanistan. However, neglecting the problem will not lead to any solution. Perhaps, collaboration on issues of key concern to the US and its regional partners could be a step forward. Drugs and illicit arms trafficking, transnational terrorist threats, and weak border security are pressing problems that cannot be effectively dealt with without having any contact with the Taliban.

Second, it is in the US and Western interest to support and cooperate closely with the neighbouring regions (Central and South Asia) on Afghanistan. Despite regular exchanges between the regional countries and the West, there are still many gaps in their mutual understanding of the Afghan situation. The development and prosperity of the region is overwhelmingly dependent on improving connectivity. Western countries have found ways to send regular humanitarian support to Afghanistan without violating existing sanctions against the Taliban. Therefore, funding regional connectivity projects could go a long way in building security and stability in Afghanistan.

The main attention of the US and its allies should be on socio-economic reconstruction and infrastructure development in Afghanistan. Sustainable development of the Afghan economy and improvement in living conditions of the Afghan people will contribute to greater support for the US policy, reduce the influence of the Taliban and decrease inter-ethnic tensions. Close cooperation with the regional countries would ease the expected burden of wider interaction with the Taliban movement. No country today wants a new phase of civil war in Afghanistan. However, letting a global power like US focus on other immediate risks and challenges arising from Afghanistan should not turn into a new conflict in the region.

## Central Asian Response: Policies of Uzbekistan and Tajikistan

It is a common perception that Central Asia is divided on how to view the Afghan situation, how to approach the challenges posed by the change of regime in the country, and what kind of policy is required to deal with the Taliban. On the surface it looks like that Tajikistan's position is not in line with the rest of Central Asian countries. Four Central Asian countries, especially Uzbekistan and Turkmenistan as direct neighbours of Afghanistan, and to a lesser extent Kazakhstan and Kyrgyzstan, are engaging with the Taliban, providing humanitarian support, conducting bilateral meetings and keeping regular contacts. There have been several visits of official representatives from the Central Asian countries to Kabul, especially from Uzbekistan and Turkmenistan.[15] Both the countries have sent high level delegations to Kabul, and have established working relations with the Taliban government.

However, Tajikistan has kept up its anti-Taliban rhetoric, questioning the Taliban's lack of inclusive approach, resulting in the marginalisation of non-Pashtun ethnicities, particularly the Tajiks. At the same time, despite its anti-Taliban rhetoric, Tajikistan continues to supply electricity to Afghanistan and maintain trade relations.[16] Tajik companies are not completely banned from conducting business with their counterparts in Afghanistan. In this context, Tajikistan's approach is similar to that of the other Central Asian countries. There are several factors determining Dushanbe's stance.

First, there are internal factors, such as the role of the leader of the country who is regarded as the "saviour of Tajik people."[17]

Second, at the same time, it is important to underline the fact that Tajikistan is the only immediate neighbour of Afghanistan that has not engaged in any high-level official meetings with the Taliban before. It does not have the experience of dealing with the movement. If one looks at the history of the Taliban and its relations with Central Asian countries or the other neighbours of Afghanistan, one finds that the Taliban had some exchanges and meetings at official level with Iran, Pakistan, China, Uzbekistan and Turkmenistan, before their takeover in August 2021, but not with Tajikistan.

Third, Tajikistan's experience back from the 1990s when during the civil war period, part of the Tajik opposition groups had training and supply bases in Afghanistan which they used for conducting operations against military groups led by Emomali Rahmon.[18] Therefore, Tajikistan is very cautious in its approach when it comes to dealing with radical movements like the Taliban. The possibility of radical groups finding a convenient support in the Taliban-led Afghanistan and using it to conduct terrorist attacks remains of concern to Dushanbe.

Finally, it is a good cause for Tajikistan to get an advanced agency in international relations. Dushanbe is actively involved in almost all international meetings and exchanges related to Afghanistan. The Tajik leader was officially invited by several European countries despite previous criticism of his actions and position on democracy issues. Tajikistan has become an important partner for many Western countries due to its current anti-Taliban rhetoric.[19] But, at the end of the day, there is no substantial difference between the Tajik perspective on Afghanistan and those of Uzbekistan, Turkmenistan, or the other Central Asian countries. There are differences in their specific approaches but there is also a common regional understanding that the Taliban must ensure security and stability especially in the northern regions of the country, which borders Central Asia, and complete elimination of drug trafficking. Dushanbe is interested in having a reliable partner in Afghanistan to deal with terrorist groups, including of Central Asian origin, which have a presence in Afghanistan, like the Islamic Movement of Turkistan (IMT), Tehrik-e Taliban Tajikistan (TTT)[20] and Daesh. The fact that Daesh is now active in Afghanistan is of huge concern to Central Asian states.

One should not forget the fact that Western forces, while withdrawing in 2021, left a huge amount of weapons behind in Afghanistan. The fate of these weapons has since not been clear.[21] As the Taliban claims to be governing the country, it is for them to prevent any kind of weapons transfer to the terrorist groups of the Central Asian origin.

In parallel to these differing stances, Central Asian governments have adjusted their political posture towards the Taliban, reflecting broader dynamics across the region. First, some of the Central Asian countries have quietly removed the Taliban from their official terrorist blacklists—a formal prerequisite for deeper engagement. Kazakhstan led the way in late 2023 by delisting the Taliban as a banned organisation, citing expanding economic ties with Kabul. Kyrgyzstan followed suit in September 2024, a decision indicating "warming ties" and cementing of a regional trend towards normalising relations with the Taliban.[22] Second, the Taliban-led Afghan diplomatic missions have resumed in all the six neighbouring countries. Uzbekistan, Turkmenistan and others have hosted the Taliban-appointed diplomats at the Afghan embassies, although they have not extended the official recognition to them. This de facto acceptance of the Taliban-appointed diplomats helps implement bilateral agreements and streamline consular issues. Third, regional organisations such as the Shanghai

Cooperation Organisation (SCO) and the Commonwealth of Independent States (CIS) have followed suit by inviting the Taliban to certain forums, giving the Taliban an observer status that further weaves them into Central Asia's diplomatic and economic dialogues.

Viewed collectively, these shifts illustrate how even countries with different official attitudes—particularly Tajikistan that has a more guarded approach—can converge on the pragmatic need for a constructive engagement with Afghanistan. Despite rhetorical or diplomatic variations, all Central Asian states share an interest in limiting cross-border security risks, maintaining or expanding trade relations, and in ensuring that Afghanistan does not become a haven for radical movements. The absence of any formal recognition for the Taliban underscores that a definitive consensus on Afghanistan's political future remains elusive. However, the regional consensus on practical cooperation—from basic trade to counterterrorism coordination—indicates that Central Asia is responding to the realities in Afghanistan by balancing caution with engagement.

There are also expectations that connectivity projects and trade relations will revive to the pre-2021 levels. All the Central Asian countries had extensive and favourable trade relations with Afghanistan as it mainly consisted of exports rather than imports. Private entrepreneurs in Central Asia benefited considerably from these trade relations. Moreover, Central Asia is now trying to connect with South Asia via Afghanistan. A major conference on Central and South Asian connectivity was hosted in Tashkent in July 2022, whichwas supported by other Central Asian countries. Any initiative on South-Central Asian connectivity is impossible without Afghanistan connecting these regions and providing transit opportunities for the whole of Eurasia. Be it theTrans-Afghan railway project, connecting Uzbekistan to Pakistan, or the long-discussed Turkmenistan–Afghanistan–Pakistan–India (TAPI) gas pipeline, Central Asian countries have been trying to reach a deal with the Taliban on their implementation.

On 26 July 2022, Uzbekistan hosted an international conference on 'Afghanistan: Security and Economic Development', which was attended by more than 100 delegates from nearly 30 countries.[23] This was the third conference in a row organised by Tashkent in the last four years to discuss the problems facing Afghanistan. The Uzbek Government has been consistently advancing its cooperation with Afghanistan no matter which political force represented it. The July 2022 conference brought together mainly special representatives and policy experts on Afghanistan from different countries. The conference provided an opportunity for a more nuanced discussion on the current situation in Afghanistan and further coordination of international efforts to deal with the Taliban government and the humanitarian crisis facing the country. It also gave the participants the opportunity to conduct a series of bilateral meetings to discuss the most pressing issues in Afghanistan.

Representatives of various countries and international organisations tried to push the Taliban to respect the rights of girls to education and women's to work, to form a more inclusive government and cut ties with terrorist groups. Acting Taliban Foreign Affairs Minister Amir Khan Muttaqi while not acknowledging the existence of any significant problems with the Taliban governance pledged to 'transform Afghanistan into the centre of peace, stability and economic cooperation.'[24] It is important to understand as to why Uzbekistan has been actively trying to engage both bilaterally and multilaterally with the Taliban and what are its achievements and challenges.

First, geography matters in determining the priorities of the country's foreign policy. Uzbekistan as a neighbour of Afghanistan has a vital interest in its peaceful and stable development. For decades, Tashkent considered Afghanistan a security threat and limited its engagement with the international community on conflict resolution in Afghanistan, focusing on bilateral cooperation with Kabul. However, in recent years, Uzbekistan has been rethinking its approach towards Afghanistan and has emphasised more on economic cooperation as a key to its sustainability.

Second, post-US withdrawal, the global attention has shifted from Afghanistan to other geopolitical developments. The Afghanistan issue has also undergone a certain routinisation in world news. Uzbekistan has been concerned about the waning global attention on Afghanistan, as it would require more than regional efforts to resolve issues related to Afghanistan. By organising and hosting large international conferences on Afghanistan, Uzbekistan has sought to keep Afghanistan at the top of the international agenda and also bring together major donors to deal with Afghanistan's pressing issues.

Third, Afghanistan is crucial to Tashkent's strategic plans to connect Central and South Asia. Uzbekistan is actively promoting the construction of the 760-km railway line from Termiz to Mazar-i-Sharif and onward via Kabul to Peshawar, and the 245-km power transmission line from Surkhon to Puli Khumri, to improve connectivity between the regions.[25] With respect to regional railway connectivity, the most strategically significant initiative is the proposed Trans-Afghanistan Railway linking Uzbekistan to Pakistan through Afghanistan. In 2023, Uzbekistan, Afghanistan and Pakistan reached an agreement in Islamabad to conduct technical studies for the Termez–Mazar–Kabul–Peshawar route, projected to cost about \$5–\$6 billion.[26] While progress on the project has been gradual, both Tashkent and Kabul appear committed. A joint project office was opened in Tashkent in May 2023 to coordinate the feasibility study.The Uzbek authorities have stated that the construction on the next segment could begin imminently, and Taliban's Deputy Prime Minister Mullah Baradar has suggested a spur extending from Mazar-i-Sharif to Herat to connect with Iran's railway network. Although project financing remains a concern, Uzbekistan's leadrole in implementing the project reflects its vision of positioning Afghanistan as a vital transit hub between Central and South Asia.

Recently, Uzbekistan's Minister of Transport Ilhom Mahkamov announced that the construction of the Trans-Afghanistan Railway is planned to begin in 2025, following President Shavkat Mirziyoyev's review of key transport infrastructure projects on 3 February 2025. The latest update includes an 80-kilometer extension to connect with Pakistani and Iranian ports, with preliminary cost estimates ranging between $4.6 billion (as assessed by Uzbekistan's "BOSHTRANSLOYIHA" institute) and $8.2 billion.[27]

Both the projects were initially agreed upon during the previous Afghan government but could not be implemented as the government fell and the Taliban took over. Soon thereafter, due to the sanctions against Russia and Belarus and the ongoing war in Ukraine, the northern transport corridors became both complex and risky for Central Asia. Alternative shipping routes across the Black Sea were also compromised by the Russian naval blockade against Ukrainian ports. Therefore, the opening of new transport corridors to South Asia was considered critical for the diversification of regional trade and connectivity. Meanwhile, in the realm of electricity and energy, Uzbekistan has continued to supply over 50 per cent of Afghanistan's imported electricity, thereby preventing blackouts in northern Afghan cities. Both sides have also pushed to complete the new 260-km Surkhan–Pul-e Khumri power line, which would raise Uzbek power exports to Afghanistan by an estimated 70 per cent.[28] In 2024, Uzbekistan signed a 10-year contract to develop Afghanistan's Tooti Maidan gas field, committing $100 million per year to tap the field's extensive reserves. This project is expected to secure much-needed natural gas for Uzbekistan while generating revenue and supplying energy to Afghanistan.[29]

The discussions during the July 2022 conference also revealed a number of challenges to Uzbekistan's policy towards Afghanistan.

First, despite multidimensional cooperation between Tashkent and the de facto Taliban authorities in Kabul, the latter could not demonstrate the ability to provide security on the Uzbek–Afghan border. According to reports, in the first half of 2022, three missile attacks were conducted from the Afghan territory on Uzbekistan.[30] In response to these and similar threats, Uzbekistan bolstered its border defences and regional security cooperation. In August 2022, Uzbekistan and Tajikistan conducted joint military drills (Commonwealth–2022) near the Afghan frontier, simulating the neutralisation of infiltrating militant groups. Heavy weaponry and rapid reaction units were employed in the exercises to rehearse sealing of the border against incursions.[31] US officials have likewise noted a "deeply" shared concern with Uzbekistan about terrorists in Afghanistan, as evidence suggests that some extremist outfits have gained strength since the Taliban came to power. To mitigate these risks, Uzbekistan has strengthened intelligence cooperation with partners and likely with the Taliban authorities as well, pressing Kabul to act against groups that could target neighbouring states.

Regardless of the Taliban reassurances on full control of the situation in the north of the country, these security incidents indicated the challenges of guaranteeing the provision of security in the border areas with the neighbouring countries. Furthermore, the emergence of the Tajik Taliban in the Badakhshan Province of Afghanistan in July 2022 was an alarming signal for Central Asia,[32] given the possibility of the Afghan Taliban blackmailing countries in the region with terrorist groups on their borders and demanding various concessions.

Second, the complicated dialogue between the international community and the Taliban on the issue of recognition of the latter's de facto government in Kabul. Due to the fact that Taliban is not recognised by the international community, funding from international financial institutions to the infrastructure projects in Afghanistan has been completely paused. Therefore, Tashkent has been keen to facilitate dialogue and mutual understanding between various countries and the Taliban. However, the statements of the delegations participating in the Tashkent Conference exposed deep disagreements between the international community and the Taliban on the issue of inclusivity in the Taliban government, and its policy towards the provision of the rights of women and girls, ethnic and sectarian minority groups, and the media freedom.[33] The discussions on human rights and inclusivity have been going on but without any substantial progress in reaching a compromise.

Third, the Taliban is now facing both internal factional divisions and resistance from many opposition groups, which have been questioning their style of governance. The movement looks fractured on many crucial issues. Inconsistent decisions and internal ideological differences have resulted in the Taliban adopting conflicting policies on girls' school education, media freedom, and in other spheres. Therefore, agreements reached in negotiations with some representatives of the movement may not necessarily transform into real policy decisions. There are several resistance groups operating in northern Afghanistan that disagree with the Taliban ideology and have not accepted their governance. Under the current conditions, these resistance groups are unlikely to overthrow the Taliban government, but are able to create regular security challenges for the Taliban.

Fourth, the Taliban have finished the first phase of the construction of the Qosh Tepa Canal in Balkh Province,[34] which diverts water from Amu Darya to improve irrigation facilities in northern Afghanistan.[35] Once the canal is completed, almost 10 cubic kilometres, which is a third of the river's water, will flow into the interiors of Afghanistan.[36] This can have serious consequences for Turkmenistan and several provinces of Uzbekistan like Khorezm, Bukhara, Surkhandarya and Navoi, as well as for the Republic of Karakalpakstan. The canal passes through a sandy area, and the efficiency of the canal is low as it is not lined or covered, so much of its water would be lost to seepage in the region's dry soil. The biggest issue is that the Taliban leadership kicked off this huge project without holding any consultations with the neighbouring countries affected by its construction.

In recent years, Uzbekistan has become one of the major international drivers of peace and reconciliation in Afghanistan. Tashkent has also emerged as a credible partner of Kabul, notwithstanding who is in power in Afghanistan. The relations between the two countries developed substantially both during the Ghani Government and the current de facto Taliban government. The hosting of a large international conference in Tashkent was another sign of Uzbek Government's effort to keep Afghanistan under the international spotlight. The Uzbek officials frequently describe this policy in terms of "pragmatism" and shared economic opportunity. For instance, President Mirziyoyev has referred to Afghanistan as a natural part of Central Asia and stressed that 'Afghanistan's problems are our problems', urging other neighbouring countries to integrate it, and not isolate it.[37]

Following the July 2022 conference, several bilateral visits that took place resulted in agreements on electricity supply, development of the Trans-Afghanistan Railway, and commitments to expand trade. Both sides also agreed to set up joint working groups to coordinate transit fees and investment in infrastructure, streamline visa procedures for businesspeople, and encourage private sector partnerships in the energy, agriculture, and the manufacturing sector.

Even before the Taliban's 2021 takeover, Mirziyoyev had advocated the incorporation of Afghanistan into regional projects—citing plans like the Surkhan–Pul-e Khumri power line and a railway to the Indian Ocean—as vital for regional peace and development.

Following the Taliban's return to power in August 2021, Uzbekistan kept its embassy in Kabul open and quickly established dialogue with the new authorities. Uzbek officials acknowledged the Taliban as the de facto reality and sought a working relationship no matter who was in power in Kabul.[38] Tashkent has since positioned itself as a key interlocutor—hosting high-level talks and humanitarian hubs—while *not* granting formal recognition to the Taliban's "Islamic Emirate" absent an international consensus. As presidential envoy Ismatulla Irgashev explains, Uzbekistan sees engagement as the only viable path: 'Imagine what happens if we don't engage...more conflict, another civil war...threats to the neighbors and the international community'.[39]

In sum, Uzbekistan's policy reflects a blend of realism and regionalism: On one hand, Tashkent engages the Taliban diplomatically and economically to promote stability, while on the other, it stays alert to a possible spill over of security threats from Afghanistan. Building on this twofold approach, the Uzbek Government focuses first on maintaining continuous dialogue with the Taliban to ensure that the Afghan territory is not used for terrorism, drug trafficking, or any form of cross-border destabilisation. The Taliban leadership has reassured Tashkent that Afghan soil would not be used to threaten its neighbours and even pledged to repay overdue debts from import of Uzbek electricity once assets were unfrozen.[40] In parallel, Uzbekistan has steadily expanded its economic outreach, laying the foundation for greater trade and infrastructure initiatives to complement the security-focused dialogue.

In October 2023, Uzbekistan's Deputy Prime Minister Jamshid Khojaev led a large delegation (including the ministers of energy, transport, water, and agriculture) to Kabul to expand trade and transit cooperation. During the visit, the Taliban side, led by Deputy Prime Minister Baradar, praised the "balanced" relations between the two countries and proposed increased Afghan exports to Uzbekistan, for which the Taliban side asked Tashkent to lower the transit fees for Afghan goods. The two countries agreed to form a joint working group on transport tariffs to promote cross-border trade. Uzbekistan also announced a "roadmap" to boost bilateral trade to as much as $3 billion (up from roughly $600 million) in the coming years, easing of visa procedures for Afghan traders and opening of a dedicated business centre in Termez for Afghan commerce.[41] This centre was later officially inaugurated by senior Afghan and Uzbek officials to facilitate cross-border trade, streamline logistics, and expand market access for Afghan exporters.

In the area of trade and industry, the two sides agreed, during the visit of Mullah Baradar to Tashkent in February 2025, to expand the import of

Afghan products into Uzbekistan in exchange for broader business opportunities for Afghan firms. Uzbek investors are also exploring the Afghan industrial sector, for instance the proposed establishment of a cement plant in Samangan Province.[42] Kabul has actively encouraged Uzbek participation in mining projects, and although no specific contracts have been concluded, Uzbekistan has signaled an interest in Afghanistan's oil and gas resources.

However, these facilitated negotiations have not yet brought the expected concessions from the Taliban authorities. History teaches us that the best way to resolve any disagreements between countries is through diplomacy and dialogue, so these means should stay in priority to find solutions to the issues of governance, security, economic development and humanitarian crisis in Afghanistan. However, if Kabul responds inadequately to the kind gestures of the neighbours, the latter would need to work on leverage mechanisms to influence any unacceptable and unconstructive moves by the former.

The de facto Taliban government is facing many problems when it comes to building relations with the neighbours, particularly as its ability to deliver on commitments made remain doubtful. While the Taliban is seeking international recognition, they are missing the fact that they have yet to secure legitimacy at the domestic level. From the Taliban perspective, they have the required religious legitimacy to govern and represent the country, but from the perspective of the international community, the government in Kabul represents the Taliban movement and not the whole Afghan nation. The Taliban needs to make some compromises and conduct an internal legitimisation exercise through a vote in *Loya Jirga* or any other alternative mechanism. However, the Taliban leaders have refused to make ideological compromises under any pressure from the international community.

The next issue Central Asia is concerned about is how independent is the Taliban. Is it fully independent in its decision making or it has to confer with some external actors before making policy commitments? There are many signs pointing to their inability to organise public institutions, deliver effective governance to the people, and control challenging situations. Daesh is more active now and it frequently carries out terrorist attacks. In addition, the Taliban needs internal de-securitisation. Simply conducting military parades will not bring any credibility or domestic and international support to the Taliban.

Finally, despite all the positive engagements with the Taliban, it is best to be cautious and not to put all eggs in one basket. It is still not very clear as to what kind of a situation will emerge in the short and medium term considering the numerous challenges facing Afghanistan and whether the Taliban would be able to deal with those challenges in the coming times. The Taliban have inherited a lot of challenges from the previous government, but if they claim to be governing the country, they need to find ways to address the complex challenges facing the country.

The governance failures of the Taliban and the lack of reliable security in Afghanistan can have a direct impact on the prospect of attracting new investments and technologies vital for the sustainable development of the region, including Central Asia. The Central Asian countries need external development partners to achieve comprehensive development. Afghanistan has to be a part of the overall regional development endeavour. However, the external participants in the development processes in Central Asia should avoid engaging in a zero-sum game to establish their spheres of influence in the region. Stability and sustainable development of Central Asia will benefit all the neighbouring regions and the international community as a whole.

## NOTES

1. 'Remarks by President Biden on a Successful Counterterrorism Operation in Afghanistan', The White House, 1 August 2022, at https://www.whitehouse.gov/briefing-room/speeches-remarks/2022/08/01/remarks-by-president-biden-on-a-successful-counterterrorism-operation-in-afghanistan/ (Accessed 30 August 2022).
2. Shahabullah Yousafzai, 'The First Eight Months of the Taliban Regime', *The Express Tribune*, 17 April 2022, at https://tribune.com.pk/story/2352890/the-first-eight-months-of-the-taliban-regime (Accessed 31 August 2022).
3. 'Taliban Govt Promises "Good News" on Girls' Education', *Global Times*, 17 May 2022, at https://www.globaltimes.cn/page/202205/1265869.shtml (Accessed 28 August 2022); Mohammad Farshad Daryosh, '"We Want Cordial Relations" With World: Mullah Yaqoob Mujahid', *Tolo News*, 3 June 2022, at https://tolonews.com/afghanistan-178311 (Accessed 29 August 2022).
4. Shishir Gupta, 'Why Will Afghanistan Remain Unstable, Violent and in an Economic Mess?', *Hindustan Times*, 16 July 2022, at https://www.hindustantimes.com/world-news/why-will-afghanistan-remain-unstable-violent-and-in-an-economic-mess-101657984607464.html (Accessed 1 September 2022).
5. Jennifer Brick Murtazashvili, 'Northern Afghanistan Once Kept Out the Taliban. Why Has It Fallen So Quickly This Time?', *The Washington Post*, 28 July 2021, at https://www.washingtonpost.com/politics/2021/07/28/northern-afghanistan-once-kept-out-taliban-why-has-it-fallen-so-quickly-this-time/ (Accessed 29 August 2022).
6. Scott Peterson, 'Afghanistan: How the Taliban Won Over Northern Ethnic Minorities', *The Christian Science Monitor*, 20 August 2021, at https://www.csmonitor.com/World/Asia-South-Central/2021/0820/Afghanistan-How-the-Taliban-won-over-northern-ethnic-minorities (Accessed 1 September 2022).
7. Sudarsan Raghavan, 'A Popular Uzbek Commander Fought for the Taliban for More Than Two Decades. He Was Arrested Anyway', *The Washington Post*, 1 February 2022, at

https://www.washingtonpost.com/world/2022/02/01/taliban-uzbek-afghanistan/ (Accessed 2 September 2022).

8. Muhammad Jalal (@MJalalAf), 'Respected Haji Mali Khan Haqqani Has Been Appointed as Deputy Chief of Army Staff of the Armed Forces of the Ministry of Defense of IEA', *Twitter* (now *X*), 4 March 2022, 1:04 AM, at https://twitter.com/MJalal700/status/1499468233023311873 (Accessed 3 September 2022).
9. 'Taliban Atrocities Reported in Crackdown on Rebel Hazara Commander', *RFE/RL Gandhara*, 1 July 2022, at https://gandhara.rferl.org/about-gandhara (Accessed 1 September 2022).
10. Jennifer Brick Murtazashvili, 'The Collapse of Afghanistan', *Journal of Democracy*, Vol. 33, No. 1, January 2022, pp. 40–54, at https://journalofdemocracy.org/articles/the-collapse-of-afghanistan/ (Accessed 25 August 2022).
11. Akram Umarov, 'When Dealing With the Taliban, Remember That Central Asia Matters', *The National Interest*, 22 August 2022, at https://nationalinterest.org/blog/middle-east-watch/when-dealing-taliban-remember-central-asia-matters-204361 (Accessed 3 September 2022).
12. Jennifer Brick Murtazashvili, 'The Endurance and Evolution of Afghan Customary Governance', *Current History,* Vol. 120, No. 825, 1 April 2021, pp. 140–145, at https://doi.org/10.1525/curh.2021.120.825.140 (Accessed 1 September 2022).
13. Tim Craig, 'Ghani Named Winner of Afghan Election, Will Share Power With Rival in New Government', *The Washington Post*, 21 September 2014, at https://www.washingtonpost.com/world/ghani-abdullah-agree-to-share-power-in-afghanistan-as-election-stalemate-ends/2014/09/21/df58749a-416e-11e4-9a15-137aa0153527_story.html (Accessed 31 August 2022).
14. Kristian Berg Harpviken and Shahrbanou Tadjbakhsh, 'Afghanistan and its Neighborhood: Continuity and Change', in *A Rock between Hard Places: Afghanistan as an Arena of Regional Insecurity*, Oxford University Press, New York, 2016, pp.139–160.
15. Elena Izteleuova, 'The Afghan Issue on the Agendas of Uzbekistan and Kazakhstan', *Central Asian Bureau for Analytical Reporting*, 7 January 2022, at https://cabar.asia/en/the-afghan-issue-on-the-agendas-of-uzbekistan-and-kazakhstan (Accessed 2 September 2022).
16. Catherine Putz, 'Central Asia Continues to Supply Electricity to Afghanistan', *The Diplomat*, 13 January 2022, at https://thediplomat.com/2022/01/central-asia-continues-to-supply-electricity-to-afghanistan/ (Accessed 5 September 2022).
17. 'President Emomali Rahmon Called Saviour of Tajik People', *CentralAsia News*, 17 November 2021, at https://centralasia.news/12340-president-emomali-rahmon-called-saviour-of-tajik-people.html (Accessed 6 September 2022).
18. R. Grant Smith, 'Tajikistan: The Rocky Road to Peace', *Central Asian Survey*, Vol. 18, Issue 2, 1999, pp. 243–251, at https://www.tandfonline.com/doi/abs/10.1080/02634939995704.
19. Temur Umarov, 'Why Tajikistan is Taking a Stand Against the Taliban', *The Moscow Times*, 26 October 2021, at https://www.themoscowtimes.com/2021/10/26/why-tajikistan-is-taking-a-stand-against-the-taliban-a75413 (Accessed 16 September 2022).

20. Giuliano Bifolchi, 'Tehrik-e Taliban Tajikistan and Terrorist Threat in Tajikistan and Central Asia', *Special Eurasia*, 25 July 2022, at https://www.specialeurasia.com/2022/07/25/tehrik-e-taliban-tajikistan/ (Accessed 6 September 2022).
21. Jack Detsch, 'The U.S. Left Billions Worth of Weapons in Afghanistan', *Foreign Policy*, 28 April 2022, at https://foreignpolicy.com/2022/04/28/the-u-s-left-billions-worth-of-weapons-in-afghanistan/ (Accessed 12 December 2022).
22. Masood Farivar, 'Kyrgyzstan Follows Regional Trend, Takes Taliban Off Terrorist List', *VOA News,* 7 September 2024, at https://www.voanews.com/a/kyrgyzstan-follows-regional-trend-takes-taliban-off-terrorist-list/7775060.html (Accessed 10 March 2025).
23. Navbahor Imamova, 'Nearly 30 Nations Engage with Taliban at Tashkent Conference', *VOA News*, 27 July 2022, at https://www.voanews.com/a/almost-30-nations-engage-with-taliban-at-tashkent-conference-/6676107.html (Accessed 10 September 2022).
24. Akram Umarov and Jennifer Brick Murtazashvili, 'What Are the Implications of Uzbekistan's Rapprochement With the Taliban?', *The Diplomat*, 8 August 2022, at https://thediplomat.com/2022/08/what-are-the-implications-of-uzbekistans-rapprochement-with-the-taliban/ (Accessed 10 September 2022).
25. Akram Umarov, 'The "Afghan Factor" in Uzbekistan's Foreign Policy: Evolution and the Contemporary Situation', *Asian Affairs*, Vol. 52, Issue 3, 2021, pp. 536–553, at https://www.tandfonline.com/doi/abs/10.1080/03068374.2021.1957321.
26. 'Afghanistan Reports Sixfold Increase in Trade with Uzbekistan', *Eurasianet*, 11 January 2024, at https://eurasianet.org/afghanistan-reports-sixfold-increase-in-trade-with-uzbekistan (Accessed 10 March 2025).
27. 'Trans-Afghan Railway Construction Set to Begin in 2025', *Kun.uz,* 5 February 2025, at https://kun.uz/en/news/2025/02/05/trans-afghan-railway-construction-set-to-begin-in-2025 (Accessed 11 March 2025).
28. 'Uzbekistan Continues to Cover Over 50% of Afghanistan's Electricity Imports', *Gazeta.uz*, 19 December 2024, at https://www.gazeta.uz/en/2024/12/19/uzb-afg/ (Accessed 11 March 2025).
29. 'Uzbekistan to Invest $1 Billion in Afghanistan's Energy Sector', *Afghanistan International*, 11 October 2024, at https://www.afintl.com/en/202410112107 (Accessed 11 March 2025).
30. Saqalain Eqbal, 'Uzbekistan Denies Reports of Missile Attack from Afghanistan', *The Khaama Press*, 18 July 2022, at https://www.khaama.com/uzbekistan-denies-reports-of-missile-attack-from-afghanistan-74832/ (Accessed 13 September 2022).
31. Josephine Freund, 'Uzbekistan and Tajikistan Conduct Joint Military Exercises Amid Afghanistan Border Concerns', Caspian Policy Center, 16 August 2022, at https://www.caspianpolicy.org/research/security-and-politics-program-spp/uzbekistan-and-tajikistan-conduct-joint-military-exercises-amid-afghanistan-border-concerns (Accessed 11 March 2025).
32. Yasir Rashid, 'Afghanistan's Badakhshan: New Security Threat for Tajikistan', Center for Iranian Studies (IRAM), 5 October 2022, at https://iramcenter.org/en/afghanistans-badakhshan-new-security-threat-for-tajikistan_en-814 (Accessed 15 December 2022).
33. Dipali Mukhopadhyay, 'The Taliban Have Not Moderated', *Foreign Affairs*, 28 March 2022, at https://www.foreignaffairs.com/afghanistan/taliban-have-not-moderated (Accessed 14 September 2022).

34. 'Work on Phase I of Qosh Tepa Canal Finished Ahead of Deadline', *Amu TV*, 11October 2023, at https://amu.tv/68490/ (Accessed 24 October 2023).
35. 'The Taliban Are Digging an Enormous Canal', *The Economist*, 13 February 2023, at https://www.economist.com/asia/2023/02/16/the-taliban-are-digging-an-enormous-canal (Accessed 20 February 2023).
36. 'Water of Amudarya May Decrease Sharply Due to Kushtepa Canal Being Built by Taliban', *Kun.uz*, 17 February 2023, at https://kun.uz/en/news/2023/02/17/water-of-amudarya-may-decrease-sharply-due-to-kushtepa-canal-being-built-by-taliban (Accessed 19 February 2022).
37. Nargiza Umarova, 'Uzbekistan's Approach to Afghanistan in the Context of Strengthening Regional Security', *The Diplomat,* 12 September 2024, at https://thediplomat.com/2024/09/uzbekistans-approach-to-afghanistan-in-the-context-of-strengthening-regional-security/ (Accessed 11 March 2025).
38. Navbahor Imamova, 'Uzbekistan Seeks to Engage Taliban Without Alienating West', *VOA News*, 4 May 2022, at https://www.voanews.com/a/uzbekistan-seeks-to-engage-taliban-without-alienating-west/6557338.html (Accessed 11 March 2025).
39. Ibid.
40. Fozil Mashrab, 'Economic Interests at Core of Uzbekistan's Pragmatic Approach Toward Taliban', The Jamestown Foundation, *Eurasia Daily Monitor*, Volume 18, Issue 169, 8 November 2021, at https://jamestown.org/program/economic-interests-at-core-of-uzbekistans-pragmatic-approach-toward-taliban/ (Accessed 12 March 2025).
41. Catherine Putz, 'Trade and Transit Top Agenda as Uzbek Delegation Visits Afghanistan', *The Diplomat,* 2 November 2023, at https://thediplomat.com/2023/11/trade-and-transit-top-agenda-as-uzbek-delegation-visits-afghanistan/ (Accessed 12 March 2025).
42. 'Baradar's Visit to Uzbekistan: Investments in Gas and Cement Plant in Afghanistan, Tariff Reductions and Trade Preferences', *Gazeta.uz*, 24 February 2025, at https://www.gazeta.uz/en/2025/02/24/uzb-afg/ (Accessed 12 March 2025).

# 5

# Tajikistan's Policy Towards Taliban-controlled Afghanistan

*Sherali Sh. Rizoyon and Makhmud F. Giyosov*

The development of the situation in Afghanistan over the past three decades has had a significant impact on the Central Asian region. The security agenda of Tajikistan, which shares a 1344,15-km long border with Afghanistan in the south,[1] is inextricably linked to the political and security processes in Afghanistan. The Afghan factor, as discussed in the chapter, has long been of concern to the country's political elite, research experts, journalists, and the Tajik community.

Dushanbe's special interest in Afghanistan is driven by the fact that there are many promising transit projects that could open avenues of economic diversification, as well as access to the economies of South Asia and the Middle East through Afghanistan. Stabilisation of the situation in Afghanistan can thus significantly enhance prospects of Tajikistan and other Central Asian states deepening cooperation with South Asian countries. It can contribute to the expansion of political, trade, economic, cultural and humanitarian relations between Tajikistan and the countries of South Asia.

Since the early days of its independence, Tajikistan has given due importance to Afghanistan, an immediate neighbouring country that has demanded constant attention from policymakers. This has also been the case with most other Central Asian states since the early 1990s. Over the years, the Central Asian states have developed their approaches based on their respective interpretations of national interests and potential prospects in seeking cooperation with Kabul. Therefore, the policies and approaches of Central Asian countries have differed. The policies of countries bordering

Afghanistan, i.e., Tajikistan, Turkmenistan and Uzbekistan, differ from those of Kazakhstan and Kyrgyzstan, which do not have direct borders with Afghanistan. However, there is a common thread running through the policies of all the five Central Asian states: they are the most constructive neighbours of Afghanistan and unlike the other neighbouring countries they have never tried to interfere in the internal affairs of Afghanistan.

The failure of modernisation efforts in Afghanistan and the return of the Taliban to power on 15 August 2021 came as a surprise to global and regional powers. They quickly changed their approaches and tried to pursue a policy, sometimes opportunistic and based on new Afghan realities. Tajikistan and other Central Asian countries had to also adapt to the changing realities on the ground and recalibrate their policies towards Afghanistan.

It should be noted that since August 2021, many articles and reports have reflected on the potential negative impact of the current situation in Afghanistan on neighbouring states in the medium and long term. The sense of shock that followed the developments in Afghanistan immediately after the Talban's return has since been replaced with a sense of pragmatism. There is a desire in the region to evolve appropriate policies and approaches to deal with the changing reality. Another important development, the Ukraine War, has gradually pushed the problem of Afghanistan to the sidelines and turned international attention away from it since February 2022. Over the past three years, during which the eyes of the entire world community were directed towards Ukraine, terrorist organisations such as Islamic State–Khorasan or Daesh–Khorasan and Al-Qaeda have quietly strengthened their presence in Afghanistan. Foreign terrorist fighters of Central Asian origin are reported to be active mainly in the north of Afghanistan.

These and other problems, as well as the existing potential risks and threats to neighbouring states emanating from the territory of Afghanistan, require close attention and regular assessment, and analysis and monitoring of the situation. The experience of studying political processes in Afghanistan shows that it is impossible to predict what will happen next there. Since the most unexpected and unpredictable events can occur due to the idiosyncratic nature of the Afghan political culture, the role and policies of the involved powers and regional players will have to constantly readapt to such changes.

## Assessment of the Situation in Afghanistan

For Tajikistan's foreign policy perspective, developments in Afghanistan in 2021 were a big shock and a challenge. President of Tajikistan Emomali Rahmon has repeatedly stressed that the government was ready to face any challenges emanating from the unfolding situation in Afghanistan. The current situation shows that the nature of threats and challenges from the territory of Afghanistan remain significant. To date, the Taliban have not fulfilled any of the fundamental demands of the international community.

### *1. Formation of an Inclusive Government*

Since August 2021, the main expectation from the international community has been the formation of an inclusive government or an inclusive system of political power, including the participation of women and all peoples of Afghanistan. In fairness, it should be noted that President Emomali Rahmon was the first to formulate and express these demands in a clear form on 25 August 2021 during a meeting with the visiting Pakistani Foreign Minister Shah Mahmood Qureshi. According to the official statement issued after the meeting, President Rahmon stressed the need to establish an inclusive government in Afghanistan, representing all ethnic groups of the country, and ruled out the possibility of Dushanbe recognising a government formed by the Taliban alone.[2] The importance of an inclusive government lies in the fact that it can become a factor in ensuring stability and security in the country. If all Afghan groups are involved in the political process and represented in the political system, the likelihood of destabilisation will decrease, and peace in Afghanistan can be achieved. Today, there are various interpretations of an inclusive government formulated by Afghan intellectuals[3] that reflect the current reality and are aimed at ensuring the interests of all Afghan political groups in the short term:

- Inclusive government is not a division of power between individual groups, but implies a broader involvement of all citizens in the decision-making processes. Thus, in order to form an inclusive system of government, it is necessary to work with all groups;
- Inclusive government in Afghanistan means rejection of centralised power; because only in a decentralised power structure can all groups and nationalities of Afghanistan find their place.

By strengthening stability, Afghan political groups can take the next step forward and create a democratic government. An important element here is to hold free and fair elections without violence and pressure, and thus determine the type of political system that is essentially representative.

The statements and actions of the Taliban show that they are convinced that they already have an inclusive government, and believe that international community have no right to interfere in the internal affairs of Afghanistan. An analysis of the current situation shows that the Taliban does not want to form an inclusive government. This is because key decisions made in Kandahar are crucial, while the absence of constitutions and an established government in Kabul is largely irrelevant. There are also significant contradictions within the Taliban, with most influential groups not wanting an inclusive government.

### *2. Perception of the Taliban*

It is useful to ask whether the Taliban have changed or not? This is the key to understand both the current processes in Afghanistan and the policies and approaches of the external powers towards the country. The way countries or groups perceive the processes in Afghanistan reflect their interests and expectations from the Taliban. It is clear that the Taliban have not changed, for i) they have not taken any of the demands and expectations of the international community seriously—the creation of an inclusive government, the involvement of women in public administration, education for girls and employment for women; ii) in internal political processes, the rights of ethnic and confessional groups are being infringed; iii) apartheid of women, and eviction of other ethnic and confessional groups from their homes; iv) Taliban's interpretation of Islam militates against generally accepted form of Islam in Afghanistan, and they have also changed sharia laws in accordance with their understanding; v) The Taliban have always shown their opponents less Islamic than them: Professor Burhanuddin Rabbani's government was called the Northern Alliance, the Hamid Karzai and Ashraf Ghani administrations—the Kabul office, and they completely dismissed the existence of various resistance groups inside Afghanistan; vi) they are now beginning to learn the laws of modern diplomacy and are ready to conduct lengthy negotiations. However, it is quite another thing that they do not guarantee results and consensus and therefore, to interact with them is to only recognise their "rightness".

There is a perception in expert circles that the Taliban are a proxy group representing the interests of a particular country or a group of countries because (i) certain countries seek to maintain their presence and influence in Afghanistan through the Taliban, (ii) the Taliban are a group imposed on the people of Afghanistan by outside powers, and (iii) they are the manifestation of external interference in the internal affairs of Afghanistan.

Against this background, the Taliban have put forward resolution of problems by force as the leitmotif of their policy, and there is no unity in their ranks and there are many contradictions within them; they are divided into different factions and they are all hostages of circumstances of their own making. It should also not be forgotten that, along with other factors, the Taliban came to power as a result of the signing of the Doha peace agreement with the United States.

### *3. Prospects for Recognition of Taliban and Lifting of International Sanctions.*

In the fourth year of their rule, the Taliban have not achieved the international recognition, and they do not also have any internal legitimacy (in the sense that there is no way one can prove that they enjoy it). Political and military opponents of the Taliban are not reconciled to the Taliban's return to power and the women and the youth are struggling for their rights. All this has created conditions that make it difficult for the Taliban to gain the international recognition. During their first time in power in the 1990s, the Taliban were recognised only by Pakistan, Saudi Arabia, and the UAE.

Today, despite lacking legitimacy and political recognition from the international community, the Taliban have managed to establish diplomatic, trade, and economic relations with several countries. They have been receiving weekly financial assistance of US$ 40 million from the United States. Their close friends too are not yet ready to recognise them, even if they have already recognised the embassies of Afghanistan run by the representatives of the Taliban and consider it important to negotiate with them, hold consultations on combating terrorism and drug trafficking support trade and economic cooperation, and provide humanitarian assistance. These countries are also calling for the unfreezing of the international reserves of the Central Bank of Afghanistan. The position taken by these countries can be described as a tactical approach in their relationship with the Taliban, which is based on their political and economic interests. Russia, based on such considerations, recognised the Taliban as the legitimate authority in Afghanistan in July 2025. However, at the same time, Moscow reiterated the conditions set by the international community for the Taliban.

It should be noted that there has been a shift in global attention away from Afghanistan in the aftermath of the Ukraine War and the conflict in Gaza. Such a situation favours the Taliban and they are focusing on consolidation of their power in Afghanistan. Sensing the lack of close attention of the international community, they are slowly turning Afghanistan into a country where terrorists, including those of foreign origins, can take shelter and plan their actions.

Another important fact that should not be missed is that the Taliban may not necessarily need international recognition at the moment, because there are already 17 embassies of various countries that are actively operating in Afghanistan. Moreover, offices of international organisations are functioning smoothly in Kabul. Today's reality shows that all the involved actors and the Taliban are satisfied with this status quo.

### *4. The Possibility of Terrorist Threats Emanating from Afghanistan*

As has been emphasised above, with the coming to power of the Taliban, terrorism has become firmly rooted in the country. This is linked to the very character of the Taliban, whose leaders are under international sanctions and the organisation itself is recognised as 'terrorist' by a number of countries. It is also a fact that the Taliban released all kinds of prisoners after coming to power, including leaders and supporters of extremist organisations; and created a favourable condition for foreign terrorist organisations to strengthen their presence in the country, with external powers involved using them in their proxy wars. Some countries view the presence and strengthening of the Taliban power in Afghanistan as favourable to their interests. These countries are engaged in the soft propaganda of the Taliban. Despite this, the terrorist threats emanating from the territory of Afghanistan have not abated.

Today there are more than 22 foreign terrorist organisations operating inside Afghanistan. Members of several of these organisations are operating freely in the country. The Taliban government has given a breathing space to all of them. They are engaged in increasing their strength by recruiting new supporters, and taking part in the management and control of some areas on behalf of the Taliban. The fact that al-Zawahiri, the leader of Al-Qaeda, lived in an elite administrative district of Kabul, where he was killed in a drone strike in the summer of 2022, proves this point. According to various estimates, about 12,000 militants belonging to various terrorist groups were released by the Taliban.

The current situation in Afghanistan is not favourable for the Central Asian countries in terms of security. Terrorist organisations such as Al-Qaeda, Daesh–Khorasan, East Turkistan Islamic Movement (ETIM), the Islamic Movement of Uzbekistan (IMU), Jamaat Ansarullah and others have become more active in Afghanistan.The most active among these is Daesh–Khorasan, whose suicide bombers blew themselves up at the Kabul Airport in August 2021 and in front of the Russian Embassy in September 2022. Then on 2 December 2022, the Pakistani ambassador was attacked, and on 12 December 2022, Daesh–Khorasan suicide bombers carried out a terrorist attack in a hotel where mainly Chinese entrepreneurs were staying. In total, in 2021 to date, Daesh–Khorasan suicide bombers have carried out numerous terrorist attacks inside Afghanistan. The main threats emanating from Afghanistan for Tajikistan and other Central Asian countries are: terrorist organisations of Central Asian origin, Al-Qaeda, Daesh–Khorasan, etc., and smuggling of drugs and precious metals, which act as a fuel for revitalisation of terrorism in the region.

### *5. The Situation of Women in Afghanistan*

The situation of women and especially girls in Afghanistan has deteriorated over the past three years. Women were earlier involved in all spheres of life in Afghanistan. Afghan women's activism is observed at two levels. It is seen in the activity of former members of parliament, civil servants and representatives of civil society who emigrated from Afghanistan after 15 August 2021. They are working actively in host countries, have opened foundations, registered organisations, held events and met diplomats to bring the problems of Afghan women to the attention of the international community. At the domestic level, women continue to demand the restoration of their most basic rights.

Today, women in Afghanistan face discrimination in all forms. They do not have the right to employment and education. On 21 December 2022, the Taliban Ministry of Education decided to ban women from studying at universities for an indefinite duration. They are not allowed to acquire modern knowledge and skills. Afghan women have continually questioned the several restrictions imposed by the Taliban authorities. Women have held demonstrations and taken out protest marches, and have also taken to social media networks to highlight their worsening condition in the country.

## Tajikistan's Current Policy Towards Afghanistan

The current Foreign Policy Concept states that Tajikistan 'is in favor of a quick restoration of lasting peace in the Islamic Republic of Afghanistan and affirms that enduring peace, security and political stability of the neighboring state meets its national interests.' It is of the view that 'mutually beneficial cooperation' with Afghanistan is 'based on historical, linguistic and cultural affinities between the two nations.'[4]

Tajikistan's policy toward Afghanistan has undergone some changes over the past two years. Dushanbe has softened its rhetoric and facilitated contacts between the business community and residents of border areas. The message of the executive body of the state authority of the Gorno-Badakhshan Autonomous Region, published on its *Facebook* page, states that on 2 September 2023, the work of border markets resumed in the Tem micro-district of Khorog, as well as in Darvaz, Vanj and Ishkashim districts, which border the Badakhshan Province of Afghanistan.[5] This step is primarily aimed at improving the well-being of residents along both sides of Amu Darya, and especially the population of the districts of Afghan Badakhshan, which contributes to their access to essential goods. In turn, the Taliban and their official and unofficial speakers no longer make threatening statements regarding Tajikistan.

Tajikistan's principled position on the Taliban has remained unchanged since 1996. Tajikistan has never recognised their power, and continues to hold the opinion that the activities of terrorist organisations on the territory of Afghanistan can create serious threats and potential challenges for the entire international community. In the late 1990s, President Rahmon had proposed a security belt around the borders of Afghanistan in order to coordinate joint measures to combat terrorism after the September 2001 terrorist attacks in the United States, complementing the global anti-terrorism campaign launched in Afghanistan. Tajikistan's proposal about the need to form a security belt around Afghanistan still remains relevant.

Tajikistan's policy towards the Afghan crisis is also influenced by the approaches of its closest neighbours and strategic partners. Russia plans to create a G5, a new regional mechanism for resolving the crisis in Afghanistan with the involvement of China, India, Pakistan and Iran. According to Russian media reports, this idea was supported by Beijing.[6] It became obvious that the path taken by Russia, aimed at playing with the Taliban and diligently whitewashing them in the Russian information space, did not lead to the expected results. In the Russian official media, the approach towards the Taliban had been changing. Since August 2021, the Russian Foreign Ministry has emphasised the expansion of relations with the Taliban. It hoped that cooperating with the Taliban would serve their interests. However, very soon Kremlin realised that the Taliban have not changed and will pose a significant threat to Russian interests in the foreseeable future. Today, Russia's approach is mixed and it is pursuing friendly relations with the Taliban while doubting their reliability. Such change in Russia's policy may have a significant impact on Central Asian countries' policies toward Afghanistan.

Uzbekistan is a close neighbour and a strategic partner of Tajikistan. Despite this, Tashkent and Dushanbe have different approaches towards the Taliban. In January 2023, Uzbek policy towards Afghanistan faced a very serious challenge due to the implementation of the Kosh-Tepa irrigation canal by the Taliban authorities. This channel is intended for irrigation of 500 thousand hectares of land in Afghanistan. Earlier, the Soviet Union and Afghanistan had agreed that the latter could use up to 10 cubic kms of water per year from the Amu Darya basin. In the following years, Afghanistan did not use its share, and Uzbekistan and Turkmenistan had been utilising the water from Amu Darya for agricultural purposes. As water is fast becoming a scarce commodity in these countries, the building of the Kosh-Tepa canal has come as a shock for Tashkent and Ashgabat.

Once this canal is constructed, Uzbekistan and Turkmenistan will face an acute shortage of water. Water is becoming a sensitive issue among countries in Central Asia and therefore, Taliban's initiative will impact the process of engagement by its northern neighbours in the long run. The Taliban have also accused Tashkent of cutting electricity in the winter season, which was probably linked to their decision to construct this canal. In this context, putting pressure on the Taliban may not also yield expected results. Be that as it may, it is obvious that in the near future, the policy of Uzbekistan and Turkmenistan towards the Taliban may undergo significant changes.

Today, close cooperation has been established between Uzbekistan and the Taliban government in trade, economic, transport and transit areas, as well as in the security sphere. In recent years, high-ranking delegations from both countries have been received in Kabul and Tashkent. Uzbekistan attaches great importance to the trans-Afghan transport corridor to increase trade flows to the countries of South Asia.

Another problematic case for Tajikistan and Uzbekistan is the fate of the Afghan aircraft flown into these countries by the Afghan pilots fleeing the Taliban in August 2021. While the Afghan pilots and their family members were evacuated by the United States from Tajikistan and Uzbekistan, these aircraft remain parked in the two countries. The Taliban have repeatedly demanded their return, to which Tashkent and Dushanbe have replied that they could only return them to a legitimate and recognised authority in Kabul, much to the chagrin of the Taliban. In February 2025, Uzbekistan transferred seven Black Hawk helicopters to the United States.[7]

Tajikistan's policy towards Afghanistan in the current situation can be comprehended from the following observations:

*First,* today Tajikistan is the only neighbour of Afghanistan that has not held open official talks with the Taliban leadership. The exception is the prolongation of the agreement on the purchase of electricity with representatives of *Da* Afghanistan *Breshna Sherkat* (DABS) in Tashkent in December 2021[8] and in Istanbul in January 2023,[9] and the meeting of the Deputy Chairman of the Gorno-Badakhshan Region of Tajikistan with representatives of the Badakhshan Province of Afghanistan.[10] For more than 27 years, Dushanbe has consistently adhered to the approach, including during the first rule of the Taliban (1996–2001), of cooperating only with a legitimate and recognised government in Kabul.

*Second,* Tajikistan has made a lot of efforts since August 2021 to draw the attention of international leaders and the public to the large-scale humanitarian crisis in Afghanistan. To mitigate the humanitarian crisis in Afghanistan, it has offered its territory through which international aid can be sent.

*Third,* Tajikistan is progressively changing its policy to find ways to coexist with a Taliban-controlled Afghanistan. It is aimed at maintaining ties with economic entities and entrepreneurs of Afghanistan.

Tajikistan's concern over the events in Afghanistan and the non-recognition of the Taliban's authority is linked to the following factors:

*First,* since independence, the Central Asian states at the bilateral and multilateral levels have considered countering international terrorism as a factor in ensuring regional security. Tajikistan's concerns over the Taliban's policies stem from its realisation that under their control, Afghanistan is harbouring terrorist groups which are a threat to regional peace.

*Second*, forceful seizure of power by the Taliban and the formation of an Islamic emirate runs the risk of emboldening like-minded elements (or groups) in different countries in the region who might want to repeat this example in their countries, including in the states of Central Asia. The case of the "Taliban" significantly impacts the security system in Central Asia, as it has the potential to convert potential threats into real ones.

*Third*, Tajikistan has the second longest border with Afghanistan (after Pakistan), and today the northern provinces of Afghanistan are completely controlled by the Taliban. Foreign fighters, including those of Central Asian origins (IMU in Uzbekistan, Jamaat Ansarullah in Tajikistan and others), have great influence in these regions and echo the sentiments of the Taliban. The leaders of the IMU and Ansarullah, after the signing of the peace agreement in Doha, had congratulated the Taliban on their "victory" over the United States and its allies and threatened the authorities in their respective countries of origin that they would 'repeat the success of the Taliban in the near future'.[11] It is pretty much evident that foreign fighters in Afghanistan are protected by the Taliban. Today, the Taliban issues them Afghan passports, supports them in every possible way, and almost all foreign fighters are under the care of the Taliban[12] so that their potential and combat experience can be used at any time. Therefore, Tajikistan is ready for any turn of events in Afghanistan.

## Bilateral Trade and Economic Relations

Tajikistan's external trade turnover with Afghanistan was about US$ 111 million in 2022, $98 million in 2023,[13] and $114.7 million in 2024.[14] An analysis of various resources showed that the bilateral trade with Afghanistan amounted to US$ 99 million in 2015, $81 million in 2016, $113 million in 2017, $99 million in 2018, $106 million in 2019, $70 million in 2020, and $84.1 million in 2021.The press service of the President of Tajikistan reports that from 1997 to 2020, the total bilateral trade amounted to US$ 1 billion 549 million,[15] i.e., for over 20 years, the average was about US$ 77.45 million.

An analysis of data from 2015 to 2024 also shows a decline in the bilateral trade, from US$ 114.7 million in 2024 to $70 million in 2020. The dip in 2020 was associated with the COVID-19 pandemic, when all states closed their borders and there was a decline in trade around the world. During the period the Taliban held power in Kabul for the first time (1996–2001), thereafter the 20-year period of the Republic (2002–2021), and since the return of the Taliban in August 2021, the trade between Tajikistan and Afghanistan has had similar indicators. Thus, the change of regimes in Kabul did not have any significant impact on trade and economic relations between both countries.

Traditionally, food products, electricity, cement, coal and other types[16] of goods have been exported from Tajikistan to Afghanistan for more than 10 years and this trend has not changed. This caters to the real needs of the people of Afghanistan and Tajikistan has limited products to export. As per the data mentioned earlier, the bilateral trade between Tajikistan and Afghanistan increased from US$ 70 million in 2020 to $84.1 million in 2021. This was more because in 2021, trade leapt back to normal after the pandemic came under control. Tajikistan imports from Afghanistan mainly fresh and dried fruits, vegetables, seeds, some types of plants and mineral fertilizers.[17]

The approach of Tajikistan on bilateral trade with Afghanistan has been most succinctly captured by Khayriddin Usmonzoda, Director of the Center for Strategic Studies under the President of the Republic of Tajikistan. Arguing that Tajikistan cannot stop cooperation with Afghanistan in all areas, Usmonzoda stated in February 2023:

> The president of the country [Emomali Rahmon] emphasized that we do not interfere in the events taking place in the neighboring country [Afghanistan], but we also cannot be indifferent...Tajikistan is interested in our neighboring country [Afghanistan] being safe, stable and developing. Security cannot be ensured without economic development. Economy has a humanitarian aspect. Therefore, Tajikistan *distinguishes between political and economic and humanitarian cooperation*. Currently, our cooperation is established in economic and humanitarian direction.[18]

Thus, the trade turnover between Tajikistan and Afghanistan is more because of traditional relations among private companies and entrepreneurs who maintain mutually beneficial trade between the two countries. The government hardly interferes in this domain.

However, the purchase of Tajik electricity by Afghanistan's DABS has been problematic. As noted earlier, in December 2021 in Tashkent and in January 2023 in Istanbul, *Barqi Tojik* (Tajik electricity producer) and DABS extended agreements on the terms of purchase of electricity. According to the Tajik media, Tajikistan exported 1.7 billion kWh of electricity to Afghanistan in 2022. 1.7 billion kWh of electricity also was exported to Uzbekistan.[19] In 2022, Tajikistan earned total amount of US$ 73 million from its sale of electricity to Afghanistan, with an average price of 4.3 cents per kWh.[20] Tajik journalists in February 2023 asked the management of *Barqi Tojik* about the debt of DABS to the company, but did not receive an exact answer. The head of *Barqi Tojik*, Mahmadumar Asozoda, did not give any specific figure, but noted that DABS' debt service capabilities have improved. At the beginning of 2022, DABS' debt to Barqi Tojik was US$ 33 million, and inmid-2022, the debt decreased by only US$ 5 million. This situation was explained by the difficulties of transferring money from accounts in Afghan banks.[21]

According to Abdullo Kurbonzoda, the deputy head of *Barqi Tojik*, DABS paid off the remaining debt of $28 million in the first half of 2023. He once again stressed that the debt was because of the problem of transferring funds from the company's accounts in Afghanistan.[22] The volume of electricity exports from Tajikistan to Afghanistan amounted to 1.6 billion kWh in 2023[23] and 1.53 billion kWh in 2024.[24]

Regardless of the abovementioned considerations, Tajikistan continues to supply electricity to Afghanistan for mainly three reasons. First, it fulfills earlier commitments (the agreement between *Barqi Tojik* and DABS on the export of Tajik electricity to Afghanistan for a period of 20 years signed in 2008); second, Afghan market is a promising area for the sale of Tajik electricity, and after the completion of the construction of large hydroelectric power plants, it has been possible to increase the volume of exports; third, the export of electricity to Afghanistan has a serious humanitarian dimension, and in the winter season, it meets the requirements of ordinary people in Afghanistan.

## Tajikistan's Infrastructure Priorities in Relation to Afghanistan

Tajikistan's priorities and expectations regarding the situation in Afghanistan are determined by the country's interests. The following can be identified as the key priorities of Tajikistan:

*Connecting Energy Systems of Central and South Asia:* Tajikistan occupies a leading place in the world in terms of producing environment-friendly electricity. Dushanbe is a major supplier of electricity to Kabul and sells its products at a lower price than its neighbours. Another important project is the

CASA–1000 transmission line, which will connect the countries of Central Asia and South Asia through Afghanistan. Pakistan and India (in the future) are potential buyers of Tajikistan's electricity, which will be exported through power lines. The search for potential electricity markets is a priority for Tajikistan. Against this background, a stable and friendly Afghanistan promises huge economic opportunities for Tajikistan.

*Transit Potential of Afghanistan for Direct Access to Pakistan, Iran and India:* It is important for Tajikistan to expand its transit potential, and Afghanistan opens up great opportunities for its implementation. Through the territory of Afghanistan, Tajikistan can reach the seas, that is, the ports of Gwadar (Pakistan) and Chabahar (Iran). Both these ports are of particular importance for Tajikistan. Another interesting project is about accessing Pakistan through the Wakhan Corridor. The construction of a highway between Chitral (Pakistan) and Ishkashim (Tajikistan) will connect the road infrastructure of both countries and will enable both Tajikistan and other Central Asian countries to have an alternate route to the port of Gwadar. Tajikistan is interested in expanding relations with the countries of South Asia, since it would contribute to the achievement of the country's strategic goals. It would break the transportation deadlock and turn Tajikistan into a transit country. For this, Afghanistan is of particular importance. Six bridges have been built over the Panj/Amu Darya River, and, according to the Minister of Transport of Tajikistan, the capacity of the Panji Poyon–Sher Khan Bandar checkpoint is second only to the Fatekhabad–Oybek checkpoint (the border in the north with Uzbekistan).[25]

Tajikistan in its *National Development Strategy-2030* has identified ways to overcome transportation and communication impasse, and turn the country into a transit hub, ensure energy independence, and make the country an exporter of electricity. In this regard, the southern vector plays a key role, since the shortest route to the seaports of Gwadar (Pakistan) and Chabahar (Iran) passes through the territory of Afghanistan. The transit potential of Afghanistan's Wakhan corridor to connecting Tajikistan with Pakistan thus assumes significance. During Karzai and Ghani's administration, direct transit through the corridor could not materialise due to tensions between Kabul and Islamabad. Post-2021, the scenario remains the same. Finally, the completion and operationalisation of the CASA–1000 transmission line, which connects the power systems of Central Asia and South Asia, would be impossible without the cooperation of the current Afghan authorities.

According to Daler Juma, Minister of Energy and Water Resources of Tajikistan, the CASA–1000 project will be launched in 2027. The construction work on the Tajik and Kyrgyz routes has now been completed, and in the coming days, the power transmission lines between Tajikistan and Kyrgyzstan will be connected.[26] The Taliban also has high hopes from this project. According to Mutaullah Abid, a representative of the Taliban government's Ministry of Energy and Water Resources, work on the CASA–1000 project in Afghanistan has been completed by 70 per cent and more than 95 per cent of the necessary equipment has already been delivered to the construction site.[27]

In December 2022, President Rahmon paid an official visit to Pakistan, and in a joint statement issued it was noted that the countries intend to bring their cooperation to the level of a strategic partnership. It was reported that a "Strategic Partnership Agreement" will be finalised and the parties will sign it soon during the visit of the Prime Minister of Pakistan to Dushanbe.[28] In July 2024, during the official visit of the Prime Minister of Pakistan Shehbaz Sharif to Tajikistan, the "Strategic Partnership Agreement between the Republic of Tajikistan and the Islamic Republic of Pakistan" was signed. Thus, Tajikistan is trying to ensure its priorities and deepen cooperation with the states of South Asia. In order to ensure Tajikistan's interests in the long term, it would be advisable to initiate the signing of a strategic partnership agreement between Dushanbe and New Delhi. Such an approach will provide an opportunity to expand and strengthen relations in all areas with Pakistan and India and can have a positive impact on the socio-economic situation in Afghanistan.

## Conclusion

Tajikistan's position on Afghanistan is dictated by the peculiarities of its own national interests and perceptions. The difference in the policy of Dushanbe from that of other Central Asian states makes it possible to assess the situation from a different point of view and take a decision on how to engage Afghanistan.

The fate of the Afghan Republic shows that all countries, especially the Central Asian states, need to take comprehensive measures to strengthen the foundations of their statehood and national security. The key lesson from the events in Afghanistan is that assistance from external partners can be temporary and situational. In protecting and strengthening a State, no other factor plays as important a role as the interests and security of the citizens. Therefore, it is necessary to take into account the Afghan experience and understand that the interests of Central Asian states and their citizens are best served by ensuring stability, security, and sustainable development.

The Central Asian states need to think seriously about the reality of terrorist threats from Afghanistan, coordinate their security policies, and evolve effective mechanisms to neutralise security challenges and threats to the region. *One thing is clear: no one but the states and the people of Central Asia have the greatest stakes in the stability and security of their region.*

## NOTES

1. 'General Information', Ministry of Foreign Affairs, Republic of Tajikistan, 26 January 2021, at https://www.mfa.tj/en/main/tajikistan/general-information (Accessed 24 February 2025).
2. 'Meeting with Pakistani Foreign Minister Shah Mahmood Qureshi', Press Service of President of the Republic of Tajikistan, 25 August 2021, at http://president.tj/en/node/26369 (Accessed 5 March 2025).
3. Sherali Sh. Rizoyon and Makhmud F. Giyosov, 'Афганистандо и послевозвращения Талибан' [Afghanistan before and after the Taliban's comeback], Donish, Dushanbe, 2023, pp. 428–431.
4. 'Concept of the Foreign Policy of the Republic of Tajikistan', Approved by the Decree of the President of the Republic of Tajikistan on 27 January 2015, No. 332, Ministry of Foreign Affairs, Republic of Tajikistan, at https://mfa.tj/en/main/view/4255/concept-of-the-foreign-policy-of-the-republic-of-tajikistan (Accessed 5 March 2025).
5. Khiromon Bakozoda, 'На таджикско-афганской границе возобновили работу совместные рынки. ТаджикистанначалсотрудничествосТалибаном?' [Joint markets have resumed operation on the Tajik–Afghan border. Has Tajikistan started cooperation with the Taliban?], *Ozodi*, 2 September 2023, at https://rus.ozodi.org/a/32575770.html (Accessed 30 September 2025).
6. 'Россияпредложиласоздатьпятистороннийформат G5 дляурегулированияв Афганистане' [Russia proposed to create a five-party G5 format for settlement in Afghanistan], *TASS*, 12 February 2023, at https://tass.ru/politika/17030 891 (Accessed 13 March 2025).
7. 'Ташкент передал США 7 вертолетов Black Hawk. В 2021 г. афганскиепилотыспасалисьнанихотталибов' [Tashkent transferred 7 Black Hawk helicopters to the US. In 2021, Afghan pilots used them to escape from the Taliban], *GolosAmeriki*, 7 February 2025, at https://www.golosameriki.com/a/uzbekistan-hands-helicopters-from-pre-taliban-afghan-army-to-us/7966804.html (Accessed 13 March 2025).
8. Mullorajab Yusufi, 'Тоҷикистонимсолба Афғонистон 1.5 млрдкиловатсоатбарқмедиҳад' [Tajikistan will provide 1.5 billion kWh of electricity this year], *Ozodi*, 14 February 2022, at https://www.ozodi.org/a/31702842.html (Accessed 5 March 2025).
9. 'Душанбеи Кабулдоговорилисьобэкспортеэлектроэнергиив 2023 году' [Dushanbe and Kabul have agreed to export electricity in 2023], *Sputnik–Tajikistan*, 11 January 2023, at https://tj.sputniknews.ru/20230111/taliby-dushanbe-elektroenergiya-1054116580.html (Accessed 5 March 2025).
10. Khiromon Bakozoda, no. 5.
11. Uran Botobekov, 'Central Asian Salafi-Jihadi Groups and the US-Taliban Peace Agreement', *The Central Asia-Caucasus Analyst*, 3 June 2020, at https://www.cacianalyst.

org/publications/analytical-articles/item/13621-central-asian-salafi-jihadi-groups-and-the-us-taliban-peace-agreement.html (Accessed 5 March 2025).

12. Sherali Sh. Rizoyonand Makhmud F. Giyosov, 'How Relevant is the Threat of Central Asian Militants from Afghanistan?', *New Geopolitics Research Network*, 12 August 2021, at https://www.newgeopolitics.org/2021/08/12/how-relevant-the-threat-of-central-asian-militants-from-afghanistan/ (Accessed 5 March 2025).
13. Sergey Venyavsky, 'ТорговляТаджикистанасталибами: фактыицифры'[Tajikistan's Trade with the Taliban: Facts and Figures], *Sputnik–Tajikistan*, 29 January 2024, at https://tj.sputniknews.ru/20240129/torgovlya-tajikistan-taliby-afganistan-tsifry-1061466044.html (Accessed 5 March 2025).
14. Stanislav Krasilnikov, 'РоссиясталаглавнымимпортеромТаджикистана'[Russia has become Tajikistan's main importer], *Sputnik–Tajikistan*, 12 February 2025, at https://tj.sputniknews.ru/20250212/russia-glavny-importer-tajikistan-1066199397.html (Accessed 5 March 2025).
15. 'СуханронӣдарнуҳуминКонфронсивазирони "ҚалбиОсиё – Раванди Истамбул"' [Speech by the President of the Republic of Tajikistan at the Heart of Asia–Istanbul Process 9th Ministerial Conference], *Press Service of President of the Republic of Tajikistan*, 30 March 2021, at https://www.president.tj/event/speeches/22872 (Accessed 5 March 2025).
16. Sergey Venyavsky, no. 13.
17. Ibid.
18. 'Директор ЦСИ: ТаджикистаннеможетпрекратитьсотрудничествосАфганистаномвовсехсферах' [Director of the CSS: Tajikistan cannot stop cooperation with Afghanistan in all areas], *Asia-Plus Tajikistan*, 9 February 2023, at https://asiaplustj.info/ru/news/tajikistan/politics/20230209/direktor-tssi-tadzhikistan-ne-mozhet-prekratit-sotrudnichestvo-s-afganistanom-vo-vseh-sferah (Accessed 5 March 2023).
19. 'Оҷонсииомори Тоҷикистонмаблағифурӯшибарқбахориҷароэълонкард' [The Statistics Agency of Tajikistan has published the volume of electricity sales abroad], *Ozodi*, 14 February 2023, at https://www.ozodi.org/a/32270437.html (Accessed 5 March 2023).
20. 'Тоҷикистонба Афғонистончӣқадарбарқдод?' [How much electricity has Tajikistan given to Afghanistan?], *Ozodi*, 8 February 2023, at https://www.ozodi.org/a/3226 2034.html (Accessed 5 March 2023).
21. 'КакранееоткрытыесведениявТаджикистанетеперьстановятсясекретными' [How previously open information in Tajikistan is now becoming a secret], *Asia-Plus Tajikistan*, 31 January 2023, at https://asiaplustj.info/ru/news/tajikistan/society/20230131/kak-ranee-otkritie-svedeniya-v-tadzhikistane-teper-stanovyatsya-sekretnimi (Accessed 5 March 2025).
22. Sayfiddin Karaev, 'Афганистанпогасилдолгв 28 миллионовдолларовзаэлектроэнергиюперед Таджикистаном' [Afghanistan has repaid a debt of $28 million for electricity to Tajikistan], *Asia-Plus Tajikistan*, 10 August 2023, at https://asiaplustj.info/ru/news/tajikistan/economic/20230810/afganistan-pogasil-dolg-pered-tadzhikistanom-za-elektroenergiyu (Accessed 5 March 2025).

23. 'Таджикистанможетувеличитьэкспортэлектроэнергиив Афганистан' [Tajikistan May Increase Electricity Exports to Afghanistan], *Sputnik–Tajikistan*, 14 February 2024, at https://tj.sputniknews.ru/20240214/tajikistan-eksport-elektroenergiya-afganistan-1061681416.html (Accessed 5 March 2025).
24. Payrav Chorshanbiev, 'Кудаисколькоэлектроэнергии Таджикистанэкспортировалв 2024 году' [Where and how much electricity did Tajikistan export in 2024], *Asia-Plus Tajikistan,* 30 January 2025, at https://asiaplustj.info/ru/news/tajikistan/economic/20250130/kuda-i-skolko-elektroenergii-tadzhikistan-eksportiroval-v-2024-godu (Accessed 5 March 2023).
25. Payrav Chorshanbiev, 'Минтранс Таджикистана: «Никаких преград для грузоперевозок с Афганистаном не существуют»' [Ministry of Transport of Tajikistan: 'There are no barriers to cargo transportation with Afghanistan'], *Asia-Plus Tajikistan,* 14 July 2021, at https://asiaplustj.info/ru/news/tajikistan/economic/20210714/mintrans-tadzhikistana-nikakih-pregrad-dlya-gruzoperevozok-s-afganistanom-ne-sutshestvuyut (Accessed 5 March 2023).
26. Ahmad Azizi, 'Tajikistan Expects CASA-1000 Power Line to be Operational by 2027', *Amu TV,* 3 March 2025, at https://amu.tv/160881/ (Accessed 13 March 2025).
27. Ilya Naymushin "'Талибан": работы по CASA-1000 на афганской территории завершены на 70%' ["Taliban": CASA-1000 work on Afghan territory is 70% complete], *Sputnik–Tajikistan*, 6 March 2025, at https://tj.sputniknews.ru/20250306/taliban-casa-1000-afganistan-1066471331.html (Accessed 13 March 2025).
28. 'Joint Communiqué on Official Visit of President of the Republic of Tajikistan, H.E. Emomali Rahmon to Islamic Republic of Pakistan', Press Service of President of the Republic of Tajikistan, 14 December 2022, at http://president.tj/en/node/29786 (Accessed 5 March 2025).

# 6

# Iran and the Revival of Taliban Emirate

*Mohsen Shariatinia and Hamed A. Kermani*

If one defines political order as lack of violence and anarchy on the one hand and the presence of an enduring and stable democratic regime on the other,[1] then such an order is being challenged as a result of the Taliban's re-emergence in Afghanistan. Since the so-called "Islamic Emirate" has reclaimed its dominance in Afghanistan after the withdrawal of foreign troops in August 2021, Iran's relations with Afghanistan have become more complicated. The paper argues that the Taliban's presence in power has challenged the political order in Afghanistan to the extent that, one, Iran has been facing practical issues with the new rulers of Kabul since September 2021, and, two, some of Iran's fundamental interests have been severely challenged in Afghanistan, both of which are a result of the collapse of the democratic political order in Kabul that Iran had learned to work with for two decades. To unpack these shifts, the paper analyses the evolving dynamics across three levels: national (local political structures and actors), regional (neighbourhood alignments and rivalries), and systemic (interactions with great powers and global norms).

## Local (national) Level

Iran has had complicated relations with the Taliban. After 9/11, Iran tacitly supported the overthrow of the Taliban government. However, gradually the conflict between Iran and the US in Afghanistan increased and Iran found common interests with the Taliban. Iran demanded the withdrawal of foreign forces from Afghanistan and cautiously welcomed the Taliban's return to power. However, the two former rivals' definition of the political order in Afghanistan is conflicted.[2] Iran had an essential role in the formation of the democratic order in Kabul following the 2001 Bonn Conference. For Iran, it was an optimal political regime for Afghanistan, even though it was unsteady and vulnerable.[3] Therefore, from Tehran's perspective, the best option was that the Taliban engaged with the democratic political system without transforming it.[4]

However, despite international pressure, Taliban changed Afghanistan's political system to an "Islamic Emirate" and deprived all political groups of political participation. The revival of the "Islamic Emirate" posed strategic and ideological threats to Iran.[5] In such an order, the form of law would be based on a *Talibani* narrative of political Islam. Consequently, minorities' rights, especially rights of Afghan Shias, who are considered as Iran's allies and strategic depth in Afghanistan, have been compromised. The Taliban government not only prohibited groups close to Iran, such as the Northern Alliance, from any political participation in the government, but also engaged in a conflict with forces loyal to Ahmad Massoud (son of former commander Ahmad Shah Massoud) for control over Panjshir, eliminating the conditions for any compromise.[6] The Taliban's narrative of Islam, which is called the "Qeshri"[7] narrative in Iran, is regressive and fanatical from the perspective of Iranian leaders and is in opposition to the official Iranian Shiite narrative of Islam. Such a narrative also has important implications for the nature of the state and its relationship with the people in Afghanistan.[8]

However, one must note that all of Iran's foreign policy elites do not agree with the above-mentioned understanding. There is a debate in this regard, and some influential people, including members of the parliament, suggest that the Taliban have changed and could be helpful to Iran's anti-West policy. Therefore, they could be subject to a cooperative and constructive approach.[9] The other side of this argument usually put forth by Iranian reformists, points to the Taliban's totalitarian, violent, and dogmatic approach toward politics, and considers it to be an existential threat to Iran and its interests in the region.[10]

After the fall of Kabul in August 2021, a heated debate broke out in Iran between two reformist and fundamentalist factions regarding Iran's relations with the Taliban. This ongoing debate is getting more heated with the developments that are happening in the relations between Iran and the Taliban. The border conflicts between Iran and Afghanistan, the differences between the two countries over the 1973 Helmand River Water Treaty, and the Taliban's treatment of political and ethnic groups in recent months have fueled this debate. Despite Tehran's concerns regarding the political situation in Afghanistan and differences with the Taliban, Tehran has put cautious engagement with the Taliban on its agenda,[11] without extending formal recognition to their regime.[12] When it comes to economic relations and the bilateral trade, this cautious engagement seems to be paying off.

When the Taliban took power, bilateral trade between Iran and Afghanistan fell dramatically. In 2019, during the Ashraf Ghani Government, Iranian exports to Afghanistan stood at $2.308 billion and in return Iran imported a small amount of goods.[13] In 2020, Iran's exports to Afghanistan decreased by 20 per cent compared to 2019.[14] In 2022, the trade between the two countries grew marginally, reaching to $1.634 billion. The bilateral trade volume has since continued to grow. In November 2023, Taliban Deputy Prime Minister Mullah Abdul Ghani Baradar visited Iran at the head of a high-level delegation, which also visited the Chabahar Port. The Afghan delegation expressed its desire to increase the value of bilateral trade to $10 billion,[15] which seems unrealistic under the current circumstances. The main issue in this area is that with the Taliban's domination of Afghanistan, the major part of international aid to this country has been cut off, and with the withdrawal of foreign forces, an important part of the country's financial circulation has also been diminished. In addition, Iran–Afghanistan–India trilateral cooperation on the Chabahar Port has faced major challenges. Therefore, the return of the trade relations between the two countries to the situation before the Taliban took over is facing major challenges.

**Regional Level**

At the regional level, Afghanistan's evolving political order intersects with longstanding strategic rivalries, many of which shape—and are shaped by—Iran's interests in the country. A productive analytical framework is to assess these rivalries through dyadic relationships of amity and antagonism. To the extent that Iran is concerned, three main dyadic rivalries in the region are connected to Tehran's interests in Afghanistan: *Iran–Pakistan*, *Iran–Saudi Arabia*, and *India–Pakistan*. These dyads relate to Afghanistan's political order around one or more of three different concepts: *nature of the state*, *social dynamics* (internal to Afghanistan), and *economy*.

As regards the first case, the Iran–Pakistan dyad demonstrates rivalry in two particular realms related to the nature of the state and social dynamics. Pakistan, enjoying religious and ethnic similarities with the majority Sunni Pashtun population in Afghanistan, clearly stands in favour of a government run by the Taliban, which has long been considered the re-Talibanistion of Afghanistan.[16] Therefore, Pakistan has tried to legitimise Taliban's *de facto* state in the international community as a normal state and gradually provide the grounds for recognising this group. It will give Pakistan an upper hand in Afghanistan against Iran.

Therefore, it is not surprising that Iranians, who traditionally are in favour of the Northern forces (comprising ethnic minorities such as Tajiks and Hazaras), watch Pakistan's attempts suspiciously.[17] Thus, the nature of the future state will not just affect social dynamics and balance of forces internally but also the regional rivalries. However, one should give serious considerations to the developments in the Taliban's relations with Islamabad. The killing of Ayman al-Zawahiri in Kabul by a US drone launched from the Pakistani soil,[18] Tehrik-e-Taliban Pakistan's (TTP) attacks on Pakistani troops from Afghanistan,[19] and the resurfacing of old territorial issues between the two countries, have led to serious tensions in bilateral relations.

Another dilemma in the Iran–Pakistan dyad in Afghanistan is the way US relates to it. Pakistan played a pivotal role in convincing the Taliban and the US to enter into negotiations that led to the Doha Agreement in February 2020. Also, there were speculations that Pakistan and the US were locked in talks over locating the US military bases on Pakistan's soil.[20] Cooperation against terrorism was mentioned as the main aim for these proposed military bases.[21] Even though Pakistani officials, particularly during the Imran Khan government and also the Shahbaz Sharif government, opposed the possibility of such a demand, it seems that after Khan's ouster, the US–Pakistan security cooperation increased.[22] Such cooperation, especially the presence of American intelligence and military forces on Iran's eastern borders, bothers Tehran in two ways. First, the US activities in Pakistan will add to Iran's security dilemma at its eastern borders in a region that is even more sensitive than Iran's border with Afghanistan due to the presence of Baloch insurgents and terrorist groups such as Jaish-ul Adl. Second, the US–Pakistan cooperation in the region, including in Afghanistan, will add to the Iran–Pakistan tensions.

The Iran–Saudi dyad is chiefly concerned with the nature of the state in Afghanistan. While the Taliban are supposed to be more affiliated with Qatari's brotherhood, their ideological ties with Saudi Jihadists and extremists are strong. The first generation of Taliban leaders, including Mullah Umar, the group's founder, studied in madrasas supported by Saudi Wahhabis.[23] Saudis also financed the jihadists' primary military efforts against the Soviets.[24] After the establishment of the "Islamic Emirate" in Afghanistan, Iran has repeatedly expressed its concerns and emphasised the establishment of an inclusive government. Part of Tehran's concern is related to the ideological nature of the Taliban and their links with anti-Shia ideological movements. In other words, Iran's disapproval of an Islamic Emirate in Kabul was in some part because of the ideological threat it posed to Tehran's narration of political Islam,[25] which within the context of the Iran–Saudi rivalry meant more footprint for the Kingdom on Iran's eastern borders.

With regard to the India–Pakistan dyad, economy and social interaction are at the centre. India has always been a crucial factor for Iran–Pakistan and Iran–Afghanistan relations.[26] Considering the importance of security dynamics that an India–Pakistan rivalry generates within the region, bringing this dyad into account is vital for understanding the regional implications of the new developments in Afghanistan from an Iranian perspective. Afghanistan is the third regional area of conflict between the two countries next to Kashmir and the Indian Ocean, and Iran happens to be on India's side in this matter.

Briefly, India considers Afghanistan—and Central Asia—as the first ring of extended neighbourhood to its strategic core—Indian Ocean.[27] Therefore, New Delhi tries to diminish Pakistan's strategic depth there and wishes to reach out to the market and natural resources of the region.[28] For India, Iran is its only logical alternative route to Central Asia, Russia, and East Europe. Economically speaking, the trilateral agreement in 2016 between Iran, India, and Afghanistan provided a foundation for Iran's economic ties with Afghanistan during the previous government, as well as bolstering Iran–India ties. The route is aimed at bypassing Pakistan and escaping China's strategic encirclement,[29] and to the extent that it enhances Iran–India ties, it causes anxiety for Pakistan. In terms of social dynamics, in the 1990s and after the invasion of foreign troops in Afghanistan in 2001, India, coupled with Iran, stood against the Taliban,[30] which then was the most trusted and powerful ally of Islamabad in Afghanistan. However, the relations between Islamabad and Kabul have not been steady since the Taliban seized power in Afghanistan. Issues such as the close ties between the Taliban and the TTP,[31] illegal migrants,[32] and conflict over shared water resources,[33] have deteriorated relations between old allies.

The Taliban has chosen Pakistan as the most important transit route and has signed important trade and customs agreements with Islamabad.[34] In addition, the Taliban has shown interest in joining the China–Pakistan Economic Corridor (CPEC) and has prioritised the implementation of the Trans-Afghan Corridor, the 573-km railway that is supposed to connect Uzbekistan to Pakistan through Afghanistan's soil.[35] Such a move is an economic loss for both Iran and India and alters regional strategic dynamics due to Afghanistan's dependence on Islamabad, tying India's hands in the region.[36] Without Kabul on board, developing the Chabahar Port by India makes less sense and causes issues for Tehran–Delhi relations as well, all in favour of Pakistan's regional interests. Even though the Taliban leaders have been trying to explore other options and diversify the Afghan trade routes, partly due to the disagreements with Islamabad, a combination of India's decreasing incentive to reach out to Afghanistan through Chabahar and Kabul's diversifying options to access the Indian Ocean and Oman Gulf means that Iran and India need to redefine their cooperation in Chabahar under the current circumstance.

The Afghanistan issue has also witnessed non-traditional regional actors seeking to play a role in recent years. Turkey and Qatar are the most important ones. The Islamic Brotherhood-bound leaderships in Istanbul and Doha seem more engaged on the Afghanistan issue than they have been in the past. Hosting the US–Taliban negotiations, despite strong interests of Riyadh and Abu Dhabi,[37] and the Taliban's office by Qatar, and longstanding efforts in intra-Afghan negotiations by Turkish President Recep Tayyip Erdoğan,[38] are signs of the emergence of new important actors in the Afghan arena. In other words, after the fall of Kabul, Turkey and Qatar tried to expand relations with the Taliban and supported them in establishing a new political order. Iran's understanding of the Turkey–Qatar axis is not very clear-cut, but imagining Tehran's threat perception from yet another ideological rival in the form of the Muslim Brotherhood in Afghanistan is not far-fetched.

### At the Level of Great Powers

Iran approaches the role of great powers in the Afghanistan crisis very cautiously, and at different levels, while looking for opportunities to deal with the crisis-prone country in cooperation with them. Iran has acknowledged great powers' role in state-building and strengthening of political order in Afghanistan throughout history but at the same time, it has looked at their presence at its eastern borders with anxiety and concern.[39] Paradoxically, United States was Tehran's most important partner in establishing the new political order in Kabul post-2001.[40] Taliban posed a severe threat to Iran before US invaded Afghanistan. On some occasions, the tension between the two escalated to the threshold of war, and Iran even considered a military advance on Herat.[41] The International Force's invasion of Afghanistan removed this threat and opened up a strategic opportunity for Tehran. Iran collaborated with the US, India, Russia, and some other powers to topple the Taliban's Islamic Emirate and establish the new political order, which benefited them in crucial ways.[42]

However, the Iran–US relations in Afghanistan became complicated later, creating a triangle of complex inter-relationship between Iran, Taliban and the US, and particularly between Iran and the US. The Doha Agreement of February 2020 brought about a new development in the triangle. The US exit strategy envisaged in the agreement presented Iran with a security dilemma: on the one hand, it removed the perceived threat from US military presence at its eastern border[43] and Iran stepped up its new regional strategy, called 'Dismiss the Americans,' while on the other hand, the American withdrawal paved way for the collapse of the Afghan Republic and the return of the Taliban hegemony in Afghanistan.

With the fall of the Ghani Government, Iran was presented with a complex opportunity. On the one hand, the threats caused by the US presence in Iran's eastern neighbourhood disappeared, while on the other, it became difficult for Iran to manage relations with the Taliban. In addition to this, thousands of Afghan refugees arrived in Iran, and Iran's bilateral trade with Afghanistan, its third largest export partner after Iraq and China, decreased dramatically. Though the trade revived slowly, the refugee issue became more severe after 2021. Official statistics indicated the presence of about four million Afghan immigrants in Iran, while the unofficial reports estimated the number to be much higher and closer to six to eight million people.[44] The presence of Afghan immigrants in large cities and with many of them committing crimes and violence in recent years made the issue of Afghan immigrants a daily concern for Iranian society and policymakers.[45] In October 2023, the Pakistan government's ultimatum to 1.7 million undocumented Afghan migrants to leave the country by 1 November fuelled fears of a new wave of Afghan migrants entering Iran after leaving Pakistan.[46]

The paper has mentioned the correlation between the Iran–US tension and its relation to Afghanistan before. Though following a sinusoidal pattern post-2001,[47] the relationship experienced escalated tensions during the first Donald Trump administration. President Joseph Biden de-escalated tensions to some extent but with the return of Trump, bilateral animosity is back in play again. After October 2023, the conflict between Hamas and Israel and the tension between Iran and the US heated up again. As the relations between the two parties stand, and despite mutual benefits in maintaining the status quo in Afghanistan for Tehran and Washington, Iran has concentrated on cooperation with Russia, China, and India in recent years.

Iran's collaboration with China and Russia in Afghanistan has endured since the 1990s. However, Iran's relationship with Moscow has further strengthened in recent years. In other words, Russia has become Iran's most crucial partner in Afghanistan amongst great powers. Both sides consider America's withdrawal a strategic opening to greater collaboration, including on Afghanistan. Even as Iran has looked forward to collaboration with Russia on Afghanistan, it has also tried to reach a mutual strategic understanding with Beijing to deal with post-2021 Afghanistan. Despite the efforts of both Iran and China, such an understanding has not yet been reached. Islamabad has been Beijing's most important partner in Afghanistan. Differences between the interests of Tehran and Islamabad in post-2021 Afghanistan have been a major obstacle to building a strategic understanding between Beijing and Tehran. But the strategic understanding between Tehran and Moscow on post-2021 Afghanistan has been established to some extent.

Historically, Iran's policy in Afghanistan has been swinging between resisting against and collaborating with great powers. Since the Taliban returned to power and the US forces withdrew from Afghanistan, working with Russia has been central to Iran's approach to Afghanistan and the region. Iranian leaders consider it an opportunity to expand Tehran's influence and take forward its 'Dismiss the Americans' strategy that gained prominence after Gen Qasem Soleimani's assassination in January 2020. Iran undoubtedly considers America's withdrawal from Afghanistan a victory. But at the same time, Iran has been worried about the nature of the Taliban State, its ideological and geopolitical agenda, and the management of relations with it.

Afghanistan's democratic political system, which provided the space for political participation of groups close to Iran, has completely disappeared and the Taliban's "Islamic Emirate" has gained a hegemonic position, and Afghan economy is facing a serious risk of collapse. Tehran is trying hard to "adapt" to the new Afghanistan while playing a role in "shaping" it. However, with Kabul's new political system in place for over three years now, Iran finds itself in a complicated situation. Iran neither favoured US's deep engagement and nor its rapid disengagement from Afghanistan, and is now facing practical challenges arising from certain ideological and political disparities with an abnormal state in its immediate neighbourhood.

## NOTES

1. Bertrand Badie, Dirk Berg-Schlosser and Leonardo Morlino (eds), *International Encyclopedia of Political Science*, Sage Publications, Los Angeles, 2011, p. 675.
2. Mohsen M. Milani, 'Iran's Policy Towards Afghanistan', *Middle East Journal*, Vol. 60, No. 2, Spring 2006, pp. 235–256.
3. Former Iranian Foreign Minister Javad Zarif has frequently spoken about Iran's key role in the Bonn Conference and also the merits of the political order that emerged from the Bonn Process in Afghanistan. For example, see 'Transcript of TOLOnews Interview with Iran's Javad Zarif', *Tolo News*, 21 December 2020, at https://tolonews.com/afghanistan-168674. The original Farsi transcript of the interview is available at https://tolonews.com/fa/afghanistan-168675.
4. Former Iranian Foreign Minister Javad Zarif had proposed accommodation of the Taliban in Afghanistan's political order. See 'Zarif Urges Taliban to Engage in Diplomatic Process for Peace in Afghanistan', *Tasnim News Agency*, 17 April 2021, at https://www.

tasnimnews.com/en/news/2021/04/17/2486122/zarif-urges-taliban-to-engage-in-diplomatic-process-for-peace-in-afghanistan. Also see 'Iran Supports Inclusive Afghan Government, Zarif Tells Taliban', *Tasnim News Agency*, 31 January 2021, at https://www.tasnimnews.com/en/news/2021/01/31/2443623/iran-supports-inclusive-afghan-government-zarif-tells-taliban.

5. Former Iranian Ambassador to Kabul Mohammad Reza Bahrami identified the legitimizing of the Taliban and delegitimising of the Afghan Republic as one the most critical weaknesses of the Doha Agreement. He also expressed Iran's concerns about the Taliban hegemony in Afghanistan and stressed on multilateralism to deal with the challenges arising from post-2021 Afghanistan. See 'رفتارآمریکابود/ القایروحیهپیروزیبهطالباننتیجه :توافقدوحهروندصلحرابهمحاقبردسفیرپیشینایراندرافغانستان' [Iran's former ambassador to Afghanistan: Instilling the spirit of victory in the Taliban was the result of America's behavior/Doha agreement brought the peace process to an end], *Jamaran News*, 15 August 2021.
6. Keyhan Cultural and News Institution, an influential news agency, recently referred to the Taliban as a 'totalitarian' movement that seeks 'domination,' and one that will violate 'minorities' rights' in Afghanistan if it manages to establish control over the entire country. See Saadullah Zarei, '**افغانستان امارت اسلامی آمریکا (یادداشت روز)**' [Afghanistan, Islamic Emirate, America (note of the day)], *Kayhan*, 9 July 2021.
7. A Persian word with an Arabic root, describing a shallow and superficial understating of religion in which the person fanatically believes in religious rules without a deep understanding of them.
8. Dr Seyed Mohammad Ali Hosseinizadeh, Assistant Professor of Political Science at Shahid Beheshti University, in an interview to the authors stated that the dominance of Deobandi narration of Islam in Afghanistan would be a threat to the Shia population of Afghanistan as well as to Iranian interests.
9. 'کندهاییهمچونداعشجلوگیریمیهمکاریباطالبانازنفوذگروه :نادری' [Naderi: Cooperation with the Taliban prevents the infiltration of groups such as ISIS], *Iranian Students' News Agency* (ISNA), 2 December 2020.
10. 'طالبانیکگروهتروریستیاستنهسیاسی /اشتباهنکنید' [Make no mistake/Taliban is a terrorist group, not a political one], *Etemad Online*, 24 June 2021.
11. For example, despite border conflicts and severe differences with the Taliban over the implementation of the 1973 Helmand River Water Treaty, Tehran has tried to manage these issues through negotiations and has avoided conflict with the Taliban. See 'ازحقوقملتایرانکوتاهنخواهیمآمد /دستوررئیسیبهوزرایخارجه و نیروبراپیگیریحقآبهایرانازهیرمند' [President's order to foreign and defence ministers to pursue Iran's water rights over Hirmand/We will not neglect the rights of the Iranian people], *Tasnim News Agency*, 27 July 2022.
12. See Fatima Koshnit, 'هارابهرسمیتنشناختیمباطالبانتعاملکردیماماآن :کاظمیقمی' [Kazemi Qomi: We interacted with the Taliban, but we did not recognise them], ISNA, 17 August 2022.
13. Sara Karimianfar, '۵ میلیارددلاریایرانباهمسایگاندرسال ۹۹.تجارت ۳۶' [Iran's $36.5 billion trade with neighbors in 2019], *The Islamic Republic News Agency* (IRNA), 1 May 2021.
14. https://www.farsnews.ir/af/news/14010123000433.
15. 'خیزافغانستانبرایتجارت ۱۰ میلیارددلاریباایران' [Afghanistan's push for $10 billion trade with Iran], at https://irannewspaper.ir/8150/7/9988.

16. Harsh V. Pant, 'Pakistan and Iran: A Relationship in Search of Meaning', in Usama Butt and Julia Schofield (eds), *Pakistan: The US, Geopolitics and Grand Strategies*, Pluto Press, 2012, p. 221.
17. Iran has always opposed efforts to give international legitimacy to the Taliban. For example, Iran's Foreign Minister Hossein Amirabdollahian considered the establishment of a comprehensive government as a condition for recognising the Taliban. See 'امیرعبداللهیان: فقطدرصورتتشکیلدولتفراگیردرافغانستان هیئتحاکمهسرپرستیکشوررابهرسمیتمیشناسیم' [Amir Abdollahian: We will recognise the ruling body in charge of the country only if an inclusive government is formed in Afghanistan], *Donya-e-Eqtesad*, 13 April 2022.
18. David Smith, Joanna Walters and Jason Burke, 'Ayman al-Zawahiri: al-Qaida Leader Killed in US Drone Strike in Afghanistan, Joe Biden Says', *The Guardian*, 2 August 2022, at https://www.theguardian.com/world/2022/aug/01/us-strike-afghanistan-kills-al-qaida-leader-ayman-al-zawahiri.
19. 'Pakistani Soldiers Killed in Firing from Afghanistan: Military', *Al Jazeera*, 6 February 2022, at https://www.aljazeera.com/news/2022/2/6/firing-from-afghanistan-kills-five-pakistan-troops-pakistan-army.
20. Mark Mazzetti and Julian E. Barnes, 'C.I.A. Scrambles for New Approach in Afghanistan', *The New York Times*, 6 June 2021, at https://www.nytimes.com/2021/06/06/us/politics/cia-afghanistan-pakistan.html.
21. 'Press Briefing by Press Secretary Jen Psaki and National Security Advisor Jake Sullivan, June 7, 2021', The White House, 7 June 2021, at https://www.whitehouse.gov/briefing-room/press-briefings/2021/06/07/press-briefing-by-press-secretary-jen-psaki-and-national-security-advisor-jake-sullivan-june-7-2021/.
22. 'No Military Bases, Have to Look After Our Own Interests: Pakistan Tells US', *The News International*, 8 June 2021, at https://www.thenews.com.pk/latest/846420-no-military-bases-for-us-pakistan.
23. C. Christine Fair, 'Insurgency, Instability, and the Security of Afghanistan', in Sumit Gangulay, Andrew Scobell and Joseph Chinyong Liow (eds), *The Routledge Handbook of Asian Security Studies*, Routledge, London, 2018, p. 192.
24. Alireza Nader, Ali G. Scotten, Ahmad Idrees Rahmani, Robert Stewart and Leila Mahnad, 'Iran's Influence in Afghanistan: Implication for the U.S. Drawdown', Rand Corporation, 2014, p. 8, at https://www.rand.org/content/dam/rand/pubs/research_reports/RR600/RR616/RAND_RR616.pdf.
25. 'Iran UN Envoy Hails Rejection of Islamic Emirate in Afghanistan', *Tasnim News Agency*, 11 December 2020, at https://www.tasnimnews.com/en/news/2020/12/11/2408021/iran-un-envoy-hails-rejection-of-islamic-emirate-in-afghanistan.
26. Zahid Shahab Ahmed and Stuti Bhatnagar, 'The India–Iran–Pakistan Triad: Comprehending the Correlation of Geo-economics and Geopolitics', *Asian Studies Review*, Vol. 42, Issue 3, 2018, pp. 7–8, at https://www.tandfonline.com/doi/full/10.1080/10357823.2018.1479728.
27. C. Raja Mohan, 'India and the Balance of Power', *Foreign Affairs*, July/August 2006, at https://www.foreignaffairs.com/articles/asia/2006-07-01/india-and-balance-power.
28. Mehreen Zahra-Malik, 'It's Afghanistan, Stupid', *Newsweek Pakistan*, 6 May 2011, at http://newsweekpakistan.com/the-take/312.

29. Rorry Daniels, 'Strategic Competition in South Asia: Gwadar, Chabahar, and the Risks of Infrastructure Development', *American Foreign Policy Interests*, Vol. 35, Issue 2, 2013, p. 94.
30. Shah Alam, 'Iran–Pakistan Relations: Political and Strategic Dimensions', *Strategic Analysis*, Vol. 28, No. 4, October–December 2004, p. 537, at https://idsa.in/system/files/strategicanalysis_salam_1204.pdf.
31. Samina Ahmed, 'The Pakistani Taliban Test Ties between Islamabad and Kabul', International Crisis Group, 29 March 2023, at https://www.crisisgroup.org/asia/south-asia/pakistan/pakistani-taliban-test-ties-between-islamabad-and-kabul.
32. 'Taliban Urges Pakistan to Grant More Time for Undocumented Afghans to Leave', *Al Jazeera*, 1 November 2023, at https://www.aljazeera.com/news/2023/11/1/taliban-urges-pakistan-to-grant-more-time-for-undocumented-afghans-to-leave.
33. P.K. Grover, 'Af-Pak Issue Over Kabul River Water Simmers', *The Tribune*, 7 September 2022, at https://www.tribuneindia.com/news/comment/af-pak-issue-over-kabul-river-water-simmers-429198.
34. Bibi Amina Hakimi, 'China, Pakistan Mull Afghan Membership in CPEC', *Tolo News*, 10 February 2022, at https://tolonews.com/index.php/business-176659.
35. The corridor connects Uzbekistan's railway with the Afghan railway at the moment, but has yet to materialise its aim to link Pakistan through the Afghan railway system. See Sophia Nina Burna-Asefi, 'After Temporary Suspension, What's Next for the Trans-Afghan Railway?', *The Diplomat*, 17 February 2023, at https://thediplomat.com/2023/02/after-temporary-suspension-whats-next-for-the-trans-afghan-railway/.
36. Waheguru Pal Singh Sidhu, 'The United States, India and Iran: Managing a Delicate Balance', Policy Brief, Center on International Cooperation, New York University, February 2016, p. 11, at https://cic.nyu.edu/wp-content/uploads/1662/65/sidhu_iran_india_final_1.pdf.
37. Samuel Ramani, 'Saudi Arabia's New Taliban Strategy', *The Diplomat*, 10 May 2018, at https://thediplomat.com/2018/05/saudi-arabias-new-taliban-strategy/.
38. Guney Yildiz, 'Biden–Erdoğan Meeting: Can Turkey's Post-NATO Role in Afghanistan Help Reset Turkish–U.S. Ties?', *Forbes*, 14 June 2021, at https://www.forbes.com/sites/guneyyildiz/2021/06/14/can-turkeys-post-nato-afghanistan-role-help-reset-turkeys-ties-with-the-us/?sh=3d69a9a04e17.
39. Mohsen Shariatinia and Hamed A. Kermani, 'Iran, China and the Persian Gulf: An Unfolding Engagement', *Global Policy*, Vol. 14, Issue S1, February 2023 (First Published Online on 15 September 2022), pp. 1–10, at https://onlinelibrary.wiley.com/doi/10.1111/1758-5899.13122.
40. Former Iranian Foreign Minister Javad Zarif, in his interviews published as a book, has spoken in detail about the close collaboration between Iran and the US in toppling the Taliban regime in 2001 and establishing the new government in Bonn Conference. See Mohammad-Mehdi Rāji (ed.), *Āqā-ye Safir: Goftogubā Mohammad-Javād Zarif, Safir-e Pishin-e IrāndarSāzemān-e Mellal-e Mottahed* [Mr Ambassador: A Dialogue with Mohammad Javād Zarif, the former Ambassador of Iran to the United Nations], Nashr-e Ney, Tehran, 2013. Also see Zalmay Khalilzad, *The Envoy: From Kabul to the White House, My Journey Through a Turbulent World*, Palgrave Macmillan, New York, 2016.

41. 'Iran Asks Taliban to Ensure Safety of Diplomats in Herat', *Reuters*, 13 August 2021, at https://www.reuters.com/world/asia-pacific/iran-asks-taliban-ensure-safety-diplomats-herat-2021-08-13/.
42. Shahram Akbarzadeh and Niamatullah Ibrahimi, 'The Taliban: A New Proxy for Iran in Afghanistan?', *Third World Quarterly*, Vol. 41, Issue 5, 2020, pp. 764–782, at https://www.tandfonline.com/doi/full/10.1080/01436597.2019.1702460.
43. Colin P. Clarke and Ariane M. Tabatabai, 'What Iran Wants in Afghanistan', *Foreign Affairs*, 8 July 2020, at https://www.foreignaffairs.com/articles/afghanistan/2020-07-08/what-iran-wants-afghanistan.
44. Wajid Rouhani, 'تعدادمهاجرانافغاندرایرانبهبیشازششمیلیوننفر :رسیدهاستکاظمیقمی' [Kazemi Qomi: The number of Afghan immigrants in Iran has reached more than six million people], *Independent Persian*, 17 July 2023.
45. 'افزایشتعدادمهاجرانافغانستانپساز ۱۴۰۰، یک :حقیقتاستارشناسانعلوماجتماعی' [Social science experts: The increase in the number of Afghan immigrants after 2021 is a fact], IRNA, 21 October 2023.
46. *Al Jazeera*, no. 32.
47. Rangin Dadfar Spanta, *Afghanistan Politics: A Narrative from Within*, Betascript Publishing, New York, 2017.

# 7

# Russian Imperatives in Afghanistan

*Alexey Kupriyanov*

In order to understand Russia's position on Afghanistan, it is necessary to grasp the underlying imperatives. This requires a historical and sociological analysis that would allow us to consider the development of relations between the Afghan and Russian societies over time, their mutual perception of each other and the incorporation of ideas about each other into their historical myth and their perception of the world around. In my article, I will touch on only one side of the issue, namely, how Afghanistan and the Afghans and Russian-Afghan relations as a whole are perceived in the Russian public consciousness. These relations have a relatively short, but extremely eventful history.

Unlike Russian-Indian ties, Russian-Afghan relations were established relatively late and initially had a completely different character. India was of interest to the Russian government primarily from a trade and economic point of view, but relations with Afghanistan initially had a serious component of security. Russia hoped to establish contacts with the Durrani Empire in order to act together against the raids and slave trade of the Central Asian tribes and polities and the threats from Qing China. However, despite a number of promising contacts (the visit of Bogdan Aslanov to Afghanistan in 1764, Shahzadeh to Orenburg in 1831, Hussein-Ali to St Petersburg in 1836, Jan Witkiewitz to Kabul in 1837, and so on), relations between St Petersburg and Kabul were actually interrupted after the defeat of Afghanistan in the Second Anglo-Afghan War 1878-1880.

Having retained its independence, Afghanistan was forced to subordinate the interests of its foreign policy to the orders of the British, who were primarily concerned with the security of British India and suspected Russia of trying to use Afghanistan as a springboard for the invasion of India. These fears were actually groundless, since the Russian military leadership was well aware of the complexity and impracticability of this undertaking, noting that the plan to march on India through Afghanistan lies more in the field of psychiatry than strategic planning. This fully applies to the strange idea of Tsar Paul to send the Cossacks on a campaign to India through Afghanistan to help Napoleon.

From the British point of view, however, things looked completely different. The gradual annexation and vassalisation of the Central Asian polities were perceived by them as a potential threat to India. This perception led to the beginning of the Great Game between Russia and Great Britain in Central Asia, with Afghanistan taking an ambivalent position: on the one hand, it was essentially a British outpost (which was confirmed during the infamous Panjdeh incident, 1885), on the other, the Afghan emirs dreamed of overthrowing from the yoke imposed by the British and make Afghanistan a fully independent state. In this situation, Russia looked like a natural ally of Kabul, because, although Afghanistan had become a playground for the Great Game, it was never the goal of this game for St. Petersburg. Historically Russia never had territorial claims on the territorial core of Afghanistan and did not perceive it as a zone of its influence.

After the October Revolution of 1917, Afghanistan became the first country to establish diplomatic relations with Soviet Russia. For Moscow this act of international recognition was of great importance, and the Soviet leadership provided all possible support to Kabul during the Third Anglo-Afghan War of 1919. Unfortunately, this support was mainly moral, since a civil war was going on in Russia at that time, and Soviet Russia could not send troops to help Afghanistan. A small number of weapons sent from Moscow were confiscated by the Turkestani Bolsheviks, who fought hard against the advancing Whites.

In the decades that followed, Moscow looked at Afghanistan through two prisms: ideology and security. Through the first prism, Afghanistan was seen as a promising post-colonial country, throwing off the unequal treaty imposed by the British, and waging a legitimate struggle against the legacy of colonialism. This approach gave rise to a natural problem that Moscow faced not only in relation to Afghanistan, but also in relation to most other post-colonial countries. The original Soviet ideological prerequisites required betting on the progressive class, i.e. the proletariat, while at the same time a pragmatic and realistic approach assumed consideration of the real situation, which prompted the Bolsheviks to ally with the ruling feudal elites in countries where the proletarian revolution remained the subject of pure theory and could not be implemented in the foreseeable future. This predetermined the eternal duality of Soviet politics: on the one hand, the USSR had to support the progressive ruling elites against the imperialists, on the other hand, the even more progressive proletariat and peasantry against the ruling elites. In each specific case, this contradiction was solved in different ways.

Through a second prism, Afghanistan was seen as the key to the security of the southern borders of the USSR. After the end of the civil war in Russia in general and in Turkestan in particular, a large number of Basmachi (participants in the rebel movement against the Soviet regime) found refuge in Afghanistan, from where they made regular raids on Soviet territory. Considering that the main forces of the USSR were concentrated in other, more threatened directions (the European and Far Eastern borders), the Soviet government tried to solve the problem in the Central Asian direction, mainly through diplomacy using the carrot and stick. For example, in 1924-1927, Moscow sent Emir Amanullah airplanes, anti-aircraft guns and experienced pilots who supported the Afghan troops in the battles against the rebels in Khost, while at the same time exerting diplomatic pressure on Kabul, demanding that the emir refuse to support the Basmachi.[1]

At the same time, Soviet intelligence was active in Kabul, counteracting the efforts of hostile intelligence services, primarily British.[2] In 1929, Soviet troops intervened directly in the situation in Afghanistan in order to keep Emir Amanullah in power: a detachment of Vitaly Primakov entered Afghanistan, defeated the Basmachi and Habibullah Kalakani troops in several battles and captured Mazar-i-Sharif, Balkh and Kholm. However, Amanullah Khan, whose troops in the south of the country were defeated, fled the country. Soviet troops were withdrawn from Afghanistan. The following year, with the permission of Muhammad Nadir Shah, who overthrew Kalakani, Soviet troops raided Afghanistan and defeated the Basmachi who did not have time to escape.[3]

Relations with the moderate reformer Mohammed Zahir Shah, who regularly visited the USSR and was friends with Nikita Khrushchev and Leonid Brezhnev, lay in line with this paradigm and completely suited Moscow. The coup d'état of Mohammed Daoud Khan and the proclamation of the republic in 1973 were also met in the USSR quite calmly, since when he was prime minister, Daoud showed himself to be a pragmatic politician, ready to move closer to the Soviet Union. The early years of Daoud's rule seemed to confirm this impression, but in 1977 he began to purge pro-Soviet elements from the government. Moscow, however, hoped to normalise relations with Daoud, but in 1978 he was overthrown and killed in the Saur Revolution. For the USSR, it came as a complete surprise.

For those who looked at the situation through an ideological prism, this surprise was a pleasant one, since the USSR received an ideologically close state on the southern borders that copied the Soviet model. For those who perceived it through the prism of security, it was rather unpleasant, since the reliable and comfortable system of interaction with the Afghan elites, which guaranteed the existence of a friendly-neutral state and the security of the southern border, was destroyed. This split in the Soviet leadership became clear after the new Afghan leaders, faced with the resistance of conservative forces as a result of rash and abrupt reforms, asked Moscow for military assistance.[4] For a long time, this assistance was provided in an extremely limited amount, and only the removal and assassination of Nur Muhammad Taraki, a personal friend of Brezhnev, by Hafizullah Amin, pushed the Soviet leadership to a full-fledged intervention and change of power in Afghanistan.[5] By that time, a new factor appeared: in the event of the fall of the pro-Soviet regime, counter-revolutionaries could come to power, and Afghanistan, as Moscow believed, could become a springboard for the United States or pro-American puppets, such as Pakistan.The result was the involvement of the USSR in the war in Afghanistan. During the ten-year conflict, the Soviet Union, trying to help the friendly regime to stabilise the situation, suffered significant economic and military losses. The Afghan war became a factor that accelerated the collapse of the USSR.

As a result, Russian society acquired a rather specific view of the Afghan war. It is considered, on the one hand, as a clearly erroneous and voluntaristic decision of the country's leadership. On the other hand, a decade after the end of the war, an opinion was formed that intervention was justified, since it helped to secure the southern borders of the USSR and interrupted drug imports. The actions of the army are regarded as fully justified: at one time, "Afghans" (people who served in Afghanistan) became objects beyond criticism, which allowed them to occupy a specific position in the societies of post-Soviet states. Although now all this is in the past, the "Afghan syndrome" still persists: any mention of a possible military operation in Afghanistan is perceived sharply negatively in Russia, while at the same time, Russian society is following what is happening in Afghanistan with deep interest. This defines the limitations of the Russian reaction to any Afghan events: the need to stabilise the situation and have a friendly Afghan population in the south, while not intervening in the situation by force. This predetermined Russian policy in the 1990s, which was to repel attacks on border outposts, and limited Russian assistance to the Northern Alliance. The idea of military intervention was categorically unacceptable to Russian society and political and military circles and remains so to this day.

## Imperatives and Missed Opportunities

On this historical basis, a set of imperatives was formed that determined Russian policy towards Afghanistan. The first key imperative is stability and tranquility. This imperative is driven by several concerns.

First, Russia is worried about a possible invasion by militants from Afghanistan.[6] It has every reason for this, since in the 1992 militants supporting the armed Tajik and Uzbek opposition have repeatedly crossed the border between Afghanistan and the CIS, attacking border outposts. Now the situation looks precarious. On the one hand, the Taliban declares its non-expansionism, and this seems to be true, because, despite the inclusion of representatives of national minorities in its composition, the Taliban still remains a Pashtun movement at its core. On the other hand, there are fears about the radicalisation of the Taliban, which, becoming more institutionalised and deprived of an enemy, may lose internal coherence and effectiveness, become corrupt and allow individual warlords to exercise more autonomy and even split.

Secondly, Russia is concerned about the problem of refugees. After the seizure of power by the Taliban, there were fears that mass migration to Central Asia from Afghanistan would now begin. They, fortunately, did not come true, the influx of refugees turned out to be relatively small, but there is no guarantee that this will not happen in the future, given the ongoing resistance of a number of social groups to the Taliban, which may intensify in the event of failures in domestic politics and the economy. Mass migration can cause a humanitarian catastrophe in the Central Asian republics, the repercussions of which will reach Russia.

For Russia, this issue is of particular importance, since the Russian border with the countries of Central Asia is not equipped with protective equipment, ditches, walls and barbed wire. This means that if refugees or terrorists enter Central Asia, they can easily enter Russia. The equipment of this border all along is a long and rather pointless business, because the border often runs in an open field. Therefore, it would be much more reasonable for Russia to keep and strengthen the natural border between Afghanistan and Central Asia, which runs mainly along the Panj River and along the mountains, which will not allow for a large-scale invasion of the countries of the region. Russia cannot allow the supply of weapons or people with weapons to cross this border.[7]

However, it is obvious that instead of having a constant war on the southern frontier, it is much easier and more reasonable to take care that Afghanistan ceases to be a potential source of militants and refugees. This can be achieved if the economic situation in Afghanistan improves and there is a responsible and strong government in power that understands Russian concerns and is ready to cooperate.

The second imperative is predominantly geopolitical. In the 1990s Russia was going through a period of decline: its economy crumbled as a result of the collapse of the USSR and the inept reforms that led to massive impoverishment of the population. At the same time, the political and part of the intellectual elites retained illusions about the West. They began to dissipate gradually, first under the influence of the position that the Western countries took regarding the Russian war in Chechnya, then after the bombing of Yugoslavia. However, at the time of the American intervention in Afghanistan, anti-Western sentiments in Russia were still not strong enough, so the Russian leadership actively cooperated with the United States and its allies, providing, in particular, assistance in transporting goods and even opening a logistics hub for non-lethal cargo and for ferrying personnel in Ulyanovsk.

But the growing mutual irritation caused by the relative decline of the power of the United States and the growth of the power of Russia, which sought to play an increasing role in the international arena, led to an open break. The first signal sounded in 2007. It was the Munich speech of Vladimir Putin, who announced the beginning of the end of the unipolar world, Russia's unwillingness to subordinate its foreign policy to the interests of other countries, criticised the expansion of NATO and the policy of economic inequality supported by Western countries. The unwillingness of the Western elites to listen to the words of the Russian leader led to the fact that the crack that had arisen widened more and more. After the reunification of Crimea with Russia in 2014, mutual discontent grew into open confrontation. The beginning of the Ukrainian conflict, active military and diplomatic support for Ukraine from the West, pumping it up with many types of weapons, further aggravated the situation.

Russia, faced with economic sanctions, open pressure from the West and unwillingness to take into account its legitimate interests in the immediate neighborhood, perceives the US, the EU and the players supporting them as hostile states. They use unfriendly rhetoric, openly declare the intentions not to recognise Russian elections and try to oust Russia from the markets and from the regions and almost directly threaten military conflict. In this situation, Russia has an extremely negative perception of the presence of the United States and NATO on its southern border and gladly accepted the US withdrawal from Afghanistan, while reproaching the US for invading the country and not fulfilling its obligations. Now, after the beginning of the

Ukrainian campaign, for Russia the issue of the absence of the United States on the southern borders of the CIS is of critical importance.[8]

Finally, the third imperative is Russian concerns about drug trafficking from Afghanistan. In Russia, the level of drug consumption is quite high, and this has become a big problem. Russia is interested not only in that drugs do not go through its territory, but also in that its citizens do not consume them.[9]

In fact, Russia would be more comfortable with a secular and friendly government in Kabul. Moscow has a positive experience of cooperation with similar regimes in Afghanistan since the government of Amanullah Khan, and, as history shows, the best result was achieved when a relatively moderate and non-radical regime ruled in Kabul, which would at the same time recognised the need for careful reforms.

Therefore, it would seem logical for Moscow to support the government of Ashraf Ghani. But he has shown himself openly anti-Russian, accused Russia of having links with the Taliban and groveled in front of the United States. Perhaps Ghani had no other option, given the clientele nature of his regime and the need to follow the general anti-Russian narrative promoted by the United States after the confrontation with Russia began. But in doing so, he signed his regime's death warrant: only Russia could save him after the Americans abandoned the government in Kabul to its fate, and he imprudently quarreled with this only possible ally.

Theoretically, Russia could bet on anti-Taliban resistance not associated with the Ghani regime. But this resistance collapsed faster than the most pessimists expected, and the National Resistance Front of Afghanistan which claims to be the main anti-Taliban force, is too weak for Russia to afford the luxury of cooperating with it, given how much it is interested in establishing stability and calm in Afghanistan.

So, for pragmatic reasons, we now have no other alternative but to develop relations with the Taliban. The presence of a Taliban government in Kabul fits all three Russian imperatives: the Taliban can establish a stable regime in Afghanistan and pacify the country, they are not connected to the United States and, paradoxically, they have so far been the most consistently combating drug smuggling compared to other Afghan governments of the last three decades.

Russia is not sure that the Taliban will fulfill the obligations, and for this reason, Moscow does not remove the Taliban status as a terrorist organisation. But so far everything indicates that the victory of the Taliban is perceived by the population calmly and with the hope of ending this endless war.

So, we must proceed it seems to me from two possible scenarios. The first implies that the Taliban will not be able to cope with the internal problems and either a new round of war will begin in Afghanistan between the factions or Taliban or we will see maybe a new insurgency. The second one implies that Taliban will be stable and will be able to organise a working system of government. The implementation of these scenarios depends not only on the internal reasons but also on the Taliban neighbours. If Russia and other neigbouring countries fight against the Taliban, training anti-Taliban militants and camps in their territory and supply weapons to them, then probability of the first scenario will increase. If they help the Taliban to establish themselves by gently influencing them, the likelihood of the latter will increase.

In Russian political discourse, the second option is still considered more likely because, from Moscow's perspective, New Delhi and other actors overestimates the Taliban's dependence of Pakistan. If the Taliban really tries to become an Afghan national government, the very course of policy will sooner or later lead them to a final break with Pakistan.[10] The unresolved border issue, the problem of refugees, the need to take into account national interests and build relationships with neighbours whose interests are not identical to the interests of Pakistan, will contribute to this break.

So, Afghanistan neighbours can help the Talban to become a full-fledged power. And it seems that it is a key issue that should be discussed with each other by the neighbours of Afghanistan. Afghanistan where the war has just ended and is facing a humanitarian crisis is very vulnerable. But the neighbouring countries also are very vulnerable to the possible expansion of radical ideas, weapons and drugs from this territory. From the Russian point of view, the main task now is to build a balance of interests in and around Afghanistan and maintain it constantly. It is difficult but necessary.

## Long-Term Processes

So far only short-term processes and their results have been described. But in order to build a stable society in Afghanistan, it is necessary to take into account more global and long-term processes, covering not only Afghanistan, but the whole world.

Afghan society is one of the least modernised societies in Asia. This happened due to various reasons, the key of which is the remoteness of Afghanistan from trade routes, the absence of easily extracted and transported minerals on its territory, its difficult terrain and the warlike nature of its inhabitants. These reasons did not allow Afghanistan to be involved in the general processes of modernisation in the 19th century that swept Asia. Afghanistan came to them belatedly during the years of Amanullah's reign, but the force of inertia was so great that Amanullah's modernisation failed. Afghan modernists made a second attempt only in the 1970s, but at first glance it also ended in failure. The modernisation under American influence in 2001-2020 also turned out to be a fiasco.

These recurring attempts at modernisation are prompted to be treated as part of a larger process, the active phase of which began in the 19th century. This process of capitalist globalisation and modernisation gradually drew in almost all countries and regions of the world, except for those archaic societies like the Afghan one, where it met with serious resistance. At the same time, Afghan society is also in the process of transformation: it has agents of modernisation, such as the army, bureaucracy, secret services, industrial workers, urban residents in general - that is, those who in one way or another interact with the processes of modernisation in the wide world and benefits from them. Gradually, modernisation also penetrates the more archaic structure of rural society. The slow, generational nature of this process is disappointing to Western observers accustomed to rapid change, and is therefore often interpreted as a failure of modernisation policies. Meanwhile, it is this long-term process, quite possibly, that causes sluggish conflicts caused by the collision of agents of modernisation with the rigid, difficult-to-transform fabric of Afghan society.

It is possible, however, that we are now seeing a change in the nature of this process: modernisation and archaism are mutually adapting, finding opportunities not only for coexistence, but also for mutual reinforcement. A kind of conservative revolution is taking place. Perhaps this is a regional trend, because we have already seen something similar in Iran and now, we see it in China and India, where society, on its way to the nation, turns to traditional values, building its identity around them. In Afghanistan, where society is the most archaic, this process takes on somewhat ugly forms.

Thus, both Afghanistan's neighbors and the whole world are facing a difficult choice. They can either try to support these conservative and at the same time revolutionary processes in Afghanistan, making sure that they do not take on ugly forms. This means gently influencing the Taliban regime and gradually supporting modernisation in the hope that its agents will become more powerful and not expecting them to change the very structure of Afghan society. Or other countries may try to support the anti-Taliban forces in the expectation that the Afghans' consciousness will suddenly change and they wholeheartedly embrace secular democratic values. Historical experience shows that the second option has so far only led to wars and bloodshed.

## NOTES

1. Yuri Tikhonov (ed.), *Soviet Russia in the Struggle for the Afghan Corridor (1919-1925), Collection of Documents*, Kvadriga, Moscow, 2017. (In Russian)
2. Yuri Tikhonov, *Afghan War of Stalin. Battle for Central Asia*, Yauza & Exmo, Moscow, 2008. (In Russian)
3. Pavel Aptekar, *The Red Sun. Secret Eastern Campaigns of the Red Army*, 5th Rim, Moscow, 2021. (In Russian)
4. A.Z. Hilali, 'The Soviet Decision-Making for Intervention in Afghanistan and Its Motives', *The Journal of Slavic Military Studies*, Vol. 16, Issue 2, 2003. pp. 113–144. DOI: 10.1080/ 13518040308430562.
5. David N. Gibbs, 'Reassessing Soviet Motives for Invading Afghanistan: A Declassified History', *Critical Asian Studies*, Vol. 38, Issue 2, 2006. pp. 239–263. DOI: 10.1080/14672710600671228.
6. Ekaterina Stepanova, 'Russia and the Search for a Negotiated Solution in Afghanistan', *Europe-Asia Studies*, Vol. 73, Issue 5, 2021. pp. 933–934. DOI: 10.1080/09668136.2020. 1826908.
7. Aron Cohen, 'How the U.S. Withdrawal from Afghanistan Will Affect Russia and Eurasia', in Stephen J. Blank (ed.), *Central Asia after 2014*, Strategic Studies Institute, US Army War College, 2013, pp. 13–32.
8. Of particular interest in this sense is the development of relations between Russia and Pakistan. A number of clearly unfriendly actions on the part of Islamabad (for example, the supply of shells to Ukraine) caused an extremely negative reaction in Russian public opinion. Considering that Pakistan is an important player in Afghanistan, this may in future affect Russia's strategy for developing relations with external actorson the Afghanistan issue.
9. Andrei Dörre & Tobias Kraudzun, 'Persistence and Change in Soviet and Russian Relations with Afghanistan', *Central Asian Survey*, Vol. 31, Issue 4, 2012. pp. 425–443. DOI: 10.1080/02634937.2012.738851.
10. Rajiv Dogra, *Durand's Curse. A Line Across the Pathan Heart*, Rupa Publications, New Delhi, 2017, p. 224.

# 8

# The Impact of Afghan Factor on Central Asia

*Irina Zvyagelskaya and Ilya Zimin*

The Taliban's return to power in Afghanistan in August 2021 caused predictable reactions from the Central Asian states. The political shift in Afghanistan was seen as holding both challenges and opportunities for the region. Central Asian states had earlier dealt with the Taliban-ruled Afghanistan in the 1990s, when the country's northern regions, bordering Central Asia, suffered from violent conflict and increased drug trafficking. The grey zone was widely used then by all sorts of extremist groups from Central Asia to establish training bases for their fighters in Afghanistan.[1] These extremist groups also found audience in the Central Asia states, which were faced with grave social and economic challenges, such as the rising poverty and unemployment levels, in the first years of their national independence.[2]

As the threats emanating from Afghanistan could not have been prevented by military means alone, the Central Asian states have been fully aware of the need to simultaneously develop contacts with the Taliban authorities and strengthen their military capabilities. In short, the current policies of the Central Asian states have to a certain extent been shaped by their past experiences and wider understanding of the Afghan situation.

## Security Challenges

A deficit of security has become a key challenge for the Central Asian states. The most serious threat is the spread of extremist ideology, which can encourage domestic destabilisation. Individual terrorist groups can use the situation to strengthen their position and to cause military tension on the borders. The expected mass influx of Afghan refugees into Central Asia did not occur—over 99 per cent of the limited 21,000–22,000 arrivals settled in Tajikistan, while Uzbekistan and Kazakhstan declined to accept them.[3] However, concerns over smuggling persist, though the Taliban's 2022 opium ban led to a sharp decline in heroin production. Direct military aggression from the Taliban against Central Asia has not been observed. The Taliban leadership has consistently assured its neighbours of its commitment to non-interference, and so far, it has adhered to this stance.[4]

At the same time, other organisations cooperating with the Afghan Taliban are posing a terrorist threat at the international and regional levels, in particular, the Pakistani branch of the Taliban or Tehrik-e Taliban Pakistan (TTP), al-Qaeda, Islamic State-Khorasan (IS-K), Jaish-e-Mohammad (JeM), Lashkar-e-Taiba (LeT), etc. These organisations are linked to the Afghan Taliban not only by some common goals (like proclaimed anti-American jihad and sharing of the drug market in the region), but also by family ties and personal loyalty oaths, the so-called *bayat*. Even the Inter-Services Intelligence (ISI) of Pakistan, whose efforts largely created the Taliban, has not been able to make its Taliban protégés sever their ties with terrorist groups that have now turned hostile to Pakistan.[5] Moreover, despite the efforts of the new Taliban government to develop neighbourly relations with Pakistan, "the deep Taliban" in Afghanistan consider the Pakistan State a *taghout*, meaning "fake", and therefore supposed to be toppled.[6]

IS-K is the most notorious international terrorist organisation in Afghanistan. The massive infiltration of the ISIS-linked militant groups into Afghanistan and the defection of a part of the Taliban fighters were the result of a large-scale operation launched by the Pakistani Army in 2014. Then a large number of Pakistani Taliban fighters and other terrorist groups were ousted from the Pakistani provinces into Afghanistan. The Pakistani Taliban swore allegiance to al-Baghdadi, the head of the ISIS.[7] Later, they were joined by IS fighters from Syria and finally in 2021 by former soldiers of the Afghan national army threatened by the Taliban hunting for them.[8] The additional incentive for them was the allowance provided by the IS-K.

Even though the Taliban declared a war on IS-K back in 2015, it has been maintaining contacts with the group, at least at the level of mid-level commanders. After the defeat of ISIS in Iraq and Syria, many militants were transferred to Afghanistan. Some of their supporters (about several thousand people) were from Central Asia.[9]

While the turmoil in Kazakhstan in January 2022 was mainly caused by intra-elite showdowns, interference of external actors could be traced as well. The clashes emphasised a potentially destructive role that radical youth formations can play if mobilised through extremist slogans.

The threat to the Central Asian states are also posed by radical opposition groups, like the Islamic Movement of Uzbekistan (IMU) that took roots and set up a base of operations in Afghanistan. One can add to it the Jamaat Bulgar, a group of Russian citizens mainly from the Volga region (Idel–Ural) and the Caucasus, which left for jihad in Afghanistan, as well as the Islamic Movement of East Turkestan, a militant-terrorist organisation whose goal is to create a fundamentalist Islamic State of East Turkestan within the Xinjiang Uyghur Autonomous Region of China. All of them can act as a potential reserve for destabilisation in Central Asia and beyond. They can provide shelter to the Central Asian extremists and facilitate their infiltration back into the countries of their origin.

The case of the Tajik organisation Jamaat Ansarullah is indicative. Initially, Ansarullah's members were former Tajik opposition fighters who refused to accept the 1997 reconciliation agreement between the government in Dushanbe and the Islamist-led opposition. The so-called new generation—children and relatives of the initial members and supporters—have since joined the group. In 2021, Tajik and Afghan sources had reported that at least 200 militants from Tajikistan based along the border of the two countries were preparing to invade Tajikistan.[10]

Border clashes occur most often on the Afghan–Pakistani border, and in smaller numbers on the Iranian border. The shelling of the Uzbek border on 18 April 2022 from the Afghan side was shocking, particularly since both sides were determined to develop good-neighbourly relations.[11] The shelling of the Tajik border was seen in Dushanbe as another proof of the Taliban's inability to ensure security. The responsibility for cross-border shellings, however, was later claimed by the IS-K.[12]

Cross-border drug trafficking had long been a key source of income for the Taliban, but their April 2022 ban on opium poppy cultivation led to an unprecedented decline in production. By 2023, opium cultivation in Afghanistan had dropped by 93–95 per cent, from 233,000 hectares in 2022 to just 10,000 hectares. As a result, the flow of Afghan heroin through Central Asia has significantly decreased, contrary to earlier expectations. However, there are concerns that this decline may be offset by a rise in synthetic drug production, particularly methamphetamine, which is increasingly emerging as an alternative illicit trade.[13]

In Central Asia, the control over drug smuggling is often in the hands of criminals or a corrupt part of the bureaucracy. In case of serious clashes, the first could provide an additional channel for the infiltration of jihadists into the region.

Afghan refugees are a minor problem for Central Asia, especially in comparison to Iran or Pakistan. There are no entrenched Afghan Diasporas in the region and local officials are not willing to allow refugees for security reasons. The Central Asian countries are not a very attractive destination for the refugees seeking a better life, especially Kyrgyzstan and Tajikistan that have a lot of social and economic problems themselves.

## Role of External Players

The global powers have always been concerned with security issues in the region. Russia is the main security provider for Central Asia: Moscow provides weapons, military assistance, training, and participates in joint exercises. There is a Russian base in Tajikistan, and Moscow is paying special attention to the Tajikistan–Afghanistan border reinforcement. It was additionally fortified, and military exercises were carried out within the framework of the Collective Security Treaty Organization (CSTO), which encompasses the three Central Asian states of Kazakhstan, Kyrgyzstan, and Tajikistan. The Shanghai Cooperation Organisation (SCO) is also playing an important role.

While the Taliban government remains internationally unrecognised, by 2024 all Central Asian states had established working-level diplomatic relations with it. Turkmenistan and Uzbekistan were the first to accept Taliban-appointed diplomats in 2022, followed by quiet engagement from Kyrgyzstan and Tajikistan—where, despite initial resistance, Taliban representatives were eventually allowed to access the Afghan consulate in Khorog. Kazakhstan took a more formal step by officially accrediting a Taliban representative in 2024.[14] Though none of these countries have officially recognised the Taliban regime, de facto diplomatic cooperation is fully operational, with Afghan embassies in all Central Asian capitals now functioning under the Taliban-appointed staff. This marks a shift from the initial expectations of complete regional isolation.[15]

The threat posed by Afghan radical organisations is well acknowledged in Central Asia and Russia. At the end of June 2022, a meeting of the defence ministers of Russia and Central Asian countries, namely, Kazakhstan, Kyrgyzstan, Tajikistan, and Uzbekistan took place in Moscow. Sergei Shoigu, the then Russian Minister of Defence, referred to 'the growing activities of international and regional terrorist organizations in Afghanistan, primarily the Islamic State of Iraq and Levant and Al-Qaeda.' He pointed to the terrorists' plans to use the Afghan territory as a base for getting into neighbouring countries and creating a network of jihadist cells. The minister noted the spread of drug trafficking, crime, and the ideology of religious radicalism in the region. Further consultations are needed to develop steps to stabilise the situation in Afghanistan and to neutralise existing threats.[16]

The United States (US) is trying to bring back its military bases into the region. Washington had a foothold in Central Asia during its campaign in Afghanistan in the beginning of 2000s, but later on the Central Asian states demanded the withdrawal of the NATO bases. After August 2021, the US military surveillance infrastructure in Afghanistan no longer exists: the nearest base from which it is possible to conduct reconnaissance by drones, as well as potential strikes, is in Qatar. Its relative distance from Afghanistan (American drones need about 10 hours to fly to Afghanistan, with the maximum operating time of 30 hours) calls into question the effectiveness of its use. In this connection the issue of alternative bases in Central Asia is coming back into US agenda. American officials had stressed the need for the deployment of such a base in the region even before the collapse of the government in Afghanistan.[17]

According to a report of the Council on Foreign Relations, the US should negotiate basing access in the region. 'The United States should jumpstart negotiations with countries in the region—such as Kyrgyzstan, Pakistan, Tajikistan, Uzbekistan and possibly even India—to house manned and unmanned aircraft to conduct intelligence, surveillance, and reconnaissance over Afghan territory,' the report stated.[18] In this context, Uzbekistan has been considered by the US as a possible host country for American bases, especially since Tashkent is not a member of the CSTO and adheres to a multi-vector policy. However, the idea is a non-starter, taken the Uzbekistan authorities' unwillingness to irritate the Taliban by siding with US on the issue. It also goes without saying that such military initiatives in the Central Asia region will be met with active opposition from Russia and China.

China itself has been playing an important role in providing regional security, mainly within the SCO framework. In the fall of 2021, China presumably gained control of a former Soviet military base in the Gorno-Badakhshan Autonomous Region of Tajikistan near the border of Afghanistan. However, the reports had never been confirmed. On the contrary, the Tajik authorities announced that they plan to use this base to deploy their forces, and Beijing will provide investments.[19]

India's role deserves a special mention. The first India–Central Asia Summit hosted by Prime Minister Narendra Modi took place at the end of January 2022 in virtual format. India and five Central Asian countries discussed the evolving situation in Afghanistan and its impact on security in the region and decided to establish a joint working group on Afghanistan at the senior officials level.[20]

The security in the region will remain a concern for global powers. The issue may be used by the US in its overall competition with Russia and China even though its hasty evacuation from Afghanistan has put into question the American reliability.

## Interests and Concerns of Central Asian States

***Uzbekistan.*** Uzbekistan has long seen Afghanistan not as a problem but as an opportunity. It was one of the few countries that started talks with the Taliban in Doha. Tashkent has been considered as another platform for Afghan negotiations since 2018; a number of meetings and international conferences were held there from 2019 to 2022.[21] Uzbek leadership is determined to develop good relations with Afghanistan under the Taliban, including trade, investments, humanitarian assistance, and infrastructure projects that were planned to be implemented under the previous Afghan Government.

Uzbekistan supports the unfreezing of assets of the Afghan Central Bank by the West; it is interested in pushing forward a post-conflict reconstruction plan for the Afghan state. Misunderstandings about a lack of electricity supply from Uzbekistan at the beginning of 2023 can hardly be an obstacle to this.

A challenge to the relatively warm Afghan-Uzbek relations is the construction of the Qosh-Tepa canal, which started in spring 2022 in northern Afghanistan (Balkh and Faryab provinces). The project aims to develop the local agriculture and create a large number of jobs. At the same time, if constructed, the canal is expected to take up to 20 per cent of Amu Darya's flow, which could negatively affect Turkmenistan's and Uzbekistan's economies. By 2024, both countries had publicly expressed concerns over the canal's long-term implications for regional water security. The situation highlights a shift in Afghanistan's role in Central Asia—not just as a source of traditional security threat but also as a key actor influencing transboundary water resources. This has added a new dimension to the regional diplomacy, with Tashkent and Ashgabat seeking engagement with the Taliban government on water management issues.[22]

Not only the end of the first phase of the construction of the canal but also the use of primitive building methods, which are fraught with significant water losses, are currently of great concern to Tashkent. President Shavkat Mirziyoyev of Uzbekistan urged that Afghanistan be included in the regional dialogue on water use. Uzbekistan is expected to sign an agreement on the most effective regime for sharing water resources.[23] Thus, despite Tashkent's obvious concern, one can note its intention to resolve the issue in the most favourable way for both sides.

To sum up, Uzbekistan is interested in the pacification of Afghanistan, as well as in the boosting of its economy at the earliest, and Tashkent is ready to cooperate with other powers to this end.

***Tajikistan.*** The Afghanistan–Tajikistan border is the longest (about 1,350 km long) in Central Asia. Tajikistan has been facing problems given the unstable situation in the bordering northern provinces of Afghanistan. In Panjshir, and partially in Baghlan and Badakhshan, there are Tajik groups that continue to fight against the Taliban.

For Tajikistan, the main concern is the spread of radical ideology among its youth, some of whom are either willing to leave for Afghanistan or to remain in their native country to carry out subversive activities. Tajikistan's social problems can only add fuel to the radicalisation of youth in the country.

In the fall of 2021, President Emomali Rahmon stated that Tajiks make up 46 per cent of the population of Afghanistan and repeatedly called on the world community to protect half of the population of Afghanistan from oppression by the Taliban.[24] While some international experts believe that the actual number of Tajiks in Afghanistan does not exceed 20–25 per cent, the accurate estimates are not available, since the only population census in Afghanistan was conducted back in 1979 and remained incomplete.[25] Moreover, the term "Tajik" is used to refer to the Persian-speaking population of Afghanistan. They lack a common national identity and are represented by separate regional and clan communities speaking Persian (or Dari), each pursuing its own goals.

It is worth noting that among the Taliban are a considerable number of members from traditionally Persian-speaking regions (Panjshir, Takhar, Badakhshan and Herat), some of whom hold prominent positions in the Taliban government. For example, Noureddin Azizi, Minister of Commerce and Industry; Abdul-Hamid Khorasani, former Chief of Police of Panjshir; Maulavi Qudratullah, former Governor of Panjshir; and Qari Fasihuddin, head of the General Staff of the Taliban Armed Forces.[26]

Tajikistan has a long tradition of aiding the anti-Taliban forces, particularly the Northern Alliance. The leaders of the National Resistance Front of Afghanistan, the main armed group from the north opposed to the Taliban, which operates mainly in the provinces of Panjshir and Baghlan, is reported to have strong ties with Tajikistan.[27]

At the same time, there is a Tajik military wing inside the Taliban called Jamaat Ansarullah, which has intensified its activities in the areas bordering Tajikistan in the Afghan province of Badakhshan. According to some reports, the members of Ansarullah are radical immigrants from Tajikistan associated with cross-border drug trafficking, rather than Persian-speaking natives of Afghanistan.[28]

Despite the existing basic mistrust in relations,[29] the two countries continue to interact at least in the humanitarian sphere and trade. According to the Taliban's Office of Statistics, about 70,000 tonnes of cargo transited Afghanistan to Tajikistan.[30] The news about the transfer of Afghan consulate general under the control of the Taliban-led Afghan foreign ministry was confirmed by the Afghan consul general himself, Naqibullah Dehkanzada, in November 2023.[31]

***Turkmenistan.*** The Turkmenistan–Afghanistan border, although fortified after August 2021 (President Gurbanguly Berdimuhamedov ordered heavy military equipment to be pulled there), is vulnerable to infiltration. In the spring of 2021, the military department of Turkmenistan repeatedly held consultations with its Russian colleagues and discussed the prospects of military cooperation (Turkmenistan signed a cooperation agreement with Russia back in 2003). The leadership of Turkmenistan pays great attention to the issues of rearmament—mainly with the help of Turkey and China.[32] The border clashes remain a serious threat to Turkmenistan's security, though the activities of radical Islamic groups of Turkmen origin in the Mary and Tejen oasis were mostly suppressed.[33] Turkmenistan is also interested in the Turkmenistan–Afghanistan–Pakistan–India (TAPI) gas pipeline project, but its construction has not started in full earnest for security reasons.[34] At the same time, in 2023, Turkmenistan started to transport LNG to Pakistan by trucks through Afghan territories (Kandahar, Spin Buldak), at least partially realising the potential of the trans-Afghan route.[35]

***Kyrgyzstan.*** Kyrgyzstan, due to its relative remoteness and lack of shared border with Afghanistan, is not so much concerned about a spill-over effect. It is a member of the Eurasian Economic Union (EEU) and the CSTO, and the latter's forces can be called upon to suppress any eventual threat emanating from Afghanistan. In September 2024, it announced the removal of the Taliban from its list of prohibited organisations. Kyrgyzstan is not very noticeable in Afghanistan and manifests itself mainly through the irregular dispatch of humanitarian supplies.[36]

***Kazakhstan.*** Like Kyrgyzstan, Kazakhstan is a member of the CSTO and the EEU and is separated from Afghanistan by the territories of other states that have their armed forces on alert. The military structure of the CSTO also remains on high alert. Kazakhstan delisted the Taliban from its list of terrorist organisations in late December 2023, and has raised the level of economic interaction with Afghanistan.

The radical and terrorist groups, whose supporters could infiltrate into Central Asia from Afghanistan, although not without difficulty, pose a potential threat. The spread of radical ideas also remains a challenge as long as acute social and economic problems remain unresolved.[37]

**Hopes and Opportunities**

After the Taliban's return, the discussions on restarting trans-Afghan infrastructure projects have come back to the fore in Central Asia. Their implementation would have resulted in an increased connectivity of Central and South Asia. The construction of roads and railways crossing Afghanistan will be the shortest route connecting the regions; it can push forward not only economic cooperation but also political, cultural and humanitarian contacts. The implementation of connectivity projects can stimulate the creation of jobs and add revenues to the state budgets.

The most ambitious plan is the expansion of railway networks, the primary beneficiaries of which would be Uzbekistan and Iran due to the existing routes linking them to Afghanistan, and also Pakistan. The Central Asian states are placed in the Asian heartland. The new logistical links will provide much needed access to the Indian Ocean ports. Among the key connectivity projects discussed in Central Asia are:

- Mazar-i-Sharif–Herat–Khaf–Chabahar railway (from Afghanistan to Iran).
- Atamurat–Akina–Andkhoy–Mazar-i-Sharif–Kunduz–Sherkhan Bandar–Nizhny Panj (Turkmenistan–Afghanistan–Tajikistan);
- Karachi–Quetta–Kandahar–Herat (from Pakistan to Afghanistan and Iran); and
- Herat–Mazar-i-Sharif–Kunduz–Sherkhan Bandar–Nizhny Panj (from Afghanistan to Tajikistan).

In the coming years, there are plans to build a railway line from Termiz to Peshawar, a power line along the route, and 1,212 infrastructure objects. It is estimated that the volume of cargo transportation along this trans-Afghan route could amount to 10 million tonnes.[38]

At first, the most perspective project is the Termez–Mazar-i-Sharif–Kabul–Torkham–Peshawar railway line. On 2 February 2022, Uzbekistan, Pakistan and Afghanistan agreed in Tashkent to a roadmap for the construction of a 600-kilometer-long rail project connecting the three countries. The first section is already working and humanitarian goods are being sent from Uzbekistan to the Balkh Province. Turkmenistan has offered to connect it through its section link to Herat, and from there to Mazar-i-Sharif.[39]

In summer 2023, Pakistan, Uzbekistan and Afghanistan signed a new agreement to build a railroad with a slightly modified route: the rail route will pass through Termiz in Uzbekistan, Mazar-i-Sharif and Logar provinces in Afghanistan, and culminate in Pakistan via the Kharlachi border crossing in the Kurram tribal district near the Afghan border. The immediate challenge for the three countries involved in the project is to get the required funding. Earlier, prior to 2021, the World Bank, the Asian Development Bank and some other organisations seemed interested to finance these projects, but since 2021, finding the investors has been greatly complicated by the doubtful status of the Taliban regime.[40]

It is expected that with the full implementation of the Mazar-i-Sharif–Kabul–Peshawar railway project, it will take only 3–5 days (instead of 35–40 days) to transport goods from Pakistan to Uzbekistan and vice versa. The cost of transporting a container from Tashkent to Karachi is estimated to be up to US$ 1,400–1,600, while on the existing Tashkent–Bandar Abbas route, the cost can reach US$ 2,600–3,000. The construction of the railway from Mazar-i-Sharif to Peshawar will require a new infrastructure—264 bridges, 7 tunnels and 641 culverts, which may give a new impetus to the economic development of the Afghan and Pakistani territories.[41]

The main obstacles to the abovementioned infrastructure initiatives are lack of security and investments. The trade and economic cooperation of the Central Asian states with the Taliban is hindered by uncertainty and instability.

The relations of the Central Asian states with Afghanistan are formed under the influence of the following two opposite factors:

1. Security threats to be contained both by military methods and by providing humanitarian support to the population of Afghanistan; and
2. The potential of turning Afghanistan into a bridge between Central and South Asia.

The dominance of one or another factor will depend on the ability of the Taliban to pursue a pragmatic state-building policy. As long as the inter-clan struggle dominates the ranks of the Taliban and their excessive traditionalism and backwardness blocks the national development, the ability of the Taliban government to ensure development and security both inside the country and for their Central Asian neighbours will remain doubtful.

# NOTES

1. Bayram Balci, 'آسیای مرکزی در عصر طالبان' [Central Asia During the Taliban Rule], *Orient XXI*, 18 November 2021, at https://orientxxi.info/magazine/article5192 (Accessed 18 July 2022).
2. Svetlana Mamiy, 'Эксперт: Самаябольшаяугроза в Узбекистане—ростради кализациимолодежи' [Expert: The Biggest Threat in Uzbekistan is the Growth of Youth Radicalisation], Center for Studying Regional Threats, 12 June 2021, at https://crss.uz/2021/06/12/ekspert-camaya-bolshaya-ugroza-v-uzbekistane-rost-radikalizacii-molodezhi/ (Accessed 18 July 2022).
3. 'Migration Data in Central Asia', *Migration Data Portal*, 31 January 2025, at https://www.migrationdataportal.org/regional-data-overview/central-asia#:~:text=As%20of%20mid,4%20per%20cent%20of (Accessed 28 February 2025).
4. Temur Umarov, 'Do the Taliban Pose a Threat to Stability in Central Asia?', *Carnegie Endowment,* 3 September 2021, at https://carnegieendowment.org/posts/2021/09/do-the-taliban-pose-a-threat-to-stability-in-central-asia?lang=en (Accessed 28 February 2025).
5. Barbara Ellas, 'Why the Taliban Won't Quit al Qaeda', *Foreign Policy*, 21 September 2021, at https://foreignpolicy.com/2021/09/21/taliban-al-qaeda-afghanistan-ties-terrorism/ (Accessed 18 July 2022).
6. Jean-Luc Racine, 'The Taliban in Power: Pakistan Torn Between Satisfaction and Anxiety', Translated from French by Jim Muir, *Orient XXI*, 1 October 2021, at https://orientxxi.info/magazine/the-taliban-in-power-pakistan-torn-between-satisfaction-and-anxiety,5078 (Accessed 28 January 2023).
7. Zokhidzhon S. Sarimsokov, 'О возможных угрозах безопасности Узбекистана со стороны джихадистскихдвиженийАфганистана' [Possible Threats to the Security of Uzbekistan from the Jihadist Movements of Afghanistan], *Postsovetskieissledovaniya* (Journal Post-Soviet Studies), Vol. 5, No. 1, 2022, p. 43.
8. Yaroslav Trofimov, 'Left Behind After U.S. Withdrawal, Some Former Afghan Spies and Soldiers Turn to Islamic State', *The Wall Street Journal*, 31 October 2021, at https://www.wsj.com/articles/left-behind-after-u-s-withdrawal-some-former-afghan-spies-and-soldiers-turn-to-islamic-state-11635691605 (Accessed 18 July 2022).
9. Richard Barrett, 'Beyond the Caliphate: Foreign Fighters and the Threat of Returnees', The Soufan Center, 31 October 2017, at https://thesoufancenter.org/wp-content/uploads/2017/11/Beyond-the-Caliphate-Foreign-Fighters-and-the-Threat-of-Returnees-TSC-Report-October-2017-v3.pdf (Accessed 18 July 2022).
10. 'Commander of Jamaat Ansarullah Radical Group Declares His Readiness to Invade into Tajikistan', *Asia-Plus*, 7 October 2021, at https://asiaplustj.info/en/news/tajikistan/security/20211007/commander-of-jamaat-ansarullah-radical-group-declares-his-readiness-to-invade-into-tajikistan (Accessed 15 July 2022).
11. 'В Узбекистанерассказалиправду о перестрелкенагранице с Афганистаном' [Uzbekistan Told the Truth About the Shootout on the Border with Afghanistan], *Sputnik Tajikistan*, 4 May 2022, at https://tj.sputniknews.ru/20220504/uzbekistan-afghanistan-perestrelka-granica-1048170006.html (Accessed 19 July 2022).
12. 'Власти Таджикистанавысказались о ракетномударесостороны Афганистана' [Tajik Authorities Speak Out About Rocket-Shelling from Afghanistan], *Sputnik Tajikistan*, 8 May 2022, at https://tj.sputniknews.ru/20220508/tajikistan-afghanistan-udar-1048287810.html (Accessed 19 July 2022).
13. 'Afghanistan Opium Survey 2023 - Cultivation and Production After the Ban: Effects and Implications', *Relief Web*, 5 November 2023, at https://reliefweb.int/report/afghanistan/afghanistan-opium-survey-2023-cultivation-and-production-after-ban-effects-and-im

plications#:~:text=Afghanistan%20opium%20survey%202023%20,Vienna%2C%205%20November%202023 (Accessed 28 February 2025).

14. Bruce Pannier, 'Central Asia in Focus: Kazakhstan Officially Accepts Credentials of Taliban Envoy', RFERL, 27 August 2024, at https://about.rferl.org/article/central-asia-in-focus-kazakhstan-officially-accepts-credentials-of-taliban-envoy/ (Accessed 28 February 2025).
15. Catherine Putz, 'Taliban's Diplomatic Presence Growing in Central Asia', *The Diplomat*, 29 March 2023, at https://thediplomat.com/2023/03/talibans-diplomatic-presence-growing-in-central-asia/ (Accessed 28 February 2025).
16. 'Очнаявстречаминистровобороны РФ и Азиивпервыепрошла в Москве' [A Face-to-Face Meeting of the Russian and Asian Defence Ministers Was Held in Moscow for the First Time], *Argumentyi Fakti* (Arguments and Facts), Moscow, 24 June 2022, at https://aif.ru/politics/vstrecha_ministrov_oborony_rossii_i_centralnoy_azii_vpervye_proshla_v_moskve (Accessed 19 July 2022).
17. 'United States Discusses with Central Asian Countries Deployment of its Military Base', *First Channel News,* 15 June 2021, at https://www.1lurer.am/en/2021/06/15/United-States-discusses-with-Central-Asian-countries-deployment-of-its-military-base/495719 (Accessed 19 July 2022); Leo Shane III, 'CENTCOM Needs More Resources to Counter Afghanistan Terror Threat: Nominee', *Defense News*, 8 February 2022, at https://www.defensenews.com/flashpoints/afghanistan/2022/02/08/centcom-needs-more-resources-to-counter-afghanistan-terror-threat-nominee/ (Accessed 19 July 2022).
18. Seth G. Jones, 'Countering a Resurgent Terrorist Threat in Afghanistan', Center for Preventive Action, Council on Foreign Relations, 14 April 2022, at https://www.cfr.org/report/countering-resurgent-terrorist-threat-afghanistan (Accessed 19 July 2022).
19. Ananth Krishnan, 'Eye on Afghanistan, China to Build Military Base in Tajikistan', *The Hindu*, 28 October 2021, at https://www.thehindu.com/news/international/eye-on-afghanistan-china-to-build-military-base-in-tajikistan/article37221418.ece (Accessed 19 July 2022).
20. 'India, 5 Central Asian Nations to Set Up Joint Working Group on Afghanistan', *Business Standard*, 28 January 2022, at https://www.business-standard.com/article/international/india-5-central-asian-nations-to-set-up-joint-working-group-on-afghanistan-122012800047_1.html (Accessed 27 January 2023).
21. 'فراخبر: نشست تاشکند درباره افغانستان' [FARAKHABAR: Conference in Tashkent on Afghanistan Discussed], *Tolo News*, 13 July 2022, at https://tolonews.com/fa/farakhabar-178922 (Accessed 19 July 2022); and 'Страны ЦА и США подвелиитогимеждународнойконференции в Ташкенте' [Central Asian Countries and the USA Summed Up the Outcomes of the International Conference in Tashkent], *Sputnik Uzbekistan*, at 17 July 2021, at https://uz.sputniknews.ru/20210717/strany-tsa-i-ssha-podveli-itogi-mejdunarodnoy-konferentsii-v-tashkente-19721374.html (Accessed 19 July 2022).
22. Andrew Kuchins, Elvira Aidarkhanova, 'Could Afghanistan's Qoshtepa Canal Worsen Water Scarcity in Central Asia?', *The Diplomat*, 7 January 2025, at https://thediplomat.com/2025/01/could-afghanistans-qoshtepa-canal-worsen-water-scarcity-in-central-asia/ (Accessed 28 February 2025).
23. Ibid.
24. 'Meeting of the President of Tajikistan with the Foreign Minister of Pakistan', Ministry of Foreign Affairs of the Republic of Tajikistan, 25 August 2021, at https://mfa.tj/en/main/view/8470/meeting-of-president-of-the-tajikistan-with-pakistani-foreign-minister. The Russian version is available at https://mfa.tj/ru/main/view/8470/ vstrecha-prezidenta-respubliki-tadzhikistan-s-ministrom-inostrannykh-del-islamskoi-respubliki-pakistan (Accessed 19 July 2022).

25. 'Afghanistan: New Census Key to Progress', *Relief Web*, 24 January 2003, at https://reliefweb.int/report/afghanistan/afghanistan-new-census-key-progress (Accessed 19 July 2022); 'Breakdown of Afghan Population As of 2020, by Ethnic Group', Statista, August 2020, at https://www.statista.com/statistics/1258799/afghanistan-share-of-population-by-ethnic-group/ (Accessed 19 July 2022).
26. Ramzia Mirzbekova, 'Панджшеровец в правительстве «Талибан». Ктоон?' [A Panjsheri in the Taliban Government. Who is he?], *Asia-Plus*, 28 September 2021, at https://asiaplustj.info/ru/news/centralasia/20210928/pandzhsherovets-v-pravitelstve-taliban-kto-on (Accessed 19 July 2022).
27. 'Location of Ahmad MassoudRevealed', *Khabar Online*, 1 November 2021, at https://www.khabaronline.ir/news/1569044/حل-اقامت-احمد-مسعود-اعلام-شد (Accessed 19 July 2022).
28. Mukhtar Wafai, 'کند یک تروریست تاجیکستانی،□نج شهرستان افغانستان را در بدخشان کنتر□می' [A Tajikistani Terrorist is Controlling Five Districts in Badakhshan], *Farsi Independent*, 26 May 2022, at https://www.independentpersian.com/node/241271/سیاسی-و-اجتماعی/یک-تروریست-تاجیکستانی،-□نج-شهرستان-افغانستان-را-در-بدخشان-کنتر□-می‌کند (Accessed 19 July 2022).
29. After a meeting in the frames of the Moscow Format in September 2023, the Tajik delegation refused to sign the Kazan Declaration that emphasised the success of the Taliban in fighting the drugs and terrorist threats.
30. '۲۴ کشور از طریق افغانستان اجناس‌شان را به ۸ کشور دیگر □ادر کرده است' [24 States Exported Their Goods to 8 Others Countries via Afghanistan], *The Khaama Press*, 18 October 2023, at https://www.khaama.com/persian/archives/125642 (Accessed 10 November 2023).
31. Hafiz Zia Ahmad [@HafizZiaAhmad], MoFA Director of Public Communication and Deputy Spokesman, Kabul, 'د تاجکستان□ه خاروغ ښار کې د هیواد جنرا□ کونسل ښاغلي نقیب الله دهقان .. زاده' [General Consul of Afghanistan in Tajikistan city Khorugh Naqibullah Dehqanzada], *X*, 9 November 2023, 10:03 PM, at https://x.com/HafizZiaAhmad/status/1722 65377280 1872063 (Accessed 10 November 2023).
32. Alexander Knyazev, 'КтогарантируетбезопасностьТуркменистана?' [Who Guarantees the Security of Turkmenistan?], *Informatsionno-Analytichesky Center* (Information and Analytical Centre), Moscow State University, 2 September 2021, at https://ia-centr.ru/experts/aleksandr-knyazev/kto-garantiruet-bezopasnost-turkmenistana/ (Accessed 19 July 2022).
33. Ibid.
34. Daniel Onyango, 'Pakistan to Move Forward with TAPI Gas Pipeline Project Even Without India', *Pipeline Journal*, 10 February 2023, at https://www.pipeline-journal.net/news/pakistan-move-forward-tapi-gas-pipeline-project-even-without-india (Accessed 9 November 2023).
35. Aygerim Sarymbetova, 'Turkmenistan Begins Exporting Gas to Pakistan via Afghanistan', *Caspian News*, 2 May 2023, at https://caspiannews.com/news-detail/turkmenistan-begins-exporting-gas-to-pakistan-via-afghanistan-2023-5-2-0/ (Accessed 10 November 2023).
36. 'В Бишкекепрошла Кыргызско-Российскаяконференциянатему: Новаяреальность Афганистана: угрозы и вызовыдля Центральной Азии и России' [A Kyrgyz–Russian Conference Was Held in Bishkek on the Topic: 'The New Reality of Afghanistan: Threats and Challenges for Central Asia and Russia'], Интернет-ПорталСНГ: Prostranstvo Integracii (CIS Internet Portal–Integration Space), 27 November 2021, at https://e-cis.info/news/568/96535/ (Accessed 20 July 2022).
37. Alexander Kadyrbaev, 'Влияниеафганскогофактораведущиестраны ШОС' [The Impact of the Afghan Factor on the Leading SCO States], *Afghanistan.ru*, 14 September 2011, at https://afghanistan.ru/doc/20882.html (Accessed 20 July 2022).

38. 'Зачемнасамомделепроводиласьконференцияпо Афганистану в Ташкенте' [Why Was the Conference on Afghanistan Actually Held in Tashkent?], *Asia-Plus*, 27 July 2022, at https://asiaplustj.info/ru/news/tajikistan/politics/20220727/zachem-na-samom-dele-provodilas-konferentsiya-po-afganistanu-v-tashkente (Accessed 27 January 2023).
39. Alexander Knyazev, 'Александр Князев: О судьбахтрансафганскихпроектов' [On the Fate of Trans-Afghan Projects], *Informatsionno-Analytichesky Center* (Information and Analytical Centre), Moscow State University, 29 June 2021, at https://ia-centr.ru/experts/aleksandr-knyazev/aleksandr-knyazev-o-sudbakh-transafganskikh-proektov/ (Accessed 20 July 2022).
40. Aamir Latif, 'Pakistan, Uzbekistan, Afghanistan sign tripartite railway link project', *Anadolu Ajansı*, 18 July 2023, at https://www.aa.com.tr/en/asia-pacific/pakistan-uzbekistan-afghanistan-sign-tripartite-railway-link-project/2949015 (Accessed 13 November 2023).
41. 'Pakistan, Afghanistan & Uzbekistan Agree 573 km Connecting Railway', Silk Road Briefing, 5 March 2021, at https://www.silkroadbriefing.com/news/2021/03/05/pakistan-afghanistan-uzbekistan-agree-573km-connecting-railway/ (Accessed 20 July 2022).

# 9

# Return of Taliban in Afghanistan: A View from Bangladesh

*Shamsher M. Chowdhury, B.B.*

Afghanistan is located close to India, and closer to Pakistan, in South Asia. The country is not an immediate neighbour of Bangladesh but is located in the same neighbourhood, and is a fellow member state of both the South Asian Association for Regional Cooperation (SAARC) and the Organisation of Islamic Cooperation (OIC). At the time when Afghanistan was invited in as a SAARC member, things were looking promising for the country. In spite of a lot of challenges on issues like corruption, governance, etc., it was believed that Afghanistan was moving towards a situation where the country would be able to play a meaningful role; that a country, with the population of about 40 million people, would have much to contribute to South Asia. It was in this backdrop that Afghanistan became the eighth member of SAARC.

## Afghanistan Heads Towards Uncertainty

Over time, especially in more recent times, things have changed dramatically in Afghanistan. At this point of time, it can be said that the only thing certain about Afghanistan is uncertainty and the situation on ground is evolving on a daily basis.

This is rather unfortunate. The writer was a junior foreign service officer in the early1970s and in 1975 had been witness to the then Afghan president, Daoud Khan, visiting Bangladesh. Understandably, as a mid-level protocol officer, he was not part of the top-level talks that were going on between President Daoud and then Prime Minister and Father of the Nation, Bangabandhu Sheikh Mujibur Rahman. But being the fly on the wall, as all protocol officers are, he did have enough access to the discussions that were going on between the two leaders. At that time, one got the feeling that both sides were talking of a peaceful, prosperous and democratic South Asia working together. Both the countries had a very positive and progressive mindset and the message that was coming across was of keeping our channels of communication open as the two countries moved forward.

For Bangladeshis of course Afghanistan had a very special place. Historically, Bangladeshi writers had travelled to Afghanistan in the past. Famous literary personalities like late Syed Mujtaba Ali, a not too distant relative of the author, had been to Afghanistan many years ago and had written about the country and its people in great detail. In fact, he was impressed with what he had seen in Afghanistan.

Importantly, in 1973, when thousands of Bangladeshis were being repatriated from Pakistan, the airline that was chosen for the repatriation was Ariana Afghan Airlines. The United Nations had thought it prudent to use Afghanistan's national flag carrier to ship thousands of families and children and others from Pakistan to Bangladesh. Such was the positive image that Afghanistan had projected for itself in the region and to the outside world.

However, things changed dramatically with the Soviet invasion of Afghanistan in 1979. That meant a long period of uncertainty and suffering. Instability began to take root in the country. The tribal culture that had characterised Afghanistan for long began to manifest itself more openly.

US President Ronald Reagan at that time looked at the mujahideen fighting the occupying Soviet military and their puppet regime as "the enemy of my enemy". He began the process of arming and using them against the Soviet military. By the time the Soviets left in humiliation in 1989, a major section of the mujahideen had turned into forces that were not palatable to anyone, any country, or to the global society as a whole. The hope was to see an Afghanistan that did not turn violent. Sadly, that hope proved to be premature. Afghanistan did turn violent and divisions along tribal and ethnic lines began to take concrete and violent shapes. Things turned worse when narrow and short-sighted policies and geo-politics came into play. Anybody who has read Steve Coll's brilliant book *Ghost Wars*, a *New York Times* bestseller, will see how the American foreign policy on Afghanistan was being guided more by energy requirements for the United States. Coll, also a Pulitzer Prize winning writer, says in his book that it was like a powerful US energy company deciding with which force the US should align itself. It opted for the more militant Southern forces and not with the relatively moderate Northern Alliance because such an approach served its narrow interests. This not only proved to be a major mistake, in fact it was a disaster.

The question that now occupies the mind of all stakeholders, big and small, is the future of Afghanistan and what it means for the future of the region as a whole. Proxy states are never a comfortable dispensation to deal with.

The military takeover of Afghanistan by the Taliban and the "government" established following the takeover does not enjoy international recognition. This is something that needs to be kept in mind. The somewhat hurried and totally chaotic pull out of the US-led NATO (North Atlantic Treaty Organization) forces from Afghanistan created a huge vacuum and the security and economic situation remains at best fluid, if not unstable. Social disharmony seems to be becoming the norm. The general idea is to see an Afghanistan that is inclusive, that represents the mind of the Afghan people and is the legitimate representative of all the people of Afghanistan. Today, Afghanistan is a very divided society, it has powerful tribes and ethnicities that mostly do not agree with each other. What is also worrisome is that when the Taliban took over, they walked into Kabul and the Presidential Palace with surprising ease, without any resistance. Having done that, the early promises that the Taliban had made, or the assurances given, now seem empty.

## The Way Forward

An inclusive administrative set up, an inclusive society, women being able to go to school unhindered, Afghanistan not becoming a source of terrorism—none of that has happened, at least not until now. The question that remains is, will Afghanistan become a sanctuary for regional terrorism and instability again? That is a very valid concern. There are some other factors that may be important. The Islamic State Khorasan Province (ISKP) for example, the Haqqani Network, Tehrik-e-Taliban Pakistan (TTP), and some other smaller armed groups, are a strange mix. Some are more palatable than others or some are less so. It is important for all to realise that a failed Afghanistan is in no one's interest. This is something all stakeholders have to keep in mind. Such a scenario can have far-reaching political, geostrategic and socio-economic implications for the region.

Afghanistan is already experiencing the dire effects of a financial meltdown. This provides an environment for radicalisation and terrorism to thrive. This is alarming. Furthermore, neighbouring states are already engaged in a regional competition to court the Kabul ruling dispensation. This can compound the negative implications for peace and security. Pakistan, Iran, Central Asian countries, and India, albeit from a different angle, are engaging in this game. There is also the emerging role of China in the neighbourhood. Any involvement with the Taliban, or with the present setup in Afghanistan, has to be on a purely objective basis, not a self-serving one. Engaging the Taliban-led regime in Kabul for narrow, self-serving goals will not serve the purpose of achieving stability, lasting peace and security. In addition, the role of major powers like China and Russia will be of critical importance, depending on the kind of role they want to play. If they are only looking for strategic locations there or seeking a "strategic depth", it could be counterproductive in the long run. Going by past experience, one also does not know the life span of the Taliban. They were there in the 1990s and they did not last very long. One does not know how long the present one will last or what kind of threats there are for the people. Afghanistan must not become the battleground for major powers, as it had been in the past. Rather, it is the responsibility of all these powers and regional players to ensure a stable and democratic Afghanistan. The battle should be for the welfare of the Afghan people, and that is what all should work for.

In such an evolving situation, it is important to keep some key points in consideration.

One needs to monitor the situation in Afghanistan very carefully and closely because whatever happens there has direct implications and bearings on South Asia, Southeast Asia, Central Asia, and beyond. The fluidity of the situation makes it difficult to assess from the outside. It is important therefore to engage from the inside. It is important for countries in South Asia, in particular, to understand the complexities of the developments.

The other point is that the international community must engage with Afghanistan to save its people from the looming humanitarian disaster and the country's very basic survival, let alone progress. Historically, of course, many had tried to venture into Afghanistan to rule. However, none of them could last, perhaps due to the failure to understand the Afghan people's psyche and expectations. There was no sense of humility, social understanding, or appreciation of religious beliefs. Some of the key actors, notably, the United States and its allies, China, Pakistan, India and Iran will have an influence on what might happen in the future. They must remain engaged. This does not necessarily mean immediate recognition as such but remaining engaged with Afghanistan, and with the Central Asian countries that are neighbouring Afghanistan. Importantly, this approach would be in the interest of the Afghan people.

Regional organisations have a bigger role to play for a stable and peaceful Afghanistan. Afghanistan should not be in the hyphenated relationship of the India–Pakistan rivalry. Pakistan should not look at Afghanistan as its proxy and as a base to create disturbances in India and the other regional countries. Those who seek to exploit Afghanistan's natural resources must be aware that it is not economically feasible to extract much of the mineral resources. There are talks of making Afghanistan the centre for renewable resources. It is a mountainous region. It can take years before the extraction of these resources can even begin. So, there is a much bigger and long-term game some actors are playing but there has to be a convergence of goals, a convergence of thought in order to move forward in the interest of a stable peaceful Afghanistan.

As far as Bangladesh is concerned, it needs to remain alert. Bangladesh has had a long relationship with Afghanistan. But in the prevailing situation, Bangladesh needs to remain vigilant and protect itself from the menace of violent extremism and religious radicalism. It is important to remember that in the past, there had been the odd Bangladeshi who had lined up with the Haqqani Group and the other terrorist elements. It is imperative, therefore, that all stakeholders, big and small, far and near work together to create deradicalised Afghanistan. This calls for cohesion, not competition. The need of the time is to work together, not necessarily in a manner that brings out the best from Afghanistan and in Afghanistan and is in everybody's interest.

The situation is very fluid and there is every reason, why the international community has not yet recognised the Taliban administrative dispensation. It is because they have not been able to deliver the right message and given the right assurances to other countries, which can facilitate a more serious and institutionalised interaction. There have been the Doha group meetings but how much impact that has had on the mindset of the Taliban is still unclear. The Taliban leadership in Kabul has actually gone back on many of the things they had said earlier. And this is the big concern.

# 10

# Education in Afghanistan: Optimism to Pessimism

*Mirwais Balkhi*

## Introduction

Following the fall of the previous Taliban regime and the establishment of a new government in Afghanistan in 2001, education emerged as a national priority. The aspirations of a young generation, long deprived of any formal learning system, placed immense pressure on schools and universities. The demand for education, however, outpaced the new government's capacity, compelling authorities to temporarily reinstate the existing pre-2001 educational system as a stopgap measure. Amid pressing need for urgent reforms, the drafters of Afghanistan's new Constitution recognised education as a cornerstone of national reconstruction. They enshrined it as a fundamental right, embedding clear and explicit provisions across multiple articles in the Constitution. Notably, Article 43 guaranteed free access to education for all Afghans—irrespective of gender—up to the bachelor's level, reflecting both a practical response to societal needs and a commitment to inclusive development.

While the new Constitution of Afghanistan did not explicitly differentiate between modern and religious education, historically, the country's sociocultural fabric and policies of previous governments supported both. Thus, the Islamic Republic of Afghanistan, through its constitutional framework, sought to define a progressive stance on women's right to education—drawing both from Islamic principles and international human rights instruments such as the Universal Declaration of Human Rights.

Beyond affirming the fundamental rights of all citizens, the architects of the new Constitution viewed youth education as of critical need for nation's reconstruction and long-term development. In a country where prolonged conflict had severely weakened the capacity of the nation and destroyed all critical infrastructures, nurturing human capital became a strategic imperative. The government recognised that sustainable progress demanded an educated and professionally skilled workforce—men and women alike—capable of improving social conditions and driving national growth. Accordingly, over the past two decades, successive Afghan administrations made concerted efforts to expand access to education, with particular emphasis on empowering women.

Recovering from the conservative approach of the Taliban regime, there was a national hunger for education among the people across Afghanistan. Bolstered by international support and government's initiatives, the country witnessed a rapid expansion of educational services—from elementary schools to universities, both public and private. Institutions sprang up in urban centres and remote villages alike, welcoming hundreds of thousands of new students.

Yet during the early 2000s, the educational infrastructure remained severely underdeveloped. Many schools operated without basic resources—lacking textbooks, chalk, blackboards, and often even buildings. Classes were frequently held outdoors under trees or in makeshift tents. In the face of acute teacher shortages, individuals with minimal literacy were hired to instruct, despite receiving little to no formal training or pedagogical support.

Despite these constraints, Afghanistan experienced dramatic quantitative growth in education. From a base of roughly one million students in the early 2000s, enrollment reached 10 million by 2021. That year, approximately 10,017,000 students were enrolled across schools, teacher training institutes, and private institutions—6,201,000 boys and 3,816,000 girls—representing a 60:40 gender ratio. Between 40 and 45 per cent of girls were in the first to sixth elementary grades, and 55 to 60 per cent were in the middle and high schools, i.e., seventh to twelfth grades. There were 23,3515 teachers working in schools across Afghanistan, of which 147,187 were male and 86,328 female, which indicated that about 37 per cent of these teachers were women. In higher education, the number increased from dozens to 350,000, of which 100,000 were girls.[1]

However, education remained problematic in Afghanistan in terms of access and infrastructure. About 3.7 million children did not go to any school. Young people were less attracted to universities due to their low academic capacity. Although the new government in Kabul had started in right earnest to rebuild the country's education system that was completely destroyed during the first Taliban rule, there were still serious obstacles that deprived millions of young people of education services.

This paper examines the principal obstacles to education in post-2001 Afghanistan. While the return of the Taliban to power poses a critical challenge, the analysis extends beyond their influence to encompass structural, political, and socio-economic factors that contributed to both the widespread deprivation of children and youth from educational access, and the persistently low quality of education nationwide.

## Obstacles from 2001 to Present

Despite notable strides in improving the educational environment in the country after 2001, the country's education system was unable to meet the growing educational needs of the people. Over 20 million children and youth were deprived of access to schools and universities—an alarming indicator of systemic exclusion.[2] On the qualitative front, Afghanistan lacked a coherent education system and curriculum capable of delivering meaningful learning outcomes, especially in marginalised and conflict-affected regions.

This fragile progress deteriorated further with the Taliban's resurgence. Educational setbacks intensified, not solely due to ideological suppression, but also because of entrenched structural deficiencies. The crisis in education stems from a constellation of interrelated factors—ranging from political instability and chronic underinvestment to cultural barriers and governance failures—each of which is outlined in the sections that follow.

### *Social Misconceptions and Cultural Barriers to Girls' Education*

Afghanistan's educational challenges are deeply embedded in its social and cultural landscape. A majority of the population resides in rural areas, where illiteracy remains widespread and traditional mindsets dominate. Many communities continue to perceive modern social norms as taboo, and the importance of formal education—especially for girls[3]—is poorly understood or actively contested.

Even in urban centers such as Balkh, Herat, Kandahar, and Nangarhar, low literacy persisted across economic classes. Although 62 per cent of non-poor families reportedly sent their children to school,[4] enrollment remains uneven, and many children—boys and girls alike—never attended school. The resistance to girls' education is particularly pronounced, driven by entrenched customs that confine women to domestic roles. Across both rural and urban settings, harmful gender norms discourage education for girls. Some tribal elders and religious authorities label female education as dishonorable, using cultural and religious rhetoric to legitimise exclusion. In their view, a woman's primary duty is homemaking and child-rearing, and schooling threatens to disrupt these roles. Ironically, while household management itself requires knowledge and skills, the dominant discourse continues to oppose women's formal learning.

These deep-rooted beliefs, reinforced by poverty and limited awareness, had left a substantial number of girls without access to education.[5] As of the most recent estimates, Afghanistan's female literacy rate stood at a mere 37 per cent—a stark reflection of both systemic neglect and ongoing socio-cultural resistance.[6]

### *Poverty as Barrier*

Poverty remains one of the most pervasive barriers to education in Afghanistan. A significant proportion of the population has long lived below the poverty line, with agriculture and livestock forming the backbone of most families' livelihoods. In such conditions, economic survival demands that all able members—men, women, and children—contribute to daily labour, leaving little room for formal schooling.

For countless Afghan children, the pursuit of education has been overshadowed by the imperative to earn. Boys and girls across villages engage in farming, animal husbandry, embroidery, and domestic crafts, while urban youth increasingly work on the streets, undertaking gruelling tasks or resorting to begging. These children often describe their lives as a trade-off between survival and the chance at a better future—compelled to sacrifice learning for bread, in the absence of adequate state support.[7]

Street children have proliferated nationwide, symptomatic of both urban poverty and systemic neglect.[8] According to the World Bank, as of 2017, only 48 per cent of poor families in Afghanistan had enrolled their children in school—a sobering statistic that underscored the depth of economic exclusion.[9] This reality illustrates how poverty not only perpetuates educational inequality, but also shapes the social fabric of future generations.

### *Uncertainty & Insecurity*

The unsafe situation and insecurity prevailing in Afghanistan since 2004, as well as the activity of armed organisations against the then government and against the Taliban, created uncertain conditions for children to attend schools, with girls, in particular, facing a more serious threat. A substantial number of girls' schools were closed in different parts of Afghanistan confronted with violence, and incidents such as acid spraying on female students, murder, and kidnapping prompted fear and worry among female students and their families.[10] On many occasions, the Taliban and opponents of the Afghan Government set fire to schools and stated their hostility to girls' education, which resulted in a drop in the attendance of female students in educational centres. Unfortunately, there were several cases of poisoning of hundreds of pupils at girls' schools. It was part of a scheme launched to prevent the presence of girls in educational institutions.[11]

From 2018 to 2021, insecurity prevailed across the country because of the Taliban militancy. For example, the 2018 report of the UN Assistance Mission in Afghanistan (UNAMA) indicated that the year 2018 was the bloodiest year for the people of Afghanistan, with over 10,000 civilians killed or injured during the year. Around 400 schools remained closed due to insecurity.[12] The opening and closing of schools in most rural areas of Afghanistan went unrecorded. About one thousand schools faced this problem. For example, when the war reached Farah in western Afghanistan or Ghazni in central Afghanistan, hundreds of schools remained closed for months.

### *Scarcity of Educational Facilities for Girls*

There are both infrastructural and cultural constraints hindering girls' access to education in Afghanistan for long. The scarcity of dedicated girls' schools which led to female students either sharing limited facilities or travelling long distances—sometimes for hours—to reach the nearest girls-only institution.[13] Such long-distance travels for girls raise serious security concerns and are culturally discouraged, especially in areas, where conservative forces hold their sway, leading many families to withdraw their daughters from schools altogether.

Compounding the issue, mixed-gender schooling is unacceptable to many Afghan families due to prevailing social norms. In schools where boys and girls must study together due to limited resources, traditional beliefs often prevent parents from enrolling their daughters. In some cases, girls are explicitly excluded or expelled—underscoring the tangible impact of cultural resistance on educational access.[14]

### *Low Quality Education Offered*

After concerns over safety and administrative inefficiency, one of the most significant difficulties facing Afghanistan was the country's generally dismal educational system, which suffered from low quality levels. According to the statistics provided by the Afghan Ministry of Education (MoE) during the Ashraf Ghani administration, only 27 per cent of the 17,000 teachers possessed the minimum eligibility criterion for a professional teacher, which was graduation from the 14th grade. In addition to other factors, this directly affected the quality and level of education provided throughout the country.

In addition to this, based on the statistics provided by the MoE, there was a shortage of more than 70,000 educators and teachers and a deficit of 90 million books before 2021.[15]

Poor management was another issue that affected Afghanistan's education system, and it manifested both at the central and provincial levels as there was clear lack of executive capacity in the education sector. The lack of adequate staff and specialised work force, as well as the appointment of non-professionals due to rampant administrative corruption, were contributing factors in the education sector's struggle in Afghanistan.[16]

Although the fundamental obstacles and challenges facing Afghanistan's education system caused the quality of education to remain poor, the previous Afghan Government was trying to solve these challenges with the support of international partners. The Afghan Government sought to address these gaps with development programmes. Plans were afoot in cultural, economic, and educational administration fields. Reforms were undertaken in schools and universities. The Ministry of Education launched the 'Decade of Education' project to carry out extensive educational reforms. However, the fluid political and security situation came in the way of implementation of these reforms.

During the republican rule, a great sense of optimism drove the government's approach towards education. The government, civil society, private sector, people, and international partners were positively inclined. Regular attempts were made to address problems facing education. Both quantitative and qualitative approaches were being encouraged in this regard.

## Education under Taliban 2.0

Despite the above-mentioned obstacles to education in Afghanistan, there were honest attempts to correct the system and provide education to all. However, when the Taliban came to power in Afghanistan, the coefficient of obstacles increased to an uncertain and unbelievable level. The Taliban themselves became the biggest obstacle to education in Afghanistan. During the last few years under the Taliban rule, all political, economic, social, and cultural infrastructures including those at the level of primary and higher education have suffered irreparable damage. In fact, the entire structure raised during the republican period has collapsed.

On 15 August 2021, Afghanistan witnessed a wholesale change. It led to changes at every level: society, government, market, socio-cultural institutions, media, etc. Afghanistan has returned to the 1990s, a decade that the people of Afghanistan had bitter memories of. The dark period of the erstwhile Taliban rule had not been completely erased from the minds of men and women. Leave apart the adults, those who were children at that time have now come of age and carry the bitter memories of regressive rule of the Taliban from 1996 to 2001.

Post-Taliban takeover, educational institutions went into coma. Afghanistan slipped into the medieval period. High-ranking employees of the Ministry of Education and the Ministry of Higher Education either chose to stay home or went into exile for fear of Taliban reprisal. University professors and teachers fled the country in large numbers. A report stated that from the universities of Kabul, Balkh and Herat, 229 professors quit their positions and left the country.[17] Of the eight professors at Master's level courses at the University of Afghanistan, seven left the country within one week of the Taliban's return. Those who stayed back did not have the courage to send their children to school. Their livelihood was in question with disruptions in economy, and most of the teachers, the only breadwinners of their families, were deprived of their salaries.

One of the most important educational sectors in Afghanistan under the rule of the Taliban, which has suffered serious damage, is the non-governmental education sector. This sector was new in Afghanistan and had been able to shoulder some responsibilities in the education sector. During the Covid quarantine period in 2019, this sector faced serious financial challenges. People were deprived of income and could not afford to pay fees to the private schools. Virtual education needed infrastructure that had not been built before in Afghanistan.

Why has the field of education, especially women's education, suffered the most compared to any other sector under the Taliban rule? To answer this question, the Taliban's view on education, particularly their view on women's education, and the issue of reforms in the educational curriculum are discussed below.

### *The Taliban's Concept of Education*

It is difficult to get a unified and coherent view of the Taliban on education. Because on the one hand, there is no uniformity among the Taliban leadership; on the other hand, fewer works and writings have been published by the Taliban ideologues on the issue. The Taliban's view on education can be recognised from the nature of the group. The Taliban ideology is a mixture of traditionalism, tribalism, and Islamism. They rely on retrogressive traditions and radical Islamic ideology. Therefore, education is an anathema for such a group.

In Taliban's view, traditional social and cultural relations are to be based on the standards set in the Golden Age of Islam, in the 8th and 9th centuries

AD. For this reason, education in science and technology is unnecessary. Islam as interpreted by the Taliban jurists is sacrosanct and can take care of all human needs. Islamic principles, enforced by Taliban, are sufficient for running market, governance, foreign policy, jurisprudence, and any other matter of consequence. All knowledge beyond it is either harmful or leads society to disaster. If at all such knowledge is required, only men, and not women, can be allowed to acquire it for running the affairs of the state.

Taliban leadership considers religious teachings to be primary, and modern ones to be secondary. They have changed the education curriculum in educational institutions adding religious principles to the curriculum while modern education has been sidelined. The quality of education has been called into question more than ever.[18] The certificates issued by religious schools are now recognised by educational institutes across the country and social science teachers are being drawn from the same pool for the universities.[19]

### *Taliban on Girls' Education*

No section of Afghanistan has suffered more than women and girls after the return of the Taliban. The Taliban do not recognise women's freedom, especially their right to work and education. Education, one of the most important of all the fundamental rights of a human being, has been taken away from them. Women were the first group to protest for the restoration of their rights, the day after the Taliban arrived in Kabul. Compared to men and young male students, women and female students were more apprehensive about Taliban usurping their rights.[20]

One of the Taliban publications that best clarifies the Taliban's view on girls' education is the book titled *Islamic Emirate*, written by Abdul Hakim Haqqani, which was published in Arabic. This book has the backing of the Amir of Taliban, Mullah Haibatullah Akhundzada, and the author himself is one of the main decision makers responsible for laying down Taliban's national policies. According to him, women's education is a must as per the explicit decree of the Quran and the hadith of the Prophet Muhammad, but because women are not allowed to go outside the house, therefore, there is a problem in evolving the right method and mechanism for executing this decree on women's education.[21]

But this is lame excuse. During the republican period, girls and boys were separated from 6 to 12 standards in the schools. In many girls' high schools in Afghanistan, female teachers were employed. The Taliban also argue that the rural folks in Afghanistan do not want girls' education, which is again an excuse to deny girls their right to education. During the republican period again, in the remotest areas of the country, some of the tribal leaders had set a fine of 5,000 afghanis per month for families that did not send their daughters to school,[22] which disproves the Taliban argument.

Based on these misinterpretations and policies, around 2,350,000 girls have been stopped from going to school. Out of about 3.7 million children who have stopped going to school, 68 per cent are girls. All in all, about five million girls have discontinued their studies since the Taliban returned to power, if the number of female university students too is taken into account.[23]

The Taliban have also reduced the number of female teachers in the educational institutions, especially in professional education, which is a serious problem affecting the country's education system. Most female teachers have faced serious problems of poverty. A large number of them are the sole breadwinners of their families. The Taliban did not pay their salary, forcing a significant number of them to leave their duties. They were also prevented from going out of the house for various reasons and therefore they are facing grinding poverty.

In addition to these, the Taliban's ambivalence about the employment of female teachers in the body of the MoE has led to reduction in the number of women serving in the education sector. Earlier, at least one per cent of the teaching positions would fall vacant every year for various reasons. The MoE had a specific policy to fill the vacant positions. In addition to contract teachers who were hired annually based on the need and on a temporary basis, the ministry had allocated 50 per cent seats for women candidates in the national teacher recruitment examination. The MoE had also hired around 7,000 female teachers for girls' schools through international institutions between 2018 and 2020. Since the advent of the Taliban, all contract teachers have been staying at home.[24]

### *Taliban's View on School Curriculum*

The Taliban's educational philosophy is deeply curriculum-centric, rooted in the pedagogical models of traditional religious schools. Their approach prioritises ideological transmission over interdisciplinary and literary engagement, with limited emphasis on skill development, artistic expression, or adaptive capacity. In this view, the curriculum functions not merely as a tool for instruction but as the central mechanism of ideological continuity. For the Taliban, the ideal curriculum serves two core purposes: neutralise perceived threats to their worldview and cultivate a resilient mindset among Afghan youth that affirms their legitimacy and ensures long-term survival. They have consistently criticised the school curricula implemented under the republican government, urging reforms that align more closely with their interpretation of Islamic principles.[25]

Following the 2020 Doha Agreement with the US, the Taliban initiated a systematic overhaul of Afghanistan's school curriculum. This process included the review of 136 textbooks—45 for elementary, 48 for middle school, and 43 for high school—in both Farsi and Pashto. A self-appointed body of religious scholars, referred to as the "Technical Team," was tasked with evaluating the materials. The Taliban argued that the republican era curriculum had been manipulated, asserting that its development—funded by foreign governments—embedded "non-Islamic and non-Afghan standards" modelled after Western ideals. In the introduction to their report on curriculum review, the Taliban acknowledged the Islamic veneer of the contents during the republican era, but claimed it concealed "superstitions" introduced under the guise of faith, driven by motives they described as "ugly." Notions such as democracy, gender equality, civil liberties and the renunciation of violence were explicitly condemned. In the Taliban's ideological framework, these concepts—core to international human rights discourse—are rebranded as incompatible, illegitimate, and morally offensive.[26]

The Taliban removed the three subjects of "graphic art," "civil education," and "culture" from the curriculum. Board members of the Taliban believed that almost all of the arts subject [drawing and art] and civil education themes are useless. The textbook proposed by the Taliban delegation, removed the subject "Culture" from the curriculum. The Taliban delegation said: 'This topic is optional, and not necessary to study. It would be good if another useful topic is taught instead.'[27]

The process of reforming and changing the curriculum does not stop here. The Taliban are planning to change the entire curriculum of schools and universities in Afghanistan. These changes will be based on the Taliban's approach and their views on the necessity of education in Afghanistan.

## Conclusion

Afghanistan's enduring crisis in the education sector has its roots in a complex web of domestic and regional factors. However, the main question that begs a convincing answer is: How do Afghans educate their next generation? While the country's political and security landscape may shift over the coming decade—potentially ending war and terrorism—a deeper crisis looms. The deliberate closure of schools and universities for girls, besides restricting boys from accessing formal education and higher learning, risk inflicting lasting harm on the Afghan society for generations.

The systematic erosion of educational opportunity in the country is already stunting the social, professional, and intellectual development of

Afghan youth. One shudders at the thought of a future in which an entire generation enters adulthood without the skills, capacities, or critical agency required to build or sustain a functioning society. The consequences of alternative education that the Taliban have tried to introduce are not hypothetical—they include rising unemployment, deepening social fragmentation, loss of direction, increased addiction, and the resurgence of extremism. This may lead to the collapse of cultural, civic, and value-based institutions which will create a fragile state and a fractured society. And the cost of such unthinking changes in the important area of education, if left unchallenged, will surpass anything one can currently imagine.

In the face of the deteriorating educational landscape in Afghanistan since the return of the Taliban, international institutions, national agencies, and non-governmental organisations (NGOs) have been seeking alternative pathways to support Afghan children, particularly girls. Online and distance education (in a clandestine manner) have emerged as emergency mechanisms—not as viable substitutes for formal schooling, but as stopgap solutions aimed at ensuring quality learning at least for those few who can form a critical mass for quality change in future. Even these efforts risk being undermined by opportunistic behaviour. A growing concern is that many NGOs, under the guise of educational service delivery, may exploit the crisis to attract funding and expand operations with little accountability. While a handful of organisations operate with genuine compassion and caution, most lack expertise, commitment, and operational capacity to deliver meaningful educational support at scale.

A pragmatic solution would be formation of a consortium of countries committed to education in Afghanistan. Well-established international actors—such as the Swedish Committee, the Aga Khan Foundation, and Save the Children—could jointly manage and coordinate the delivery of aid. Such a mechanism could mitigate misuse of resources by organisations seeking to benefit from donor attention without substantive educational engagement.

It is also essential to underscore that Afghanistan's national curriculum was neither anti-religious nor opposed to national identity. In fact, the 2019 competency-based redesigned curriculum sought to cultivate committed, capable, and socially engaged citizens. During the pilot phase in select provinces, the MoE produced Persian and Pashto reading textbooks rooted in Islamic and patriotic values for students of first, second and third grade, with inputs from both curriculum experts and religious scholars. This process added relevance and religious legitimacy to the curriculum.

However, the Taliban are now working—under various pretexts—to impose an ideologically rigid and extremist curriculum across schools and universities. Their aim is to educate a generation that internalises a doctrine of religious authoritarianism, thereby entrenching their rule and claiming long-term legitimacy. Such a trajectory threatens to transform Afghanistan into a breeding ground for terrorism and extremism, with devastating implications for the country's future and regional stability.

## NOTES

1. 'Educational Situation in Afghanistan; A Conversation with Former Minister of Education of Afghanistan', *Farsi Times*, Washington, DC, January 2023.
2. Minister of Education's Speech on the Decade of Educational Reforms to the Civil Service Commission, Ministry of Education, Islamic Republic of Afghanistan, 12 November 2019.
3. 'Field Studies in Girls Access to Education; Challenges and Opportunities and Situation Analysis', Fieldwork, p. 6.
4. Human Rights Watch Report 2017, p. 57.
5. 'Educational Restrictions for Women in Afghanistan: Factors and Solutions', *Jomhor News*, May 2013, at https://www.jomhornews.com/fa/news/29932/.
6. 'Top 10 Facts About Girls' Education in Afghanistan', The Borgen Project, 9 February 2023, at https://borgenproject.org/facts-about-girls-education-in-afghanistan/.
7. *Jomhor News*, no. 5.
8. Fieldwork, p. 10, no. 3.
9. Human Rights Watch, no. 4.
10. Fieldwork, no. 8.
11. *Jomhor News*, no. 5.
12. 'New Education Year in Afghanistan and an Assessment of the Education Situation in the Country', Center for Strategic and Regional Studies, Kabul, 22 March 2019, at https://csrskabul.com/?p=4946.
13. 'Afghan Father Travels for Miles and Waits for Hours Every day to Educate Daughters', *Voice of America News,* 24 December, 2019, at https://www.voanews.com/a/extremism-watch_afghan-father-travels-miles-and-waits-hours-every-day-educate-daughters/6181591.html.
14. *Jomhor News*, no. 5.
15. Center for Strategic and Regional Studies, Kabul, no. 12.
16. Ibid.
17. 'Brain Drain after Taliban Takeover; 229 Professors From Just Three Universities Have Left the Country', *BBC News,* 4 February, 2022, at https://www.bbc.com/persian/afghanistan-60200786.
18. 'The Taliban and Women Education', *Salam Watandar Radio,* 17 June 2019, at https://swn.af/taliban-and-womens-education/.
19. Nida Mohammad Nadim, Taliban Higher Education Minister, 'The Criteria of a Scholar is Decided by his Jihad Activities, and Madrasa Ulema Don't Need to Give Any Exam for Their Scientific Degrees', X Post, 17 December 2022, 10:21 AM, at https://twitter.com/nda_ndym/with_replies (Accessed 3 February 2023).
20. Fawzia Koofi, 'Afghanistan Women Raised their Voice Immediately after the Taliban Control of Kabul', Herat Security Dialogue, Dushanbe, 29 November 2022.
21. Abdul Hakim Haqqani, *Islamic Emirate*, Darul Uloom al-Sharia, 2022, p. 89.
22. 'Even in the tribal areas the demand for education is strong and we have to respond to their expectations', Minister of Education's Address at the Teachers Gathering in Kabul, Loya Jirga Hall, Ministry of Education Monthly Report, 28 July 2018.
23. *Farsi Times*, no. 1.

24. *Farsi Times*, no. 1.
25. In the summer of 2018, the self-proclaimed Taliban head of education in Paktika Province issued a message to the Afghan Ministry of Education, threatening to close schools nationwide unless a subject titled 'History of Islam' was formally included in the curriculum. The threat raised serious concerns at the time, as it appeared that the Taliban were seeking to shut down schools on the pretext of religious aberration in the text books. In response, the MoE compiled and sent a comprehensive list of chapters already present in the curriculum that addressed Islamic history and values. It also clarified that the content the Taliban claimed to be missing was, in fact, reflected in the existing textbooks. Upon reviewing the material, the Taliban expressed satisfaction and allowed the schools to remain open. This episode revealed that the curriculum itself was not at odds with Islamic principles. Rather, it highlighted how education policy was being politicised—used by the Taliban not as a matter of doctrinal integrity, but as a tool of leverage. The incident underscores the fragility of access to education in conflict zones, where ideological actors may invoke religion not to improve learning, but to justify restriction.
26. 'Details of the Taliban's Educational Curriculum; Blood and Hatred Return to Books', *Hasht-e-Subh Daily,* 17 December, 2022, at https://8am.media/details-of-the-talibans-curriculum-hatred-and-bloodshed-return-to-books/.
27. Ibid.

# 11

# Taliban and Education in Afghanistan: Relevance of Bacha Khan's Legacy

*Bilquees Daud*

Afghanistan has been experiencing violent, armed conflict for over four decades now, which apart from inflicting human and material losses has left a deep social and psychological impact on the Afghan society. It has given rise to a "new normal," which is, a growing culture of violence at both the political as well as inter-personal and community levels. Moreover, this is also mirrored amongst others, notably in the educational curriculum of the country that ironically over years of conflict was moulded with the intention of condoning or justifying the systematic use of violence. The immense significance attached to the educational system to establish "ideological hegemony" can be gauged from the fact that regime changes were accompanied by drastic curricular changes, while the Islamist resistance opened several schools for Afghan refugees in Peshawar and in territories controlled by it in years of conflict.

This pattern appears to be unfolding yet again with the Taliban's return to power on 15 August 2021, with many of the fragile gains made in the field of education between 2001 and 2021 being steadily reversed. The Taliban have appointed mullahs to positions of leadership, sought to tinker with the curriculum to align it with their narrow interpretation of Islam, and have denied women access to education beyond grade six. Afghanistan has become the only country in the world to deny women access to education, defying calls by Islamic theologians and leaders to reverse the ban. These developments show that the Taliban's opinion on Islamic teachings and

Sharia law is inaccurate and it yet again drives home the challenge posed by the radicalisation of youth through educational curriculum.

The paper draws upon the legacy of Khan Abdul Ghaffar Khan, the first Muslim and Pashtun who became an icon for practicing non-violence and championing the cause of education for girls, and argues that a credible counter-discourse to the Taliban must be rooted in the local socio-cultural milieu.

Khan Abdul Ghaffar Khan or Badshah Khan or Bacha Khan, also famously known as the Frontier Gandhi and *Fakhr-e-Afghan* (Pride of the Afghans), believed that Islam preaches gender equality, peaceful coexistence with other faiths, and stands for social progress. In sharp contrast to it, the Taliban project a totally different version of Islam based on conservative ideas of banning women from work, education, and social mobility. The stark disparity between these two worldviews appears more striking since Bacha Khan came from the same ethnic background as bulk of the Taliban's core leadership.

## Education System in Afghanistan

Up to the nineteenth-century, Afghanistan was a centre of developed civilisation, literature, and science in the region. The country produced great scholars and philosophers, such as, Ibn Sina Balkhi, Maulana Jalaludin Rumi, Khushal Khan Khatak, etc. These scholars used a combination of secular and religious expertise to promote learning. As observed by Mansory, 'Islam has been dominating most parts of the country for 1,200 years or more, which implied that Islamic education has reached great parts of the population, also rural people living in remote areas.'[1] Madrasas emerged as centres of religious learning and were promoted by communities and religious leaders through private funding.

Soon after Afghanistan got its independence in 1919, King Amanullah Khan paid special attention to education. He was in favour of supporting modern and secular education throughout the country, and for the first time sent female students abroad for studying. The king's reforms were considered one of the crucial developments in the education system in Afghanistan. When the king was overthrown by the conservative mullahs, he was replaced by Habibullah Kalakani in 1929. The first step Kalakani took was to ban the female education in the country. He also called back the female students who were sent abroad for education.[2] It was for the first time in the history of the country when women were not allowed to get education.

Following Kalakani's brief rule of nine months, Amanullah's reforms were continued by his successor, King Nadir Shah, in 1930. As noted by

Samady, 'A new constitution, adopted in 1931, made primary schooling compulsory for all Afghans, and placed all modern educational institutions under the control of the State. Education at all levels—primary till tertiary—was provided for free for all Afghans.'[3] Therefore, the 1930s is considered the era of educational reforms in terms of building schools in all provinces and unifying the educational system of the country by incorporating madrasas in the formal education system.

However, throughout history, education system in Afghanistan relied on foreign financial aid, mainly from Germany, France, United States (US), and the Soviet Union's financial aids applied through countries like Pakistan, Iran, and Saudi Arabia during the periods of conflict. This dependency shaped Afghanistan's education curriculum to favour the type of education each foreign donor country supported. For instance, the April 1978 coup d'état, which was followed by the Soviet invasion of Afghanistan, ushered in a period of "Sovietisation" of Afghanistan, including its education system. But 'the Marxist ideology...seems to have little effect either on the village people in the provinces, who are deeply rooted in their popular and religious traditions, or on the highly educated intellectuals, who have a good knowledge of Western culture.'[4] As a result, modern secular education faced resistance in the rural areas where people feared for their traditions and religious beliefs under an atheistic communist ideology.

In the first few years of the Soviet invasion, it was said that approximately six million people fled the country, more than a million were killed, and the enrolment in educational institutions fell from over a million in 1979 to around 700,000 pupils in 1985.[5] Among the people who left the country, the highly-educated Afghans mostly went to the West whereas the illiterate and poor ones became refugees in Pakistan and Iran, where often radical forms of religious education were provided for their children to promote Jihad against the Soviet Army in Afghanistan.

In 1992, three years after the withdrawal of the Soviet Army, the last communist government in Kabul was replaced by a Peshawar-based coalition of seven Afghan mujahideen parties that proclaimed Afghanistan as an "Islamic Republic" for the first time in its history. The new government faced an acute lack of resources, insecurity, and a unified curriculum for education. Moreover, in an ideologically charged environment, a high degree of external meddling in the country's affairs, priority was given not merely to religious education but one favouring a radical interpretation of the faith, largely not known to Afghans.

The undermining of the education system was facilitated by the anarchy and chaos that dominated the Afghan landscape in the 1990s. During the first

Taliban rule (1996–2001), women were strictly denied the right to education and work. However, there were some underground schools that tried to provide education to the young girls. Even after the overthrow of the Taliban regime in 2001 and the establishment of a democratic system in 2004, schools and teachers continued to be targeted. In 2007, about 226 schools were burned down and 110 teachers assassinated.[6]

## Politicisation of Education in Afghanistan

Afghanistan's political instability has damaged social constructs and lifestyles. The education system has always been manipulated by foreign donors and local rulers. That is why the dependency of the country's education sector on foreign aid opened doors for various political agendas to be propagated among young minds. Initially Sovietisation and then Islamisation affected the educational system and encouraged violence and use of children as instruments to win the war.

The communist governments considered education 'an important instrument for fostering the economic and social transformation of Afghanistan. Its educational policies, adopted in 1980 with the assistance of Soviet advisors, aimed at promoting literacy and basic education and the development of vocational training and higher education.'[7] However, the communists, as Yusuf Elmi believes, created an environment of distrust and lack of self-confidence among the people and the students. For instance, students were not allowed to speak against the government and air their grievances.

Though Kabul University had been a centre of political activity, during the initial years of communist rule, social gatherings and informal meetings among the students to exchange ideas had disappeared. Instead, politics became an important part of the student life. Students conducted violent demonstrations against the Soviets and disliked their compatriots who supported the Soviets.[8] The students were divided into two categories, ones who favoured the regime and the others who were in opposition.

On the other hand, Olivier Roy believes that the Soviets aimed to create a young generation alien to the past traditional Afghan society. They wanted the youth to adopt the modern "Soviet way of life," not necessarily politically but socially. Further, he mentions, the Soviets not only changed the curriculum but also the structure of educational institutions. He defines "Sovietisation" of Afghanistan as an effort to make the country look like a "Soviet Muslim Republic," focusing on urban society and youth, which was carried 'through institutions, educations and ideology'.[9]

The French model of education system was replaced with the Soviet model and young students were sent for education to the Soviet Union, East Germany, and India. The amendments took place notably in the middle schools, colleges and universities where Russian language became mandatory and religious education was replaced with new subjects such as 'historical materials, dialectical materialism, and history of working-class movement'.[10] Though, they also built kindergartens (for working women's kids) and nurseries (for orphans), which was a new concept for the Afghan education system. Finally, in the whole process, orphans became more Sovietised than others as they lacked parental care and family protection, rendering them more vulnerable to propaganda.

Additionally, since Sovietisation took place mostly in the cities, the growing gap between rural and urban people not only divided Afghan society but also increased resistance against the communist regime. The rural population that lived in total isolation had no access to governmental facilities and thus was influenced by the mujahideen to stand against the communists who were projected as a threat to their religious beliefs and social norms. Therefore, many families left the country as they did not want to live under the communist rule, nor did they wish to pursue jihad against them. Among all, poorer families' children and youth who immigrated to Iran and Pakistan have suffered the most because in refugee camps they neither had access to food, housing, and health nor to proper education. The children in refugee camps in Pakistan attended schools run by international organisations that provided traditional and religious education. According to Samady, '...The curricula of these schools have varied in quality and scope and have not been based on a unifying national vision for Afghan society and culture, as a reaction to communist ideology.'[11]

To further strengthen the resistance against the Soviets, the mujahideen parties in Iran and Pakistan ignored the importance of national agenda in the schooling at refugee camps and instead emphasised the religious dimension of education. Sayyid Bahaouddin Majrooh states that the mujahedeen parties either 're-opened the old religious Madrasas' or built 'institutions to train militants for revolutionary Islam' that were also funded by Saudi Arabia. Also, 'the host country Pakistan having been found in the name of Islam, officially undergoing the process of Islamization and also having had trouble since its creation with Afghanistan' was not keen to promote Afghan national education.[12] Moreover, Pakistan hoped to create a new breed of Islamists ruling Kabul who would be friendly to Pakistan considering Islamic affinity and give up the demand for Pashtunistan and be less close to rival India.

In fact, Islamisation as a response to communism was funded by the West, particularly the US, to be undertaken in Afghan refugee camps in Pakistan. Afghan children were taught in the schools to kill infidels and fight for the country's freedom from un-Islamic rulers. In other words, 'in the twilight of the Cold War the US spent millions of dollars to supply Afghan school children with textbooks filled with violent images and militant Islamic teachings.'[13] These books, published in the Nebraska University at Omaha in US, were used for ideological propaganda. Pages from one such book taught to children in Afghan refugee camps in Pakistan are given below.

**Image 1: Pages from Textbook Taught in Refugee Camps in Pakistan**

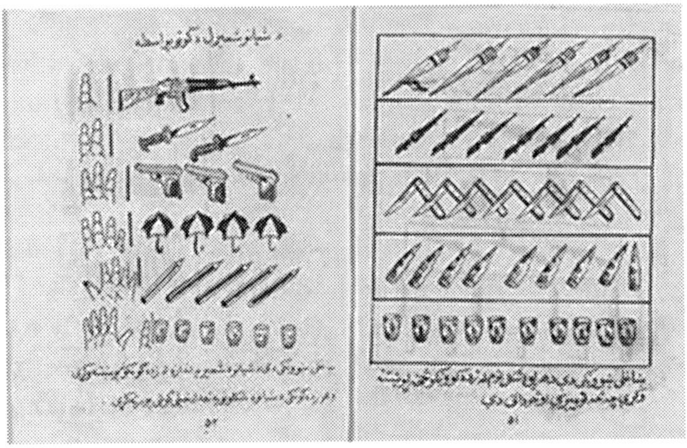

*Source:* https://www.reddit.com/r/AfghanCivilwar/comments/q9wukz/in_the_80s_usaid_funded_militarized_children/.

Similarly, the Taliban used the American-produced books to teach children in madrasas and to promote anti-American sentiments. They focused mainly on orphaned and refugee children to be educated as extremists since they themselves had been exposed to US books earlier. In contrast, Pia Karlsson and Amir Mansory stated, 'Taliban aimed at educating students with a correct and strict view on Islam [based on their ideology] while simultaneously training them in modern subjects and thus making them able to compete with what was called the secular school students.'[14] However, the bitter reality is that the Afghan children and youth have over the years been indoctrinated with violence through textbooks, which has contributed towards inculcating among them a culture of violence and aggression.

What is even more astonishing is the fact that following the toppling of the Taliban regime by the US and its allies in its "war on terror," the same books continued to be in print and circulation in many Afghan schools. In 2002, the United States Agency for International Development (USAID) provided $6.5 million to print textbooks for Afghan schools. These were the same books used in the Afghan refugee camps 'forcing Islamic fundamentalist texts on Afghan kids for 20 years'.[15] After much discussion among the US policymakers and the people, the public opinion in the US weighed in, arguing to the effect that it is illegal to promote religious education with taxpayers' money. In response the USAID removed its logo and references to the US Government from the books and said that they 'left the Islamic materials intact because they feared Afghan educators would reject books lacking a strong dose of Muslim thought'.[16] Eventually the circulation of old schoolbooks by USAID came to an end in early 2003.

Even though education became the top priority of the Afghan Government, the establishment of a common school programme lagged. Instead, education remained limited to non-governmental organisations (NGOs) making efforts to use diverse curriculum to teach children, but most of them used the syllabus adopted by the mujahideen focusing on religious and traditional teaching.[17]

Finally, the Islamic Republic of Afghanistan adopted a new unified national curriculum in 2005 to be implemented in all schools throughout the country. Yet, the new curriculum, though much improved from the past, lacked peace education to effectively replace violence depicted in textbooks taught to children for so many years.

## Taliban and Education in Afghanistan

Following the toppling of the Taliban regime by the US in late 2001, boosting education was one of the most significant achievements in Afghanistan. Despite challenges, female enrolment showed a secular increase across the board. It rose from nearly zero to 2.5 million at the school level and registered a phenomenal 20-fold increase in higher education from 5,000 girls' students in 2001 to 100,000 by 2021.[18] The focus on education, particularly girls' education to enhance women's rights in the country was a top priority of international community. However, the recent developments have demonstrated that the hard-won gains made over the past 20 years by Afghan women remain reversible. Following their return to power and contrary to the phony promises made earlier, the Taliban have moved swiftly to orchestrate a systemic elimination of Afghan women and girls from all spheres of public life, including education. Afghan girls were initially denied access to education beyond grade six but soon the ban extended to women at the university level. The Taliban sought refuge for the decision in the name of Islam and what they perceived to be "Afghan culture".[19]

However, this is not borne out by empirical evidence. Consider for instance the fact that data for women's participation in the national university entrance exams known as *Kankor* show a steady increase in female participation from a measly 1,000 female aspirants in 2003 to 78,000 by 2013. Notably in provinces such as Herat, female participation in the entrance exams outpaced that of males by the ratio of 53 to 42 per cent.[20] It clearly demonstrated the desire and legitimacy in Afghan society for access to education cutting across the gender divide. If anything, the Taliban's ban on education for women reveals that not only their decision is not in sync with the Afghan socio-political milieu but it also shares uncanny ideological similarities with the likes of Habibullah Kalakani, who after toppling Amanullah Khan from power in 1929 sought to undo his educational reforms by banning women from accessing education.

Historically speaking, it would be fair to argue that Afghanistan has always been a traditional society but not a conservative one bound by strict religious dogmas. Consider for instance, the Taliban's claim that co-education system promotes vice. Nothing could be further from the truth as historically co-education has been followed only until grade five under regimes of various hues, barring the initial period of the communist rule. From grade five onwards, female and male students have studied in different sections and/or shifts. Apart from that, girls' school uniform always remained the same with black dress/skirt and a white *chadar* (a cloth to cover the head). In the school curriculum too, religious subjects were always present even during the communist era. Therefore, there is no evidence to support the Taliban's fallacious claim that schools in Afghanistan did not follow Islamic standards.

Besides curtailing women's access to education, the Taliban has imposed restrictions on women's dress, mobility and employment. Consider for instance the new morality law, called "Law on the Promotion of Virtue and the Prevention of Vice", enacted in July 2024 that forbade women's voice to be heard in public, explicitly prohibiting women from singing and reciting poems. The new law thus is 'effectively attempting to render them into faceless, voiceless shadows'.[21] The codified law, receiving ratification from the Supreme Leader, Hibatullah Akhundzada, justified the harsh treatment of women under the Taliban's rule. Another article of the new morality law states that women must cover their bodies, including their faces, and requires women and men to avoid eye contact. The attempt to police women's body and sexualise them is further attested to by the law which prevents women from '.... befriending non-Muslims, sex outside of marriage, lesbianism, anal sex, paedophilia, and missing one's religious prayers and fasts.'[22] These measures have effectively erased half of the population from public life, disproportionately impacting a society where a large number of households are run by single women who lost their male members in the long years of war.

A critical discernment of both Islam and Afghan history tells us that in reality the Taliban's treatment of women finds no precedence and justification in either Islam or Afghan culture that have been perversely used to justify such measures. Traditionally, women in rural Afghanistan enjoyed social mobility and participation in public life. This is seen in women's role on the battlefield, embodied most potently in the legend of Malalai of Maiwand, who took on the British in the second Anglo–Afghan War (1878–1880). It shaped oral traditions through folk poems known as *Landay* and singing of songs in the community festivals. Afghan women also had the liberty to leave home without a male companion and bring water from *Godar* or "water places" in the villages of southeast Afghanistan.[23]

The fact remains that in practice the socio-cultural and religious milieu in Afghanistan has been far removed from the Taliban's worldview, which draws on a narrow Sunni-Deobandi interpretation of Islam as taught in conservative religious seminaries of Pakistan. This ignores the diverse and syncretic schools of theological thought that have thrived in Afghanistan. The Taliban seek to bring about a socio-political and cultural re-engineering of Afghan society for which education provides the most potent and effective tool. They seek to use the educational curriculum to preach violence and hatred. This is evident by the recent establishment of the suicide museum in the country, which showcases the materials used for destruction by the group in the recent years.[24] It reiterates the long-held view by many critics of the Taliban, including the author, that the Taliban normalise and encourage violence. Consider for instance the fact that Sirajuddin Haqqani in the opening ceremony of the suicide museum with the family members of suicide bombers '... congratulated the men for their loved ones' divine sacrifice and gifted them with clothes, cash, and the promised allocation of land plots.' And in October 2021, amid increasing tensions with Tajikistan, the group announced the deployment of 3,000 suicide bombers to the border between the two countries.[25]

In addition, Taliban's assessment board for the modification of education curriculum has already published its version of the revised school curriculum in 26 paragraphs. Among other things, the committee emphasised that textbooks should talk about the Muslim world only, disregarding the West and denouncing importance figures such as Amanullah Khan, Faiz Mohammad Kateb Hazara, and Abdul Ghani Khan. Moreover, the Taliban recommendation on curriculum focuses on their interpretation of Islam, the importance of jihad and stresses that 'the sharia rules of killing in war, retaliation in kind, stoning, and other cases should be explained'.[26] These developments are contradictory to what Bacha Khan, a devoted Muslim and a Pashtun leader, advocated to his followers. His ideological legacy teaches peace, co-existence, tolerance, non-violence, equality, and non-discrimination.

## Bacha Khan's Legacy and its Relevance

Bacha Khan's background as a Muslim and a Pashtun made his non-violent struggle unique since he was able to challenge the conventional discourse, which portrayed the Pashtuns as "wild" people pre–disposed to violence. Hailing from the North-West Frontier Province (NWFP) of British India, now Khyber Pakhtunkhwa (KPK) Province of Pakistan, Bacha Khan promoted the creed of non–violence and the cause of girls' education in a culture that privileged patriarchy and martial qualities. He argued:

> We would have fared ill if we had not learnt the lessons of non-violence. We are born fighters, and we keep the tradition by fighting among ourselves... [thus]...this non-violence has come to us as a positive deliverance.[27]

To promote his cause, he set up *Azad* schools in the NWFP region, inviting the ire of the British who saw empowerment through education as a threat. Notably, Bacha Khan and his *Khudai Khidmatgar*'s political philosophy dealt with the ideas of jihad in a way that would appear inconceivable to many modern political movements of the day. He regarded dealing with the internal "greater jihad" (jihad-i-akbar) as indispensable to embarking upon the external "lesser jihad" (jihad-i-asghar) against colonial oppression. The former in Bacha Khan's conception was seminal to cultivate virtues of service, restraint, and patience.[28]

Bacha Khan's followers held on to their vow of non-violence even when Mahatma Gandhi's followers dithered. Essentially, for Bacha Khan, preserving the non-violent protest was much more important for Afghans than the Indians because 'the Pathans had been characterised by the British as wild, ungovernable and uncivilised and hence it was doubly important that their protest demonstrate political maturity and fitness for self-rule'.[29] For that reason, Bacha Khan and his followers were able to challenge the British stereotype and uphold moral high ground in the history of the region.

Bacha Khan said: 'to me non-violence has come to represent a panacea for all the evils that surround my people.... therefore, I am devoting all my energies towards the establishment of a society that would be based on its principles of truth and peace.'[30] Mukulika Banerjee argues that Bacha Khan though very much inspired by Mahatma Gandhi, had adopted a non-violent dogma before Gandhi '… through his own reflections on the needs and short comings of Pathan society'.[31] To achieve that aim, he initially started a non-political organisation, *Anjuman-Islah-ul-Afghania*, aimed at encouraging 'economic, social and educational improvement in Frontier' as he wanted his people to take professions other than agriculture only.[32]

Bacha Khan realised the potency of education as a medium to not only uplift his people but also to help realise his goals of inculcating maturity, restraint, and service amongst the Pashtuns. His propagation of gender equality was firmly rooted in the framework of Islam. He fervently believed in men and women being granted equal rights under Islam, arguing '…in the Holy Quran, you have an equal share with men. You are today oppressed because we men have ignored the commands of God and the Prophet'.[33]

Bacha Khan's respect for women sourced from his close attachment to his mother. He valued his mother's views and never liked the concept of *purdah* in his society, which meant 'isolation of women from men'. His mother also had high expectations and trust in him. She would say, 'he is a strong man…and he will be Badshah, a king.'[34] And he proved to be the king of non-violent resistance in the Subcontinent's northwestern region. However, seeing today's political situation both at the Afghanistan–Pakistan frontier and the region, his efforts to promote the philosophy of non-violence, the education of women, and women's involvement in efforts for justice appear to have been overshadowed by forces of radicalisation and Islamisation triggered by regional and international geopolitics.

It is imperative that to counter the challenge of radicalisation through education, as well as to bridge the gender divide in education, interventions must draw on the history and legacy of figures such as Bacha Khan who envisioned non-violence as a means of social and political change. Unfortunately, his legacy has been either forgotten and/or has been deliberately suppressed in contemporary narratives. To not repeat the mistakes of the past and have a brighter future, work in rehabilitating the history of non-violence in the educational, social, and political discourse of Afghanistan is seminal. Such interventions will be sustainable, socio-culturally hard to challenge and help in the long run to build societies based on values of tolerance and equity.

The political scientists divide non-violent resistance into three kinds: Hindu pacifism, Christian pacifism, and secular pacifism.[25] But Bacha Khan based his idea of non-violence action on Islam. Given Afghanistan's socio-political context, the country is not yet ready to adopt a secular form of non-violent protest. Instead, a practice closer to the local realities needs to be applied to achieve the expected results. For this reason, Bacha Khan's work and experiences that could be called Islamic pacifism will be successful if incorporated in the curriculum since it matches the local context, language, religion, and the culture of the country. Students should be taught that social and political change can also happen by non-violent means as Bacha Khan wrote about. Particularly, Bacha Khan's ways of dealing with non-Muslims, raising social awareness on the importance of education for all, especially for women, and of encouraging people to avoid negative cultural practices and work for the betterment of their community voluntarily, need to be passed on to future generations.

However, the task at hand is excruciatingly challenging given the Taliban's intention to mould the educational curriculum in line with their political worldview. This is seen for instance, among other things, in the disparaging statements made about the secular education by the Taliban minister of education, as also in their opening of a suicide bombing museum.[36] It will rear a generation committed to violence. Public education curriculum offers to the Taliban a potent tool to brainwash and control younger generations for their political agenda. Thus, while banning women from access to education is a matter of grave concern and needs to be challenged, what is equally if not more alarming are changes being made to the education curriculum as it will have reverberations well beyond Afghanistan. As Gandhi said, 'If we are going to bring about peace in the world, we have to begin with the children.'[37] Thus, the right to education, not physical presence in schools but provision of quality education to enable a competent and peaceful individual, can play a key role in building children's personalities to avoid violent and discriminatory behaviour.

A useful starting point in this context is provided by the strategies adopted by the Pashtun *Tahafuz* Movement (PTM),[38] which has emerged as the only force that is able to challenge the Taliban effectively on its own turf in the frontier region through non-violent mass mobilisation. It is worth mentioning that the PTM has gone a step further, and under very challenging circumstances, by mobilising people in the tribal areas. Receptivity for interventions along these lines exists at the grassroots level in Afghanistan. This can be gauged from the work being done specifically in the field of education by activists such as Matiullah Wessa through his organisation, Pen Path, which remains steadfastly committed to propagating girls' education through grassroots mobilisation.[39]

## Conclusion

Education can serve as a powerful tool to work towards establishing a society that is based on the principles of social justice and equity, which is key to realising sustainable peace. To achieve this end, it is imperative that the education system be protected from political manipulation for it to be able to inculcate among the younger generations social values and morals that contribute towards peace and inclusivity.

Unfortunately, in Afghanistan, regimes of various political hues have used education to fulfill their ideological and geo-political agendas and those of their foreign patrons. In this context, it is worth drawing particular attention to the fact that while the Taliban's decision to deny women access to education is deplorable, what is even more concerning is the concerted attempt to re-engineer the curriculum to reflect their regressive and narrow interpretation of Islam. The active and passive resistance against these attempts being led by women needs to be supported. The ramifications of this attempt at social re-engineering through education will be felt beyond the borders of Afghanistan. The voices of Afghan women, as well as religious scholars and grassroots activists resisting such attempts, need to be adequately and effectively amplified.

The socio-cultural milieu of the region offers sufficient socio-cultural capital to effectively challenge the discourse of the Taliban on religious and cultural grounds and produce legitimate counter-narratives rooted in the philosophy of non-violence. The preaching and practices of figures like Bacha Khan provide an anchor for actions to this end. The strength of his teachings lay in his ability to ground his radical ideas within the framework of Islam and the cultural setting of the region. His advocacy for access to modern education for all, based on values of equity and tolerance, resonates to this day, as seen in the struggle of the likes of Malala Yousafzai and Matiullah Wessa.

The only force in the region that has managed to muster a counter-narrative to the violence whipped up by the Taliban and the excesses of the Pakistan Army has been the PTM, which like Bacha Khan draws on the philosophy of non-violence. The potency of the PTM's message can be gauged from the scale of mass mobilisation it has managed to achieve in the notorious tribal areas of Pakistan, despite an unofficial media ban on covering its activities. It is time for the international community to invest in grassroots movements of such nature. Otherwise, one is likely to see history repeat itself, as the Taliban were raised in madrasas in Pakistan funded predominantly by the Saudis and on a curriculum designed and disseminated earlier by the US. If steps are not taken to intervene in the unfolding situation in Afghanistan, one is likely to see another generation being raised on the same ideology, propagating what they perceive to be traditional values. Thus, the international community must intervene urgently and effectively to challenge the revisionist curriculum being implemented by the Taliban as a means for social and political re-engineering of Afghanistan.

## NOTES

1. Pia Karlsson and Amir Mansory, 'Islamic and Modern Education in Afghanistan—Conflictual or Complementary?', Institute of International Education, Stockholm University, 2002, p. 2.
2. Mehtarkhan Khwajamir, 'History and Problems of Education in Afghanistan', SHS Web of Conferences, Vol. 26, Article No. 01124, 2016, pp. 1–4, at https://www.shs-conferences.org/articles/shsconf/pdf/2016/04/shsconf_erpa2016_01124.pdf.
3. Saif R. Samady, 'Modern Education in Afghanistan', *Prospects*, Vol. XXXI, No. 4, December 2001, p. 589.
4. Inger W. Boesen, 'Ten Years of War and Civil War in Afghanistan—An Educational Catastrophe for an Entire Generation', Danish Refugee Council, Copenhagen, 1988, p. 4.
5. Saif R. Samady, no. 3, p. 592.
6. Hanif Yazdi, 'Education and Literacy in Afghanistan: Lessons of History and Prospects for Change', *The Monitor*, Vol. 14, Issue 1, Fall 2008, p. 43.
7. Saif R. Samady, no. 3, p. 592.
8. Yusuf Elmi (ed.), *Afghanistan: A Decade of Sovietisation*, Afghan Jehad Works Translation Centre, Peshawar, 1988, p. 65.
9. Olivier Roy, 'The Sovietization of Afghanistan', in Milan Hauner and Robert L. Canfield (eds.), *Afghanistan and the Soviet Union: Collision and Transformation*, Westview Press, San Francisco, 1989, p. 48.
10. Ibid, p. 54.
11. Saif R. Samady, no. 3, p. 601.
12. Sayd Bahaouddin Majrooh, 'Education in Afghanistan: Past and Present—A Problem for the Future', *Central Asian Survey*, Vol. 6, Issue 3, 1987, p. 114.
13. Joe Stephens and David B. Ottaway, 'From U.S., the ABC's of Jihad', *The Washington Post*, 23 March 2002, at https://www.washingtonpost.com/archive/ politics/2002/03/23/from-us-the-abcs-of-jihad/d079075a-3ed3-4030-9a96-0d48f63 55e54/.
14. Pia Karlsson and Amir Mansory, no. 1, p. 13.
15. Jared Israel, 'Bush & the Media Cover up the Jihad Schoolbook Scandal', Global Issues, 9 April 2002, at https://www.globalissues.org/article/431/bush--the-media-cover-up-the-jihad-schoolbook-scandal.
16. Joe Stephens and David B. Ottaway, no. 13.
17. Pia Karlsson and Amir Mansory, no.1, p. 15.
18. 'UNESCO Dedicates the 2023 International Day of Education to Afghan Girls and Women', United Nations Educational, Scientific and Cultural Organization (UNESCO), 19 January 2023, at https://www.unesco.org/en/articles/unesco-dedicates-2023-inter national-day-education-afghan-girls-and-women#:~:text=Audrey%20Azoulay%2C%20 Director%2Dgeneral%20of,their%20fundamental%20right%20to%20education.

19. Sirajuddin Haqqani, 'What We, the Taliban, Want',*The New York Times*, 20 February 2020, at https://www.nytimes.com/2020/02/20/opinion/taliban-afghanistan -war-haqqani.html.
20. Laiq Zirack, 'Women's Education: Afghanistan's Biggest Success Story Now at Risk', *The Diplomat*, 1 September 2021, at https://thediplomat.com/2021/09/wo mens-education-afghanistans-biggest-success-story-now-at-risk/.
21. United Nations Human Rights Office of the High Commissioner, 'Commission Afghanistan: Repressive Law Must be Immediately Repealed', 27 August 2024, at https://www.ohchr.org/en/press-briefing-notes/2024/08/afghanistan-repressive-law-must-be-immediately-repealed.
22. Mariam Safi and Ayesha Khan, 'New morality law in Afghanistan is not just silencing women's voices: it's gender apartheid', ODI, 11 October 2024, at https://odi.org/en/insights/new-morality-law-in-afghanistan-is-not-just-silencing-womens-voices-its-gende r-apartheid/?form=MG0AV3.
23. Bilquees Daud 'Pashto *Landay*: A Mirror of Folk Life', *IIC Quarterly*, Vol. 44, No. 2, Autumn 2017.
24. Natiq Malikzada, Twitter (now X), 14 January 2023, 4:29 PM, at https://twitter.com/natiqmalikzada/status/1614215563672453121.
25. Atal Ahmadzai, 'Why the Taliban Still Love Suicide Bombing', *Foreign Policy*, 7 December 2021, at https://foreignpolicy.com/2021/12/07/taliban-suicide-bombing-parade-violence-afghanistan/.
26. Haseeb Bahesh, 'Exclusive: Taliban Modify Education Curriculum to Propagate Violence and Bigotry', *Hasht-e Subh*, 17 December 2022, at https://8am.media/ eng/exclusive-taliban-modify-education-curriculum-to-propagate-violence-and-big otry/.
27. D.G. Tendulkar, *Abdul Ghaffar Khan: Faith is a Battle*, Gandhi Peace Foundation, Popular Prakashan, Bombay, 1967, p. 295.
28. Mukulika Banerjee, *The Pathan Unarmed: Opposition and Memory in the North West Frontier*, Oxford University Press, Bangalore, 2000, p. 148.
29. Mukulika Banerjee, 'Justice and Non-Violent Jihād: The Anti-Colonial Struggle in the North West Frontier of British India', *Études Rurales*, EHESS, No.149/150, January–June 1999, p. 192.
30. Eknath Easwaran, *A Man to Match His Mountains: Badshah Khan, Nonviolent Soldier of Islam*, Nilgiri Press, New York, 1985, p. 196.
31. Mukulika Banerjee, *The Pathan Unarmed: Opposition and Memory in the North West Frontier*, Oxford University Press, Bangalore, 2000, p. 146.
32. Eknath Easwaran, no. 30, p. 82.
33. Rajmohan Gandhi, *Ghaffar Khan: Nonviolent Badshah of Pakhtuns*. Penguin Books, Delhi, 2004, p. 104.
34. Eknath Easwaran, no. 30, p. 42.
35. Gene Sharp, 'The Meanings of Non-Violence: A Typology (Revised)', *The Journal of Conflict Resolution*, Vol. 3, No.1, March 1959, p. 43.
36. Natiq Malikzada, no. 24.
37. Ashley J. Ward, 'Developing a Culture of Peace and Non-Violence Through Education', Bombay Sarvodaya Mandal & Gandhi Research Foundation, at http://www.mkgandhi.org/articles/peace4.htm.

38. PTM is a non-violent movement in the Khyber Pakhtunkhwa Province of Pakistan aiming to provide justice for the Pashtuns. It demands 'basic human rights' for Pashtuns and 'seeks an end to the atrocities of the armed forces against the Pashtuns in the name of security, extrajudicial killings, enforced disappearances, and policies such as "good Taliban and bad Taliban". It also demands the removal of military checkpoints and the establishment of a truth and reconciliation commission…to investigate extrajudicial killings, land mines in former federally administered tribal areas region and enforced disappearances.' See 'Manzoor Pashteen's Arrest: The Pakistani Military Establishment's Vile Attempt at Regaining Lost Face May Backfire', EFSAS Commentary, 31 January 2020, at https://www.efsas.org/ com mentaries/manzoor-pashteen-arrest-the-pakistani-military-establishment-vile-attem pt-at-regaining-lost-face/.
39. 'Activist Matiullah Wesa Calls to Reopen Girls' Schools', *TOLOnews*, 11 April 2022, at https://tolonews.com/afghanistan-177527.

# 12

# Taliban Regime and Afghan Opium Industry

*Shreyas Deshmukh*

In April 2022, six months after regaining power in Afghanistan, Taliban Chief Hibatullah Akhundzada declared a nationwide ban on poppy opium cultivation. It was stipulated that the violation of the decree will result in crop destruction and punishment under Sharia law.[1] In March 2023, the Taliban issued another edict prohibiting cannabis cultivation.[2]

The Taliban had a similar policy during their previous reign. In the last two decades, the Taliban, while acting as an insurgent force, concurrently administered a shadow government by appointing shadow governors in the provinces they controlled and endorsed opium production. It constituted a primary revenue stream for sustaining the insurgency.

The combination of Afghanistan's weak economic foundation and persistent political instability enabled flourishing of narcotics trafficking, thus establishing its reputation as a narco-state. Over time, it became a critical component of the nation's revenue generation. This ecosystem comprised multinational groups involved in narcotics and arms trafficking, as well as other organised crime syndicates with the capacity to exert influence over the state apparatus. Nevertheless, numerous states and international entities have committed resources to counternarcotics initiatives within Afghanistan for an extended period. The ramifications of the Taliban's policy decision on this matter will affect all stakeholders, the future trajectory of Afghanistan, and regional stability. Assessing the ramifications of the Taliban's return for Afghanistan's opium-based ecosystem is of paramount importance.

## Background

The Soviet invasion of 1979 precipitated a correlation between opium production in Afghanistan and persistent instability, resulting in heightened poverty and a governance deficit. This process resulted in the shift of opium and cannabis production from Pakistan and Iran to Afghanistan.[3]

Decades of attempt to eradicate narcotics cultivation in Afghanistan have been hindered by insecurity, economic instability, and a lack of political resolve. Afghan opium and heroin steadily increased their market share over the last four decades, accounting for 80 per cent of global demand in 2022,[4] which highlighted the growing strength of drug traffickers. With the emergence of new supply routes and markets, traffickers adapted to the changing conditions by improving the quality of their products. They transitioned from raw opium and cannabis to processed morphine-based substances with varying purity levels, which facilitated easier smuggling and higher profit margins.

The number of opioids increased twofold between 2010 and 2019, particularly in South and South West Asia.[5] For the suppliers, these are the closest geographical areas with low risk. The Arabian Sea and Indian Ocean serve as routes for larger shipments to Africa, Southeast Asia, and Europe. The Balkan route has become a popular choice for shipments bound for Eastern Europe. According to the UNODC, 42 per cent of opiate that exited Afghanistan transits through Pakistan while Iran has reported that 90 per cent of morphine and 85 per cent of heroin seized in its territory in 2018 had been trafficked via Pakistan, and very small percentage smuggled directly from Afghanistan.[6] The trafficking of most narcotics produced in Afghanistan is controlled by well-connected traffickers from Iran and Pakistan, who have operated in the shadows for decades and reap the majority of profits.

As a result, opiate seizures around Afghanistan increased in 2021, with the exception of Pakistan, which also suffers from governance deficit (see Map 1).

The map illustrates the correlation between the high level of opiate addiction in Iran and the large number of seizures, as well as the country's role as a major route for narcotic traders to smuggle their products to Eastern Europe. Central Asian neighbours of Afghanistan foresaw more violence and instability in the region following the 2020 Doha agreement and took measures to deal with such contingencies. Northern drug smuggling networks were disrupted due to the additional protective security measures and strengthened border security in Tajikistan, Uzbekistan, and Turkmenistan.[7] In South Asia, India witnessed a sharp rise in heroin seizures in 2021

**Map 1: Opiate Seizures Around Afghanistan since August 2021**

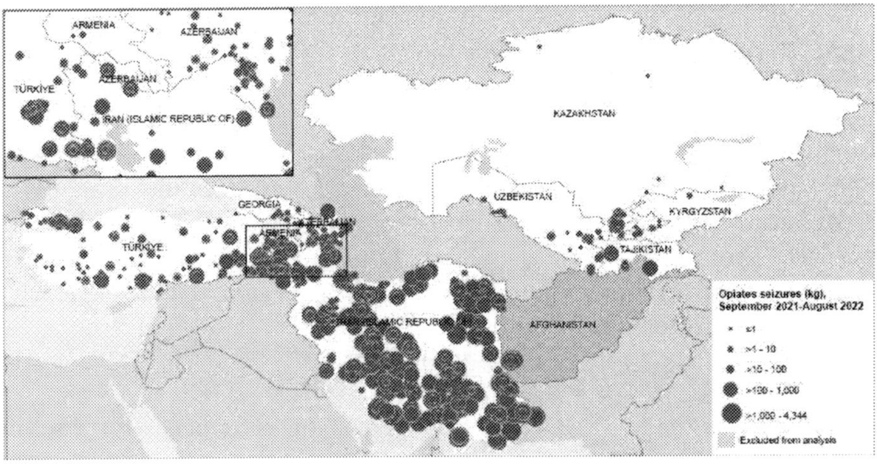


*The boundaries and names shown and the designations used on this map do not imply official endorsement or acceptance by the United Nations. Dotted line represents approximately the Line of Control in Jammu and Kashmir agreed upon by India and Pakistan.*

*Source:* 'Opium Cultivation in Afghanistan: Latest Findings and Emerging Threats', UNODC, November 2022, p. 8, at https://www.unodc.org/documents/crop-monitoring/Afghanistan/Opium_cultivation_Afghanistan_2022.pdf (Accessed 3 February 2023).

immediately after the Taliban takeover of Afghanistan but subsequently it reduced over the years (see Graph 1 below).

**Graph 1: Heroin Seizures in India from 1998 to 2023**

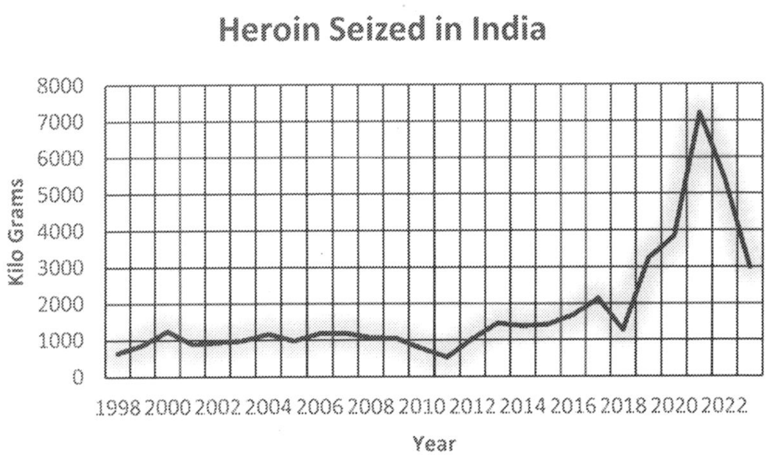


*Source*: Annual Report of the Narcotics Control Bureau of India, at https://narcoordindia.in/periodicals.php (Accessed 2 February 2023).

The majority of these potent psychoactive substances such as heroin and methamphetamine that emerged in the market in 2021–22 were manufactured under the previous Afghan administration. In expectation of the Taliban's counternarcotics policies, such substances were hastily moved out of Afghanistan. Moreover, the Afghan opium market's competitiveness and its geographical location as the "heart of Asia" have made entering and exiting relatively easy.[8] The involvement of political actors in the drug trade strengthened the supply chain during the last two decades.[9] The 2018 report by the US Special Inspector General for Afghanistan Reconstruction (SIGAR) revealed that no counter-drug efforts in Afghanistan achieved lasting results in reducing poppy cultivation or opium production.[10]

**Afghanistan as a Narco-state and Taliban Insurgency**

Data from multiple UNODC reports demonstrates a persistent rise in Afghanistan's overall opium production, excluding the period of first Taliban rule in the late 1990s when the Taliban demonstrated their determination to enforce counter-narcotics policies. The ban on opium by the Taliban in August 1997 and 1999, as mentioned in the US State Department reports, had resulted in a one-third decrease in poppy farming in Afghanistan.[11] The UNODC report also noted a significant decrease in opium poppy cultivation from 82,000 hectares in 2000 to just 8,000 in 2001.[12]

As per the UN Security Council (UNSC) report of March 1999, the Taliban had destroyed about 34 heroin-processing labs in Nangarhar Province following a decree by Mullah Omar.[13] The UN officers conducted surveys in southern and eastern provinces, even during such a tumultuous period.[14] The UNSC reports of 1999 and 2000 suggest that the Taliban were sincere about their counter-narcotics efforts, but the documents do not point to the ability of the regime to regulate the policies in the longer term.

The Taliban's early achievements were ultimately undermined by their deficient human rights record, rigid religious policies, lack of economic expertise, and tolerance of extremism, all of which hindered efforts to reduce opium poppy cultivation in Afghanistan. Thus, the policy was short-lived as the US ousted the Taliban regime in late 2001 after the 9/11 attacks. The continued instability in Afghanistan in the aftermath led to an increase in narcotic production and trafficking.

In the wake of the 2014 departure of most of the coalition troops from Afghanistan, the Taliban—dominant in the south and southwest—expanded their offensive into the eastern and northern provinces.[15] Increased violence in these previously stable and opium-free provinces led to a significant rise in poppy cultivation.[16] A correlation existed between the Taliban's control and the rise in opium production in these areas; it remains unclear whether the former caused the latter or vice versa. Reports suggest that the Taliban provided support to the drug traffickers and also offered convoy protection against the Afghan National Security Forces (ANSF).[17] The sustained increase in poppy cultivation after 2001 also questioned the seriousness of the ANSF, Counter-narcotics Police of Afghanistan, and coalition forces in eradicating it.[18]

The Taliban's approach to narcotics is paradoxical, considering their dual role as insurgents and governing authority in parts of the country. The discrepancy underscored the debate on the Taliban's reliance on revenue derived from opium and affiliated businesses. The conclusions of the UNODC reports are contested by the extensive research of Barnett Rubin and David Mansfield, American political scientists with expertise in Afghanistan, who have focused on the impact of opium poppy cultivation on rural Afghan communities. They presented empirical evidence, which strongly suggests that the Taliban did not primarily rely on opium for income.[19] Despite the author's inability to reach a definitive conclusion, a comparative analysis of these divergent perspectives reveals Taliban's involvement in the narcotics trade.

(a) The Taliban insurgency aggravated insecurity, thus providing a favourable climate for manufacturing and processing of narcotics.
(b) Afghanistan's opium production was increasing sufficiently to satisfy the global demand.
(c) A significant number of powerful entities from diverse governing structures were complicit in and profited from this undertaking.
(d) The opium industry in Afghanistan had a decentralised nature, involving multiple stakeholders.
(e) Afghan farmers' cultivation of opium poppies was motivated by economic hardship, not profit-seeking.

The insecurity fuelled by the Taliban's insurgency trapped Afghanistan in a loop where the country was likely to 'remain insecure, politically fragmented, weakly governed, poor, dominated by the informal or illicit economy, and a hostage to the drug industry'.[20] The steady rise in opium production particularly in areas under the control of the Taliban in the past, such as the Helmand Province, proved the point (see Graph 2 below).

**Graph 2: Opium Poppy Cultivation in Helmand Province, 2006–2022**

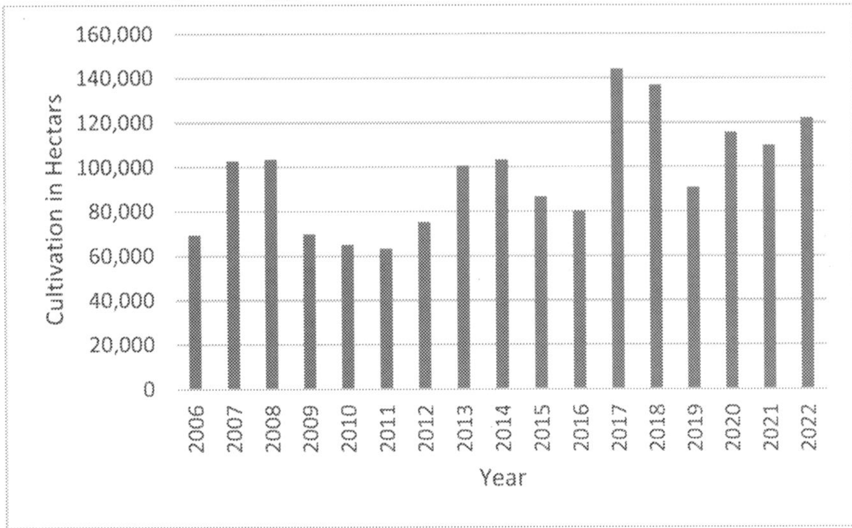


*Source:* 'Opium Cultivation in Afghanistan: Latest Findings and Emerging Threats', UNODC, November 2022; 'Afghanistan Opium Survey 2019', UNODC, February 2021.

After Taliban's return to power in August 2021, a significant reduction in poppy cultivation occurred in southern states, specifically Helmand, from 67.3 per cent of the national average in 2021 to 0.4 per cent in 2023.[21] The northeastern provinces, particularly Badakhshan, became the primary location for poppy cultivation, replacing the southwestern provinces.[22] Taliban forces encountered resistance from local farmers during clashes that ensued following attempts to eliminate opium cultivation.[23] In 2024, cultivated acreage expanded by an estimated 19 per cent year-on-year, reaching 12,800 hectares, following a 95 per cent decrease in the 2023 growing season.[24] Despite this, opium production in 2024 exhibited a 93 per cent reduction from 232,000 hectares recorded in 2022 before the ban.[25] This demonstrates the Taliban's capacity for legal enforcement. In November 2024, the Taliban announced the formation of the High Commission on Anti-Narcotics.[26] The Taliban's counter-narcotics strategy remains unclear; however, their primary approach involves a two-pronged tactic of enforcing a poppy cultivation ban and offering substitute crops.[27] This policy is primarily motivated by the enforcement of ideology, bringing economic stability and the eradication of competing power structures.

## Opium Economy under Taliban Rule

The opium economy has played a crucial role in Afghanistan's national revenue for many years.[28] The UNODC estimates that the opiate economy accounted for 7 to 11 per cent of the country's GDP in 2021.[29] More than 10 per cent of the Afghan population depends on the opium economy. Additionally, local businesses like real estate rely on the financial liquidity from the illegal drug trade.

In the wake of the 2021 Taliban takeover, a significant increase in opium sales by Afghan farmers occurred, with a 32 per cent rise generating US$ 1.4 billion for farmers in 2022.[30] Zabihullah Mujahid, the Taliban spokesperson, declared at a press conference two days after the Taliban seized Kabul that the "Islamic Emirate" would put an end to the drug trade.[31] In April 2022, Taliban chief Akhundzada announced the ban on the cultivation of poppy.[32]

The regime had warned the farmers eight months prior to implementing the ban[33] and also provided a two-month grace period for harvesting the standing opium crop to reduce the losses of farmers.[34] The ban demonstrably led to a sharp decline in poppy cultivation and a rise in the cost of narcotics internationally, as evidenced by reports from independent analysts like David Mansfield[35] and the United Nations.[36] Despite an increase in income, farmers' purchasing power remained unchanged as inflation rose from 4.2 per cent in 2021 to 17.9 per cent in 2022.[37] The inflation reduced after the initial phase of uncertainty. In July 2023, World Bank reported that the year-on-year inflation had been negative in May and June.[38] The same report further provides a reason for declining inflation, which is, 'over 50 per cent of Afghan households struggle to maintain their livelihoods and consumption,' as they lost the purchasing power due to lack of income.[39]

Despite farmer compliance with the ban,[40] it was clear that incentives for opium cultivation have risen due to increased political, social, and economic vulnerability. Severe food insecurity affects roughly half the Afghan population, with 30 million people urgently requiring humanitarian aid.[41] The absence of alternative income sources has resulted in acute food insecurity for 20 million citizens, with 2.7 million facing famine, according to the International Federation of Red Cross and Red Crescent Societies. Since 2020, the sustained drought has intensified the crisis affecting the entire country.[42] Given its drought resistance, established market, and high yields, poppy cultivation may remain the optimal choice.[43] High-value crops like pomegranates, almonds, pistachios, and asafoetida require extended periods of growth to reach maturity. Drastic reduction in Opium cultivation will reduce the supply of opium and export quality heroin in the near future.[44] This was confirmed by both the US State Department and UNAMA reports, but the reports also acknowledged the ongoing trafficking and sale of processed opiates and synthetic drugs from Afghanistan.[45] The drug traffickers rely on strategic reserves[46] to sustain their operations.[47]

## Social Factors

For centuries, Afghan people have derived a sense of collective security from their tribal identity. The recent wars in Afghanistan have weakened the country's social fabric, resulting in the rise of terrorist groups and drug lords.[48] During his tenure, former Urozgan Governor Jaan Muhammad Khan, a member of the Durrani tribe, manipulated the preceding administration's poppy eradication programme to stifle competition from the Ghilzai tribe and perpetuate inflated prices.[49] Some mujahidin leaders during the Afghan civil war, such as Gulbuddin Hekmatyar of Hizb-e-Islami, depended on illegal profits from opium and heroin smuggling, with the support of Pakistan's Inter Service Intelligence (ISI).[50]

The Taliban's rise to power means that individuals who control agricultural lands might have to pay protection money for a portion of their earnings. In certain regions, the Taliban overcame their traditional foes from the former northern alliance and gained dominance over opium/heroin production sites in northern provinces.

The transborder opiate trafficking is structured along ethnic lines, primarily engaging Pashtun and Baluch populations inhabiting regions adjacent to the eastern and western frontiers. This is significant due to the preponderance of Afghan narcotics trafficked through Iran and Pakistan.[51] Within the Loya Paktia region, which is situated on the border with Pakistan, the Haqqani network had established a considerable presence and is actively involved in narcotics trafficking and heroin production.[52] Though smaller in scale than the Kandahari Taliban faction, the operation provided significant financial resources to the Haqqani network.[53] The decision by the Taliban in April 2022 to ban poppy cultivation demonstrated the Kandahari faction's strategic effort to consolidate power via the regulation or eradication of the decentralised opium trade. Intentions behind the policy could sow division within the ranks of the Taliban. Acting Interior Minister Sirajuddin Haqqani, who is also the head of the Haqqani Network, was found criticising Akhudzada for monopolising power.[54] Previously, the Taliban helped smuggle opium and collected taxes on it.[55] The exact figure of their yearly revenue is not available, but it could be in the range of US$ 100 to 400 million.[56] Thus, the policy contradiction is due to the economic requirement versus ideological compulsion.

**Reality vs. Compulsion**

The Taliban, driven by their ideology, confront complex dilemmas in their pursuit of Sharia implementation, disregarding present-day political and economic realities. One such challenge involves the control of poppy cultivation.

International organisations and the previous regime viewed opium production as a socio-economic problem, leading to the adoption of counter narcotics policies similar to those used in South America and East Asia. However, the Taliban's engagement with drug cultivation and use is underpinned by religious and ideological factors. The Taliban's actions are driven by religiously motivated insurgency, or the governance of an emirate pursuing a utopian vision. Shia and Sunni schools of Islamic jurisprudence provide ample justification for a ban on narcotics.[57] Thus *Amir-ul-Mu'minin*, a title held by both Mullah Omar and subsequently Hibatullah Akhundzada, issued an edict prohibiting the production and consumption of narcotics, emphasising the policy's religious foundation in Sharia law.

In the view of the "Islamic Emirate," a ban on drugs is essential to address the significant societal challenges stemming from drug addiction within Afghanistan. The goal is to redirect societal progress, eradicate Western cultural effects, and establish a truly Islamic society. In essence, the Taliban's efforts focus on rehabilitating drug users and apprehending those involved in smaller drug smuggling operations in Afghanistan.[58]

A long-term approach is necessary for drug eradication, hinging on political stability and security as the key to success. There seems to be little attention given by the international community to a counter-narcotics strategy bearing in mind the scenario of the return of the Taliban regime.[59] The strict application of Sharia law under the Taliban has rendered the continued functioning of international organizations increasingly problematic.[60] Stringent limitations on women's rights, coupled with an anti-democratic agenda and the Taliban regime's tolerance of extremism, have engendered considerable international concern about Taliban's future.[61] The Taliban's strict adherence to their interpretation of Islamic law hinders the acceptance of direct international aid subject to external oversight and conditions. The Taliban are obligated to grant access, ensure the safety of surveyors, and transparently share financial transaction data with oversight bodies, including the UNODC and FATF, for anti-money laundering purposes. Transparent and accountable governance is fundamental for receiving international aid. The former Taliban regime was more amenable to addressing this issue. The Taliban today are pursuing international engagement, seeking aid, recognition, and investment predicated on the acceptance of their terms.

In contrast, the Taliban's insurgent activities against the Western coalition were financed for twenty years via the narcotics trade. Their financial support, like that of other terrorist organisations, stemmed from both legitimate trade taxation and illegitimate mining endeavors. The essential function of any politically driven organisation is the acquisition and retention of territorial control for political ends. However, this outcome is contingent upon the cessation of resident distress. This funding model's long-term viability is compromised by its erosive effect on relationships with those it governs. Therefore, the Taliban regime may be diversifying its revenue streams, transitioning from those previously utilized by insurgent factions or pursuing economic integration. Hence the Taliban are focusing more on exploiting natural resources such as inviting regional countries to invest in strategic minerals and also using its geographical position at the heart of Asia to assimilate emerging new international trade corridors such as North–South Transport Corridor. A significant obstacle to this strategy is its southern neighbour, Pakistan.

### A Coercive Neighbour

Pakistan, a crucial transit point for Afghan goods and a major importer to Afghanistan, is experiencing economic difficulties stemming from its long-standing unsustainable policies.[62] The Durand Line's contested status, combined with their abusive treatment of Afghan nationals, led to recurrent clashes and border closures between two countries. Pakistan's newly established border policy is having a negative impact on legal trade[63] and resulting in a scarcity of essential goods in Afghanistan.[64] Drug smugglers may take advantage of this security and economic volatility to relocate drug production to Pakistan's border areas.

Thus, the lack of other resources could impede the Taliban's ability to confiscate means of sustenance and cultivate lasting opposition in the short term. While the Taliban might frame their drug trade profits as addressing the populace's necessities, their actual utilisation of the funds remains a separate matter. The temporary ban on poppy cultivation has yielded higher farmgate prices, thereby benefiting farmers. Given past experiences, the Taliban may recognize that the forceful eradication of poppy cultivation, without providing a viable alternative, will likely lead to increased cultivation nationwide.

### Conclusion

Afghanistan's increased opium production is historically linked to three key factors: instability, poverty, and a governance deficit. These factors continue to be relevant under the Taliban rule. This indicates a potential rise in opium poppy production in future. The regional surge in opioid use has shifted the focus of the narcotics trade from international to regional. The Taliban intend to consolidate their authority by prohibiting poppy cultivation and eliminating the influence of entrenched narcotics traffickers.

The Taliban's extensive control of industry provides leverage in their negotiations for international recognition and increased humanitarian assistance. Should this prove unsuccessful, the Taliban's governance may become dependent on revenue generated from the narcotics trade. Despite the regime change, prior Afghanistan-focused counter-narcotics strategies may retain relevance, given the potential for a comparable approach by the Taliban. The methodology is structured across three phases: interdiction, eradication, and the development of alternative income sources. These strategies proved unsuccessful due to the impact of poverty, political instability, escalating violence, and an extended timeframe for achieving desired outcomes. Prior successes in other countries with similar strategies can be attributed to optimised sequencing, appropriate resource allocation, and a secure operational environment. Despite establishing a degree of security, the Taliban regime lacks the requisite political, economic, and moral capacity for sustainable suppression of narcotics production.

## NOTES

1. 'Decree of Amir al-Momenin Regarding Prohibition of Poppy Cultivation in the Country', Alemarah English, 3 April 2022, at https://www.alemarahenglish.af/decree-of-amir-al-momenin-regarding-prohibition-of-Poppy-cultivation-and-any-intoxicants/ (Accessed 6 February 2023).
2. 'Taliban Ban Cannabis Cultivation Across Afghanistan', *The Express Tribune*, 19 March 2023, at https://tribune.com.pk/story/2406985/taliban-ban-cannabis-cultivation-across-afghanistan (Accessed 25 August 2023)
3. Christopher Ward and William A. Byrd, 'Afghanistan's Opium Drug Economy', The World Bank, December 2004, p. 42, at https://documents1.worldbank.org/curated/en/158651468767124612/pdf/311490PAPER0AF100SASPR0no051Dec0171.pdf (Accessed 6 February 2023).
4. 'Opium Cultivation in Afghanistan: Latest Findings and Emerging Threats', UNODC, November 2022, p. 3, at https://www.unodc.org/documents/crop-monitoring/Afghanistan/Opium_cultivation_Afghanistan_2022.pdf (Accessed 3 February 2023).
5. 'Drug Markets Trends: Cannabis Opioids', *World Drug Report 2021*, United Nations Office on Drugs and Crime (UNODC), June 2021, p. 66, at https://www.unodc.org/unodc/en/data-and-analysis/wdr-2021_booklet-3.html (Accessed 4 February 2023).
6. 'Statement of James Soiles, Deputy Chief of Operations, Drug Enforcement Administration U.S. Department of Justice Before the Subcommittees of Middle East and North Africa, and Asia and Pacific Committee on Foreign Affairs', U.S. House of Representatives, for a hearing entitled After Withdrawal: The Way Forward in Afghanistan and Pakistan (part iii), 10 December 2014, at https://www.dea.gov/sites/

default/files/pr/speeches-testimony/2014t/121014t.pdf (Accessed 1 September 2023); 'UNODC World Drug Report 2021, Drug Markets Trends: Cannabis Opioids, Volume 3', United Nations Office for Drug Control and Crime Prevention, p. 93, at https://www.unodc.org/unodc/en/data-and-analysis/wdr-2021_booklet-3.html (Accessed 1 September 2023); 'Pakistan and Narco-Trafficking a Protracted Global Challenge', *PRF Report*, 15 August 2023, at https://prfworld.org/pakistan-and-narco-trafficking-a-protracted-global-challenge/ (Accessed 1 September 2023)

7. Gavin Helf and Barmak Pazhwak, 'Central Asia Prepares for Taliban Takeover', Unites States Institute of Peace, 20 July 2021, at https://www.usip.org/publications/2021/07/central-asia-prepares-taliban-takeover (Accessed 2 February 2023).
8. UNODC, no. 4, p. 31.
9. Dexter Filkins, 'Despite Doubt, Karzai Brother Retains Power', *The New York Times*, 30 March 2010, at https://www.nytimes.com/2010/03/31/world/asia/31karzai.html (Accessed 10 February 2023).
10. 'Counter Narcotics: Lessons from the U.S. Experience in Afghanistan', Office of the Special Inspector for Afghanistan Reconstruction (SIGAR), United States Government, June 2018, p. 3, at https://www.sigar.mil/pdf/lessonslearned/SIGAR-18-52-LL.pdf (Accessed 6 February 2023).
11. 'The Taliban and the Afghan Drug Trade', The Bureau of South Asian Affairs U.S. Department of State, at https://1997-2001.state.gov/www/regions/sa/facts_taliban_drugs.html (Accessed 31 August 2023).
12. 'Afghanistan Opium Survey 2019', UNODC, February 2021, p. 7, at https://www.unodc.org/documents/crop-monitoring/Afghanistan/20210217_report_with_ cover_for_web_small.pdf (Accessed 6 February 2023).
13. Report of the Secretary General, 'The Situation in Afghanistan and its Implications for International Peace and Security', United Nations, 53rd Session, Agenda Item 45, 21 June 1999, at https://unama.unmissions.org/sites/default/files/21%20June%201999.pdf (Accessed 31 August 2023).
14. Report of the Secretary General, 'The Situation in Afghanistan and its Implications for International Peace and Security', United Nations, 53 Session, Agenda Item 45, 31 March 1999, at https://unama.unmissions.org/sites/default/files/31%20March%201999.pdf (Accessed 31 August 2023).
15. Bill Roggio, 'Mapping Taliban Control in Afghanistan', *Long War Journal*, at https://www.longwarjournal.org/mapping-taliban-control-in-afghanistan (Accessed 3 February 2023).
16. 'Afghanistan Opium Survey 2017: Cultivation and Production', UNODC, November 2017, p. 5, at https://www.unodc.org/documents/crop-monitoring/Afghanistan/Afghan_opium_survey_2017_cult_prod_web.pdf (Accessed 2 February 2023).
17. Gretchen Peters, 'How Opium Profits the Taliban', United States Institute of Peace, August 2009, p. 20, at https://www.usip.org/publications/2009/08/how-opium-profits-taliban (Accessed 8 February 2023).
18. 'Counternarcotics Police of Afghanistan: U.S. Assistance to Provincial Units Cannot Be Fully Tracked and Formal Capability Assessments Are Needed', SIGAR, October 2014, at https://www.sigar.mil/pdf/audits/sigar-audit-15-12.pdf (Accessed 1 September 2023); Rober M. Perito, 'Afghanistan's Police the Weak Link in Security Sector Reform', United State Institute of Peace, Special Report 227, August 2009, at

https://www.usip.org/sites/default/files/afghanistan_police.pdf (Accessed 1 September 2023).

19. Barnett R. Rubin and Jake Sherman, 'Counter-Narcotics to Stabilize Afghanistan: The False Promise of Crop Eradication', Center on International Cooperation, February 2008, p. 10, at http://cic.es.its.nyu.edu/sites/default/files/counternarcotics final.pdf (Accessed 8 February 2023); David Mansfield, 'A Taxing Narrative: Miscalculating Revenues and Misunderstanding the Conflict in Afghanistan', Afghanistan Research and Evaluation Unit, October 2021, p. VI, at https://areu.org.af/wp-content/uploads/2021/10/2105E-A-Taxing-Narrative-English.pdf/ (Accessed 7 February 2023).
20. Ward and Byrd, no. 3, p. 85.
21. Yogita Limaye, 'Inside the Taliban's War on Drugs - Opium Poppy Crops Slashed', BBC, 6 June 2023, at https://www.bbc.com/news/world-asia-65787391 (Accessed 22 January 2025).
22. 'Afghanistan Drug Insights, Volume 2: 2024 Opium Production and Rural Development', UNODC, November 2024, p. 6, at https://www.unodc.org/documents/crop-monitoring/Afghanistan/Afghanistan_Drug_Insights_V2.pdf (Accessed 22 January 2025).
23. 'Taliban Say Order Restored After Afghan Opium Poppy Protest', *Dawn*, 7 May 2024, at https://www.dawn.com/news/1832068/taliban-say-order-restored-after-afghan-opium-poppy-protests (Accessed 22 January 2025).
24. 'Afghanistan: Opium Cultivation Increased by 19 per cent in Second Year of Drugs Ban, according to UNODC', UNODC, 6 November 2024, at https://www.unodc.org/unodc/en/press/releases/2024/October/afghanistan_-opium-cultivation-increased-by-19-per-cent-in-second-year-of-drugs-ban--according-to-unodc.html (Accessed 22 January 2025).
25. 'Afghanistan: Opium production remains 93 per cent below pre-drug ban levels, says UNODC', UNODC, 27 November 2024, at https://unis.unvienna.org/unis/en/pressrels/2024/unisnar1492.html (Accessed 22 January 2025).
26. 'Draft Procedure for High Commission on Anti-Narcotics Finalized', *Tolo News*, 1 November 2024, at https://tolonews.com/afghanistan-191467 (Accessed 22 January 2025).
27. 'Five-Year Alternative Cultivation Plan Implemented for Afghan Farmers', *Tolo News*, 8 July 2024, at https://tolonews.com/business-189631 (Accessed 22 January 2025).
28. Afghanistan Opium Survey 2019, p.17
29. UNODC, 2021, p. 15.
30. 'Opium Cultivation in Afghanistan: Latest Findings and Emerging Threats', UNODC, November 2022, p. 3, at https://reliefweb.int/report/afghanistan/opium-cultivation-afghanistan-latest-findings-and-emerging-threats (Accessed 3 February 2023).
31. 'Transcript of Taliban's First News Conference in Kabul', *Al Jazeera*, 17 August 2021, at https://www.aljazeera.com/news/2021/8/17/transcript-of-talibans-first-press-conference-in-kabul (Accessed 6 February 2023).
32. 'Decree of Amir al-Momenin Regarding Prohibition of Poppy Cultivation in the Country', no. 1.

33. Ibid. The opium poppy crop planted in the month of November and December in Afghanistan.
34. Ghada Waly, 'UN Security Council Briefing on the Situation in Afghanistan', UNODC, 26 September 2022, at https://www.unodc.org/unodc/en/speeches/2022/unsc-afghanistan-270922.html (Accessed 6 February 2023).
35. David Mansfield, 'Truly Unprecedented: The Taliban Drugs Ban v2.0.', Alcis, 6 June 2023, at https://www.alcis.org/post/taliban-drugs-ban (Accessed 25 August 2023).
36. 'Afghanistan Opium Survey 2023', UNODC, November 2023, p. 3, at https://www.unodc.org/documents/crop-monitoring/Afghanistan/Afghanistan_opium_survey_2023.pdf (Accessed 1 December 2023); Report of the Secretary General, 'The Situation in Afghanistan and its Implications for International Peace and Security', United Nations, 77th Session, Agenda Item 34, 20 June 2023, at https://unama.unmissions.org/sites/default/files/ 230620_sg_report_on_afghanistan_s.2023.453.pdf (Accessed 31 August 2023).
37. Ibid, p. 5.
38. 'Afghanistan Economic Monitor', World Bank, 31 July 2023, at https://thedocs.worldbank.org/en/doc/556f10c93b28f880074208ad43583bf7-0310012023/original / Afghanistan-Economic-Monitor-31-July-2023.pdf (Accessed 31 August 2023).
39. Ibid.
40. Mark Green, 'Opium Poppy Cultivation in Afghanistan Appears to be Declining—At a Cost', Wilson Center, 23 August 2022, at https://www.wilsoncenter.org/blog-post/opium-poppy-cultivation-afghanistan-appears-be-declining-cost (Accessed 4 February 2023).
41. 'WFP Afghanistan: Situation Report, 21 February 2023', United Nations Office for the Coordination of Humanitarian Affairs (UNOCHA), 21 February 2021, at https://reliefweb.int/report/afghanistan/wfp-afghanistan-situation-report-21-february-2023 (Accessed 22 February 2023).
42. 'Afghanistan: Drought 2021-2023', UNOCHA, at https://reliefweb.int/disaster/dr-2021-000022-afg (Accessed 25 August 2023).
43. Christian Parenti, 'Flower of War: An Environmental History of Opium Poppy in Afghanistan', *The SAIS Review of International Affairs*, Vol. 35, No. 1, Winter–Spring 2015, p. 183.
44. UNODC, November 2023, p. 3.
45. Report of the Secretary General, June 2023, and Media Note, 'Meeting of U.S. Official with Taliban Representative', US Department of State, 31 July 2023, at https://www.state.gov/meeting-of-u-s-officials-with-taliban-representatives/ (Accessed 31 August 2023).
46. 'SIGAR Reports over 165,000 tons of opium stockpiled in Afghanistan', *The Khaama Press*, 24 August 2024, at https://www.khaama.com/sigar-reports-over-165000-tons-of-opium-stockpiled-in-afghanistan/ (Accessed 22 January 2025).
47. Malali Bashir, 'Opium Sold Openly in Afghanistan, Despite the Taliban Ban', *Radio Free Europe/ Radio Liberty*, 18 August 2023, at https://www.rferl.org/a/azadi-briefing-taliban-opium-sold-openly-despite-ban/32553913.html (Accessed 4 September 2023).

48. Tilak Devasher, *The Pashtuns: A Contested History*, Harper Collins, Haryana, 2022, p. 42.
49. Anand Gopal, *No Good Men Among the Living; America, the Taliban, and the War through Afghan Eyes*, Metropolitan Books/Henry Holt and Company, New York, 2014, p. 203.
50. Gretchen Peters, no. 17, p. 8.
51. Ward and Byrd, no. 3, p. 41.
52. Gretchen Peters, 'Haqqani Network Financing the Evolution of an Industry', U.S. Military Academy, Combating Terrorism Center at West Point, July 2012, p. i, at https://apps.dtic.mil/sti/pdfs/ADA562872.pdf (Accessed 1 September 2023)
53. Ibid, p. 45.
54. 'Taliban Minister Haqqani's Rare Rebuke of Top Leader Akhundzada Shows Infighting', *Alarabiya News*, 13 February 2023, at https://english.alarabiya.net/News/world/2023/02/13/Taliban-Minister-Haqqani-s-rare-rebuke-of-top-leader-Akhundzada-shows-infighting (Accessed 15 February 2023).
55. Gretchen Peters, no. 17, p. 20.
56. Dawood Azami, 'Afghanistan: How do the Taliban Make Money?', BBC, 28 August 2021, at https://www.bbc.com/news/world-46554097 (Accessed 1 September 2023).
57. K.M. Nejad and S.H. Hashemi, 'Status of Narcotic Drugs in Islamic Jurisprudence and Foundation of Islamic Laws', *Beijing Law Review*, Vol. 9, No. 3, September 2018, pp. 401–424, at https://doi.org/10.4236/blr.2018.93025 (Accessed 2 February 2023).
58. 'Over 20 Thousand Drug Addicts Under Treatment', Alemrah English, 30 May 2022, at https://www.alemarahenglish.af/over-20-thousand-drug-addicts-under-treatment/ (Accessed 1 February 2023).
59. 'UN to Host Talks on Afghan Drug Alternatives', *Tolo News*, 6 September 2024, at https://tolonews.com/afghanistan-190588 (Accessed 22 January 2025).
60. 'Taliban Order Bars Afghan Women From Working with UN', *UN News*, 4 April 2023, at https://news.un.org/en/story/2023/04/1135357 (Accessed 1 September 2023).
61. Report of the Secretary General, 'The Situation in Afghanistan and its Implications for International Peace and Security', United Nations, 77th Session, Agenda Item 34, 20 June 2023, at https://unama.unmissions.org/sites/default/ files/230620_sg_report_on_afghanistan_s.2023.453.pdf (Accessed 31 August 2023).
62. Sophia Saifi and Julia Horowitz, 'Blackouts and Soaring Prices: Pakistan's Economy is on the Brink', *CNN*, 2 February 2023, at https://edition.cnn.com/2023/02/02/economy/pakistan-economy-crisis/index.html (Accessed 4 February 2023).
63. Jibran Ahmad, 'Thousands of Trucks Stuck at Afghan-Pakistan Border Crossing', *Reuters*, 21 February 2023, at https://www.reuters.com/world/asia-pacific/thousands-trucks-stuck-afghan-pakistan-border-crossing-2023-02-21/ (Accessed 23 February 2023).
64. 'Explained: What is Causing Acute Food Insecurity in Afghanistan?', *The Indian Express*, 26 October 2021, at https://indianexpress.com/article/explained/explained-what-is-causing-acute-food-insecurity-in-afghanistan-7590402/ (Accessed 7 February 2023).

# 13

# Afghan Taliban: Sitting Out Global Pressures on Reforms?

*Mahendra Ved*

With the return of the Taliban to power in August 2021, after the United States-led Western forces withdrew, Afghanistan, now called the Islamic Emirate of Afghanistan, is either "liberated" or has again regressed into medieval ages—depending on how one looks at the tumultuous event. It was the biggest debacle for the United States since it quit Vietnam. The Taliban, now in full control, are more articulate, yet unchanged in the rigid application of their version of Islam on their people than they did during their first stint in power (1996–2001). The UN Analytical Support and Sanctions Monitoring Team concerning the Taliban in its 2023 report observed that the Taliban have 'reverted to the exclusionary, Pashtun-centred, autocratic policies of the Taliban administration of the late 1990s'.[1]

Yet, Afghanistan's isolation is gradually ending. China has sent an ambassador and 40 countries have accorded it de facto recognition. This underscores a complex situation: Even if it disapproves, the world community cannot ignore the miseries the Afghan people continue to face, no matter who rules them.

More important is the fact that the 'global war on terrorism' that brought the United States (US) and the North Atlantic Treaty Organization (NATO) to Afghanistan, has not been won. Indeed, it has complicated the situation for all of Afghanistan's neighbours. Afghan narcotics' cultivation and movement remain a matter of concern. Banned in 2022 by the new rulers, its production is lower than before, although it registered an increase of 30 per cent between 2023 and 2024, reaching 433 tonnes in 2024. This is because 'the Taliban's campaign against narcotics has drastically reduced opium poppy cultivation and upended Afghanistan's drug economy. Driven by ideology, the Taliban's anti-drug efforts include rounding up drug users, eradicating crops, and shuttering drug bazaars.'[2] However, the International Crisis Group's report expresses scepticism about the effectiveness and continuation of the ban which is estimated to cut US$ 1.3 billion earnings that are roughly eight per cent of Afghanistan's GDP.[3]

Afghanistan continues to be coveted for its geographical location and its untapped resources. Unsurprisingly, a new phase of the 'Great Game' has begun. The players have changed and their positions have altered, but none is likely to give up or lose interest. None of those who invaded/occupied it in modern times—the British in the nineteenth century, the Soviets, and the Americans in the 20th century—was there for Afghanistan's nation-building. Defeated, they have left the country poor and devastated but weaponised, to fend for itself.

After over four decades since the monarchy ended, the Afghans under the Taliban are on their own. Their conditions when viewed from the outside are unenviable. Few prospects exist to compensate for the lost decades and catch up with the world. The only redeeming feature is that it has remained territorially intact.

A multi-ethnic society with significant populations from the neighbourhood, it has been subjected to frequent violence and cleansing, which ensures its immediate neighbours' interest and concern. Being landlocked limits its options and it must depend upon neighbours for access to the outside world.

New factors, both geopolitical and geo-economic, impact it. One is the emergence of China as not just a regional but also a global power. Russia ruled for a decade before the Soviet Union broke up. The US marked its presence there for two decades. They would need to share their strategic space with China. Like the rest of Europe, the British, who initiated the original 'Great Game' in the nineteenth-century, are now camp followers of the US.

What has not changed, or indeed, worsened, is how the Taliban govern Afghanistan and treat women and ethnic minorities. They appear determined to sit out all the calls to change their style. The absence of diplomatic recognition and economic sanctions, even freezing of their funds abroad, have not pressured them. They do not seem to be bothered about the global odium.

However, concerns over Afghanistan's worsening humanitarian crisis, the threat of terrorism, and hard-nosed pragmatism have led to some international engagement. Three years into its rule of Afghanistan, the Taliban government has achieved some diplomatic wins and has consolidated power.

China quietly made the beginning in February 2024 when it recognised Bilal Karimi as the envoy of the Taliban regime. Earlier, in September 2023, it dispatched Zhao Sheng as the Chinese envoy. China and Russia appeared to move in tandem. In April 2024, Zamir Kabulov, the long-time special envoy of President Vladimir Putin, met the Taliban leadership. Security analysts have interpreted this as an effort to fill in the vacuum caused by the US/NATO withdrawal. Many countries did not close their missions in Kabul when the Taliban returned to power. Kabul has so far gained control of missions in 14 countries.

### India

A notable "returnee" is India which closed its mission and consulates in August 2021 but reopened its embassy in 2022 following the earthquake in the country to help in aid delivery. On 8 January 2025, Indian Foreign Secretary Vikram Misri met with Acting Afghan Foreign Minister Amir Khan Muttaqi during a visit to Dubai. Talks reportedly focused on expanding trade and leveraging Iran's Chabahar Port, which India has been developing to bypass Pakistan's Karachi and Gwadar ports.

This has been a significant move by India. It has historic ties with both Iran and Afghan people and is one of the key stakeholders in regional peace. 'Delhi has now given the Taliban leadership the de facto legitimacy it has sought from the international community since its return to power,' Michael Kugelman of the Wilson Center, an American think-tank, told BBC in January 2025.[4]

The importance of the move was underscored on 15 December 2023, when External Affairs Minister S. Jaishankar of India told parliament of "historical and civilisational ties" with Afghanistan. India has invested more than US$ 3 billion over 500 projects across Afghanistan, including roads, power lines, dams, hospitals and clinics. It has trained Afghan officers, awarded thousands of scholarships to students and built a new parliament building. Having dealt with Kabul—monarchical, communist, or Islamist—India enjoys a warm rapport with the Afghan people.[5]

For India, the deeper reason for the Afghan outreach is its aim to strengthen connectivity and access Central Asia, which it can't reach directly by land due to Pakistan's refusal of transit rights. Experts say Afghanistan is the key to this goal. One strategy is collaborating with Iran on the Chabahar port development to improve access to Central Asia via Afghanistan. India's Border Roads Organisation (BRO) developed the Delaram–Zaranj Highway, also known as Route 606, a 135-mile-long two-lane road in Afghanistan, connecting Zaranj in Nimruz Province, near the Iranian border, with Delaram in neighbouring Farah Province. India spent US$ 152 million.

However, in a missed opportunity, India could not build a railway line from Chabahar to Zaranj, Afghanistan. The project was part of a trilateral agreement between India, Iran, and Afghanistan to create a trade route to Afghanistan and Central Asia. India was later dropped from the project due to funding delays caused mainly due to the US's adversity to Iran. The cost for the 628 km rail line was estimated at US$ 1 million per kilometre.

### "Befriending Enemy's Enemy"

Significantly, Kabul's relations with Delhi appear to be easing amid rising tensions between Afghanistan and Pakistan. Pakistan, which sheltered the Taliban for over two decades and facilitated their return to power, now claims the hard-line Pakistani Taliban (TTP) are sheltered, armed and operate from sanctuaries in Afghanistan. Given their heavy dependence upon Pakistan, it is possible long-term that the Taliban may shun India at some stage. But Jayant Prasad, a former Indian ambassador to Afghanistan, justifies the move: 'Letting the Taliban stew in its juice won't help Afghan people. Some engagement with the international community might pressurise the government to improve its behaviour.'[6]

Dropping its earlier antipathy towards the Taliban, India is cautiously working in tandem with the world community and the United Nations. Notably, the Taliban government participated, for the first time, in UN-hosted talks in June 2024 in Qatar to discuss economic issues and counter-narcotics efforts. Chief Taliban government spokesman Zabihullah Mujahid, who led the delegation, said the gathering was a further proof that: 'Afghanistan has come out of isolation.'[7]

Opinions concerning dealing with the Taliban remain divided. While there is no sign of any collective move to recognise the Taliban regime, save for occasional expressions of anguish, little is said of the women and the ethnic minorities in Afghanistan despite reports of their being isolated and ill-treated keep coming up. The Taliban reject any criticism as "interference". In principle, the world community can be faulted for paying lip service to Afghan women and minorities. Global criticism has proved like Teflon on the Taliban's back. That being the reality, with each nation guarding its interests, the world has gradually moved towards doing normal business with Kabul.

The world now has to deal with the inevitable Afghan exodus. Refugees throng European cities where they are unwelcome. Thousands have left Afghanistan since the 1970s, adding to the millions who have done so during each conflict, internal as also caused by foreign intervention. Afghanistan's neighbours are fighting off the pressure on their populations and economies. Iran deported 750,000 Afghans and announced a plan to deport up to two million by March 2025. While Iran has long hosted Afghan refugees, naturalisation opportunities are rare.[8]

In October 2023, the United Nations estimated that nearly 3.7 million Afghans, registered and illegal, resided in Pakistan, while Pakistani authorities believed the number to be as high as 4.4 million. Of them, about 541,000 Afghan refugees were forced to leave Pakistan in the first phase initiated on 1 November 2023 while over 80,000 were forcefully deported in the second phase started on 15 April 2024. These Afghans were either not Pakistanis or were not registered as refugees. That army-led operation ended amidst much criticism at home, especially from human rights bodies and political parties having a Pashtun support base and charges of selective eviction and corruption.

While they deal with these returnees without protesting, the Taliban's unstated policy so far as the exodus is concerned, is to do nothing to stem it. Western nations airlifted over 120,000 Afghans abroad, as per a statement issued by the European Parliament. This may have begun early and been carried out in phases, considering that the actual evacuation in August 2021 was abrupt and chaotic. Since then, at least 300,000 Afghans have fled by land. It has continued unabated as people flee, often with families, to escape persecution and misery. As per the UNHCR (United Nations High Commissioner for Refugees) figures of June 2023, two million Afghans live outside their country as registered refugees in Iran, Pakistan, Tajikistan, Uzbekistan, and Turkmenistan. Pakistan had 300,000 more unofficial arrivals since August 2021, taking the number to 1.2 million. Some estimates put it at 1.4 million. Iran is sought after even more than Pakistan in that the Afghans find it easy to register themselves as refugees and seek to move to the West. The new arrivals could reach 500,000. Tajikistan has a small number of about 3,000, likely to touch 10,000.

## Women & Human Rights

As they did in their first regime (1996–2001), the Taliban have kept their women indoors, without work, and girls without much education, not because they see a challenge from them, but because they claim that their version of Islam prescribes it. Girls have been barred from attending schools and universities, even appearing for examinations. Their marginalisation has indeed been a continuing phenomenon. Reflecting global anguish, Nobel peace laureate Malala Yousafzai spoke at the closing session of a Pakistan-hosted international summit on girls' education in Muslim communities around the world, sharply criticising the Afghan Government for imposing sweeping curbs on Afghan women's access to education and employment.[9]

As noted by Abdulkader Sinno of Indiana University, 'The Taliban's decision-making process is opaque to many observers and policymakers in the West. While the Taliban's decisions are not necessarily good for Afghanistan, they do have organizational, doctrinal, and cultural underpinnings.'[10]

Before many countries began their back-to-Afghanistan move in 2024, the thrust, even at the UN was on human rights. Addressing the UN Human Rights Council on 15 June 2022, the then UN High Commissioner for Human Rights stated that Afghanistan was witnessing the "institutionalised, systematic oppression" of women. Unsurprisingly, on 16 May 2022, the Taliban authorities announced that they had dissolved Afghanistan's independent human rights commission as it was "not deemed necessary".[11]

Sinno offers an explanation/apologia for the Taliban's determined resistance to women's education, one of the main issues with the world community that has withheld formal diplomatic recognition, stating that 'banning girls' education or destroying the Bamiyan Buddhas as a form of protest may seem self-defeating, but Taliban leaders believe that expressing disagreement is important even if it comes at a cost.'[12]

Stray street protests by women in Kabul have been beaten back, violently. Women's groups are better organised abroad. They vehemently protested at the invitation sent to Kabul ahead of a major international conference on Afghanistan hosted by the United Nations. The 30 June–1 July 2024 event held in Qatar, the women's bodies said, provided tacit international legitimacy to the Taliban's unrecognised and internationally sanctioned government.[13] A year earlier, the Taliban hosted a men-only conference of about 3,500 mostly clerics and tribal elders from across the country in an apparent bid to demonstrate their hold on power and domestic legitimacy. The three-day meeting 'failed to address thorny issues such as the right of teenage girls to go to school.'[14]

On how the Taliban functions, Sinno writes: 'The Taliban government in Kabul plays an important role, but the supreme council in Kandahar, in the demographic Pashtun hinterland of the Taliban, is the ultimate arbiter in any decision-making. The secretive Kandahar council, or *shura*, exists to protect key leaders from assassination attempts and to provide leadership in case of another foreign invasion.'[15]

**Resistance to Taliban**

A powerful minister, Khalilur Rahman Haqqqani, who belonged to the powerful Haqqani family, was assassinated by a suicide bomb in December 2024. A designated terrorist, he was killed while leaving his ministry office in Kabul. He is the most high-profile leader to have been killed since the Taliban took power in 2021. Islamic State Khorasan Province (ISKP) claimed credit for the assassination.

Relocated from Syria to Afghanistan with its focus on Asia, the ISKP has posed the most noteworthy challenge so far. It seems unlikely that any threat could come from the ethnic minorities. According to WorldAtlas (2019 figures), the Pashtun (Pashto) are 42 per cent, Tajik 27 per cent, Uzbek 9 per cent, Hazara 8 per cent, Aimaq 4 per cent, Turkmen 3 per cent, Balochi (Baluch) 2 per cent and Other Groups 5 per cent.[16] However, these ethnic minorities remain divided, confined to large pockets in the north and the east, and are economically the weakest. Any such resistance to the Taliban would have to be engineered from outside. The Taliban can keep the ethnic minorities suppressed since even a semblance of resistance, political or military that existed in the weeks that followed their takeover has worn away. It would need Russian support. With Moscow warming up to Kabul, prospects of a Northern Alliance that forged at the turn of the last century regrouping again seem remote. The alliance was formed at the turn of the century because of different dynamics, including the US's need to chase Al Qaida. The Taliban ensured control over the northern region this time over even before they captured Kabul. Its revival seems difficult given the Sino-Pak interest in dominating the Afghan narrative and keeping out others—the Western powers, Iran, and the Central Asians.

The Taliban's exclusive and oppressive governance approach and decisions on women's education and the veil have left little room for the world community to intervene. According to a report in the Pakistani daily, *The Express Tribune*, that has found no elaboration, 'at least one dozen countries, including Pakistan, were on the verge of recognising the Afghan Taliban government in March [2022] but withheld their decision following the failure of Kabul's de facto rulers to fulfil the promises made with the international community.'[17]

'They [Taliban] missed a great opportunity. Around 10 to 12 countries were actively considering recognising their government in March,' a senior Pakistani official involved in the process revealed.[18]

Thankfully, the Taliban do not talk of democracy since they do not subscribe to its universally accepted concept. Yet, their desperation for the recognition of their government by the international community has remained the key reason they have so far shied away from implementing their agenda to the full. For these reasons, they have allowed the presence of former president Hamid Karzai and also Abdullah, so as not to offend the world community further. Gulbuddin Hekmatyar, the controversial warlord and former prime minister, has also stayed on. Karzai is forced to stay with his erstwhile political rival Abdullah, indicating that the two have been rendered ineffective. Karzai opposed the government diktat on women wearing head-to-toe "burqa" in public.[19] He also stressed a "national dialogue" as essential for Afghanistan when he met with United Nations Deputy Chief Amina Mohammed in Kabul in January 2023.[20] However, the Afghan news portal *Hasht-e Subh* had a post, calling his role "controversial" and describing him as 'A Politician in Search of Influence and Credibility Amid Contradictions and Illusions'.[21] In sum, there is no political opposition to the Taliban today.

Among the worst victims are former lawmakers and officers who worked in previous regimes and did not try to, or could not leave. As per reports, these out-of-job officials and journalists with all private outlets closed, who were relatively well-fed earlier, were seen in the streets selling food as vendors for earning daily bread.

Leaders like Ahmed Masoud, son of former commander from Panjshir Ahmed Shah Masoud, and some officials of the Karzai and Ghani governments shuffle between Iran and other countries, but with little scope, so far, for building up credible military resistance to the Taliban. Propping up Masoud's National Resistance Front (NRF) appears to suit the West. He seeks to unite the Afghan diaspora. At a conference in Vienna on 16 September 2022, he announced what he called "a new phase" in his effort to seek a "political" solution and bring the Taliban to the table for talks.[22]

The other possible source of challenge, a more potent and long-term, is from within, especially between the "moderates" based in Kabul and who are in the government and the "hardliners" in Kandahar who decide the ideology. But it is unlikely to rock the boat since power keeps everyone together. The Taliban were never a homogenous group. Reports of fights, including fisticuffs and gunfire, involving their top leaders, appearing in global media have been expectedly denied, but are not inconceivable, given their interpretation of Islam's tenets and of the gun culture that governs the lives of the Afghans.

Reports have emerged of the powerful Haqqani leader (of the Haqqani Network) publicly disagreeing with the top Taliban leadership. Sirajuddin Haqqani, the Taliban's powerful acting interior minister, lambasted for the first time the group's reclusive spiritual leader for monopolising power and damaging their government in Afghanistan. 'Power monopolization and defamation of the entire system have become common,' Haqqani said in an angry speech at the packed graduation ceremony of an Islamic religious school in the southeastern Khost Province. 'The situation cannot be tolerated any longer,' he added, without naming Supreme Leader Haibatullah Akhundzada directly.[23]

On dealing with women's status in society, while the rulers in Kabul were willing, to quote Sinno, again, 'It was the Kandahar *shura* that overruled the Kabul government's decision to let girls attend secondary school. Observers speculate that the dividing line is theological, with the younger and more open leadership in Kabul being overruled by the ultra-conservative leadership in Kandahar.'[24]

The Taliban, as well as the Haqqanis, are wary of threats from their principal adversaries, the Islamic State–Khorasan Province (ISKP), which advocates a line that is more radical than the Taliban. These threats have supposedly prevented the rulers in Kabul from showing any relaxation towards women.

The Taliban–ISKP tussle is shaping the future course the Kabul rulers may take. According to an analysis by Vanda Felbab-Brown of Brookings, 'Afghanistan in 2023 will be shaped by whether or not the Taliban's supreme leader, Haibatullah Akhundzada, retains his tight grip on all decision-making. The second crucial dynamic will be terrorism and militancy. The Taliban is unlikely to get a better handle on the Islamic State in Khorasan (ISK).'[25]

## The US/ NATO Exit

The US withdrew its forces with the last man leaving, on 30 August 2021. A fortnight earlier, the Taliban entered Kabul on 15 August, hours after President Ashraf Ghani fled the country and his government collapsed. Formations of the Afghan national army and the police swiftly surrendered in a process that had been underway, even as the US/NATO wound up their operations. Nobody anticipated this. The Taliban demanded that the Americans honour the deadline set by the Doha pact.

After much internal debate and as a worried world watched, the Joseph Biden administration implemented the Doha pact signed in February 2020 by the Trump administration. Any option to stay on in Afghanistan was ruled out by the aggressive campaign the Taliban unleashed, capturing one district after the other, once the Doha Agreement was signed. Unprecedented scenes of chaos and human misery accompanied the process as thousands thronged the Hamid Karzai International Airport in Kabul, many climbing on the wings of the American aircraft, desperately trying to leave the country.

There was no guarantee of life and safety for the people, including those who had worked for the Karzai/Ghani regimes, as the evacuation took place in the most chaotic conditions. Many foreign missions closed their operations, fearing the worst as had happened when the Mujahideen had entered Kabul on 27 April 1992, and again when former President Muhammad Najibullah was caught and killed after the Taliban seized Kabul in September 1996. History repeated in August 2021, a third time.

Since 30 August 2021, the US has gradually minimised its engagement with Afghanistan except humanitarian assistance when needed. An unresolved issue between the US and Afghanistan is that of the $7 billion of Afghan assets withheld by the US Federal Reserve. In February 2022, the Biden administration announced a process aimed at letting relatives of victims of the 9/11 (11 September 2001) terrorist attacks, who have legal claims against the Taliban, pursue $3.5 billion of those assets. The Taliban had sheltered Al Qaeda leaders who planned the 11 September attacks during the Taliban's previous rule of Afghanistan. This may be legitimate under American law, but after nearly two decades' presence in Afghanistan, when a trillion dollars were spent, this step smacks of pique and pettiness towards a poor nation, howsoever hostile.

Engaged in reviewing the performances of their respective governments, American lawmakers have, without a lament, blamed the collapse of the Ghani Government on the end of the US/NATO military support while the British lawmakers have blamed "systematic failure" to tackle the crisis, calling out the claims made by the Biden administration. While all this is factually true, in both these analyses, one discerns frustration at the failure to claim a victory of the powerful at the hands of the Taliban, a ragtag but well-armed and highly motivated force.

The Western view as a whole is that quitting Afghanistan was the best and only option. Individually and collectively, the US and NATO members failed to see what was coming or were unready to prevent it when the Taliban, taking the Doha pact as the green signal, launched an offensive in May 2020. Trump-1, and later, the Biden administration miscalculated that after settling with the Taliban keeping Kabul out of the Doha pact talks, they could lean on President Ghani to hold talks with the Taliban, to "share" power with an advancing, marauding force that he could not match, and that aware of the take-no-prisoners dynamics that usually operates in Afghanistan, he would step down when asked. Eventually, not wanting to meet the fate of Najibullah, Ghani fled, hours before the Taliban fighters entered Kabul.

US Secretary of State in the Trump-1 administration Mike Pompeo blamed Ghani 'for failing the US-led peace process and landing his people into trouble'. The US wanted Ghani's negotiations with the Taliban to be a year-long process that would have led to a peaceful transfer of power in Kabul. Pompeo said it did not happen because Ghani did not want it to succeed. Questioned if he had asked Ghani to step down, Pompeo said: 'Well, he would think I did but I didn't. I was incredibly frustrated with President Ghani.'[26] The global media, even the Americans, grudgingly admitted to this being the outcome of "hubris".

Beyond the media debates and expert analyses, there has been no official admission of the flawed, indeed, one-sided, Doha pact that sought little by way of any commitment from the Taliban representatives who signed it. It was midwifed after prolonged negotiations by Zalmay Khalilzad, a diplomat close to Trump. The US only sought assurance that the Taliban would not attack US interests. There was little by way of verification or an effective counter, to any violation. The unmistakable political side to this pact was that Trump wanted it to boost his chances of re-election to the presidency in 2020, which he eventually lost.

Criticised, the Biden administration displayed a pro-active stance like killing Al Qaida chief Ayman al-Zawahiri in a drone strike executed by the Central Intelligence Agency (CIA) in Kabul, demonstrating "over the horizon" capability to combat terrorism. Biden himself announced it on 1 August 2022.[27] The Taliban disputed it, insisting that they found "no evidence" of the Al Qaida chief dying in the attack. Later, Zabihullah Mujahid, Taliban spokesman, said, 'We have not reached a result yet. There has been no clear and decisive reason to prove that such an incident happened. It is still at a level of (the) allegation. We have not received a satisfactory reason from the US.'[28]

### Afghanistan in US Presidential Election 2024

The evacuation from Afghanistan resurfaced, briefly but prominently, during the presidential elections debate. Trump attended a Martyrs' Memorial Service at the Arlington National Cemetery on 1 September 2024, when he engaged in fierce debate with his rival Kamala Harris, who called Trump's visit to the cemetery "disrespectful" to the dead soldiers. But families of the 13 soldiers, who died during the exit on 26 August 2021, blamed the Biden administration. Harris responded by alleging, correctly, that Trump, as the president in February 2020, had tied America to the Doha pact.

Both were right—America's Afghanistan policy was wrong. Tired of what had become an expensive stay in men and material, it did not know how to exit. As President, Obama enforced a "surge" in the military presence. It did not work because the Taliban were being supported by Pakistan. Trump later accused Pakistan of "playing the double game."

By hindsight, an ill-advised Trump-1 forsook President Ghani's government, which the US had been supporting, even sustaining it with funds and soldiers. He invited the Taliban, designated as a "terror group" by the United Nations, to Camp David for talks. Encouraged, the Taliban overran half of Afghanistan. Trump's negotiators, who pressured Ghani and the Taliban to reconcile, forgot the basic human traits, strong with the Afghans, that they would kill each other rather than compromise. Afghanistan has since been in a lethal limbo.

Trump-1 alone can answer why his administration reduced the American military presence to just 2,500 combatants and forced Kabul to release from prison 5,000 of the most dreaded terrorists. Biden could have halted the process of implementing a flawed Doha pact. But the "Afghanistan fatigue" had afflicted the American mind by that time. After all, the US had lost 2,459 military personnel, with 20,769 wounded, from October 2001 to August 2021.

Overall, the US, whenever it can take time off from Ukraine and other preoccupations, may act. But beyond specific targeting of individuals, it cannot be expected to mount an all-out military operation, as it did in 2001 unless it perceives a direct threat to its interests.

**Militancy Hub**

The Afghan Taliban appear confident that they can use radical Islam and its soldiers to suppress the population, host—willingly or otherwise—terror groups of various hues, and remain in denial. As highlighted in a recently released UN report, Al Qaeda and the self-styled Islamic State–Khorasan Province (ISKP) are operating unhindered in Afghanistan.[29] Sirajuddin Haqqani denied this in the course of his interview with *CNN-News18*.[30]

This has caused a major issue with Pakistan. Even as it wielded considerable influence, including in the formation of the new government, it found the Taliban uncooperative on the question of their ties with the TTP. In his 23 September 2022 address to the UN General Assembly, Pakistan Prime Minister Shehbaz Sharif pointed to international concerns that Pakistan shared about 'the threat posed by the major terrorist groups operating from Afghanistan, especially Islamic State, ISIL-K [another name for ISKP] and TTP [Tehrik-e-Taliban Pakistan], as well as Al Qaeda, ETIM [East Turkistan Islamic Movement], and IMU [Islamic Movement of Uzbekistan].'[31]

The ISKP is, indeed, the group to watch as Afghanistan goes through its inward march to nowhere. The ISKP was weakened and reduced to a non-entity during the US-backed Ghani Government, but when it saw the power vacuum and the Afghan Taliban's internal divisions, it seized the opportunity. It intensified its recruitment drive, while at the same time transforming its combat strategy.

When the Afghan Taliban were laying siege after siege to every major city in the country, there were some major prison breaks. These prison breaks let out all the deadly terrorists belonging to the ISKP and Al Qaeda, who had been apprehended by the Ghani Government with effort and the use of state resources. Later, to the Taliban's surprise, the ISKP carried out a suicide bomb blast in the Hamid Karzai International Airport in Kabul, when Afghan people and foreigners were leaving the country in frenzy. The ISKP's intent to oppose the Taliban regime was clear. Transnational militant groups were indeed operating in Afghanistan even as the US/NATO military machine maintained a heavy footprint in that country. But like the Russians in the 1980s, they retained a presence in Kabul and were confined to their military bases.

There are legitimate fears that if the Taliban weaken for reasons discussed above, Afghanistan will again become a hotbed of international terrorism. One indication is the reported presence of Jaish-e-Muhammad (JeM) chief Masood Azhar. Pakistan claims that he is in Afghanistan, which Kabul denied.[32] There was likely a tacit understanding between Islamabad and Kabul. The latter kept its militants away each time the Financial Action Task Force (FATF) came calling to check Pakistan's performance in preventing terror financing through money laundering. The tacit arrangement has crumbled since the two sides have been clashing over TTP. Afghan Information Minister Khairullah Khairkhwa called the TTP "guests" and assured support to its members in an interview.[33]

## India–Pakistan in Afghanistan

When India made urgent efforts to rush medicine and food supplies, Pakistan prevaricated and then relented by allowing the Afghan vehicles to collect Indian supplies. It required a visit by the Taliban foreign minister to Islamabad and seek personal intervention of Prime Minister Imran Khan. It was a one-off concession but Islamabad insisted and caused further delays. All, this while Pakistan keeps appealing to the world community to rush humanitarian aid to Afghanistan.

India has long lived with the myth that it can leverage the US to keep Pakistan under check in Afghanistan. At no stage did the US forsake Pakistan which has been its ally, even while Washington under Trump-1 harshly criticised Islamabad for double-crossing. Hoping to return to the Afghan theatre, the US has repeatedly supported, in the name of fighting terrorism, Pakistan in its effort to resolve problems with Kabul over the TTP's operations staged from the Afghan territory.

The US hands now get further tied seeing Pakistan getting closer to a China that is advancing its interests in Afghanistan. Beijing has been pushing the idea of the China–Pakistan Economic Corridor (CPEC) being extended to Afghanistan as the "China–Afghanistan Economic Corridor." This explains why the US under Trump-1 earlier and later under Biden, from time to time urged regional stakeholders in Afghanistan to unite to do their bit. While such a thing may be desirable from an American standpoint, it completely ignores the strategic stakes and rivalries among the regional powers, a complex process in which the US itself is a player. While promoting development that helps the Afghan people, India has consistently declined, even wriggled out of delicate diplomatic situations, to put its boots on the Afghan soil, save to protect its mission.

The Afghan Taliban do not acknowledge it, but use the TTP as leverage against Pakistan. This has become a major bone of contention for the military and the policy planners in Pakistan. Formed in 2007 to replace the Pakistan Government with an Islamic Caliphate, the TTP finds ideological brotherhood with the Afghan Taliban. Its clout has increased manifolds since the latter returned to power in Kabul in a campaign in which 6,500 TTP fighters participated, with a nod from the Imran Khan government. The TTP is assessed as the largest group of foreign terrorists in Afghanistan. Utilising its ideological affinity with the new Kabul rulers and using Afghan soil, it has been staging violent operations in Pakistan with impunity. It is dominating the tribal belt on the Af-Pak border defying the Pakistani security forces.

Pakistan's TTP problem was serious before the Taliban regained power in Kabul, but has grown exponentially upsetting Islamabad's calculations of having a "friendly" government on its western border. In January 2021, Maj Gen Babar Iftikhar, then director general of Inter-Services Public Relations (ISPR), stated that 83,000 civilians and soldiers were killed in the fight against terrorism, costing Pakistan US$ 126 billion.[34] Since August 2021, the increased TTP-led insurgent violence has killed more than 1,500 people in Pakistan. In 2023 alone, more than 500 Pakistanis, mostly security forces, had died in militant attacks. They included at least 220 soldiers and officers, according to official data quoted by the *Voice of America* in its September 2023 report. In December 2024, the *New York Times* listed over 1,400 casualties.

This has impacted Pakistan on many fronts besides destabilising the tribal belt on the Af-Pak border. With its economy in dire straits, Pakistan is further hit by the flight of American dollars to dollar-starved Afghanistan. Traders and others bring in as much as $5 million a day.[35] Illicit flows help Afghanistan but hurt Pakistan's economy. The TTP has developed bases in Afghanistan's border areas. Reports in Pakistan media allege that the Afghan rulers have provided access to the TTP fighters to military equipment left behind by the American forces.

In December 2021 and again in December 2022, the TTP unilaterally ended the ceasefire pact reached with the Pakistan Government that was brokered by the Afghan Taliban and stepped up its activity. TTP's principal demand is that the Pakistan Government annul the merger of the tribal areas and withdraw the army. All efforts by Islamabad to get Kabul to act to evict the TTP cadres and/or at least, persuade them to hold peace talks have failed. The militant groups as an escape routine move to Afghanistan whenever pursued by the Pakistani authorities and Kabul, more than ever before, denies their presence.

The Afghan Taliban consider the TTP and its activities as Pakistan's domestic issues and ask Islamabad to fend for itself. This, in essence, underlines the failure of Pakistan's plans to have a friendly regime in Kabul that would help curb militancy, leaving alone its aspirations of such a government allowing strategic depth against other neighbours, especially India.

The report of the UN Security Council (UNSC) 1988 Taliban sanctions committee also underscored the presence of other terror outfits, particularly the TTP, in the Taliban-led regime. 'TTP has arguably benefitted the most of all the foreign extremist groups in Afghanistan from the Taliban takeover. It has conducted numerous attacks and operations in Pakistan. The TTP also continues to exist as a stand-alone force,' the report said as it estimated the number of TTP fighters to be 'several thousand'. 'The group [TTP] is estimated to consist of 3,000 to 4,000 armed fighters located along the east and south-east Afghanistan-Pakistan border areas,' the report added.[36]

The threat to the Taliban regime from ISKP is serious. In its article published in December 2021, the *South China Morning Post* stated:

> A fast-escalating wave of terrorist attacks in Afghanistan and Pakistan by the regional chapter of Islamic State (Isis) suggests the jihadist group is methodically exploiting political opportunities to establish itself as the pre-eminent resistance to the Taliban regime in Kabul and its allies in Pakistan.
>
> Since the departure of United States-led forces from Afghanistan in August, Islamic State Khorasan (Isis–K) has waged a terrorist

> campaign in Kabul and guerilla [*sic*] warfare against Taliban forces in most provinces bordering Pakistan.[37]

## Friends Turns Adversaries

While chaos caused by political and economic instability in Afghanistan dog the world, for the Taliban, the new situation points to ideological differences with Pakistan, their principal benefactor on matters of faith. Taliban spokesman Zabihullah Mujahid questioned Pakistan's democratic framework during a television interview when he stated: 'The political structure in Pakistan does not reflect the Islamic system. Their religious law does not allow for that system to operate. Religion is unimportant to them; only growth is vital.'[38]

The Taliban's relations with Pakistan are also intertwined with Islamist militancy in the region. They have enjoyed ideological proximity with other Sunni extremist groups that have used the difficult-to-govern border area that straddles both sides. Besides proscribed-but-active Lashkar-e-Taiba (LeT) and JeM, they include the TTP, easily the most formidable. This underscores the continued, and more complex, presence of the Afghan factor in Pakistan's internal affairs that goes well beyond the refugees' influx, the movement of drugs and arms, and the smuggling of goods at the expense of Pakistani traders.

The Afghanistan–Pakistan hiatus has persisted ever since the latter's birth in 1947, despite religious and cultural ties and Kabul's dire need for access to the outside world through Pakistan. Aizaz Ahmad Chaudhry, a former Pakistan Foreign Secretary, has lamented over how a Pakistan victory over Afghanistan in a cricket match at Sharjah led to violence. He wondered why "A majority of Afghans are bitter about Pakistan." He faulted the way Afghanistan as a nation has looked upon Pakistan since the latter's birth, and also the current Pakistan policy towards Kabul. He advocated a hands-off policy, resolving all issues through talks and promoting bilateral and economic cooperation. There was no hint of strategic interests, or of any warmth in the ties that began souring even before the year 2021 ended, with border skirmishes on the ground. Its many expectations from a group it hosted for two decades and helped return to power belied, Pakistan is experiencing what can be called "Afghanistan fatigue." It has no alternative but to live with the neighbour.[39]

The disappointment is particularly acute in the Taliban's failure to "deliver" on the TTP. The *Dawn* in its editorial wrote:

> Regional states—specifically Pakistan, Iran, China, Russia, and the Central Asian states—must individually and collectively put pressure

> on the Taliban to not allow Afghanistan to once more become a global base for terrorism. Instead of the flawed military adventurism undertaken by the Western bloc, regional states and the international community must warn the Taliban that trade and diplomatic ties will be impossible if groups like Al Qaeda, IS and the TTP continue to find shelter in their country.[40]

## History: Disputed Durand Line

For all the help and nurturing they received from Pakistan, the Taliban remain dogged in their refusal to recognise the British-era Durand Line that forms the disputed international border with Pakistan. The Taliban 1.0 (1996–2001) refused it and the new Taliban government is also firm about it.

Barely four months in power, Taliban soldiers exchanged mortar fire with the Pakistan Rangers guarding the border in eastern Nangarhar Province in December 2021. The Afghans destroyed the border fence being laid by the Pakistani personnel. The local Taliban official threatened “a war” if the Pakistanis persisted. According to Afghan news outlet *The Khama Press*, Pakistani soldiers unleashed artillery on the Kunar Province following the incident in Nangarhar Province’s Gushta area. At the border near Chaman across Kandahar, seven Pakistanis died and 31 were injured.[41] Such incidents have recurred in the following years, with Pakistan frequently closing the border at Torkham.

Created as a separate “homeland” for the Muslims of the Indian Subcontinent, but as many historians say, as part of the British imperial design in South and West Asia, Pakistan was born in 1947 with twin border disputes. Its forces’ invasion of Jammu and Kashmir within two months of its birth ended in a stalemate and has remained the cause of four wars with India. The dispute with Afghanistan was over the Durand Line. Afghanistan sought to meet the new entity with hostility by being the only country to oppose Pakistan’s membership in the UN. The dispute has persisted through the intervening seven decades plus. The stand of Taliban 2.0, the current Afghan regime, remains the same.

The reason for this has been overlooked by the big powers and the stakeholders in Afghanistan. The arbitrarily drawn line—that began on a map and a red pen and was formalised on the ground later to Kabul’s disadvantage—cuts through the heart of the Pashtun populace, sowing seeds of mistrust and hatred and divided political loyalties between two adversarial regimes. Named after Sir Mortimer Durand, the foreign secretary of imperial India, this invisible yet powerful cartographical reality has defined the westernmost frontier of undivided India and formed the core of the

Afghanistan–Pakistan territorial issues. It has not allowed the Pashtun issue to be settled.

In his book, *Durand's Curse: A Line Across the Pathan Heart*, former Indian diplomat Rajiv Dogra sums up its impact best by recording a comment by Khan Abdul Wali Khan. When asked about his identity, Wali Khan, son of the legendary Frontier Gandhi, Abdul Ghaffar Khan, said, he was, 'a six-thousand-year-old Pashtun, a thousand-year-old Muslim and a twenty-seven-year-old Pakistani'.[42] The Afghanistan–Pakistan border clashes began in 1949 and have recurred from time to time with varying intensity. They did not change with Pakistan playing the proxy for the Western powers against the Soviet Union and with its double game of fighting terror alongside the West and nurturing the Taliban at the same time in the last two decades.

For all the complexities that the world is grappling to deal with, the Taliban are essentially Pashtun. Given the Afghan desire to reunite the Pakhtuns or Pashtuns, they are unlikely to change now.

**Dealing with Taliban**

The world is confronted by the dilemma of having to deal with a group that it has disapproved of, was sanctioned by the UN for its violent ways, and was once ousted from power. Significantly, however, the Taliban are designated individually, but not as a group.

History has perceived the Afghans as a proud people. But the last four decades as the playground of the big powers has changed much with 47 per cent of Afghans unable to secure two square meals. There are no estimates of those dying due to hunger, lack of medical attention and other causes. The Taliban appear hopeful that the world will come around to help each time there is a natural disaster. Taliban also seem confident that many of the governments that are officially critical of the ways they rule their country will come around, unofficially and through their business enterprises. Afghanistan has considerable natural wealth that remains unexplored. They have approached China to resume exploring copper and think that other nations will join in through proxies to have a share of the Afghan economic pie and also, to keep the Chinese presence under check.

Compulsions to prevent Afghanistan's economic collapse have come to heavily influence the world community's approach. There is a serious dichotomy in the way the world expects the Taliban to govern and render humanitarian aid, without formally recognising the new government. 97 per cent of its people do not get enough to eat. Not doing so could lead to a major humanitarian catastrophe.

As was evident in the 2021 year-end debate and voting at the UNSC, the emphasis of the group led by China–Russia was more on delivering aid, without pressing a timeline for political reforms. The latter approach suits the Taliban, their benefactors like China and Pakistan, and in general, the Muslim nations for whom political reforms matter much less. For the latter, with the growing perception of Islamophobia in the West, that the Taliban are distorting and even betraying Islam does not seem to matter. Thus, the fault lies in both camps.

## Options for India

As one of the major investors in Afghanistan's development, India has earned goodwill, especially during 2002–2021. It has taken patient waiting and several months of effort for India to get around the Taliban leaders, most of them sheltered in Pakistan for many years. The only contact it had in 2021 was Sher Mohammad Abbas Stanikzai, the Deputy Minister of Foreign Affairs, who had trained in India as a young army officer. It took India almost a year of effort to speak to Sirajuddin Haqqani, the Interior Minister. Haqqani spoke to Indian television channel *CNN-News18* when he appealed to India and Pakistan to resolve outstanding issues coming in the way of reopening trade avenues in the region. He welcomed Indian development assistance.[43]

India has responded positively with projects. How far India can deploy personnel to work there on its projects seems doubtful because of the precarious security situation. Yet, working with the Taliban regime now accords it a key advantage that it is doing business with a force that had in the past hurt its interests.

India's capacity to manoeuvre is and shall remain limited—notwithstanding the goodwill among the Afghan people and its investments in their development. By similar logic, Pakistan, despite a measure of hostility among the Afghan people, will retain an advantage over India, as it has a common border unlike India, and is Afghanistan's principal source of goods and of access to the sea. That geography cannot be changed.

Indian success in the two decades, that is 2001–2021, in the form of US$ 3 billion investments in projects and in Afghan goodwill, besides its pro-active diplomacy, in effect, depended upon the US/NATO presence. Karzai and Ghani visited India frequently with their wish lists, although the Indian response was circumscribed by its interests, limitations, and caution not to over-reach in a terrain where the Haqqani network and militant groups sponsored by Pakistan's ISI were and remain strong.

India would need to revise its plans under the new circumstances where the Taliban are keen to cooperate, whether to have Indian projects, but on their own terms. Given the fluid security situation on the ground, it would require very high determination and diplomatic and security considerations for India to resume its presence the way it had earlier.

But it must wait and watch with the rest of the community—perhaps, longer, given the Pakistan factor—before it can gain more than a diplomatic toehold in Kabul under the Taliban dispensation. India did not have friends even when the Russians left and waited for its opportunity to reach out to the new rulers. It will have to, and can, do so again.

Pakistan may regain, for now at least, the Afghan market that it lost in recent years to India and China. Whether or not Pakistan gains "strategic depth" with the Taliban in power in Afghanistan, it can certainly gain some "commercial depth" now that the transportation of Indian goods via the sea and airlifts from Delhi to Kabul have been limited.

India has to stay economically and commercially relevant in the region. It needs to revitalise the Chabahar Port with Iran to retain access to Afghanistan and Central Asia. Here, Uzbekistan is crucial for India's plans to boost connectivity. The three have formed a trilateral working group on the joint use of Chabahar.

Being identified with the US in the South Asian region where the US has just ended its military presence poses a short and medium-term challenge for India. Much will depend upon how the Trump administration (2025–2029) looks at Afghanistan and the region. A return of the military presence seems most unlikely, it will need India's cooperation to promote development as it did from 2002–2021. The challenge here will be to keep its uneasy co-existence with Pakistan which would also be ready to be wooed by Trump. The situation is too complex to be analysed, how Trump would want to contain China's presence in the Af-Pak region. India's equations with China are unlikely to change, though. China, which does not favour it and is a firm Pakistan ally, emerging as the strongest regional power, poses India with its major, long-term challenge, in Afghanistan.

Since Afghanistan being ruled by the Taliban is a fait accompli, the only way of meeting this challenge squarely could well be by responding to the Taliban's overtures and without recognising their regime, start dealing with their government, to guard India's national interest.

Whatever the equations within the camps and among the camps of stakeholders in Afghanistan, all must fight the common enemy: terrorism, and the narcotics that finance it.

## NOTES

1. 'Fourteenth Report of the Analytical Support and Sanctions Monitoring Team Submitted Pursuant to Resolution 2665 (2022) Concerning the Taliban and Other Associated Individuals and Entities Constituting a Threat to the Peace Stability and Security of Afghanistan', United Nations Security Council, S/2023/370, 1 June 2023, p. 3.
2. 'Trouble in Afghanistan's Opium Fields: The Taliban War on Drugs', International Crisis Group, Asia Report N°340, 12 September 2024, at https://www.crisisgroup.org/asia/south-asia/afghanistan/340-trouble-afghanistans-opium-fields-taliban-war-drugs.
3. Ibid.
4. Soutik Biswas, 'Why India is Reaching Out to the Taliban Now', BBC, 15 January 2025, at https://www.bbc.com/news/articles/cp8ke9e27dxo.
5. Ibid.
6. Ibid.
7. AFP, 'Afghanistan's Taliban Rulers Score Diplomatic Wins, Consolidate Power', *The Economic Times*, 12 August 2024, at https://economictimes.indiatimes.com/news/ international/world-news/afghanistans-taliban-rulers-score-diplomatic-wins-consoli date-power/articleshow/112463987.cms?from=mdr.
8. Mitra Naseh, 'One of the World's Largest Refugee Populations, Afghans Have Faced Increasing Restrictions in Iran', Migration Policy Institute, 7 January 2025, at https://www.migrationpolicy.org/article/afghan-refugees-iran.
9. Ayaz Gul, 'Malala Yousafzai Asks Muslim Leaders to Reject Taliban's Treatment of Afghan Women Openly', *Voice of America* (VOA), 12 January 2025, at https://www.voanews.com/a/malala-yousafzai-asks-muslim-leaders-to-reject-taliban-s-treatment-of-afghan-women-openly-/7933980.html.
10. Abdulkader Sinno, 'Taliban Decisions Reflect Internal Disagreement', East Asia Forum, 3 September 2022, at https://www.eastasiaforum.org/2022/09/03/taliban-decisions-reflect-internal-disagreement/.
11. Mohammad Yunus Yawar, 'Taliban Dissolve Afghanistan's Human Rights Commission, Other Key Bodies', *Reuters*, 17 May 2022, at https://www.reuters.com/world/asia-pacific/taliban-dissolve-afghanistans-human-rights-commission-other-key-bodies-2022-05-16/.
12. Abdulkader Sinno, no. 10.
13. 'Afghan Talks Kick Off in Doha Amid Anger Over Taliban's Exclusion Of Women', RFE/RL's *Radio Azadi*, 30 June 2024, at https://www.rferl.org/a/afghanistan-talks-doha-taliban-women-rights/33014343.html.
14. AFP, 'Taliban Still Illegitimate Rulers Say Afghan Women Activists', *The Times of India*, 3 July 2022, at https://timesofindia.indiatimes.com/world/south-asia/taliban-still-illegitimate-rulers-say-afghan-women-activists/articleshow/92636329.cms.
15. Abdulkader Sinno, no. 10.
16. Benjamin Elisha Sawe, 'The Ethnic Groups of Afghanistan', WorldAtlas, 10 September 2019, at https://www.worldatlas.com/articles/ethnic-groups-of-afghanistan.html.

17. Kamran Yousaf, 'Afghan Taliban "Missed Opportunity" for Recognition', *The Express Tribune*, 4 July 2022, at https://tribune.com.pk/story/2364567/afghan-taliban-missed-opportunity-for-recognition.
18. Ibid.
19. 'Burqa Has Nothing to Do with Afghanistan Culture, Says Hamid Karzai', *Hasht-e Subh*, 21 May 2022, at https://8am.media/eng/burqa-has-nothing-to-do-with-afghanistan-culture-says-hamid-karzai/.
20. Fatema Adeeb, 'Karzai Stresses Need for National Dialogue in Afghanistan', *TOLOnews*, 18 January 2023, at https://tolonews.com/afghanistan-181655.
21. Sanjar Sohail, 'Hamid Karzai: A Politician in Search of Influence and Credibility Amid Contradictions and Illusions', *Hasht-e Subh*, 29 October 2024, at https://8am.media/eng/hamid-karzai-a-politician-in-search-of-influence-and-credibility-amid-contradictions-and-illusions/.
22. AFP, 'Afghan Insurgent Leader Calls for New Anti-Taliban "Political" Front', VOA, 16 September 2022, at https://www.voanews.com/a/afghan-insurgent-leader-calls-for-new-anti-taliban-political-front-/6750867.html.
23. Eltaf Najafizada, 'Taliban Minister's Rebuke of Supreme Leader Shows Infighting', *Bloomberg*, 13 February 2023, at https://www.bloomberg.com/news/articles/2023-02-13/taliban-minister-s-rare-rebuke-of-top-leader-shows-infighting.
24. Abdulkader Sinno, no. 10.
25. Vanda Felbab-Brown, 'Afghanistan in 2023: Taliban Internal Power Struggles and Militancy', Brookings, 3 February 2023, at https://www.brookings.edu/blog/order-from-chaos/2023/02/03/afghanistan-in-2023-taliban-internal-power-struggles-and-militancy/.
26. Anwar Iqbal, 'Ghani Landed Afghans in Trouble: Pompeo', *Dawn*, 15 January 2023, at https://www.dawn.com/news/1731703.
27. 'Remarks by President Biden on a Successful Counterterrorism Operation in Afghanistan', The White House, 1 August 2022, at https://www.whitehouse.gov/briefing-room/speeches-remarks/2022/08/01/remarks-by-president-biden-on-a-successful-counterterrorism-operation-in-afghanistan/.
28. Mohammad Farshad Daryosh, '"No Details Found to Prove Zawahiri Was Killed in Kabul": Islamic Emirate', *TOLOnews*, 8 February 2023, at https://tolonews.com/afghanistan-181961.
29. 'Hotbed of Militancy', Editorial, *Dawn*, 25 July 2022, at https://www.dawn.com/news/1701458; Baqir Sajjad Syed, 'Al Qaeda, IS Gaining Strength in Afghanistan: UNSC Report', *Dawn*, 21 July 2022, at https://www.dawn.com/news/1700764.
30. Manoj Gupta, 'Exclusive | Afghanistan Needs India's Help "Desperately" to Secure Peaceful Environment: Taliban Interior Minister Haqqani', *CNN-News18*, 2 August 2022, at https://www.news18.com/news/world/exclusive-afghanistan-needs-indias-help-desperately-to-secure-peaceful-environment-taliban-interior-minister-haqqani-5670295.html.
31. Barnett R. Rubin, 'Afghanistan after U.S. Withdrawal: Five Conclusions', Carnegie Corporation of New York, 31 October 2022, at https://www.carnegie.org/our-work/article/afghanistan-after-us-withdrawal-five-conclusions/.
32. Amit Baruah, 'The Curious Case of Masood Azhar and His Whereabouts', *The Hindu*, 16 September 2022, at https://www.thehindu.com/podcast/the-curious-case-

of-masood-azhar-and-his-whereabouts-in-focus-podcast/article65898675.ece; 'Kabul Denies Masoud Azhar's Presence in Afghanistan', *TOLOnews*, 14 September 2022, at https://tolonews.com/afghanistan-179847.

33. Ayaz Gul, 'Taliban Hint at Shielding Anti-Pakistan Militants in Afghanistan as "Guests"', VOA, 27 December 2024, at https://www.voanews.com/a/taliban-hint-at-shielding-anti-pakistan-militants-in-afghanistan-as-guests-/7916430.html.
34. Sana Jamal, '83,000 Lives Lost in Pakistan's War on Terrorism', *Gulf News*, 12 January 2021, at https://gulfnews.com/world/asia/pakistan/83000-lives-lost-in-pakistans-war-on-terrorism-1.76428064.
35. Eltaf Najafizada and Ismail Dilawar, 'Dollars Smuggled From Pakistan Provide Lifeline for the Taliban', *Bloomberg*, 7 February 2023, at https://www.bloomberg.com/news/articles/2023-02-06/dollars-smuggled-from-pakistan-provide-lifeline-for-the-taliban.
36. Shahabullah Yousafzai, 'TTP "Benefitted Most" from Taliban Takeover of Kabul: UN Report', *The Express Tribune*, 29 May 2022, at https://tribune.com.pk/story/2358932/ttp-benefitted-most-from-taliban-takeover-of-kabul-un-report.
37. Tom Hussain, 'ISIS-K Escalates Terror Attacks in Afghanistan and Pakistan in Show of Resistance Against Taliban', *South China Morning Post*, 8 December 2021, at https://www.scmp.com/week-asia/article/3158929/isis-k-escalates-terror-attacks-afghanistan-and-pakistan-show-resistance.
38. Sakshi Tiwari, 'Double Trouble: India, Afghanistan Halt Pakistan's Construction Work Along the Disputed Borders', *The Eurasian Times*, 25 December 2021, at https://eurasiantimes.com/india-afghanistan-halt-pakistans-construction-work-along-disputed-borders/.
39. Aizaz Ahmad Chaudhry, 'Brotherly Afghanistan?', *Dawn*, 14 September 2022, at https://www.dawn.com/news/1710043.
40. 'Hotbed of Militancy', Editorial, *Dawn*, 25 July 2022, at https://www.dawn.com/news/1701458.
41. Najibullah Lalzoy, 'Taliban Destroys Pakistan's Barbed-wire Erected on Durand Line', *The Khaama Press*, 21 December 2021, at https://www.khaama.com/taliban-destroys-pakistans-barbed-wire-erected-on-durand-line-347357/.
42. 'Review – "Durand's Curse: A Line Across the Pathan Heart"', Asian Lite, 2 May 2022, at https://asianlite.com/2022/lite-blogs/review-durands-curse-a-line-across-the-pathan-heart/.
43. Manoj Gupta, no. 30.

# 14

# Afghanistan Again Under Taliban: Present Imperfect, Future Uncertain

*Ashok Behuria*

The Taliban came, they saw, they conquered. This is how one can describe the Taliban entry into Kabul on 15 August 2021. The forces of the Kabul government, funded, trained, equipped and enabled by the most powerful nations of the world led by the US just melted away offering zero resistance, as if some invisible (and still unknown) deal was struck between the Taliban and the US on the one hand and the Kabul government and the Taliban on the other.

The successful return of the Taliban came after a year and half of the agreement signed at Doha (in February 2020), which the Americans struck with the Taliban, wherein the latter committed themselves to good behaviour.[1] Interestingly, the US signed this agreement with 'the Islamic Emirate of Afghanistan which [was] not recognized by the United States as a state and [was] known as the Taliban.'[2]

It was hard to imagine that the US would look away from its friends and associates in Kabul and finally decide to end its experiment of almost two decades to rebuild Afghanistan as a democratic state. After February 2020, however, it was clear that the US had given up on Afghanistan and was fashioning an honourable exit, notwithstanding the American hesitation to recognise the Taliban as the "Islamic Emirate". Even as the US Congress instituted a bipartisan Afghanistan War Commission in December 2021 'to conduct a comprehensive review of key decisions' taken by the US from June 2001 to August 2021,[3] basically do a forensic study of its failure in Afghanistan, the Taliban revelled at their success and a sense of euphoria overwhelmed the Islamist radical groups of all hues in the region and beyond. This was visible in the Daesh suicide attack on the Kabul Airport, 11 days after the Taliban overran Kabul, that killed around 183 people including 13 US armed personnel. The US's helplessness was evident in the fact that it was in no mood to reconsider its decision to leave Afghanistan to the Taliban, even in the face of such early backlash. The liberal democratic constituency that the US and its allies had invested in was left to the mercy of the very regressive force that they had so fervently desired to replace.

All this was happening in the days following the pandemic that had ravaged the entire world. With the departure of the US, the aid and assistance that Afghanistan enjoyed over the years also dried up very fast. The US has since tied its doles to demonstration of good behaviour by the Taliban. Things have panned out in such a manner ever since that the Afghans are being visited by a chronic humanitarian crisis that is only being marginally addressed by show of bare charity by some of the developed countries in the world.

In this context, it is useful to analyse the state-of-affairs in the war-ravaged Afghanistan and its implications for India, the region and the world.

## Return of the Taliban and the Situation on the Ground

It has been three and a half years since the Taliban returned to power. Much water has flown down the Kabul River since then. The Taliban have not behaved as moderately as they were expected to. Reports from the UN and other sources paint a rather unflattering picture of Afghanistan under the Taliban.

### *Status of Women*

With the suspension of the 2004 Afghan Constitution, women's rights are no longer protected by law. Moreover, the Taliban have disbanded Afghanistan Independent Human Rights Commission (AIHRC) and the Ministry of Women's Affairs (MoWA). The directives issued by the Taliban have impacted the life of the girls and women adversely. Soon after their return, the Taliban shut down secondary schools for girls in 24 out of 34 provinces that put a stop to education for about 850,000 girls. Apart from this, it is now mandatory for women to wear hijab, stay at home unless it is absolutely necessary to go out, and travel outside only if accompanied by a male member. They cannot wear coloured attire and their family members would be held responsible for their conduct.[4] A report by Amnesty International on 22 July 2023 said that since the Taliban took control, they had 'violated women's and girls' rights to education, work and free movement; decimated the system of protection and support for those fleeing domestic violence; detained women and girls for minor violations of discriminatory rules; and contributed to a surge in the rates of child, early and forced marriage in Afghanistan.'[5]

They have arrested women human rights activists and stopped women from attending universities and issued a directive to non-governmental organisations (NGOs) to stop their female staff from working in their concerns. Women-led businesses that used to employ a large number of women have been closed. Women have been ejected from the justice system. A fair number of women working in bureaucracy and the judicial system have been asked to stay home. The Taliban interim foreign minister obliquely referred to the criticism of such policies in an article in *Al Jazeera* in March 2023 saying that 'internal affairs' have been 'misconceived or misconstrued,' and there was a need to paint an 'accurate picture of the values and needs of Afghanistan' based on the 'religious and cultural sensibilities' of Afghan society which 'require a cautious approach.' Failure to maintain a 'proper equilibrium, pertaining to such sensibilities' has led to 'serious difficulties' in the past and they have drawn their own lessons from history, he would argue.[6]

### *State of Economy*

On the economic front, Afghanistan is facing 'intersecting economic and humanitarian crises.'[7] This is partly because of multiple reasons but mainly because of the withdrawal of international assistance after Taliban's return and pegging their help to demonstration of good behaviour by the Taliban. In the financial year the Taliban came to power (2020–21), the gross domestic product per capita income dropped by 34 per cent. The Central Bank of Afghanistan under the Taliban has been cut off from the international banking system and the US would not let it access its assets including foreign currency reserves. The cumulating adverse impact of US sanctions on the Taliban, the after-shocks of the pandemic, the tremors of the Ukraine war and mismanagement of political-economy by the Taliban have led to a severe economic crisis with debilitating impact on the ongoing humanitarian crisis leading to multiple problems of severe food shortage, malnutrition, infant-mortality, and starvation.

The Taliban do not consider themselves responsible for these crises and have claimed that they had inherited 'a collapsed narco-state, with an emptied treasury, unpaid bills, millions of drug addicts, rampant corruption, universal poverty and unemployment and a stagnant economy.'[8] The Taliban foreign minister cited above would rather say that they are trying their best to "Afghanise" all sectors of governance and taking steps to 'disentangle Afghanistan from the crippling reliance on foreign aid—which defined the political setup of the past decades' and they would follow a foreign policy based on equality and respect avoiding 'entanglement in global and regional rivalries.'[9]

***Security Situation***

The Taliban would claim that since their return the security situation has improved. In fact, the Taliban were the principal actors engaging in attacks on the previous government and therefore it was natural that the level of violence would come down. Data from independent sources would also prove that. From the table given below from South Asian Terrorism Portal it is clear that incidents of violence came down sharply from 1180 in 2021 to 406 in 2024 with the number of deaths also going down from 8469 in 2021 to 856 in 2024 and there is a continuous decline in numbers since 2021.

**Table 1: Yearly Terrorist Incidents and Fatalities in Afghanistan**

| *Year* | *Incidents of Killing* | *Civilians* | *Security Forces* | *Terrorists/ Insurgents/ Extremists* | *Not Specified* | *Total* |
|---|---|---|---|---|---|---|
| 2018 | 1788 | 1284 | 1557 | 11883 | 137 | 14861 |
| 2019 | 1723 | 817 | 728 | 10634 | 6 | 12185 |
| 2020 | 1156 | 847 | 1217 | 5529 | 86 | 7679 |
| 2021 | 1180 | 1122 | 788 | 6386 | 173 | 8469 |
| 2022 | 416 | 657 | 0 | 83 | 913 | 1653 |
| 2023 | 268 | 290 | 0 | 75 | 136 | 501 |
| 2024 | 406 | 206 | 0 | 29 | 621 | 856 |
| 2025 | 54 | 14 | 0 | 3 | 138 | 155 |
| Total* | 6991 | 5237 | 4290 | 34622 | 2210 | 46359 |

* Data till 15 March 2025.

*Source:* Datasheet–Afghanistan: Yearly Fatalities, South Asia Terrorism Portal, Institute for Conflict Management, New Delhi, Last updated 15 March 2025, at https://satp.org/datasheet-terrorist-attack/fatalities/afghanistan (Accessed 17 March 2025).

This, however, may not be the whole picture. Afghanistan continues to be in the throes of violence, although on a reduced scale, with a more virulent Islamist outfit called Islamic State–Khorasan (IS–K) defying the Taliban's call for peace and launching attacks on the minority Shia population. The Taliban have taken measures to stop such violence, which does not show any sign of abating soon. Intra-Afghan differences and lack of consensus on the nature of government in Afghanistan has perhaps added to Taliban's ambivalence about launching an all-out offensive against the IS–K and allied forces. It is believed that there are elements within the Taliban empathising with the IS–K, which is inhibiting their efforts to rein in these forces.

### *Taliban Divided?*

There are reports of three groups within the Taliban, that is, the *moderates* (the politicians) led by Mullah Abdul Ghani Baradar, the *extremists* (Haqqani group; the fighters), led by Sirajuddin Haqqani, who is the acting interim minister and the *conservatives* (the mullahs) led by Haibatullah Akhundzada, who are the decision makers. What unites them is their zeal for establishing an Islamic system of governance, while they differ in the methods to be used to achieve such goal. The Taliban are Pashtun dominated and this is very clearly visible in the all-male predominantly Pashtun interim government, which lasts till date. The moderates who negotiated the deal with the Americans have been relegated to the position of 'deputies' while the cabinet berths went mostly to the Haqqani group, known for its alliance with the al Qaeda and for harbouring the Tehrik-e-Taliban Pakistan (TTP). The conservatives under Mullah Akhundzada have tried to maintain their leadership in concert with these two forces—the moderates and the extremists. This is not to deny that they do have consensus, howsoever fragile, over their approach to the women and the minorities. That is the reason why the Tajiks, Uzbeks and the Hazaras are almost absent from the corridors of power.

The Taliban are unapologetic about their non-inclusive policy, despite their profession earlier of initiating an intra-Afghan dialogue. This is a fault line that is waiting to explode in case the economic situation does not improve. However, they may not have been entirely unfazed by the fact that their government remains unrecognised, even by the very powers that backed their return, that is, Pakistan, China, Russia, Iran and Turkey. All these countries are worried about the adverse impact of Afghanistan labouring under the Taliban refusing to moderate itself on their security. Pakistan is worried about the sudden surge in attacks by TTP operating from Afghan soil especially because the Taliban have not responded to its request to initiate action against them. The Russians and the Chinese, exploring newer areas of convergence between them in the backdrop of the Ukraine war, are not too eager to step in and help the Taliban tide over the crises they are facing in Afghanistan.

### *Seeking Recognition without Moderation*

The Taliban have come to a stage where they have started seeking international recognition and expressing their willingness to work with the US and the international community. However, they are still not prepared to form an inclusive government and grant freedom to women and minorities as per international norms and practices. They do not wish to be seen to be succumbing to pressures from outside to moderate themselves. In the face of a more extremist force emerging in the horizon in the shape of the IS–K, the Taliban may not change its conservative agenda at all. At the same time, its main endeavour would be to avoid getting embroiled in any such controversial attack on the US and the West (like in the case of 9/11) that would incur their wrath again compelling them to take summary action against the Taliban like they did in 2001. They are likely to operate under the tolerance threshold of the international community precluding the possibility of any armed action against them in future. The people of Afghanistan, used to subsistence-level existence for a long time, are also unlikely to come out openly in a popular protest against the Taliban. Given these possibilities, the Taliban are likely to stay quarantined within Afghanistan while the women and the minorities are doomed to a second-class status in the state.

## Implications for India and the Region

There was a genuine fear in India that Afghanistan returning to Taliban rule would be a bad proposition because Pakistan was likely to retain its influence over them, which it could use against India like it had done in the past during the previous stint the Taliban had in Afghanistan (1996–2001). However, that has not happened so far, although some reports of India-focused jihadi groups raising their terror training camp in Afghanistan came out in the Indian media subsequent to the return of the Taliban. However, Pakistani predicament on account of intensified attacks by the TTP is there for all to see.

### *Pakistan Stumped*

Pakistan has found itself in an uncomfortable situation because it has now faced multiple attacks by TTP who are supposedly given a long rope by the Afghan Taliban. Pakistani requests in this regard, seeking Taliban's intervention against TTP, have largely fallen on deaf ears. This has, in a way, balanced the strategic threat India and Pakistan are facing separately from a Taliban-controlled Afghanistan. The Taliban action in February 2023,[10] resulting in the killing of Ejaz Ahmed Ahanger, an IS–K operative in Kunar of Kashmiri origin, responsible for planning multiple attacks on Indians and Indian facilities in Afghanistan, as well as the Taliban expression of intent to have good relationship with India, has irked Pakistan. It should, however, not mean that Pakistan and the Taliban have turned into eternal enemies of each other. However, the strain in the relations is quite visible and the Taliban's intransigence to act against the TTP continues to define the relationship. Pakistan has even taken measures that denote its displeasure with the Taliban since 2023. One of these is the decision to expel Afghan refugees on the pretext that they were security threats to Pakistan.

In fact, in October 2023, the Pakistan Government unveiled a strategy to deport what it called "foreign nationals" lacking valid visas or those who had exceeded their visa duration by more than one year. These so called "foreign nationals" meant Afghans residing in Pakistan without legal documentation. The United Nations estimated that approximately 3.8 million Afghans were present in Pakistan at the time the deportation announcement was made, while Pakistani officials suggested the figure could be as high as 4.4 million. Afghans represented 98 per cent of the foreign national population in the country. By January 2025, more than 813,300 individuals had returned to Afghanistan. The Pakistan Government attributed the mass deportations to a rise in crime and violence, including incidents of suicide attacks. However, the turn of events suggested that there were political motivations behind such abrupt deportations, suggesting that the Pakistan Army aimed to compel the Taliban to heed Pakistani request and rein in the TTP.

***Engagement India-style***

Following the Taliban's takeover of Afghanistan in August 2021, India's interaction with the regime and the nation has progressed through a pragmatic, careful, and cautious strategy of gradual engagement. This transformation underscores India's strategic imperative to preserve its influence in Afghanistan, protect national security, counter regional adversaries such as Pakistan and China, and respond to humanitarian issues—all while managing the ethical and diplomatic complexities associated with engaging an unrecognised, authoritarian government.

The overthrow of the US-backed Afghan government by the Taliban on 15 August 2021 was perceived widely in India as a considerable setback. With an investment exceeding $3 billion in various development initiatives—such as the Salma Dam, the Afghan Parliament building, and the Delaram–Zaranj highway—India had established robust relationships with the Islamic Republic of Afghanistan, particularly under the leadership of Hamid Karzai and Ashraf Ghani. The resurgence of the Taliban disrupted two decades of soft power diplomacy that aimed to counteract Pakistan's influence and foster a stable, amicable neighbour.

As the Taliban consolidated their hold, India promptly evacuated its diplomatic personnel from Kabul and shuttered its embassy and consulates, including those in Kandahar and Mazar-i-Sharif. On 31 August 2021, India engaged in its first official dialogue with the Taliban when Ambassador to Qatar, Deepak Mittal, met with Sher Mohammad Abbas Stanekzai, the head of the Taliban's political office in Doha, at India's embassy. This meeting, initiated by the Taliban, centred on the safety of Indian citizens and sought assurances that Afghan territory would not be utilised for anti-India terrorism, reminiscent of concerns stemming from the 1999 IC-814 hijacking during the Taliban's earlier governance. Subsequently, India suspended Afghan visas, including those for students and medical patients, indicating a significant withdrawal from active involvement.

India did not, however, completely sever its ties with Afghanistan following its withdrawal. Confronted with a deepening humanitarian crisis—intensified by drought, economic disintegration, and the exit of the US forces—India initiated a programme of assistance. In December 2021, it dispatched 1.6 tonnes of medical supplies, followed by 2,500 metric tonnes of wheat in early 2022, which was transported through Pakistan and delivered to the World Food Programme in Afghanistan. This represented a transition to a humanitarian-focused strategy, allowing India to avoid direct support for the Taliban while fostering goodwill among the Afghan populace. By June 2022, India cautiously moved towards re-engagement. A delegation led by J.P. Singh, who then headed the Pakistan–Afghanistan–Iran (or PAI) division in the Ministry of External Affairs (MEA) of India, travelled to Kabul to supervise the distribution of humanitarian aid following a devastating earthquake in Khost and Paktika provinces. Singh's meeting with Taliban's Acting Foreign Minister Muttaqi marked the first official visit since the Taliban's takeover. That same month, India reopened its embassy in Kabul with a "Technical Team" to facilitate aid coordination, indicating a pragmatic approach to collaborating with the current authorities without granting formal recognition. This approach stood in stark contrast to India's outright rejection of the Taliban during their previous rule from 1996 to 2001, when it had shown its predilection for the Northern Alliance.

India's involvement in Afghanistan evolved cautiously throughout 2022 and 2023, striking a balance between humanitarian assistance and security concerns. New Delhi voiced its apprehension regarding the Taliban's ban on women's university education in December 2022, which was in line with UN Security Council Resolution 2593, adopted during India's presidency in 2021, advocating for inclusivity and human rights. Nevertheless, a pragmatic approach had started shaping India's policy by then.

India continued to provide aid, including the delivery of 50,000 metric tonnes of wheat, 500,000 COVID-19 vaccine doses, and winter clothing, while also engaging with the Taliban to prevent the use of Afghan territory by groups such as Lashkar-e-Taiba and Jaish-e-Mohammed, which pose threats to India. In 2023, India took part in regional discussions involving the Taliban, including the January 2023 Regional Cooperation Initiative meeting in Kabul, where the head of its technical team spoke alongside representatives from China, Russia, and Pakistan. This participation underscored India's intention to maintain its relevance in Afghan matters amid the increasing influence of China, exemplified by Beijing's ambassador being stationed in Kabul since September 2023. By November 2023, India permitted diplomats appointed by the Taliban to assume control of abandoned Afghan consulates in Mumbai and Hyderabad, a pragmatic measure aimed at addressing the needs of the Afghan community without extending official recognition.

The most significant escalation in engagement with the Taliban came in 2024 and early 2025, driven by deteriorating Taliban–Pakistan ties and India's strategic recalibration. Pakistan's December 2024 airstrikes on alleged TTP hideouts in Afghanistan's Paktika Province—killing dozens and prompting Taliban retaliation—created an opening for India. Islamabad's fraying influence over Kabul, once a Taliban patron, contrasted with India's warming ties.

On 8 January 2025, Indian Foreign Secretary Vikram Misri met Taliban's Acting Foreign Minister Muttaqi in Dubai—the highest-level bilateral engagement since 2021. Misri, the MEA's top official, signalled India's intent to elevate relations. The meeting covered:

- *Trade via Chabahar*: Both sides agreed to boost trade through Iran's Chabahar port, which India has developed to bypass Pakistan, reducing Kabul's dependence on Karachi and Gwadar.
- *Humanitarian and Development Aid*: India pledged further support for health and refugee rehabilitation, with plans for new development projects—reviving its pre-2021 role as a major donor.
- *Security Assurances*: The Taliban reiterated their commitments not to harbour anti-India groups, addressing New Delhi's core concern.
- *Cricket Ties*: Leveraging the sport's popularity in both nations, India proposed closer ties in this field.

The statement issued by the Taliban following the meeting referred to India as a "significant regional and economic partner," suggesting Kabul's intention to expand its alliances beyond Pakistan. The MEA highlighted India's continued assistance and prospective initiatives, reaffirming its position of non-recognition while simultaneously strengthening practical relations.

Be that as it may, India's bid to supply humanitarian assistance and upgrade its contact with Afghanistan are interpreted in the media by domestic observers as steps in the right direction, especially since these are guided by political realism rather than retributive diplomacy. It is interesting to find such baby-steps being taken by all countries helping Afghanistan avert the danger of a humanitarian catastrophe while there is absolutely no stomach for cutting some slack on the issue of recognising the Taliban without them honouring their own commitments incorporated in the Doha agreement on issues of inclusive government and the rights of minorities and women.

### Menacing IS–K, Resurgent Al Qaeda

In the meanwhile, the Taliban have demonstrated some resolve for fighting out the IS–K and there have been several arrests and killings to this effect. Since a lot of these elements come from the ranks of the Taliban, and the Taliban–IS-K confrontation could degenerate into a fratricidal war, there is a possibility of the Taliban striking a deal with the IS–K. Such a deal would turn Afghanistan into a hotbed for jihadi activities because the IS–K is in no mood to scale down on its global agenda any time soon. Neighbourhood terror elements like Islamic Movement of Uzbekistan (IMU), which has already pledged its allegiance to the Islamic State, and the East Turkestan Islamic Movement (ETIM), have reportedly received a boost from the Taliban's return. Many of their cadres locked up in various jails in Afghanistan were released in the aftermath of the Taliban's return when there was a move to free all the Taliban cadres imprisoned by the previous administrations. They have now teamed up again and countries like Uzbekistan and China are worried about these groups reviving their secessionist/Islamist agenda in the region and posing a critical security challenge to these countries. The brutal IS-inspired attacks by members of a little-known National Thowheeth Jama'ath and their connections to the Islamic State cells in southern and eastern India point to the disturbing possibility of similar attacks or lone-wolf strikes by members of nascent radical groups motivated by the success of Islamist groups like the Taliban, which saw the back of a global superpower like the US.

The IS–K/ISIL (Islamic State in Iraq and Levant) affiliates are asserting themselves, with the express intent to make their presence felt globally in the post-Baghdadi (leader of ISIL who was killed on 26–27 October 2019 by US forces in a military operation codenamed Operation Kayla Mueller) scenario after receiving a setback in the Syrian theatre. While it is betraying its global ambitions through its undaunted assertions in the Afghan and African theatres, Al Qaeda has also quietly spread its tentacles in the South Asian theatre through AQIS (Al Qaeda in the Indian Sub-continent). It has like the IS–K announced its footprint in Jammu and Kashmir. Unlike the IS–K, Al Qaeda has its umbilical cord tied to Taliban and has pledged its loyalty to the Emir of Taliban, Mullah Akhundzada. Its Islamist ambition does not necessarily stay confined to Afghanistan. The Taliban, in their current edition, have chosen not to express themselves as agents of global Islam. However, Al Qaeda, despite its allegiance to the Taliban, and death of its leader Ayman

Al-Zawahiri (in July 2022) has not shunned its global agenda. The new Al Qaeda leader, suspected to be in Iran, endorses the global Islamist agenda of this outfit.[11]

Al-Qaeda maintains close connection with its offshoots in Africa (Al Shabab in Somalia, Jama'a Nusrat ul-Islam wa al-Muslimin [JNIM] has been able to expand its operations in West Africa and the Sahel) and the Middle East. There are reports of fighting between the affiliates of ISIL and Al Qaeda in most of the theatres where they are operating in Asia and Africa. As these two competing terror machines with their franchisees spread all over the Afro-Asian theatre fight the local governments and each other, the Central Asian neighbours of Afghanistan and China have shown their sensitivity to the resurgence of diasporic terror groups like IMU[12] and the ETIM that now calls itself Turkestan Islamic Party (TIP) and their assertion in the northern frontiers of Afghanistan.

There were reports of Al-Qaeda's affiliate Jamaat Ansarullah (JA), a Tajik group regarded as the Taliban of Tajikistan, joining the Taliban special units fighting resistance forces along the border of Tajikistan in the Afghan provinces of Badakhshan, Kunduz and Takhar. It was also reported that a senior leader of JA, Muhammad Sharipov (*aka* Mahdi Arsalan) has been tasked by the Taliban to look after the security of five districts of Badakhshan Province.[13] The Taliban have a tough job ahead either trying to rein in these terror groups or hiding its acquiescence with their jihadi plans in the neighbourhood. The international community also has to closely monitor the developments and ensure that the foreign fighters in Afghanistan do not carry the germs of Jihad across the borders into other states of central and southern Asia.

## The Future

An obstinate Taliban resistant to change and a fatigued international community unwilling to engage an immoderate Taliban steeped in puritanical orthodoxy makes the future of Afghanistan look gloomy and uncertain. The trend suggests that majority of Afghans, bound by tribal mores and Islamic zeal, would be content with their existence at the subsistence-level and not push for the replacement of the Taliban any time soon. The Taliban have learnt their lessons too from their earlier experience during 1996–2001 and would avoid, in all likelihood, optimal deterioration of overall socio-political condition warranting coercive external intervention. The international community led by the US has also learnt its own lesson and would not again root for wholesale transformative indulgence in a country that appears unready for liberal democratic institutions even in the face of grave provocation and would not go beyond short and swift kinetic action. In the post-pandemic and post-Ukraine world, there is also less appetite in the developing countries to waste their resources on a country like Afghanistan where after investing trillions of dollars over 20 years, the people still pined for an Islamist future and considered democracy inimical to their culture and interest.

Any effort to transform Afghanistan has to begin with recognition of the fact that the orthodox tribal leadership imbued with Islamist fervour will continue to hold sway for a considerable length of time and dictate the future course of politics in the war-ravaged country. It is this harbinger class that must be engaged and informed about the need for bringing about a wholesale change in their outlook and draw lessons from history that inflexible approach to politics often leads to disaster. While it is true the Taliban would like to get engaged on its own terms, the desperation it has shown in recent days, which comes out very clearly in Taliban's Interim Foreign Minister Muttaqi's *Al Jazeera* overtures should be taken as a soft signal and taken advantage of. A renewed dialogue with the Taliban, this time round not with Baradar and his men, but with the Haqqanis and the top leadership, could actually enliven the possibility of extracting concessions from the Taliban with regard to issues that it considers non-negotiable. The Interim Foreign Minister Muttaqi must be reminded in such a dialogue that they have to climb down from their non-negotiable positions because as he himself wrote 'one hand cannot clap'.[14]

## NOTES

1. The Taliban promised to 'prevent the use of the soil of Afghanistan by any group or individual against the security of the United States and its allies', 'start intra-Afghan negotiations with Afghan sides' and work towards 'a permanent and comprehensive ceasefire', in return for withdrawal of all foreign troops and release of combat and political prisoners 'as a confidence building measure.' See 'Agreement for Bringing Peace to Afghanistan between the Islamic Emirate of Afghanistan which is not recognized by the United States as a state and is known as the Taliban and the United States of America', US State Department, 29 February 2020, at https://www.state.gov/wp-content/uploads/2020/02/Agreement-For-Bringing-Peace-to-Afghanistan-02.29.20.pdf (Accessed 26 October 2023).
2. Ibid.
3. See 'Afghanistan War Commission', at https://www.afghanistanwarcommission.org/ (Accessed 26 October 2023).
4. 'Situation of Human Rights in Afghanistan', Report of the Special Rapporteur on the Situation of Human Rights in Afghanistan, Human Rights Council Fifty-first session, 6 September 2022, at https://www.ohchr.org/en/documents/country-reports/ahrc516-situation-human-rights-afghanistan-report-special-rapporteur (Accessed 26 October 2023).
5. Amnesty International, 'Afghanistan: UN Human Rights Council must address Taliban's

ongoing "relentless abuses"', 5 March 2023, at https://www.amnesty.org/en/latest/news/2023/03/afghanistan-un-human-rights-council-must-address-talibans-ongoing-relentless-abuses/ (Accessed 26 October 2023).

6. Mawlawi Amir Khan Muttaqi, 'Afghanistan is ready to work with the US, but sanctions must go', *Al Jazeera*, 23 March 2023, at https://www.aljazeera.com/opinions/2023/3/23/afghanistan-is-ready-to-work-with-the-us-but-sanctions-must-go (Accessed 26 October 2023).
7. Congressional Research Services, 'Afghanistan: Background and U.S. Policy', 21 June 2023, p. 2, at https://crsreports.congress.gov/product/pdf/R/R45122 (Accessed 26 October 2023).
8. Mawlawi Amir Khan Muttaqi, no. 6.
9. Ibid.
10. Praveen Swami and Amogh Rohmetra, 'Top Kashmir jihad commander who led Indian suicide bombers in Afghan IS attacks believed killed', *The Print*, 21 February 2023, at https://theprint.in/india/top-kashmir-jihad-commander-who-led-indian-suicide-bombers-in-afghan-is-attacks-believed-killed/1385976/ (Accessed 26 October 2023).
11. 'Thirty-first report of the Analytical Support and Sanctions Monitoring Team submitted pursuant to resolution 2610 (2021) concerning ISIL (Da'esh), Al-Qaida and associated individuals and entities', UN Security Council, S/2023/95, 13 February 2023, at https://www.securitycouncilreport.org/atf/cf/%7B65BFCF9B-6D27-4E9C-8CD3-CF6E4FF96FF9%7D/N2303891.pdf (Accessed 28 February 2025).
12. Lucas Webber and Bruce Pannier, 'The Islamic Movement of Uzbekistan's Enduring Influence on IS-Khurasan', Global Network on Extremism and Technology, 3 March 2023, at https://gnet-research.org/2023/03/03/the-islamic-movement-of-uzbekistans-enduring-influence-on-is-khurasan/ (Accessed 26 October 2023).
13. 'Thirtieth Report of the Analytical Support and Sanctions Monitoring Team submitted pursuant to resolution 2610 (2021) concerning ISIL (Da'esh), Al-Qaida and associated individuals and entities', UNSC, S/2022/547, 15 July 2022, at https://www.securitycouncilreport.org/atf/cf/%7B65BFCF9B-6D27-4E9C-8CD3-CF6E4FF96FF9%7D/S%202022%20547.pdf (Accessed 26 September 2023).
14. Mawlawi Amir Khan Muttaqi, no. 6.

# 15

# India's Shifting Approach to Taliban in Afghanistan

*Ajay Darshan Behera*

The Taliban's swift takeover of Kabul on 15 August 2021 marked the collapse of two decades of international efforts to establish a stable Afghan state. The Doha Agreement between the United States and the Taliban, signed in February 2020, outlined a conditional withdrawal of US and coalition forces. However, as foreign troops left, the Taliban quickly advanced, capturing key districts and border checkpoints with minimal resistance from Afghan security forces. The unexpected fall of Kabul resulted in a chaotic US–NATO withdrawal, sealing the Taliban's return to power.

For India, this development posed a profound foreign policy dilemma. Historically opposed to the Taliban, New Delhi had supported Afghanistan's republican governments and invested in development projects to counterbalance Pakistan's influence. With the Taliban now in control, India has to navigate a complex landscape—balancing security concerns, economic stakes, and regional geopolitics. This paper analyses India's predicament by examining the historical context of Indo-Afghan relations, India's economic interests in Afghanistan, India's perceived security threats, shifting regional geopolitics, and India's evolving diplomatic strategies. India's approach involves difficult trade-offs between engaging with a regime it long shunned and protecting its interests in an Afghanistan now controlled by the Taliban.

## Historical Context

India and Afghanistan have historically maintained friendly ties, though these relations have fluctuated due to Afghanistan's internal turmoil. During the

1980s, India was the only South Asian country to recognise the Soviet-backed Democratic Republic of Afghanistan, aligning with its broader policy of opposing extremist forces. However, the 1990s marked a downturn as the Afghan civil war escalated and the Taliban seized power in 1996. India did not recognise the Taliban's Islamic Emirate and instead supported the anti-Taliban Northern Alliance, led by figures like Ahmad Shah Massoud, in cooperation with Iran and Russia. India's reluctance to engage with the Taliban stemmed from concerns over the group's ties to Pakistan and its alleged support for anti-India terrorist activities.

A critical moment in India's stance against the Taliban occurred in December 1999, when Indian Airlines Flight IC-814 was hijacked and taken to Taliban-controlled Kandahar. India was compelled to negotiate with the Taliban and terrorist groups to secure the release of the hostages, reinforcing its distrust of the regime. India, to ensure passenger safety, acquiesced to the release of a jailed Pakistani terrorist, Masood Azhar. After being transferred to Afghanistan, the Taliban allowed Azhar to travel to Pakistan, where he founded Jaish-e Mohammad (JeM), responsible for a spate of high-profile attacks across India.

Following the US-led intervention in 2001 that toppled the Taliban, India quickly re-established diplomatic relations with the new Afghan government. It strongly supported the administrations of Presidents Hamid Karzai and Ashraf Ghani, viewing them as essential partners in the fight against extremism and Pakistani influence. Over the next two decades, India remained one of Afghanistan's closest regional allies, investing significantly in development projects while steering clear of direct military involvement. Indian policymakers regarded the US-backed Afghan government as a strategic buffer against regional instability.

Between 2001 and 2021, India emerged as a significant contributor to Afghanistan's reconstruction efforts, providing over $3 billion in aid. It made India the largest regional donor and one of Afghanistan's top five global donors. Its assistance materialised through high-profile infrastructure projects that symbolised the strong bilateral partnership. India financed the construction of the Afghan Parliament building in Kabul and other major projects, including roads, dams, schools, hospitals, power lines, and training programmes designed to enhance Afghanistan's human capital and governance structures.

Among India's most ambitious initiatives was the Afghan-India Friendship Dam (Salma Dam) in Herat Province. This project played a crucial role in Afghanistan's agricultural and energy sectors. India's Border Roads Organisation also constructed the 218-kilometre Zaranj–Delaram highway, which links Afghanistan's remote southwest to the Iranian border. This highway provided Afghanistan with an alternative trade route through Iran's Chabahar Port, reducing its dependence on Pakistan. Such infrastructure projects contributed to Afghanistan's development and aligned with India's strategic interests in enhancing regional connectivity and access to Central Asia.

India also played a vital role in capacity building by training thousands of Afghan civil servants, military personnel, and police officers. It provided scholarships to Afghan students, fostering long-term educational and cultural ties. By 2017, India had refurbished over 200 schools and sponsored more than 1,000 Afghan students in higher education programmes.[1] Although India did not engage in direct military action, it offered military training and non-lethal equipment to Afghan security forces.

This extensive engagement reflected India's strategic objective of preventing the resurgence of a Pakistan-backed extremist regime in Afghanistan. To achieve this, India remained committed to strengthening Kabul's government, ensuring that no radical Islamist regime beholden to Pakistan's security establishment gained a foothold in Afghanistan. Throughout this period, India maintained a policy of engaging only with Afghanistan's elected government and deliberately avoided direct interactions with the Taliban.

However, since the intra-Afghan talks in Doha on 12 September 2020, there had been indications that India might consider engaging in direct negotiations with the Taliban.[2] By mid-2021, as it became clear that the Taliban might regain power, India began to reassess its position. In a significant policy shift, Indian envoys held a meeting with the Taliban representatives in Doha, facilitated by Qatar.[3] This marked a departure from India's strict policy of non-engagement with the Taliban, signalling a pragmatic response to Afghanistan's evolving political reality.

The Taliban's swift takeover of Afghanistan in August 2021, following the US withdrawal, presented a significant challenge for India. After two decades of diplomatic engagement, financial assistance, and goodwill-building efforts toward the Afghan Republic, India suddenly found itself faced with the reality of dealing with a regime it had long opposed. In response, New Delhi evacuated its embassy in Kabul and repatriated all Indian nationals, effectively severing its on-ground presence in the country.

India's long-standing commitment to democracy, minority rights, and development in Afghanistan further complicates any prospects of recognising the Taliban-led government. The ideological gulf between the Taliban and proponents of liberal governance is stark. Rejecting Western influences, the Taliban has formed a non-inclusive government and implemented regressive policies, particularly targeting women and minorities. Girls have been banned from secondary and university education, while decrees prohibit women from working in non-governmental organisations. Reports indicate that the Taliban is cracking down on dissent, suppressing minorities, and diverting humanitarian aid to consolidate its rule. The UN Security Council has sanctioned Taliban leaders as they reinstate policies reminiscent of their previous regime.[4]

Despite these concerns, a complete disengagement from Afghanistan would come at a strategic cost, potentially ceding influence to regional rivals such as Pakistan and China. This underscores India's current dilemma: how to manage relations with a Taliban-controlled Afghanistan while safeguarding its long-term geopolitical and security interests.

### India's Investments in Afghanistan

Over the past two decades, India has made significant investments in Afghanistan's economy and development, driven by humanitarian commitments and strategic interests. These efforts aimed to integrate Afghanistan into regional trade networks while circumventing Pakistan, thereby strengthening economic ties and reducing Afghanistan's reliance on its unstable neighbour. By 2021, India had established considerable on-ground assets and long-term commitments within Afghanistan's economy.

India played a crucial role in developing Afghanistan's infrastructure, enhancing connectivity and public services. As stated earlier, one of the most notable projects was the Afghan-India Friendship Dam (Salma Dam) in Herat, which was fully funded by India at a cost of approximately $275 million. This dam generates 42 MW of power and irrigates 200,000 acres of farmland, making it a vital asset for the economy of western Afghanistan. As mentioned earlier, another significant Indian initiative was the construction of the 218-kilometre Zaranj–Delaram Road that connects Afghanistan's Ring Road to the Iranian border at Zaranj, facilitating Afghan trade through Iran's Chabahar Port.

India also constructed and renovated over 200 schools, numerous hospitals and clinics, and key government buildings. The Afghan Parliament building in Kabul, inaugurated in 2015 at a cost of $90 million, stands as a landmark project symbolising India's commitment to Afghan democracy. Beyond its functionality, this modern complex provides Afghanistan's legislature with a fully equipped venue. India also contributed to the restoration of cultural heritage by helping refurbish historic sites such as the Stor Palace in Kabul, further enhancing its soft power influence.[5]

India's aid programme extended beyond physical infrastructure to encompass critical services. Regular food aid shipments supported Afghanistan in addressing grain shortages, while Indian assistance to Afghan farmers included seeds and agricultural training programmes. In the healthcare sector, India reconstructed the Indira Gandhi Institute of Child Health in Kabul and provided medical vans and essential medicines. Additionally, thousands of Afghan students benefited from Indian scholarships and professional training programmes under the Indian Technical and Economic Cooperation (ITEC) scheme. These initiatives aimed to promote self-reliance and foster long-term goodwill, thereby strengthening Afghanistan's human capital.

With Pakistan blocking direct overland trade between India and Afghanistan, India sought alternative routes to sustain economic engagement. The most ambitious effort was the India–Iran–Afghanistan trilateral agreement to develop Chabahar Port in Iran. This initiative provided India with a crucial trade corridor to Afghanistan and beyond, circumventing Pakistan. India committed $500 million to the development of Chabahar Port and assumed control of port operations in 2018.[6]

India utilised this new route to deliver its first shipment of wheat to Afghanistan in October 2017.[7] The cargo arrived at Chabahar Port by sea and was transported to Afghan cities by truck, reducing Afghanistan's reliance on Pakistani ports. Such initiatives strategically bolstered Afghan–Indian trade, allowing Indian exports like pharmaceuticals, tea, and textiles to enter Afghan markets while enabling Afghanistan to export dry fruits, carpets, and minerals to India. Furthermore, India and Afghanistan established an air freight corridor in 2017, facilitating the direct shipment of high-value goods such as Afghan saffron and pomegranates. By 2020, bilateral trade between India and Afghanistan had reached approximately $1.5 billion annually, making Afghanistan one of the top recipients of Indian development aid.[8]

India also explored Afghanistan's resource wealth and energy transit potential. In 2011, an Indian consortium obtained rights to mine the Hajigak iron ore deposits, which were estimated to contain 1.8 billion tonnes of high-grade ore. India initially intended to invest $10 billion in the project, but security concerns hindered progress.

Another key initiative was India's participation in the Turkmenistan–Afghanistan–Pakistan–India (TAPI) gas pipeline, designed to transport Turkmen gas to Indian markets through Afghanistan and Pakistan. Although the project has remained stalled due to security and financing challenges, India's involvement underscores Afghanistan's strategic role in regional energy connectivity.

By mid-2021, India's investments had established a significant economic presence in Afghanistan. Indian-built infrastructure benefited millions of Afghans, while trade initiatives positioned Afghanistan as a vital transit hub for India's access to Central Asia's energy resources. These efforts were not mere acts of goodwill but part of a broader strategy to enhance India's influence in the region, counter Pakistan's dominance, and create new commercial opportunities.

While the Taliban's return to power in August 2021 created uncertainty regarding these investments, India's longstanding commitment to Afghanistan's development underscored its strategic interest in the country. Through diplomacy, trade partnerships, and infrastructure projects, India's engagement with Afghanistan sought to yield long-term geopolitical and economic benefits while promoting regional stability.

**Taliban's Return and India's Economic Stakes and Connectivity Issues**

The Taliban's sudden return to power in August 2021 significantly disrupted India's economic and developmental investments in Afghanistan. Overnight, India's on-ground presence vanished as diplomats, engineers, and consultants were evacuated. Ongoing projects were halted indefinitely, and future investments were put on hold. Since India, along with most countries, has not recognised the Taliban regime, formal economic engagement has been suspended, leaving Afghanistan's economy in difficulties due to aid cut-offs and sanctions.

India closed its diplomatic missions, including its embassy in Kabul and consulates in Kandahar, Herat, Jalalabad, and Mazar-i-Sharif. This also led to the withdrawal of Indian development officials overseeing infrastructure projects. Consequently, work on about 20 ongoing Indian-funded projects—ranging from roads to schools—halted. For instance, critical extensions and maintenance for the Salma Dam and major highways came to a standstill due to the absence of Indian engineers. To maintain a minimal presence, India sent a technical team back to Kabul in June 2022, primarily for humanitarian coordination.

The Taliban's takeover, combined with Afghanistan's diplomatic isolation, has impeded India's regional connectivity initiatives. Trade through Pakistan was briefly suspended in 2021 but resumed for humanitarian purposes. As an exception, Pakistan allowed India to transport wheat to Afghanistan in late 2021 and early 2022. Meanwhile, India has continued to deliver food aid through Chabahar Port, including 20,000 tonnes of wheat via Iran in March 2023. However, the broader vision of Chabahar as a major trade corridor remains unfulfilled due to global shipping concerns and US sanctions on Iran. Despite these challenges, India signed a 10-year agreement in May 2024 to maintain operations at Chabahar Port, reaffirming its commitment to the project.[9] By 2024, India had transported 2.5 million tonnes of wheat to Afghanistan via Chabahar. However, these shipments remain largely humanitarian rather than the anticipated expansion of commercial trade. Due to political uncertainty, plans for Afghan–Indian business partnerships and investments in mining and exports remain stalled.

A major strategic setback for India has been the disruption of its plans for land connectivity to Central Asia via Afghanistan. During the previous Afghan government, India maintained strong relations with both Afghanistan and Central Asian states, facilitating projects like the India–Afghanistan–Iran transit corridor. Now, without a reliable partner in Kabul, India's direct land access to Central Asia is significantly restricted.

The Taliban, however, have expressed support for regional connectivity projects, including the TAPI gas pipeline, seeking transit revenues. Yet, India remains cautious, as engaging in such projects would necessitate formal dealings with the Taliban, which could be diplomatically complex. Meanwhile, countries like Uzbekistan continue to advocate for trans-Afghan transport corridors linking to Pakistan's ports and Chabahar. China has also moved swiftly to integrate Afghanistan into its Belt and Road Initiative (BRI). Pakistan has sought the Taliban's cooperation to extend the China–Pakistan Economic Corridor (CPEC) into Afghanistan. If India remains disengaged, it risks being excluded from emerging regional transit frameworks.

With its economic investments in Afghanistan largely dormant, India faces a strategic dilemma: whether to maintain a policy of non-engagement or explore limited economic cooperation with the Taliban. While India's development projects continue to benefit Afghan civilians, its inability to exert influence over their operations limits its diplomatic leverage. The Taliban, however, have indicated a willingness to work with India, referring to it as a "significant economic partner."[10] Discussions about expanding trade via Chabahar also suggest possible openings for cautious re-engagement.

The Taliban's return has raised concerns about India's economic interests in Afghanistan. While India's previous investments continue to support Afghan livelihoods, New Delhi currently cannot utilise them for strategic gain. The broader vision of Afghanistan as a transit hub for Indian trade into Central Asia is on hold, awaiting a more favourable political climate. Meanwhile, India is pursuing a flexible strategy—one that balances cautious economic engagement with wider geopolitical realities to protect its long-term interests in the region.

## Taliban–Pakistan Links and India's Security Concerns

The Taliban's return to power in Afghanistan in 2021 reshaped South Asia's geopolitical landscape, intensifying the strategic competition between India and Pakistan. For decades, Islamabad has sought to maintain control over Afghan affairs, leveraging its ties with the Taliban to secure what it calls "strategic depth" against India. Conversely, New Delhi has historically aligned itself with the former Afghan Republic, investing billions in development projects and maintaining strong diplomatic ties with Kabul.

The collapse of the US-backed Afghan government and the Taliban's takeover initially appeared to be a strategic victory for Pakistan, eliminating India's influence in Afghanistan and bringing a long-time Pakistani ally to power. However, the complexities of governance, shifting regional dynamics, and the Taliban's growing defiance of Pakistani expectations have led to a rift in the previously close relationship, creating new challenges for Islamabad while opening limited yet significant opportunities for India.

Pakistan's role in facilitating the Taliban's rise has long raised concerns for India. The Inter-Services Intelligence (ISI) provided financial, logistical, and military support to the Taliban during its initial ascent in the early 1990s, ensuring a pro-Pakistan government in Kabul after the fall of the Soviet-backed Afghan administration. Pakistan was among the few countries to recognise the Taliban regime in 1996, cementing a relationship that endured even after the US invasion of Afghanistan in 2001. Although Pakistan officially became a US ally in the War on Terror, it continued to covertly support the Taliban, offering sanctuary to its leadership in Quetta and other parts of the country.[11] Islamabad's strategic calculus was clear: the Taliban's return to power would impede India from gaining influence in Afghanistan, limit New Delhi's ability to use Afghan territory for strategic partnerships, and provide Pakistan with an ally to counter Indian interests in the region. However, this assumption soon proved overly simplistic, as significant rifts began to emerge between the Taliban and Pakistan over several critical issues.

One of the most contentious points has been the presence and activities of the Tehrik-e-TalibanPakistan (TTP), a militant group ideologically aligned with the Afghan Taliban but engaged in an insurgency against the Pakistani state. Despite Islamabad's repeated demands, the Taliban have been reluctant to act against the TTP, which has launched numerous deadly attacks within Pakistan. The TTP has intensified its assaults on Pakistani military and intelligence targets, including the devastating Peshawar Police Mosque bombing in February 2023 that killed over 100 individuals, most of whom were security personnel. The Taliban's refusal to crack down on the TTP has severely strained relations with Pakistan, challenging the long-held belief that the Taliban would remain a compliant ally. Consequently, Pakistan has resorted to unilateral military action, including airstrikes against TTP hideouts in eastern Afghanistan in 2023 and 2024, further escalating tensions between the two governments.[12]

Compounding these challenges is the long-standing dispute over the Durand Line, the colonial-era border between Afghanistan and Pakistan, which successive Afghan governments—both republican and Taliban-led—have refused to recognise. The Taliban's unwillingness to formally acknowledge the Durand Line as the legitimate boundary has frustrated Islamabad, which expected Kabul to support Pakistan's territorial claims. Instead, the Taliban's defiance has bolstered nationalist sentiments within Afghanistan, leading to deterioration in bilateral relations. Pakistan, having long sought to exert uncontested influence in Afghanistan, now finds itself in an increasingly adversarial position with a regime it once supported, a development that has not gone unnoticed in New Delhi.

For India, the fractures in the Pakistan-Taliban relationship present both risks and opportunities. Historically, India has viewed the Taliban with suspicion due to their close ties with Pakistan and their role in providing sanctuary to anti-India militant groups during the 1990s. Under the Taliban rule, Afghanistan became a haven for anti-India militant groups, including Lashkar-e-Taiba (LeT) and JeM, both responsible for devastating terrorist attacks on Indian soil. Some analysts express concerns that Afghanistan could emerge again as a regional terrorist haven,[13] as seen in the past hosting of groups like LeT and JeM.

The 2001 attack on the Indian Parliament, orchestrated by JeM, was traced back to militant training camps in Afghanistan. The 2008 Mumbai attacks, which claimed over 170 lives, were executed by LeT operatives, further reinforcing India's concerns about Pakistan-based militant groups exploiting Afghan territory for training purposes. Additionally, the 2019 Pulwama attack, in which a suicide bomber killed 40 Indian paramilitary personnel in Jammu and Kashmir (J&K), was attributed to JeM, raising alarms about the potential resurgence of these groups under Taliban rule. The possibility that these groups could again find refuge in Afghanistan remains a primary security concern.[14]

Most of these groups are united by a rigid interpretation of political Islam rooted in Deobandi Sunni ideology. They advocate for strict enforcement of Sharia and stressed solidarity with other Jihadist movements around the world.[15] Their ideological kinship with Al-Qaeda remains strong, driven by shared religious objectives. Despite Taliban assurances, severing ties with Al-Qaeda appears unlikely. The US drone strike that killed Al-Qaeda leader Ayman al-Zawahiri in Kabul on 31 July 2022 reinforced concerns that the Taliban continues to shelter international terrorist groups,[16] raising alarms in New Delhi about Afghanistan's potential resurgence as a breeding ground for extremist activities.

Despite these concerns, the growing divide between the Taliban and Pakistan presents India with an opportunity to re-engage with Afghanistan cautiously. Indian analysts are debating whether India missed an opportunity by not engaging with the Taliban earlier, especially during the US–Taliban negotiations, when recognition could have been crucial. Some argue that India, like other countries, should have initiated contact when negotiations were underway. However, India's official stance has consistently favoured an Afghan-led, Afghan-owned and Afghan-controlled reconciliation process for lasting peace, emphasising that engagement with the Taliban should align with a strategic assessment rather than merely following the actions of others.

The official Indian position remains steadfast, articulated in the joint declaration of the Delhi Regional Security Dialogue hosted by India on 10–11 November 2021. It stated that the government should represent the will of the Afghan people, represent all sections of Afghan society, and ensure the rights of women, children and minorities. The statement emphasised the common concerns of terrorism, terror financing, radicalisation and narco-terrorism emanating from the Taliban-controlled Afghanistan. In the fifth national security advisor's meeting on Afghanistan held in Moscow on 8 February 2023, National Security Advisor Ajit Doval, while focussing on food security and medical supplies for the Afghan people, reaffirmed the importance of the UN Security Council (UNSC) Resolution 2593 (2021),[17] emphasising the denial of sanctuary to terror outfits, including those designated by UNSC Resolution 1267.[18] He stressed the importance of an inclusive and representative dispensation for the overall well-being of Afghan society and called for an inclusive setup in Afghanistan. So, there was constant messaging to the Taliban about not providing sanctuary to terror groups and forming an inclusive government.

India's reluctance to engage directly with the Taliban may stem from a desire to uphold its policy of not negotiating with "militant groups", fearing potential pressures to engage with rebel and separatist groups within India. Following the US withdrawal, India sought to safeguard its security interests and investments in Afghanistan, particularly preventing Kashmir-focused armed groups like LeT and JeM from using Afghanistan as a base for attacks in J&K. Establishing a backchannel with the Taliban became crucial for India to ensure that Afghanistan doesn't evolve into a significant security threat in the future.[19] However, the uncertainties surrounding the credibility and reliability of any assurances from the Taliban pose challenges to any policy of engagement.

While it is difficult to assess a definitive attitudinal change, there have been indications that the Taliban had sought outreach with India. In 2016, Syed Akbar Agha, a cousin of Mullah Syed Tayyab Agha, the former chief of the Taliban's Doha office, expressed the Taliban's willingness to reconcile with India and send a message of peace and friendship. Signals were reportedly sent through informal channels, suggesting that a relationship with India would have bestowed legitimacy on the Taliban in the international community. In 2018, during Russia's regional forum on Afghanistan, where the Taliban was present, the group reportedly reached out directly to Indian diplomats attending the event, expressing a desire to mend fences.

The engagement between the Taliban and India increased once the Taliban came to power. Since then, the Indian side has engaged the Taliban leadership both in Kabul and in third countries. Between August 2021 and January 2025, India gradually enhanced its engagement with the Taliban through a combination of diplomatic, security, and regional channels, ensuring it continued to be a relevant player in Afghanistan's evolving landscape. At the diplomatic level, India has established high-level political contacts with the Taliban by participating in key international forums, such as the Moscow Format consultations. The renewed engagement has not gone unnoticed by Islamabad, which views India's re-entry into Afghan affairs with suspicion.

India's involvement in Afghanistan is also influenced by its long-standing relationships with the country's ethnic minorities, particularly the Tajiks, Hazaras, and the Uzbeks, many of whom remain sceptical of both the Taliban and Pakistan. These groups played a crucial role in the former anti-Taliban Northern Alliance. While India has not openly supported any armed opposition, speculation persists regarding potential covert involvement should the Taliban regime face significant internal challenges. The Taliban is not a homogeneous group and there are differences between the various factions within it. India's interests align more with those of former Northern Alliance leaders, who continue to resist the Taliban's more extreme policies and have traditionally opposed Pakistan's influence in Afghanistan.

The central question in India's Afghanistan strategy is whether the Taliban can truly act independently of Pakistan or if its historical ties will ultimately keep it aligned with Islamabad. If the Taliban continue to provide a safe haven for Pakistan-based terrorist groups targeting India, New Delhi may be compelled to adopt a harder stance. Former Afghan intelligence chief Rahmatullah Nabil had warned that even if India had good meetings and was greeted warmly by Taliban's acting interior minister Sirajuddin Haqqani or other Taliban ministers, India should know that anti-Indian sentiment is inherent in the Taliban.[20] India, therefore, must keep channels open with former leaders, acknowledging that the Taliban's nature may not have fundamentally changed. India's approach should balance pragmatic engagement with the Taliban to safeguard long-term interests.[21] If the Taliban show a willingness to assert an independent foreign policy—especially by addressing India's security concerns—India may pursue further diplomatic and economic engagement.

The evolving Afghanistan–Pakistan dynamic marks a significant shift in the regional balance of power. Pakistan, once confident that the Taliban's return would advance its strategic interests, now faces an increasingly uncooperative regime in Kabul. Conversely, India, which initially feared losing all influence in Afghanistan, is gradually finding avenues to re-engage. Given the fluidity of the situation, India must remain adaptable—seizing opportunities for engagement while preparing for potential security risks. Navigating this complex landscape requires a strategy that balances pragmatism with caution, safeguarding India's strategic interests without inadvertently legitimising a regime whose long-term trajectory remains uncertain.

## Strategic Competition, Shifting Alliances and Regional Geopolitics

The Taliban's takeover of Afghanistan has significantly altered the geopolitical dynamics of South and Central Asia, presenting India with new challenges in a complex regional landscape. India's policy on Afghanistan is now shaped by the actions and interests of key regional and global players—Pakistan, China, Iran, Russia, and the United States—each pursuing its strategy toward the Taliban. This section examines how these regional dynamics impact India's approach and its role in multilateral frameworks such as the Shanghai Cooperation Organisation (SCO). The strategic competition with Pakistan regarding Afghanistan has been discussed in the previous section.

### *China's Expanding Role in Afghanistan and Its Impact on India*

Since the Taliban's return to power in 2021, China has positioned itself as a key player in Afghanistan, engaging pragmatically with the new regime in ways that sharply contrast with India's cautious approach. Unlike New Delhi, which had no formal ties with the Taliban before their takeover, Beijing maintained a steady line of communication with the group and quickly moved to establish diplomatic and economic relations following the US withdrawal. While most countries, including India, closed their embassies in Kabul amid the uncertainty of the Taliban's rule, China chose to keep its diplomatic mission operational. It has since provided economic assistance and engaged in high-level talks with Taliban officials, treating them as the de facto rulers of Afghanistan without extending formal recognition.

China's engagement with Afghanistan is driven by two primary objectives: security and economic interests. The main concern for Beijing is the potential use of Afghan territory by Uighur militant groups to bolster separatist movements in Xinjiang. China has long perceived the East Turkestan Islamic Movement (ETIM) as a direct threat to its internal security, fearing that extremist factions could take advantage of Afghanistan's instability to regroup and coordinate attacks against Chinese interests. The Taliban, aware of China's sensitivities, have promised Beijing that they will not offer safe haven to ETIM militants, striving to maintain stable relations with one of the few major powers willing to engage with them. However, China remains cautious, given Afghanistan's history as a refuge for transnational jihadist groups, and continues to monitor the Taliban's actions closely.

Beyond security concerns, China views Afghanistan as an untapped economic opportunity, especially regarding natural resources. The country's vast reserves of copper, oil, and rare earth elements have attracted Chinese investment, with Beijing seeking ways to incorporate Afghanistan into its broader economic strategy. In January 2023, a Chinese company signed an agreement to extract oil from the Amu Darya basin, marking one of the first significant foreign investment deals under Taliban rule. Discussions have also resumed about the long-stalled Mes Aynak copper mining project, a site estimated to contain one of the world's largest untapped copper deposits. If these projects materialise, they could further entrench China's economic presence in Afghanistan, providing the Taliban with much-needed revenue while enhancing China's access to critical raw materials.

China's growing involvement in Afghanistan presents challenges and opportunities for India. On one hand, Chinese investments could contribute to Afghan stability, reducing the risk of Afghanistan becoming a hub for terrorism. If China pressurises the Taliban to combat extremist groups such as the Islamic State–Khorasan (IS–K) and ETIM, it could indirectly align with India's security interests. On the other hand, China's expanding economic and diplomatic influence could push India further to the sidelines.[22] If Afghanistan becomes integrated into China's BRI, India risks exclusion from regional connectivity networks. Moreover, the prospect of China's alignment with Pakistan, enabling them to shape Afghanistan's geopolitical trajectory and sidelining Indian interests jointly, should not be ruled out altogether despite the current strained relations between Pakistan and Afghanistan.

India remains wary of China's role in multilateral forums such as the SCO, where Beijing has advocated for deeper engagement with the Taliban while minimising concerns about terrorism linked to Pakistan. Furthermore, China has occasionally blocked UN sanctions against terrorists based in Pakistan, which has frustrated India. To counterbalance China, India has strengthened its ties with Russia, Iran, and the Central Asian states, highlighting a regional consensus on counterterrorism and stability in Afghanistan. Given these developments, India has to navigate its Afghan strategy carefully, ensuring that it remains an active player in the region while countering the growing influence of its two main strategic rivals.

### *Iran, Russia, and the United States: Regional and Global Players*

Iran's relationship with Afghanistan and the Taliban is complex. While Iran seeks to protect the Shia community within its traditional spheres of influence, it also harbours deep ideological differences with the Taliban due to their anti-Shia stance. Tehran views the Taliban's takeover of Kabul as an expansion of Sunni Wahhabi influence and closely monitors the group's treatment of the Shia population.

Despite these tensions, Iran has adopted a pragmatic approach, balancing engagement with caution. Although it has not formally recognised the Taliban government, it has maintained diplomatic ties and continued trade with Afghanistan. Additionally, Iran has facilitated Indian humanitarian aid shipments through Chabahar Port, positioning itself as a crucial intermediary between India and the Taliban. Both India and Iran share a strategic interest in countering Pakistan's influence in Afghanistan and curbing the spread of Sunni extremism.

Russia, like India, opposed the Taliban in the 1990s but has since adjusted its policy. Moscow has hosted multiple Taliban delegations and allowed Taliban-appointed diplomats to take over Afghanistan's embassy in Moscow. While Russia initially saw the Taliban as a stabilising force, concerns over IS–K attacks and Central Asian security have made its stance more cautious. India and Russia cooperate on counterterrorism efforts within the SCO, but Moscow's increasing alignment with China and Pakistan complicates India's position.

The United States withdrew its military presence from Afghanistan in August 2021. However, Washington continues to exert influence in

Afghanistan through sanctions, aid policies, and counterterrorism operations. India closely coordinates with the US on Afghanistan, particularly regarding security threats posed by Al-Qaeda, IS–K, and Pakistan-backed terrorist groups. While both India and the US oppose recognising the Taliban, Washington's evolving approach—especially if it seeks counterterrorism cooperation with the Taliban—could lead to policy divergences with India.[23]

India's Afghanistan policy is influenced by regional competition, security concerns, and economic interests. While Pakistan aims to exclude India, tensions between Islamabad and the Taliban create potential opportunities for Indian engagement. At the same time, China's increasing presence presents both security threats and economic challenges. India continues to work with Iran, Russia, and the US, using multilateral platforms like the SCO to advocate for counterterrorism commitments and regional stability.

Going forward, India has to carry out a delicate balancing act: engaging cautiously with the Taliban while ensuring that Afghanistan does not become a hub for anti-India terrorism. India's broader strategic objective remains to prevent its adversaries from dominating Afghanistan's geopolitical and economic future, thereby safeguarding its interests in this volatile region.

### India's Diplomatic Outreach

India's diplomatic outreach towards the Taliban is characterised by caution, pragmatism, and adaptability in response to evolving security, economic, and geopolitical challenges. Although India has not recognised the Taliban government, it acknowledges the de facto reality of their rule and has gradually engaged in limited diplomatic and humanitarian interactions. This approach balances the protection of India's interests with assistance to the Afghan people while strategically withholding formal legitimacy to maintain diplomatic leverage. The key elements of India's evolving engagement include discreet outreach, humanitarian diplomacy, a partial diplomatic presence in Kabul, and carefully managed high-level interactions.

After the Taliban's return in August 2021, India's immediate focus was the safe evacuation of its diplomatic staff and citizens. However, rather than severing ties completely, India kept backchannel communication open. On 31 August 2021, just two weeks after Kabul fell, India's Ambassador to Qatar Deepak Mittal met Sher Mohammad Abbas Stanekzai, head of the Taliban Political Office in Doha, marking the first publicly acknowledged contact with the Taliban. The meeting took place at the Embassy of India on the request of the Taliban. This meeting, although limited to discussions about the safety of Indian nationals, signalled India's willingness to maintain dialogue.

Shortly thereafter, India supported UNSC Resolution 2593, which outlined global expectations from the Taliban, including the need to uphold human rights and prevent Afghanistan from becoming a safe haven for terrorism. In late October 2021, a delegation of Indian diplomats, led by Joint Secretary J.P Singh—head of the Pakistan–Afghanistan–Iran desk in the External Affairs Ministry—engaged with the Taliban's Acting Deputy Prime Minister, Abdul Salam Hanafi. This interaction took place on the sidelines of a regional conference on Afghanistan hosted by Russia, which brought together diplomats from 10 countries, including India, Pakistan, and China, along with a Taliban delegation. These talks marked the first high-level contact between India and a senior member of the Taliban's interim cabinet, reportedly focusing on addressing mutual concerns.

By early 2022, the worsening humanitarian crisis in Afghanistan prompted India to enhance its engagement. India facilitated emergency aid shipments, working with the Taliban to ensure that food and medical supplies reached those in need. Notably, following negotiations with Pakistan, India sent 50 trucks carrying 2,500 tonnes of wheat to Afghanistan through land routes. The Taliban collaborated with the UN World Food Programme to distribute this aid, marking a practical yet indirect partnership between India and the Taliban.

In June 2022, India took a significant step by dispatching a delegation led by Joint Secretary J.P. Singh to deliver humanitarian aid and engage with the Taliban's acting foreign minister, Maulavi Amir Khan Muttaqi. As part of its assistance efforts, New Delhi provided Afghanistan with 20,000 metric tonnes of wheat, 13 tonnes of medicines, 500,000 COVID-19 vaccine doses, and winter clothing.[24] Following this, India reopened its mission in Kabul deploying a technical team to oversee aid distribution and monitor developments on the ground. The Taliban provided security for this mission, indicating their interest in maintaining engagement with India. However, India emphasised that this action did not imply recognition of the Taliban government but was necessary to support the Afghan people.[25]

India reaffirmed its commitment to Afghanistan's stability and development at the Security Council meeting on the UN Assistance Mission in Afghanistan (UNAMA) on 10 March 2025. India's permanent representative to the UN, Ambassador P. Harish, emphasised India's long-standing historical and people-to-people ties with Afghanistan and reiterated its proactive role in regional and international peace efforts. He stated that India remains engaged in humanitarian assistance and since August 2021, India has provided 27 tonnes of relief material, 50,000 tonnes of wheat, 40,000 litres of pesticides, and over 300 tonnes of medical supplies to

Afghanistan. India has also collaborated with various UN agencies in health, food security, education, sports, and capacity building, implementing more than 500 projects across Afghanistan since 2001.[26] Thus, India remains committed to constructive engagement with all stakeholders for peace, stability and the well-being of the Afghan people.

India has maintained backchannel security dialogues with influential Taliban leaders, particularly those seen as pragmatic, such as Mullah Abdul Ghani Baradar.[27] These discussions were reportedly centred on counterterrorism assurances and intelligence-sharing, with a focus on monitoring and curbing the presence of Pakistan-based militant groups like JeM and LeT. By fostering these security dialogues, India aimed to prevent Afghanistan from becoming a base for anti-India militancy while assessing the Taliban's evolving stance on regional security.

To complement these efforts, India has also engaged with regional intermediaries, leveraging its strong ties with countries such as Qatar, the United Arab Emirates, and Turkey to facilitate indirect communication with the Taliban. This multilateral approach ensured that India remained an active stakeholder in Afghanistan's political landscape, influencing key decisions while mitigating risks associated with direct engagement. Through these carefully calibrated measures, India successfully positioned itself as a pragmatic actor, balancing its security imperatives with the need for diplomatic caution in its dealings with the Taliban regime.

The clearest indication of India's evolving approach emerged in January 2025 when Foreign Secretary Vikram Misri met Taliban Acting Foreign Minister Muttaqi in Dubai—the highest-level official meeting between the two sides to date—signalling a pragmatic shift in India's approach. The Taliban praised India as a "significant regional and economic partner," while Indian officials confirmed discussion on trade, connectivity, and humanitarian aid. The talks specifically focused on expanding commercial routes via Chabahar Port, underscoring India's strategic interest in maintaining Afghanistan's connection to its trade networks.

While India remains unwilling to grant formal recognition to the Taliban regime, it has shown a willingness to engage selectively, particularly in areas such as trade, security assurances, and economic cooperation. However, India has carefully maintained a distinction between engagement and diplomatic recognition. It has refused to allow the Taliban-appointed ambassador to assume control of the Afghan Embassy in New Delhi, reinforcing its policy of dealing with the Taliban as de facto authorities without legitimising their rule. Eventually, India might not be averse to establishing consular relations to facilitate the visa process for ordinary Afghans.

India's diplomatic strategy toward the Taliban involves a delicate balancing act—one that aims to protect its security interests, maintain regional influence, and support the Afghan people while avoiding the premature legitimisation of the Taliban government. This approach is anchored in a thoughtful calibration of engagement, ensuring that India remains an active participant in Afghanistan's future without sacrificing its principles. At the heart of this strategy is the choice to engage without formal recognition. By maintaining dialogue with the Taliban, India creates opportunities for practical cooperation, allowing it to tackle key security concerns and protect its interests in Afghanistan. However, it deliberately refrains from granting diplomatic legitimacy, using recognition as a strategic tool rather than an automatic concession.

Alongside this cautious engagement, India continues to utilise its humanitarian and soft power diplomacy to foster goodwill among the Afghan people. Through ongoing efforts in humanitarian aid, education, and medical assistance, India enhances its presence in Afghanistan in ways that transcend political considerations. This not only alleviates the suffering of ordinary Afghans but also ensures that India's long-standing ties with the country remain strong, regardless of shifts in political leadership.

Furthermore, India actively works to shape regional and global consensus on Afghanistan's future. By collaborating with both international and regional powers, it aims to prevent Afghanistan from becoming a hub for terrorism while ensuring open pathways for economic and strategic connectivity. This multilateral engagement allows India to influence broader policies toward Afghanistan, ensuring its interests align with the evolving geopolitical landscape.

While challenges persist—especially in navigating the unpredictability of the Taliban's actions and the competing interests of other regional actors—India's carefully calibrated approach ensures it neither isolates itself from developments in Afghanistan nor rushes into premature commitments. By balancing pragmatism with principled diplomacy, India keeps its options open and protects its strategic interests in a volatile and uncertain regional environment.[28]

## Conclusion

The Taliban's return to power in Afghanistan in August 2021 marked a profound shift in the region, presenting significant political, economic, and security challenges. The prospect of an inclusive, power-sharing government seems unlikely as the Taliban consolidates an Islamic theocracy without a clear economic strategy for sustainability. Historically dependent on foreign aid, Afghanistan now confronts worsening poverty and hunger, exacerbated by a severe humanitarian crisis.

The geopolitical landscape has undergone notable changes. The withdrawal of Western forces and the lack of significant internal resistance have strengthened the Taliban control. This power vacuum has enabled China to increase its influence in Afghanistan. While the Taliban hope that Chinese investment will revive the Afghan economy, Beijing has remained cautious and provided minimal direct economic assistance.

Pakistan, which once viewed the Taliban's return as a strategic gain, now faces an increasingly strained relationship with the regime. The TTP, backed by the Afghan Taliban, has ramped up attacks within Pakistan, leading to retaliatory airstrikes by Pakistani forces. These developments have further strained tensions between the two parties, undermining Pakistan's earlier assumption that a Taliban-led Afghanistan would align with its regional interests. As Pakistan's strategy meets challenges and tensions escalate, regional stability remains fragile. India has to remain vigilant and adaptable to these shifting dynamics.

India is reassessing its long-standing policy of disengagement with the Taliban. The risk that Afghanistan could once again become a hub for anti-India terrorism necessitates a strategic recalibration. While the Taliban have reached out to India in an attempt to normalise relations, deep-seated mistrust remains. The US–Taliban negotiations in Doha demonstrated that the Taliban are not always reliable partners, having reneged on multiple commitments. Moreover, internal divisions within the group, particularly with factions like the Haqqani Network—still designated as a terrorist organisation—continue to pose security risks for India.

India's engagement with the Taliban demonstrates a careful balance between pragmatism and principle, making limited and conditional engagement the most viable approach. A rigid policy of complete isolation may uphold India's moral clarity and commitment to democratic values, but it would also cede strategic ground to Pakistan and China, diminishing India's influence in Afghanistan and leaving it without access and options. Moreover, history suggests that isolating the Taliban does not weaken them; rather, it risks pushing them further into the sphere of hostile regional actors, increasing long-term security threats for India.

Given these considerations, a calibrated middle path—selective engagement without formal recognition—enables India to retain influence without legitimising the regime. By maintaining a technical presence in Kabul, extending humanitarian aid, and pursuing limited economic initiatives, India ensures its relevance in Afghanistan's future. This strategy allows India to adjust its level of engagement based on the Taliban's actions while using diplomatic recognition as leverage. Additionally, it helps counter Pakistan's influence without fully aligning with the Taliban, thus preserving India's long-standing goodwill among the Afghan people.

This nuanced approach, however, presents challenges. India must carefully manage its engagement to avoid inadvertently strengthening the Taliban while safeguarding its own security interests. There remains a risk that the Taliban will continue harbouring anti-India militants, rendering India's outreach ineffective. However, a complete disengagement would leave India without leverage, making it an outsider in a region where adversaries actively shape the strategic environment.

Ultimately, India's approach to Afghanistan must be dynamic and responsive to shifting realities. If the Taliban demonstrate moderation, India can expand its engagement. Conversely, if they become more hostile, India can scale back its outreach while reinforcing its security posture. By neither fully embracing nor entirely rejecting the Taliban, India preserves its strategic options without legitimising a regime that contradicts its values. In a geopolitical landscape where rigid policies are rarely sustainable, a measured and conditional engagement strategy ensures India retains influence while safeguarding its long-term security and strategic interests.

## NOTES

1. 'Strengthening India-Afghanistan Strategic Relations in an Uncertain World', Address by H.E. Shaida Abdali, Ambassador of Afghanistan to India, Brookings India, 25 April 2017, at https://www.brookings.edu/events/india-afghanistan-and-connectivity-in-south-asia-address-by-h-e-shaida-abdali-ambassador-of-afghanistan-to-india/ (Accessed 25 August 2024).
2. Harsh Pant, 'How India Came Around to Talking to the Taliban', *Foreign Policy*, 25 September 2020, at https://foreignpolicy.com/2020/09/25/how-india-came-around-to-talking-to-the-taliban/ (Accessed 14 November 2024)
3. Geeta Mohan, 'Indian Officials had a "Quiet" Rendezvous with Taliban, Says Qatari Special Envoy', *India Today*, 22 June 2021, at https://www.indiatoday.in/world/story/indian-officials-meet-taliban-qatari-special-envoy-talks-1817915-2021-06-22 (Accessed 15 November 2024).
4. Lynne O' Donnell, 'The Taliban are Losing Some of the Cash Cows', *Foreign Policy*, 10 January 2023, at https://foreignpolicy.com/2023/01/10/taliban-afghanistan-women-ban-humanitarian-aid/ (Accessed 4 September 2024).
5. 'India's Indispensable Role in Afghanistan's Development–A Tale of Friendship, Hard Work, Sacrifice', *The Statesman*, 17 August 2021, at https://www.thestatesman.com/india/indias-indispensable-role-afghanistans-development-tale-friendship-hard-work-sacrifice-1502995765.html (Accessed 23 May 2024).
6. 'India and Iran Sign "Historic" Chabahar Port Deal', *BBC News*, 23 May 2016, at https://www.bbc.com/news/world-asia-india-36356163 (Accessed 7 April 2024).

7. Kallol Bhattacherjee, 'India Ships Wheat to Afghanistan via Chabahar', *The Hindu*, 29 October 2017, at https://www.thehindu.com/news/national/india-ships-wheat-to-afghanistan-via-chabahar/article19945498.ece (Accessed 7 April 2024).
8. Aishwarya Paliwal, 'Afghanistan Crisis: Indian Trade Worth $1.5 billion Stops Abruptly as Afghans Stare at Bleak Future', *India Today*, 24 August 2021, at https://www.indiatoday.in/india/story/afghanistan-crisis-indian-bilateral-trade-stops-abruptly-afghans-bleak-future-1844493-2021-08-24 (Accessed 19 August 2024).
9. 'India Inks 10-year Deal to Operate Iran's Chabahar Port', *Reuters*, 14 May 2024, at https://www.reuters.com/world/india/india-sign-10-year-pact-with-iran-chabahar-port-management-et-reports-2024-05-13/ (Accessed 14 October 2024).
10. 'Taliban Say India is a "Significant Regional Partner"After Meeting', *Reuters*, 9 January 2025, at https://www.reuters.com/world/asia-pacific/taliban-say-india-is-significant-regional-partner-after-meeting-2025-01-09/ (Accessed 28 January 2025).
11. Matt Waldman, *The Sun in the Sky: The Relationship between Pakistan's ISI and Afghan Insurgents*, Discussion Paper 18, Crisis States Research Centre, London School of Economics and Political Science (LSE), June 2010, at https://www.lse.ac.uk/international-development/Assets/Documents/PDFs/csrc-discussion-papers/dp18-The-Sun-in-the-Sky.pdf; and Mark Mazzetti, Jane Perlez, Eric Schmitt and Andrew W. Lehren, 'Pakistan Aids Insurgency in Afghanistan, Reports Assert', *The New York Times*, 25 July 2010, at http://www.nytimes.com/2010/07/26/world/asia/26isi.html (Accessed 12 April 2024).
12. 'Amid Economic Crisis, TTP Re-emerges as Potential Threat to Pakistan: Report', *The Hindu*, 17 February 2023, at https://www.thehindu.com/news/international/amid-economic-crisis-ttp-reemerges-as-potential-threat-to-pakistan/article66520404.ece (Accessed 12 April 2024).
13. Suhasini Haidar, 'Taliban is Allowing LeT and JeM to Shift Base to Afghanistan, Claims Former Afghan Security Chief', *The Hindu*, 1 December 2022, at https://www.thehindu.com/news/national/taliban-is-allowing-let-and-jem-to-shift-base-to-afghanistan-claims-former-afghan-security-chief/article66210620.ece (Accessed 25 August 2024).
14. Aijaz Hussain, 'With Taliban's Rise, India Sees Renewed Threat in Kashmir',*The Diplomat*, 15 September 2021, at https://thediplomat.com/2021/09/with-talibans-rise-india-sees-renewed-threat-in-kashmir/ (Accessed 25 August 2024).
15. Antonio Giustozzi, *Koran, Kalashnikov and Laptop: The Neo-Taliban Insurgency in Afghanistan*, Foundation Books, New Delhi, 2007, p. 13.
16. That Al-Qaeda has a significant presence in Afghanistan and remains close to the Taliban have been reported by UN Monitoring teams. See UN Sanctions Monitoring Team Thirtieth Report, 15 July 2022, p. 16, at https://documents-dds-ny.un.org/doc/UNDOC/GEN/N22/394/29/PDF/N2239429.pdf?OpenElement and UN Sanctions Monitoring Team Thirty-First Report, 13 February 2023, p. 16, at https://documents-dds-ny.un.org/doc/UNDOC/GEN/N23/038/91/PDF/N2303891.pdf?OpenElement (Accessed 24 December 2024).
17. By the terms of the UN Resolution 2593 (2021), adopted by a vote of 13 in favour with two abstentions (Russian Federation and China), the 15-member organ demanded that Afghan territory not be used to threaten or attack any country and reiterated the importance of combating terrorism in Afghanistan.
18. UN Security Council Resolution 1267 was adopted unanimously on 15 October 1999. The Council designated Al-Qaeda chief Osama bin Laden and associates as terrorists. It established a sanctions regime to cover individuals and entities associated with Al-Qaida, Osama bin Laden and/or the Taliban wherever located.
19. Abdul Basit, 'Why Did India Open a Backchannel to the Taliban?' *Al Jazeera*, 7 July 2021, at https://www.aljazeera.com/opinions/2021/7/7/why-did-india-open-a-backchannel-to-the-taliban (Accessed 24 December 2024).

20. Ibid.
21. Don Mclain Gill, 'India, the Taliban, and the Country in Between', *The Diplomat*, 17 October 2022, at https://thediplomat.com/2022/10/india-the-taliban-and-the-country-in-between/ (Accessed 24 December 2024).
22. Sumit Ganguly, 'What the Taliban Takeover Means for India', *Foreign Policy*, 17 August 2021, at https://foreignpolicy.com/2021/08/17/afghanistan-taliban-takeover-india-security-terrorism/ (Accessed 24 December 2024).
23. Vinay Kaura, 'India's Search For a New Role in Afghanistan', Middle East Institute, 8 December 2021, at https://www.mei.edu/publications/indias-search-new-role-afghanistan (Accessed 25 January 2025).
24. Sachin Parashar, 'MEA Team in Afghanistan Oversees Aid Delivery, Engages Taliban; Kabul Seeks Resumption of Indian Projects', *The Times of India*, 3 June 2022, at https://timesofindia.indiatimes.com/india/mea-team-in-af-1st-time-since-india-withdrew-embassy-staff/articleshow/91970632.cms (Accessed 25 January 2025).
25. Ibid.
26. Statement by Ambassador P. Harish, Permanent Representative of India to the UN, at the UN Security Council Meeting on UNAMA, New York, 10 March 2025, at https://pminewyork.gov.in/IndiaatUNSC?id=NTMxMw (Accessed 11 March 2025).
27. Rezaul H. Laskar, 'In a Huge Shift, India Opens Channels with Afghan Taliban Factions and Leaders', *Hindustan Times*, 9 June 2021, at https://www.hindustantimes.com/india-news/in-a-first-india-opens-communication-channels-with-afghan-taliban-factions-101623165405972.html (Accessed 25 January 2024).
28. Vinay Kaura, 'India-Taliban Relations: A Careful Balancing Act, Driven by Pragmatism', Middle East Institute, 30 May 2023, at https://mei.edu/publications/india-taliban-relations-careful-balancing-act-driven-pragmatism (Accessed 25 January 2025).

# 16

# Seven Decades of Indian Aid and Assistance to Afghanistan

*Vishal Chandra*

*The bonds of friendship between Afghanistan and the Indian people, whether in times of their struggle for freedom or thereafter, are a continuation of the history, culture and humanism which the peoples of the two countries have shared from times immemorial.*[1]

**—Afghan Prime Minister Noor Ahmad Etemadi**,
Kabul, 5 June 1969.

*India was and is an important stakeholder in Afghanistan. The special relationship with people of Afghanistan over centuries will guide India's approach. Nothing can change this.*[2]

**—Indian National Security Adviser Ajit Doval**,
Dushanbe, 27 May 2022.

## The Early Decades

The people of Afghanistan have very much been a partner in India's seven-decade long endeavour to strengthen not only the state-to-state but also the people-to-people ties. India's development and assistance programmes in Afghanistan have had a long history. It began with the signing of the 'Treaty of Friendship' between the two countries in New Delhi in January 1950,[3] followed by the 'Treaty of Commerce' in Kabul in April 1950,[4] 'Agreement on Air Services' in Kabul in January 1952, and later, the 'Agreement on Radio Telephonic Communications' in Kabul in March 1961 and the 'Agreement on Cultural Relations' in Kabul in October 1963.

By the early 1950s, Indian vice consulates in Jalalabad and Kandahar and the Afghan consulate general in Bombay (now Mumbai) were functioning. Indian sports teams, artists and musicians were regularly invited to participate in the Afghan *Jashan* or the annual Independence Day celebration, Afghan sports teams would visit India to play friendly matches, and cultural delegations were exchanged. At the request of the Afghan Royal Government, India began to send teachers, particularly English teachers, to the Afghan schools and conduct training courses for the Afghan Air Force personnel at its facilities in India.[5]

India provided equipment and training to set up meteorological and aeronautical communication facilities at Kabul and Kandahar airports. In 1955–56, India deputed an 18-member technical team to help with the installation of meteorological and aeronautical communication facilities in both the cities. India also facilitated the training of Afghan personnel in flight mechanic airframe and flight mechanic engine courses, and in radio technician course as well.[6] This was perhaps the first major capacity building project India had undertaken in Afghanistan.

To assist the nascent Ariana Afghan Airlines, established in 1955, India de-registered four Dakota aircraft, then operating as a private air service in India, for relocation to Afghanistan.[7] By the mid-1950s, India had begun training Afghan personnel in organising small scale and cottage industries, such as handloom and textiles, salt extraction, milk production and distribution, etc. India donated *Ambar Charkha*s to the Afghan Government in 1958 and deputed instructors to train the Afghan personnel in its use. India also welcomed Afghan musicians for training with the All India Radio (AIR) under the Cultural Scholarship Scheme instituted by the Government of India, and other Afghan personnel for training in India under the UN Fellowship Schemes.[8]

Interestingly, during 1955–56, in perhaps the first instance of the two countries extending humanitarian relief to each other, the Afghan Red Crescent Society dispatched clothes for flood victims in India, and the Indian Red Cross Society donated a sum for the flood victims in Afghanistan. In June 1956, India dispatched relief material consisting of 2,800 blankets and 5,000 shirts for the victims of earthquake in Afghanistan.[9]

The two countries entered into a trade arrangement in September 1962, whereby Afghanistan agreed to export fruits (dry and fresh), asafoetida, cumin seeds, hides and skins, and medicinal herbs to India. India on its part agreed to export textiles (cotton, woollen, silk, handloom fabrics, etc.), food products (confectionary, tea, coffee, spices, dried and salted fish, preserved mango and vegetable products, tapioca, cane jaggery, etc.), agricultural products, chemical products and soaps, pharmaceuticals, engineering and electrical goods, household and building requirements, hardware, rubber and leather manufactures, handicraft and cottage industry products, and several other miscellaneous products to Afghanistan.[10] Several of these items are still being traded between the two countries.

In the 1960s, a common policy of non-alignment and Afghanistan's "friendly neutrality" brought India and Afghanistan closer. The signing of the 'Agreement on Cultural Relations' in October 1963 could be regarded as a high point in the early years of the India–Afghanistan relations, for it institutionalised the people-to-people contacts between the two countries for a long time to come.

The 1963 treaty sought to 'further strengthen the ancient cultural bonds between the two countries' by exchanging, teachers, scientists, and members of cultural institutions; instituting fellowships and scholarships for scholars and students; facilitating the training of government employees in scientific, technical and industrial institutions; promoting intellectual exchange and encouraging collaboration between scientific, artistic, literary and other learned societies and organisations; establishing chairs in universities and other institutions of higher learning; and disseminating information through books and periodicals, exhibition of films, and through radio broadcasts.[11] Later, Indian archaeological experts were deputed to work with their Afghan counterparts for the restoration and preservation of the historical monuments in Bamyan.

Soon thereafter, Indian President Dr S. Radhakrishnan paid a five-day state visit to Kabul from 5 June to 10 June 1966. India initiated its second major project in Afghanistan when Indian Vice President Zakir Husain laid the foundation stone for the construction of a 100-bed children's hospital in Kabul during his state visit from 10 July to 15 July 1966. However, the project was delayed due to Pakistan's refusal to provide India with overland transit facility to Afghanistan after the 1965 war. To overcome logistical challenges posed by it, India and Afghanistan worked to further strengthen the air connectivity between the two countries. In addition to the Srinagar–Kabul air service, Indian Airlines launched a weekly air service between Amritsar and Kabul in September 1967. India also deputed pilots and engineers to help Afghanistan improve its domestic air connectivity.[12]

During Prime Minister Indira Gandhi's five-day state visit to Afghanistan from 5 June to 10 June 1969, the two countries decided to set up a ministerial-level joint commission to explore prospects of cooperation in economic, technical and cultural fields. The joint communiqué issued identified scope for collaboration in the fields of irrigation, power, agriculture, small scale industries, education and culture. India agreed to send technical experts to work on small irrigation projects in Afghanistan.[13] Prime Minister Indira Gandhi also visited Bamyan and Salang Pass during her state visit.

During 1968–69, India allocated Rs. 92.5 lakhs for the setting up of the children's hospital in Kabul. India also decided to present agricultural implements worth Rs. 1.7 lakhs to the Afghan Government. India provided jeeps with trailers to assist the Indian irrigation experts conducting surveys in Afghanistan under the Colombo Plan. Training was also provided to Afghan personnel in flying and aircraft maintenance, and a number of Indian teachers and doctors were deputed to Afghanistan.[14] The increased air connectivity received a further boost with the signing of the September 1975 'Trade Treaty' between the two countries.[15] With the change of regime in Kabul following the April 1978 coup, another trade treaty was signed between the two countries.[16]

As stated earlier, the January 1950 'Treaty of Friendship' was followed by a series of treaties as bilateral engagements and with it the people-to-people contacts expanded and deepened. By the 1960s, Afghanistan was among the leading beneficiaries of the exchange programmes administered by the Indian Council for Cultural Relations (ICCR).[17] Similarly, by the 1970s and the 1980s, Afghanistan had emerged as a leading beneficiary of the Indian Technical and Economic Cooperation (ITEC) Programme.[18]

India continued to provide humanitarian assistance, particularly food assistance, to the people of Afghanistan as the country plunged into a civil war in the 1990s. India was among the last countries to vacate its embassy in September 1996, when Kabul first fell to the Taliban forces. Interestingly, the imprint of certain aspects of India's earlier capacity building and aid and assistance programmes can be seen in its post-2001 engagement with Afghanistan and its people.

### Post 2001*

The overthrow of the isolated Taliban regime at the end of 2001 opened avenues of unprecedented international engagement in Afghanistan for the next almost two decades. India formally reopened its embassy on 22 December 2001, the day Hamid Karzai was sworn in as the Chairman of the Afghan Interim Administration. In the following years, India emerged as a leading development partner of Afghanistan, with hundreds of Indian-

* This section has been drawn from the author's recently published monograph on the subject. For a more detailed analysis, see Vishal Chandra, *Afghans in Need: Positing India's Continued Engagement with Afghanistan*, MP-IDSA Monograph Series, No. 88, October 2024, at https://www.idsa.in/publisher/system/files/page/2015/monograph-88.pdf.

sponsored development projects spread across the country. India's development and capacity building projects in Afghanistan were notably broad-based, multi-sectoral, and abidingly people-oriented. India's Afghan outreach traversed the remarkably diverse social–cultural and geographical landscape of the country.

India's engagement in post-2001 Afghanistan can be categorised mainly under five heads: (i) large infrastructure projects; (ii) small community development projects;[19] (iii) capacity building projects, including special scholarship/fellowship and customised training programmes instituted for Afghan students, government officials and professionals; (iv) humanitarian aid and assistance, mainly comprising supply of food grains and lifesaving drugs, and more recently, the India-made COVID vaccines, and also delivery of emergency relief material in times of natural calamities; and (e) promoting Afghan trade through improved connectivity, particularly the development of Shahid Beheshti Terminal at Chabahar Port in Iran and the setting up of the India–Afghanistan Air Freight Corridor.

During 2001–2021, India–Afghanistan relations were also characterised by a regular exchange of high-level visits, including visits by heads of the two states, and consultative mechanisms instituted at various levels. Having committed development assistance worth US$ 3 billion to Afghanistan during the period, India was said to have emerged as the largest regional donor and the fifth-largest donor globally.[20]

### *India's Development and Humanitarian Outreach*

Indian development projects in Afghanistan covered a wide range of critical sectors, including power transmission, hydroelectricity, road construction, agriculture, irrigation, industry, telecommunication, transport, information and broadcasting, education, healthcare, water supply, rural development, and institutional capacity building. It ranged from:

1. Constructing the new Afghan Parliament building[21] in Kabul to supporting the establishment of first of its kind Afghanistan National Agricultural Sciences and Technology University (ANASTU)[22] in Kandahar.
2. Constructing the 218 km Zaranj–Delaram Road, linking the south-western section of Afghanistan's national highway to the Iranian border,[23] to constructing basic health clinics/centres and school buildings across various provinces to providing artificial limbs (or the Jaipur foot) for Afghan amputees from landmine blasts.[24]
3. Renovating, equipping and upgrading the 400-bed Indira Gandhi Institute of Child Health (IGICH)[25] in Kabul to extending financial

assistance to the Afghan Red Crescent Society (ARCS) for the treatment of Afghan children suffering from congenital heart disease (CHD).[26]

4. Constructing the 202 km, 220 kilovolt (kV) double-circuit power transmission line from Pul-e-Khumri to capital Kabul, and a 220/110/20 kV substation at Chimtala,[27] to building multipurpose 42 megawatt Afghan–India Friendship Dam (Salma Dam)[28] in western Afghanistan.
5. Providing regular wheat assistance to augment Afghanistan's food reserves in times of drought to sending millions of doses of India-made COVID vaccines for the Afghan people, including the Afghan refugees in Iran.
6. Donating hundreds of buses for urban transport, utility vehicles for city municipalities and military vehicles for the Afghan National Army to gifting three airbus aircraft to Ariana Afghan Airlines.
7. Restoring telecommunication infrastructure in provinces to expanding national TV network by providing an uplink from Kabul and downlinks in all 34 provincial capitals.
8. Renovating the iconic Habibia School[29] to restoring the historic Stor Palace[30] in Kabul.
9. Digging tube/bore wells and solar electrification in villages to building a cold storage facility in Kandahar.[31]
10. Training Afghan military cadets and officers, including women cadets, to providing scholarships for thousands of Afghan students and professionals at its institutions.

Thus, all along, India was a part of Afghanistan's endeavour to make up for the decades lost to wars and instability. Here it is important to also briefly mention that Indian diplomatic and project personnel often lost their lives to violent attacks by elements opposed to the Indian presence and its development cooperation with the "Islamic Republic of Afghanistan". In a deadly suicide attack on the Indian Embassy in Kabul on 7 July 2008, Indian defence attaché and counsellor were killed along with two Indian security personnel and more than 50 Afghan people waiting for their visa.[32] Similarly, 11 Indian (six in terrorist attacks and five in accident) and 126 Afghan lives were lost during the construction of the 218 km Zaranj–Delaram Road linking the Herat–Kandahar Highway to the Afghanistan–Iran border. The road was said to have reduced the travel time between the two points from about 12–14 hrs to just over two hours.[33]

### *Special Scholarship and Training Programmes*

As stated earlier, India's "people-centric" development projects traversed the geography and demography of the country. The same could be said for India's training and capacity-building programmes, including the ICCR administered Special Scholarship Scheme and the ITEC administered Fellowship Programme for Afghan Nationals implemented since April 2006, and the Department of Agricultural Research and Education (DARE) and the Indian Council for Agricultural Research (ICAR) administered Fellowship Programme for Afghan Nationals since 2010–11, all of which benefitted a cross-section of Afghan students and professionals.

India allocated 1,000 slots per year for Afghan students under the ICCR Special Scholarship Scheme, with additional 500 scholarships for the children/dependents of Afghan military martyrs implemented since 2018–19; 625 slots per year under the ITEC Fellowship Programme; and 614 slots on agricultural studies under the DARE–ICAR India–Afghanistan Fellowship Programme since 2010–11. Another 25 slots were allocated annually to Afghanistan for short-term training programmes under the Technical Cooperation Scheme (TCS) of the Colombo Plan.

India also deputed its civil servants under the UNDP's Capacity for Afghan Public Administration (CAP) Programme to assist in developing the administrative capacities of the various Afghan institutions. India was a major contributor to the World Bank's Afghanistan Reconstruction Trust Fund (ARTF) and the UNDP's National Institution Building Programme (NIBP) in Afghanistan.

Indian foreign ministry's annual report of 2020–21 informed that since 2006, more than 10,000 Afghan students, including 3,000 Afghan women students, had benefitted from the ICCR Special Scholarship Scheme.[34] The annual short-term ITEC training programmes included areas, such as: information technology; communication; English language proficiency; human resource planning and development; geo-informatics; textile mills management; development journalism; women's empowerment; and promotion of micro-enterprises.

By 2018–19, India was annually offering about 3,500 scholarships and training slots to the Afghan nationals and over 15,000 Afghan students were studying in India.[35] Afghan diplomats were also attending training courses at India's Foreign Service Institute (FSI), now Sushma Swaraj Institute of Foreign Service (SSIFS), since early 2002.[36] Just a month before the fall of the Ashraf Ghani government in August 2021, the SSIFS conducted the Eighth Special Course for Diplomats from Afghanistan from 5 July to 17 July

2021. In all, 25 Afghan diplomats, including three women diplomats, participated in it.[37] By July 2021, 218 Afghan diplomats had undergone training courses at SSIFS, New Delhi.[38]

### *'New Development Partnership'*

In September 2017, India and Afghanistan agreed to initiate a 'New Development Partnership' comprising 116 High-Impact Community Development Projects (HICDPs) in critical areas such as education, health, agriculture, irrigation, flood control, micro-hydropower, drinking water, sanitation, renewable energy, rural development, and capacity building. These projects were to be implemented across 31 provinces of Afghanistan. India further agreed to provide grant-in-aid assistance for the following:

- Building the Shatoot Dam that would provide potable drinking water to over 2 million Kabul residents and facilitate irrigation in the neighbouring districts;
- Building a low-cost housing project for the returning Afghan refugees in eastern Nangarhar Province;
- Improving the road connectivity to Band-e-Amir in central Bamiyan Province;
- Building a water supply network for Charikar city in Parwan Province;
- Establishment of a gypsum board manufacturing plant in Kabul; and
- Construction of a polyclinic in Mazar-e-Sharif, capital of northern Balkh Province.

India also agreed to further extend the ICCR Special Scholarship Scheme for Afghan Nationals by another five years (2017–22); initiate the implementation of 500 scholarships for graduate studies in India for the next-of-kin of Afghan military martyrs from the academic year 2018–19; expand the medical assistance for Afghan military personnel; explore ways to strengthen ANASTU, the first agricultural university of its kind in Afghanistan; extend assistance to Afghanistan in applications of remote sensing technology, including in agriculture and resource management; and to host India–Afghanistan Days of Culture to promote cultural and people-to-people contacts.[39]

### *Air Freight Corridor & Chabahar Port Development*

In view of Pakistan's continued intransigence on the issue of extending overland transit facility to India, which had long hampered and undermined prospects of inter and intra-regional trade and connectivity in the region, India and Afghanistan established an Air Freight Corridor in June 2017, connecting

Kabul and Kandahar to New Delhi to leverage the bilateral trade and provide Afghan goods with direct access to the Indian and other South Asian markets.[40] Subsequently, the air corridor was extended to include other Afghan and Indian cities.

By the latter half of 2020, more than 1,000 flights bringing Afghan goods to India had been conducted.[41] The main items of Afghan exports through the air corridor were dried fruits and nuts (mainly, dried raisin, walnut, almond, fig, pine nuts, pistachios and dried apricots); fresh fruits (mainly, pomegranate, apple, apricot, cherry, melon and watermelon); saffron; *heeng* (asafoetida); and medicinal herbs and spices.

At a broader regional level, India has been committed to developing and expanding the capacities of the Chabahar Port, located in the south-eastern Sistan and Baluchestan Province of Iran, as part of its efforts to improve the North–South regional connectivity and trade and provide landlocked Afghanistan and Central Asia with an alternative and a shorter access route to sea. According to a dry run study report published by the Federation of Freight Forwarders' Associations in India, the Chabahar Port is said to be 247 nautical miles (nm) closer than Bandar Abbas to India and 80 km closer to the Afghan border, which reduces the sea and land transport time to Afghanistan.[42]

According to the India Ports Global Limited (IPGL),[43] which is responsible for equipping and operating the Shahid Beheshti Port Terminal at Chabahar, the port is barely 550 nm from the Kandla Port (renamed Deendayal Port) in the western Gujarat State and 786 nm from Mumbai in the western Maharashtra State of India. It is Iran's only oceanic port with direct access to the Arabian Sea and the Indian Ocean. This also means that the port is least likely to be impacted by any challenges posed by developments in the Persian Gulf and the Strait of Hormuz.

On 23 May 2016, Iran, India and Afghanistan entered into a trilateral 'Agreement on the Establishment of an International Transport and Transit Corridor' or the 'Chabahar Agreement'. The agreement was signed in Tehran in the presence of Indian Prime Minister Narendra Modi, Iranian President Hassan Rouhani and Afghan President Ashraf Ghani. India also committed a total grant assistance of $85 million and a credit facility of $150 million for the development of the Shahid Beheshti Terminal at the Chabahar Port. Later, India supplied six mobile harbour cranes (two 140 tonnes and four 100 tonnes capacity) and other equipment worth $25 million.[44]

The key objectives of the Chabahar Agreement were: to 'create a reliable transport corridor for the smooth transport and transit of goods and passengers through Chabahar Port' among the three countries; 'increase the efficiency of the transport corridor aimed at optimizing transport costs'; 'attract transit of goods and passengers of other countries through the international transport and transit corridors'; and 'facilitate access to international markets by using land, sea and/or air transportation through Chabahar Port'.[45]

It was stated in April 2023 that since IPGL took over the operations of the Shaheed Beheshti Terminal at Chabahar in December 2018, India had despatched a total of 2.5 million tonnes of wheat and 2,000 tonnes of pulses through the port to Afghanistan.[46] India sent its first shipment of over 16,308 metric tonnes of wheat through the port to Afghanistan on 29 October 2017 from the Kandla Port.[47] The shipment finally arrived in Afghanistan's western Nimroz Province, bordering Iran, on 11 November.[48] It came just months after India acceded to the Customs Convention on the International Transport of Goods Under Cover of TIR Carnets (TIR Convention) on 15 June 2017.

The first shipment of cargo from Afghanistan under the TIR Convention, routed through the Chabahar Port, arrived at India's Nhava Sheva and Mundra ports on 13 March 2019. It was flagged off on 24 February from Zaranj, capital of Nimroz Province bordering Iran. It was said that the shipment contained 570 tonnes of dried fruits, textiles, carpets and other goods carried by 23 vehicles.[49] Subsequently, Afghanistan sent four more consignments through the Chabahar Port in 2019.[50] In all, Afghanistan shipped almost 700 tonnes of agricultural and mineral products to India through the Chabahar Port in 2019.[51]

According to the Indian foreign ministry's annual report of 2022–23, since December 2018, the IPGL-operated terminal at Chabahar Port had handled 255 vessels, 16,250 twenty-foot equivalent unit of containers and 5 million tonnes of bulk and general cargo from various countries.[52] Besides shipments from India, the port also handled shipments and trans-shipments from Russia, Brazil, Thailand, Germany, France, Ukraine, Oman, Romania, Bangladesh, Australia, Kuwait, Uzbekistan and the United Arab Emirates.[53] Afghanistan's first shipment of dried fruits to Tianjin Port in China and Iran's first shipment of aquatic products to Thailand were sent via the Chabahar Port.[54] The port was integrated with a free trade zone in April 2020.

Prior to it, the joint statement issued at the end of Iranian President Rouhani's visit to New Delhi in February 2018 had stressed on the need to include Chabahar Port within the framework of the International North–South Transport Corridor (INSTC).[55] In March 2021, Indian External Affairs Minister S. Jaishankar proposed the inclusion of the Chabahar Port in the 7,200 km-long multi-modal India–Iran–Russia INSTC, linking the Indian Ocean and the Persian Gulf to the Caspian Sea via Iran and onward to Northern Europe via St. Petersburg in Russia.[56] It basically seeks to provide sea access mainly to the landlocked Central Asian and Eurasian economies (see map below). In March 2021, External Affairs Minister Jaishankar also welcomed Afghanistan and Uzbekistan to join the 13-member INSTC.[57]

**Map 1: Route of Chabahar–INSTC**
(Map not to scale)

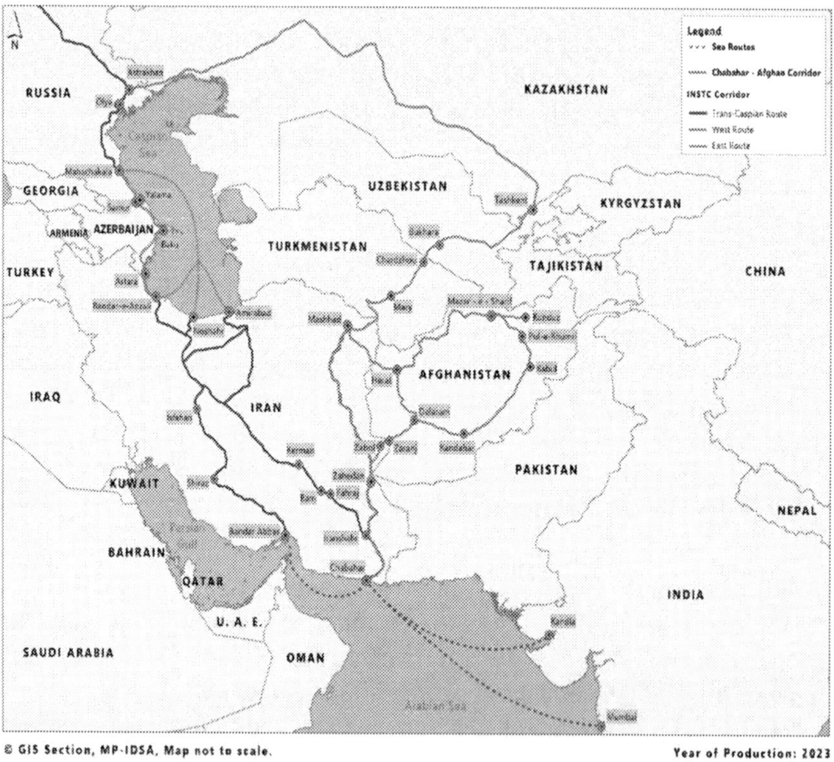


*Source:* GIS Section, MP-IDSA.

### *Bilateral Trade*

The India–Afghanistan bilateral trade crossed US$ 1 billion in 2017–18, with Indian exports to Afghanistan standing at $709.75 million and imports from Afghanistan at $433.78 million. Between 2015–16 and 2019–20, Indian exports to Afghanistan grew by over 89 per cent and imports by 72 per cent.[58] The air freight corridor established in late 2017 contributed to the rise in bilateral trade. The total bilateral trade finally crossed US$ 1.5 billion in 2019–20, with Indian exports standing at US$ 997.58 million and imports from Afghanistan at US$ 529.84 million (for details, see Table 1).

**Table 1: India–Afghanistan Trade: FY 2015–16 to FY 2020–21 (In US$ million)**

| *S. No.* | *Year* | *2015–16* | *2016–17* | *2017–18* | *2018–19* | *2019–20* | *2020–21* |
|---|---|---|---|---|---|---|---|
| 1. | **Export to Afghanistan** | **526.60** | **506.34** | **709.75** | **715.44** | **997.58** | **825.78** |
| 2. | % Growth | 24.62 | -3.85 | 40.17 | 0.80 | 39.43 | -17.22 |
| 3. | **Import from Afghanistan** | **307.90** | **292.90** | **433.78** | **435.44** | **529.84** | **509.49** |
| 4. | % Growth | 17.56 | -4.87 | 48.10 | 0.38 | 21.68 | -3.84 |
| 5. | **Total Trade** | **834.50** | **799.24** | **1,143.53** | **1,150.89** | **1,527.42** | **1,335.27** |
| 6. | % Growth | 21.92 | -4.22 | 43.08 | 0.64 | 32.72 | -12.58 |
| 7. | **Trade Balance** | **218.70** | **213.44** | **275.97** | **280.00** | **467.74** | **316.29** |

*Source*: Data drawn from Country-wise Export Import Data Bank, DGCI&S, Department of Commerce, Ministry of Commerce and Industry, Government of India, at https://www.commerce.gov.in/trade-statistics/.

### *Assistance during Pandemic*

In 2020, during the COVID-19 pandemic, India had undertaken the supply of 5 lakh tablets of Hydroxy-chloroquinine, 1 lakh tablets of Paracetamol, and 50,000 pairs of surgical gloves to the Afghan Government.[59] In February 2021, India supplied 500,000 doses of India-made Covishield vaccine (Serum Institute of India) to help Afghanistan combat the pandemic. It was said that the first stage of mass vaccination in Afghanistan began on 23 February 2021 with the arrival of the Indian vaccine. Another 468,000 doses of India-made Covishield vaccine were supplied by COVAX on 8 March 2021, making Afghanistan the first Central Asian country to receive the vaccine through COVAX.[60] On 1 January 2022, India supplied the second batch of 500,000 doses of India-made COVID vaccine (Covaxin by Bharat Biotech) to Afghanistan.[61] It was sent through Iran's Mahan Air and handed over to IGICH in Kabul.

In November 2020, Indian External Affairs Minister Jaishankar announced the launch of Phase-IV of the Indian community development projects in Afghanistan, which included around 150 projects worth US$ 80 million.[62] It is to be noted that since 2005, three phases of small community-based development projects funded by Indian grants had been implemented. Under Phase I and II implemented during 2005–09, US$ 20 million was provided for undertaking 116 projects. Under Phase III launched in 2012, funding of US$ 100 million was provided for 420 projects of which 350 had been completed.[63]

By the end of 2020, Indian had implemented more than 400 small community development projects spread across Afghanistan, with another 150 such projects planned in the next phase; supplied about 75,000 metric tonnes of wheat (April–September 2020) and more than 20 tonnes of life saving medicines and other equipment, through the Chabahar Port, to assist the Afghan people in addressing the COVID pandemic; and more than 65,000 Afghan students were said to have studied in India.[64] Afghanistan had also opened its second consulate in Hyderabad, in addition to the one in Mumbai, in January 2020.

**Post 2021**

At the time of the regime change in Kabul in August 2021, India had several ongoing development projects spread across the country; several thousands of Afghan nationals were studying on special scholarship/fellowship schemes or were visiting for medical treatment or business purposes in India; and Afghan military officers and cadets were undergoing training at Indian military institutions.

In keeping with its "people-centric" approach towards Afghanistan, India, within weeks of the power shift in Kabul, decided to resume the humanitarian aid and assistance to the Afghan people. In the coming years, as the humanitarian crisis deepened in Afghanistan, India further augmented its humanitarian outreach to its longest standing partner in the country, the people of Afghanistan.

While India had put its grant-in-aid development projects in Afghanistan on hold after the Taliban takeover, it continued with its humanitarian aid and assistance programmes and also special scholarship/fellowship schemes for Afghan students who were already enrolled in Indian educational institutes and were based in India.

India deputed a team of officials and staff at its embassy in Kabul in June 2022 to monitor and coordinate its humanitarian aid and assistance, and in due course, resume its development outreach to the Afghan people. India continued to annually allocate budget of Rs 200 crore (budget estimate) for 'Aid to Afghanistan' and Rs 100 crore for the Chabahar Project; bilateral trade, including through the land route, too continued, and as per the World Bank's reports, India remains the second largest export market for Afghan products; and there are also charter flights, scheduled and non-scheduled, carrying passengers and goods from Afghanistan to India. Recently, India also announced a new visa service for Afghan nationals under six categories—business visa, student visa, medical visa, medical attendant visa, entry visa, and UN diplomat visa.

In perhaps the first official enunciation of India's policy approach towards post-August 2021 Afghanistan, India's External Affairs Minister Jaishankar while speaking at the UN on 13 September 2021 stated that India's approach has always been guided and will continue to be guided by its historical friendship with the people of Afghanistan, and that India is willing to stand by the Afghan people as it has in the past. He identified 'normalisation of regular commercial operations of Kabul airport' and 'efficient logistics' as critical to creating an enabling environment for speedy and effective delivery of relief assistance to the Afghan people. It is essential that 'humanitarian assistance providers are accorded unimpeded, unrestricted and direct access to Afghanistan.' He added that only the UN has the capacity to ensure 'a non-discriminatory distribution of humanitarian assistance across all sections of the Afghan society.'[65]

By early October 2021, India was exploring the possibility of dispatching humanitarian assistance consisting of 50,000 metric tonnes of wheat and essential medical supplies via Pakistan land route to Afghanistan.[66] A bulk of the UN country team was also back by September to coordinate the distribution of humanitarian aid and assistance to the people in Afghanistan. As Pakistan Government continued to drag its feet on the Indian proposal, Acting Taliban Foreign Minister Muttaqi took up the issue with then Pakistan Prime Minister Imran Khan during his visit to Islamabad in November 2021. In his meeting with Imran Khan on 12 November, Muttaqi requested that the Indian wheat be allowed to be transported via Pakistan to Afghanistan. After much delay, Pakistan agreed to briefly allow Indian wheat assistance to be transported via land route to Jalalabad on an exceptional basis. Afghanistan's official state news agency *Bakhtar* stated in January 2022 that the transportation of Indian wheat assistance had to be suspended many times due to Pakistani restrictions.[67] Much of the wheat assistance had to be later transported to Afghanistan through the Chabahar Port.

### *Delhi Declaration*

On 10 November 2021, India hosted Delhi Regional Security Dialogue on Afghanistan in line with its call for 'a unified international response to address the security and humanitarian challenges facing Afghanistan.' The dialogue, third in series, brought together the national security advisors/secretaries of security councils of Iran, Kazakhstan, Kyrgyz Republic, Russia, Tajikistan, Turkmenistan, and Uzbekistan. Pakistan and China refused to participate in the regional dialogue. The first two rounds were hosted by Iran in 2018 and 2019.[68]

The *Delhi Declaration on Afghanistan* issued at the end of the dialogue emphasised that 'Afghanistan's territory should not be used for sheltering, training, planning or financing any terrorist acts'; called for a 'collective cooperation against the menace of radicalization, extremism, separatism and drug trafficking in the region'; noted that the 'United Nations has a central role to play in Afghanistan'; emphasised the importance of 'ensuring that the fundamental rights of women, children and minority communities are not violated'; underlined 'the need to provide urgent humanitarian assistance to the people of Afghanistan'; and reiterated that 'humanitarian assistance should be provided in an unimpeded, direct and assured manner to Afghanistan' and the assistance should be distributed 'in a non-discriminatory manner across all sections of the Afghan society.'[69] In December 2021, India also supported the UN Security Council resolution to grant exemption from sanctions for humanitarian assistance to Afghanistan.

### *First Official Indian Delegation in Kabul*

On 2 June 2022, India for the first time since the Taliban takeover sent a multi-member team to Kabul. It was led by the Joint Secretary of PAI (Pakistan, Afghanistan and Iran) Division in the Indian Ministry of External Affairs, J.P. Singh. According to the ministry's press release, the team was in Kabul to oversee the delivery operations of India's humanitarian assistance to Afghanistan.[70] The Indian delegation visited the Indira Gandhi Institute of Child Health and the Habibia School in Kabul, both renovated by India, and the power substation built by the Power Grid Corporation of India at Chimtala near Kabul.

The visiting Indian delegation met senior members of the Taliban, including Acting Afghan Foreign Minister Amir Khan Muttaqi and Acting Deputy Foreign Minister Sher Mohammad Abbas Stanekzai, to discuss further Indian assistance for the Afghan people. The delegation also met the representatives of international agencies like World Health Organisation and World Food Programme involved in the distribution of Indian humanitarian assistance.[71] According to the *Bakhtar News Agency*, Muttaqi described the visit of the Indian delegation as a "good start" towards the restoration of diplomatic and trade ties 'between the two friendly countries.' He was also said to have stressed on 'India resuming its stalled projects in Afghanistan…and providing consular services to Afghans, primarily for students and travellers.' It was further stated that 'both sides agreed to boost bilateral trade…and work on mutual interests.'[72]

Interestingly, just about a week before, Indian National Security Adviser Ajit Doval in his address at the Fourth Regional Security Dialogue on

Afghanistan, held in Dushanbe on 27 May 2022, had reportedly stressed the need 'to enhance capability of Afghanistan to counter terrorism and terrorist groups which pose a threat regional peace and security'. He was also said to have stated that 'the foremost priority should be the right to life and a dignified living as well as protection of human rights of all the people in Afghanistan'; emphasised 'the need for representation of all sections of Afghan society including women and minorities so that the collective energies of the largest possible proportion of the Afghan population feel motivated to contribute to nation building'; and argued that the 'provision of education to girls and employment to women and youth will ensure productivity and spur growth' and 'have a positive social impact including discouraging radical ideologies among youth.' On India's relationship with Afghanistan, he was said to have stated that 'India was and is an important stakeholder in Afghanistan.' India's 'special relationship with the people of Afghanistan over centuries will guide India's approach' and 'nothing can change this.'[73]

***Indian Technical Team in Kabul***

On 22 June 2022, a massive earthquake hit eastern Afghanistan leading to a huge loss of lives and property, mostly in the provinces of Paktika and Khost. India as a first responder had immediately dispatched two Indian Air Force aircraft with over 27 tonnes of emergency relief assistance consisting of essential supplies, including family ridge tents, sleeping bags, blankets, sleeping mats, etc., for the affected people, in coordination with the UN Office for the Coordination of Humanitarian Affairs and the Afghan Red Crescent Society.[74]

The same day, on 22 June, India deployed a technical team at its embassy in Kabul to 'closely monitor and coordinate the efforts of various stakeholders for the effective delivery of humanitarian assistance' to the Afghan people. The Indian Ministry of External Affairs in its press release stated that India's future approach to Afghanistan will continue to be guided by its 'longstanding links with Afghan society' and 'development partnership including humanitarian assistance for the people of Afghanistan'.[75]

In October 2022, it was reported that the two countries would soon reactivate the air freight corridor and that India would extend technical support to the Afghan Central Bank or *Da* Afghanistan Bank.[76] In November, it was reported that the head of the Indian technical team based in Kabul met the acting Taliban urban development minister and that India may resume work on 20 stalled development projects in various parts of Afghanistan.[77] The Taliban minister was also said to have invited Indian investments in the urban and housing sector, especially in the New Kabul City project.[78]

Interestingly, in March 2023, there were reports about Taliban officials participating, for the first time, in a four-day online ITEC course on 'Immersing with Indian Thoughts,' conducted by the Indian Institute of Management in Kozhikode (IIM–K). The institute confirmed that 18 Afghan participants had attended the online course.[79] The ITEC programme was aimed at facilitating 'a deeper understanding and appreciation of India's business environment' and providing 'participants an opportunity to experience and learn about India's economic environment, regulatory ecosystem, leadership insights, social and historical backdrop, cultural heritage, legal and environmental landscape, consumer mind-sets and business risks.' The programme was said to be open to government officials, business leaders, senior managers and executives from all countries.[80]

### *Indian Participation in Regional Cooperation Conference in Kabul*

India participated in a regional conference hosted by the Taliban-led Afghan Ministry of Foreign Affairs on 29 January 2024. Termed as 'Afghanistan's Regional Cooperation Initiative,' the conference was chaired by Acting Foreign Minister Muttaqi. It brought together special representatives and diplomats of several neighbouring and regional countries, including Russia, China, Iran, Pakistan, Turkmenistan, Kazakhstan, Uzbekistan, Kyrgyzstan, Türkiye and Indonesia, besides India. Muttaqi in his address emphasised the need to establish a 'region-centric narrative' that is 'aimed at developing regional cooperation for a positive and constructive engagement between Afghanistan and regional countries.'[81] In a report posted on the Taliban's official website, the Indian representative at the conference was said to have stated that 'India actively engages in international and regional initiatives concerning Afghanistan, demonstrating its support for all endeavors aimed at promoting stability and development in Afghanistan.'[82]

### *Second Official Indian Delegation in Kabul*

On 7 March 2024, India sent its second official delegation to Kabul, led by then Joint Secretary (PAI) J.P. Singh. The official spokesperson of the Indian Ministry of External Affairs in his weekly media briefing held on 8 March informed that the Indian delegation held meetings with senior members of the Afghan authorities. The delegation also met former President Hamid Karzai and officials of the United Nations Assistance Mission in Afghanistan, and interacted with members of the Afghan business community. The delegation held discussions on India's humanitarian assistance to the people of Afghanistan and the use of Chabahar Port by Afghan traders.[83]

According to the press release issued by the Taliban-led Afghan Ministry of Foreign Affairs, Joint Secretary Singh in his meeting with Acting Foreign

Minister Muttaqi referred to historical ties between the two countries and conveyed India's continued commitment to providing humanitarian assistance to the people of Afghanistan. He was said to have further stated that India seeks to expand 'political and economic cooperation' with Afghanistan and 'enhance trade through Chabahar Port'. Muttaqi expressed gratitude for the humanitarian assistance provided by India and emphasised his government's 'balanced foreign policy' and stated that it wants to 'strengthen political and economic relations' with India. He also urged the visiting senior Indian official to facilitate visa issuance for Afghan businessmen, patients and students.[84]

It was clear from the statement issued and also from the Indian delegation's direct interaction with the Afghan businessmen, first since the return of the Taliban to power, that the emphasis was on promoting bilateral trade through the Chabahar Port. Due to the ongoing tensions with Pakistan, leading to frequent disruptions in Afghan trade through the Pakistani land routes, Kabul had been looking to its west to Iran and its ports, particularly the Chabahar Port, to diversify Afghan trade and transit routes. It is to be noted that on 13 May 2024, India Ports Global Limited and Ports and Maritime Organization of Iran signed a long-term contract for the development of Shahid Beheshti Port Terminal at the Chabahar Port. A year earlier, in November 2013, Acting Taliban Deputy Prime Minister for Economic Affairs Mullah Abdul Ghani Baradar had visited Chabahar during his official visit to Iran. Highlighting the significance of the Chabahar Port for Afghanistan, his office had stated:

> Connecting to Chabahar Port will grant Afghanistan access to markets in Europe, the Middle East, India, and China, thereby strengthening Afghanistan's global relationships. Chabahar Port offers a more efficient route, being tens of kilometers closer than Bandar Abbas and hundreds of kilometers shorter than Karachi Port, resulting in unprecedented reductions in export costs and transit times. Situated strategically, Chabahar Port enables Afghanistan to establish new trade and transit partnerships while connecting to international markets with lower time and cost.[85]

### *Bilateral Trade Post 2021*

After a brief interruption following the collapse of the government in Kabul in August 2021, the trade between the two countries resumed. While the air freight corridor was suspended, Afghan goods, mainly dry and fresh fruits, and medicinal herbs and seeds, continued to arrive via land route at India's Attari integrated check post located on India–Pakistan border in the Amritsar

District of the Indian state of Punjab. It is the only permissible land route for direct trade with Pakistan, which remains suspended since 2019, and for importing goods from Afghanistan to India. In 2023–24, Attari integrated check post was said to have recorded its highest ever import of Afghan goods since its opening in 2012.[86] In July 2024, there were reports of Afghanistan exporting onions from Kunar Province and cherries and apricots from Maidan Wardak Province to India, through the land route via Pakistan.[87]

Indian exporters too reportedly continued to send goods, particularly sugar, via Karachi Port and onward through the land route to Afghanistan. As it was not possible to do business through the Afghan banks, Dubai, where most of the Afghan traders have been based, emerged as the payment hub.[88] Meanwhile, in early May 2022, India also extended the relaxation of fumigation regulations for import of agricultural commodities, including from Afghanistan.

According to trade figures available on the website of the Indian Department of Commerce, Ministry of Commerce and Industry, India's total bilateral trade with Afghanistan stood at $1 billion in 2024–25, with Indian exports to Afghanistan at $319 million and imports from Afghanistan at $690 million. While India's exports to Afghanistan have been declining since 2020–21, imports from Afghanistan have been growing (see Table 2).

**Table 2: India–Afghanistan Trade: FY 2019–2020 to FY 2024–25**

(In US$ million)

| *S. No.* | *Year* | *2019–20* | *2020–21* | *2021–22* | *2022–23* | *2023–24* | *2024–25* |
|---|---|---|---|---|---|---|---|
| 1. | **Export to Afghanistan** | **997.58** | **825.78** | **554.47** | **437.05** | **355.45** | **318.91** |
| 2. | % Growth | 39.43 | -17.22 | -32.85 | -21.18 | -18.67 | -10.28 |
| 3. | **Import from Afghanistan** | **529.84** | **509.49** | **510.93** | **452.81** | **642.29** | **689.81** |
| 4. | % Growth | 21.68 | -3.84 | 0.28 | -11.38 | 41.85 | 7.40 |
| 5. | **Total Trade** | **1,527.42** | **1,335.27** | **1,065.40** | **889.85** | **997.74** | **1,008.72** |
| 6. | % Growth | 32.72 | -12.58 | -20.21 | -16.48 | 12.12 | 1.10 |
| 7. | **Trade Balance** | **467.74** | **316.29** | **43.54** | **-15.76** | **-286.84** | **-370.90** |

*Source*: Data drawn from Country-wise Export Import Data Bank, DGCI&S, Department of Commerce, Ministry of Commerce and Industry, Government of India, at https://www.commerce.gov.in/trade-statistics/.

### *India's Continued Humanitarian Aid and Assistance*

Since 2021, India has provided 50,000 metric tonnes of wheat, 300 tonnes of medical supplies, 100 million polio doses, 1.5 million doses of Covid vaccines, 28 tonnes of disaster relief aid, and 40,000 litres of Malathion pesticide to help fight the locust menace in Afghanistan. India has partnered with the United Nations Office on Drugs and Crime (UNODC) to help in the rehabilitation of the drug-user population in Afghanistan, especially the women drug users. In this regard, India has provided 11,000 units of female hygiene kits that also included baby food, general-use hygiene kits, blankets, clothing, footwear, medical aid and other miscellaneous items. These kits were distributed at the UNODC run drug treatment centres across Afghanistan. India has also supplied 500 units of winter clothing and donated 1.2 tonnes of stationary kits for students at the Habibia School in Kabul which was earlier renovated by India.[89]

Following the meeting held between Indian Foreign Secretary Vikram Misri and Acting Taliban Foreign Minister Muttaqi on 8 January this year in Dubai, India provided further humanitarian assistance to Afghanistan. Most recently, in April 2025, India donated nearly 5 tonnes of life saving vaccines to the Afghan Ministry of Public Health, to help the country prevent and combat rabies, tetanus, hepatitis B, and influenza.[90] In mid-May, India sent food aid packages containing 11 food items, which were distributed by the Kabul Refugee Affairs Directorate to about 5,000 Afghan returnee families.[91] At the end of May, India donated a consignment of 11,000 vital vaccine doses to the Afghan Ministry of Public Health. The consignment included 5,500 doses of influenza vaccine and 5,500 doses of meningitis vaccine.[92]

### *Online Scholarship Scheme for Afghans*

In August 2023, ICCR sought to resolve the lingering issue of visa issuance/extension facing the Afghan students by announcing that from the academic year 2023–24, it will offer 1,000 scholarships annually to Afghan students for various online undergraduate and postgraduate courses at the participating India universities and institutions.[93] According to the Indian foreign ministry's latest annual report of 2024–25, since 2023, the ICCR scholarship scheme has provided online scholarships for 2,000 Afghan students, including 580 female students, through the e-VidyaBharti portal. The report also stated that India continues to offer online scholarships for Afghan students in agriculture related fields in collaboration with ANASTU in Kandahar.[94]

With India's Bureau of Immigration rolling out a new visa service for Afghan citizens end of April this year, which has six categories of visa, including 'student visa' for Afghan ICCR scholarship awardees and for Afghan students admitted in government educational institutes, the issue stands resolved.[95]

***Towards Development Cooperation with Afghanistan***

India has been patiently crafting its political and economic approach towards the Taliban-led Afghanistan. Several rounds of interaction have taken place in the recent months between senior Indian and Taliban foreign officials. The Joint Secretary of PAI Division in the Indian Ministry of External Affairs, J.P. Singh, following his visit to Kabul in March 2024, met Taliban's chief spokesperson Zabihullah Mujahid on the sidelines of the Third UN meeting on Afghanistan held on 30 June and 1 July 2024 in Doha. Mujahid was leading the Taliban delegation to the UN meeting in Doha.

Joint Secretary Singh led another Indian delegation to Kabul a few months later on 4–5 November 2024. Besides meeting Foreign Minister Muttaqi and former President Karzai, he also met Acting Taliban Defence Minster Mullah Mohammad Yaqoob, the son of Taliban's founder Chief Mullah Omar. This was the first such meeting between a senior Indian official and Mullah Yaqoob.

According to the statement issued by the Afghan Ministry of Foreign Affairs, the discussions between Singh and Muttaqi focussed on 'strengthening political & economic relations' and 'facilitating people-to-people movement' of the two countries. Muttaqi, similar to previous meetings, underscored the need for improved visa facilitation for Afghans. He also appreciated India's humanitarian assistance to Afghanistan and acknowledged India's commitments in the development sector. Singh was said to have stated that, in addition to humanitarian aid, 'India has initiated development assistance' and 'is currently engaged in technical discussions with concerned Afghan authorities'. He was also said to have stated that 'technical delegations from the region, including Afghanistan & India, would convene to discuss operational frameworks for the Chabahar Port' in the near future and agreed 'to further facilitate the visa process for Afghans.'[96]

Immediately following Joint Secretary Singh's visit to Kabul, India accepted a Taliban-appointed diplomat, Ikramuddin Kamil, a PhD holder from the New-Delhi-based South Asian University and a deputy director rank official in the Afghan foreign ministry, as the acting Afghan Consul General in Mumbai.[97] Also, a delegation from the Afghanistan Telecommunications Regulatory Authority, led by its Director General Mawlvi Barat Shah Aga Nadeem, visited New Delhi to attend the 25th Meeting of the South Asian Telecommunication Regulators' Council (SATRC-25) held from 11 to 13 November 2024.[98]

Soon thereafter, India's Foreign Secretary Vikram Misri met Acting Afghan Foreign Minister Muttaqi on 8 January 2025 in Doha. The acting

Taliban deputy ministers of commerce and transport were also said to be present in the meeting. According to the press release of the Indian Ministry of External Affairs, Foreign Secretary Misri 'underlined India's historic friendship with the Afghan people' and 'the strong people to people contacts between the two countries,' and 'conveyed India's readiness to respond to the urgent developmental needs of the Afghan people'. The press release stated that 'India would consider engaging in development projects in the near future, in addition to the ongoing humanitarian assistance programme.' It further stated that, in response to the request from the Afghan side, 'India will provide further material support in the first instance to the health sector and for the rehabilitation of refugees' and strengthen sports (cricket) cooperation. The two sides also 'agreed to promote the use of Chabahar port for supporting trade and commercial activities'. The press release ended stating that the Afghan side 'underlined its sensitivities to India's security concerns' and 'agreed to remain in touch and continue regular contacts at various levels'.[99]

The statement put out by the Afghan Ministry of Foreign Affairs stated that Muttaqi referred to India as "a key regional & economic player" and underlined Kabul's desire to strengthen political and economic relations with India. Referring to his government's 'balanced & economy-centric foreign policy,' he assured the Indian side that Afghanistan does not pose a threat to any nation. He expressed gratitude for India's humanitarian assistance and hoped for raising the level of diplomatic relations with India and easing of visa regime for Afghan businessmen, patients and students. It was further stated that Foreign Secretary Misri appreciated the Taliban government's 'efforts in ensuring security, and combating narcotics and corruption in the country' and 'emphasized India's interest in expanding political & economic relations with Afghanistan, and promoting trade through the Chabahar Port'. The statement ended stating that the two sides 'agreed to look into facilitating trade & visa processes'.[100]

Almost four months after Foreign Secretary Misri and Taliban Foreign Minister Muttaqi met in Dubai, the new Joint Secretary of PAI Division in the Indian Ministry of External Affairs, M. Anand Prakash, visited Kabul and met Taliban Foreign Minister Muttaqi on 27 April 2025. His visit to Kabul assumed significance in the light of the Taliban foreign ministry's quick condemnation of the 22 April terrorist attack in Pahalgam in Kashmir in which 26 people were killed. According to the statement issued by the Afghan Foreign Ministry, the two sides held discussions on 'strengthening bilateral political relations,' 'enhancing trade and transit cooperation,' and exchanged views on 'recent regional developments'. Muttaqi highlighted 'the favorable environment for investment in Afghanistan' and 'encouraged Indian investors to seize the existing opportunities'. He also called for the 'normalization of visa issuance processes for businessmen, patients, and students'. Joint Secretary was said to have 'reiterated India's intention to continue its assistance to Afghanistan' and 'conveyed India's interest in investing in infrastructure projects, including the resumption of those initiatives that had been previously halted'. Both sides were said to have stressed on 'enhancing bilateral engagements, streamlining visa procedures, promoting the exchange of delegations, and strengthening cooperation in various fields'.[101]

**Summing Up**

India's humanitarian and development assistance programmes in Afghanistan, including capacity building programmes and small development projects, have evolved over the decades. These programmes were conceptualised and designed to cater to the diverse needs of the Afghan people, spanning the length and breadth of the country. As a result, Indian presence and engagement have mostly spanned a broad spectrum of socio-economic sectors in Afghanistan.

Despite several rounds of attack on Indian diplomatic missions (embassy and four consulates) and project personnel engaged on the ground, which often lead to loss of both Indian and Afghan lives, and various logistical challenges due to Pakistan blocking the overland transit access, India has earlier successfully executed several large infrastructure and small development projects across Afghanistan.

India has been sensitive and adaptive to the local conditions and requirements and has innovatively sustained the people-to-people connect, the most enduring link in the "Indo-Afghan" engagement, and fundamental to India's Neighbourhood First Policy. This is best reflected in India's humanitarian commitments to the people of Afghanistan, post-2021. The Indian leadership has made it clear that India will continue to contribute to non-discriminatory, broad-based efforts to help Afghan people tide over the current crisis.

However, in the current scenario, for Afghanistan to have a sustainable development processes, the Taliban regime will have to adopt a socially inclusive approach to governance at various levels. It first needs to create an enabling environment for a cross section of trained, qualified, and educated Afghan workforce to return and contribute to the growth of the country.

Unlike in the 1990s, both regional countries and the broader international community have decided against abandoning the Afghan people or isolating the Taliban regime. However, the sustainability of such an approach in the long-term would depend on the Taliban regime's willingness to effectively address threat perceptions prevalent in the region, and also its ability to appreciate nuances to state governance and international commitments, and the responsibilities that come with it. It cannot be simply all about having control over the territories and borders of the country and increasing diplomatic footprint across continents.

Meanwhile, with an estimated over two million Afghans having returned from Pakistan and Iran since September/October 2023, and with many more still to follow, the humanitarian crisis in Afghanistan is unlikely to abate soon. In such circumstances, it is all the more incumbent upon the Taliban regime to create conducive environment for the flow of increased aid and assistance to the most vulnerable and neediest among all sections of the Afghan population. Kabul also urgently needs to create an enabling environment for flow of foreign trade and investments.

## NOTES

1. Bakhtar News Agency, Text of Speech by Prime Minister Noor Ahmad Etemadi at the Banquet in Honour of Mrs. Indira Gandhi, the Prime Minister of India, Kabul, 5 June 1969, *The Kabul Times*, Vol. VIII, No. 63, 7 June 1969, pp. 1 and 4, at https://digitalcommons.unomaha.edu/kabultimes/2174/.
2. 'India Important Stakeholder in Afghanistan, Nothing Can Change It: NSA Ajit Doval in Dushanbe', *News 18*, 27 May 2022, at https://www.news18.com/news/india/india-important-stakeholder-in-afghanistan-nothing-canchange-it-nsa-ajit-doval-in-dushanbe-exclusive-5258209.htm (Accessed 2 June 2023); DD News, 'The NSA's of Tajikistan, India, Russia, Kazakhstan, Uzbekistan, Iran, Kyrgyzstan and China Met in Dushanbe', Twitter (now X) Post, 27 May 2022, 10:30 AM, at https://twitter.com/DDNewslive/status/1530051279967629312 (Accessed 2 June 2023).
3. 'Treaty of Friendship between the Government of India and the Royal Government of Afghanistan', 4 January 1950, New Delhi, Ministry of External Affairs, Government of India, at https://mea.gov.in/Portal/LegalTreatiesDoc/AF50B1219.pdf (Accessed 8 April 2023). The Treaty, signed by Indian Prime Minister and Minister for External Affairs Jawaharlal Nehru and Afghan Ambassador to India Nadjibullah Khan, came into force on 30 September 1950.
4. The India–Afghanistan 'Treaty of Commerce' came into force on 24 March 1952. See 'Treaty of Commerce between the Republic of India and the Royal Kingdom of Afghanistan', 4 April 1950, Kabul, Indian Treaty Series, Commonwealth Legal Information Institute, at http://www.commonlii.org/in/other/treaties/INTSer/1950/8.html (Accessed 8 April 2023).
5. Annual Reports of the Ministry of External Affairs, Government of India.
6. Ibid.
7. According to the official website of the Ariana Afghan Airlines, 'An American commercial pilot relocated several war-surplus Dakota Aircraft to Afghanistan, which he had been operating as a private air service in India after the end of World War II.' See 'History of Ariana Afghan Airlines', at https://www.flyariana.com/Corp/history (Accessed 9 April 2023).
8. Annual Reports of the Ministry of External Affairs, Government of India.
9. Ibid.

10. 'India Afghan Trade Arrangement of 1962-63', Ministry of Commerce and Industry, Government of India, 1962, at https://elibrary.sansad.in/server/api/core/bitstreams/47699fdb-9566-4099-bd3e-7596db11e840/view (Accessed 25 July 2025).
11. 'Agreement between the Government of India and the Royal Government of Afghanistan on Cultural Relations', Kabul, 4 October 1963, Ministry of External Affairs, Government of India, at https://mea.gov.in/Portal/LegalTreatiesDoc/AF63B1448.pdf (Accessed 9 April 2023). The treaty came into force on 10 February 1965.
12. Annual Reports of the Ministry of External Affairs, Government of India.
13. Bakhtar News agency, 'Afghan–India Joint Communique' and 'India to Help Afghanistan in Small Irrigation Projects', *The Kabul Times*, Vol. VIII, No. 66, 10 June 1969, at https://digitalcommons.unomaha.edu/kabultimes/2174 (Accessed 20 July 2025).
14. Annual Reports of the Ministry of External Affairs, Government of India.
15. 'Trade Agreement between the Government of India and the Government of the Republic of Afghanistan', 3 September 1975, New Delhi, Indian Treaty Series, at http://www.commonlii.org/in/other/treaties/INTSer/1975/22.html (Accessed 20 April 2023).
16. 'Trade Agreement between the Government of India and the Government of the Democratic Republic of Afghanistan' 24 June 1978, Kabul, Indian Treaty Series, at http://www.commonlii.org/in/other/treaties/INTSer/1978/26.html (Accessed 25 April 2023).
17. The ICCR is an autonomous organisation under the Indian Ministry of External Affairs. The Council was founded on 9 April 1950 by Independent India's first Education Minister Abul Kalam Azad. For the objectives of the Council, see *Indian Horizons*, ICCR, Vol. 62, No. 4, October–December 2015, p. 1, at https://www.iccr.gov.in/sites/default/files/indian%20horizon%20vol%2062%20no.%204%20final.pdf (Accessed 14 May 2023).
18. Instituted on 15 September 1964, the ITEC Programme is the leading capacity building platform of the Indian Ministry of External Affairs. It is administered by the Ministry's Development Partnership Administration (DAP)–II Division, which was established in January 2012. ITEC is essentially bilateral in nature and demand-driven, and it has several components. For details, see 'Capacity Building and Technical Assistance as Development Partnership', Ministry of External Affairs, Government of India, at https://mea.gov.in/Capacity-Building-and-Technical-Assistance-as-Development-Partnership.htm (Accessed 15 September 2023).
19. The MoU for Small Development Projects (SDPs) was signed during Indian Prime Minister Manmohan Singh's state-visit to Afghanistan from 28 to 29 August 2005.
20. Report of Address by H.E. Shaida Abdali, Ambassador of Afghanistan to India, 'Strengthening India-Afghanistan Strategic Relations in an Uncertain World', Brookings India, New Delhi, 25 April 2017, at https://www.brookings.edu/events/india-afghanistan-and-connectivity-in-south-asia-address-by-h-e-shaida-abdali-ambassador-of-afghanistan-to-india/ (Accessed 5 October 2024)
21. The new Afghan Parliament building was jointly inaugurated by Prime Minister Narendra Modi and President Ashraf Ghani on 25 December 2015. It was constructed by India's Central Public Works Department (CPWD). The foundation stone for the new parliament building was laid by former Afghan King Mohammad Zahir Shah during Prime Minister Manmohan Singh's state visit to Afghanistan from 28 to 29 August 2005.
22. The ANASTU, located in Kandahar, was inaugurated on 15 February 2014 by Afghan President Hamid Karzai and Indian External Affairs Minister Salman Khurshid. For details about the Indian assistance to ANASTU, see 'ANASTU: India Furthers Assistance in Southern Afghanistan', Embassy of India, Kabul, 7 February 2015, at https://eoi.gov.in/kabul/?3832?000#:~:text=ANASTU%20was%20inaugurated%20on%2015,Mr (Accessed 6 May 2023).

23. The Zaranj–Delaram Road was built by India's Border Roads Organisation (BRO). It was inaugurated on 22 January 2009 by Indian External Affairs Minister Pranab Mukherjee and Afghan President Hamid Karzai.
24. 'Live with Dignity–Free Artificial Limbs Camp Started in Kabul', Embassy of India, Kabul, Press Release, 18 June 2014, at https://eoi.gov.in/kabul/?3412?000 (Accessed 16 October 2024).
25. The foundation stone for the100-bed children's hospital, initially known as the Institute of Child Health (ICH), in Kabul was laid by Indian Vice-President Dr Zakir Hussain during his visit to Afghanistan from 10 July to 15 July 1966. The institute was formally inaugurated by King Mohmmad Zahir Shah on 12 July 1972 during Indian President V.V. Giri's visit to Afghanistan from 10 July to 14 July 1972. ICH was later renamed as Indira Gandhi Institute of Child Health (IGICH) in 1985.
26. In 2015, India committed grant-in-aid of $5 million ($1 million per year) to ARCS for the treatment of Afghan children suffering from CHD at hospitals in New Delhi. By 2020–21, a total of 2,328 Afghan children had been treated at Indian hospitals. See 'Grant-in-Aid Provided by Govt of India, to Afghan Red Crescent Society, Kabul, Afghanistan for the Treatment of Afghan Children Suffering from Congenital Heart Disease (CHD)', Press Release, Embassy of India, Kabul, 28 February 2021, at https://eoi.gov.in/kabul/?12443?000 (Accessed 16 October 2024).
27. The 202 km, 220 kV double-circuit Pul-e-Khumri–Kabul power transmission line and the 220/110/20 kV substation at Chimtala, north of Kabul, was built by the Power Grid Corporation of India, under an agreement with the India ministry of external affairs signed on 12 August 2005. The transmission line, a part of the 462 km transmission line bringing Uzbek electricity to Kabul, was energised on 20 January 2009. The Chimtala substation was inaugurated by former President Karzai on 18 May 2009. Bharat Heavy Electricals Limited (BHEL) later constructed 220/20 kV substations at Charikar (capital of northern ParwanProvince) and Doshi (in northern Baghlan Province) to service the Pul-e-Khumri–Kabul transmission line.
28. The Afghan–India Friendship Dam, built on Harirud River in western Herat Province, was jointly inaugurated by Prime Minister Narendra Modi and President Ashraf Ghani on 4 June 2016. See 'PM Inaugurates Afghan-India Friendship Dam; WAPCOS Executes Landmark Infrastructure Project', Ministry of Water Resources, Press Information Bureau, Government of India, 4 June 2016, at https://pib.gov.in/newsite/printrelease.aspx?relid=145967 (Accessed 9 October 2024).
29. The renovated building of the Habibia High School in Kabul was jointly inaugurated by Prime Minister Manmohan Singh and President Hamid Karzai on 28 August 2005. The school was originally built by Amir Habibullah Khan (1901–19) in 1903.
30. The historic Stor Palace (also known as the Qasre Storay) in Kabul, originally built in the late nineteenth century, was restored by Agha Khan Trust for Culture in collaboration with India and Afghanistan. The restored palace was jointly inaugurated, via video-conferencing, by Prime Minister Narendra Modi and President Ashraf Ghani on 22 August 2016. The restoration work began in 2013 and was completed in July 2016, employing more than 300 Afghan craftsmen and labourers.
31. The 5,000 tonne-capacity cold storage facility in Kandahar was built by India's Central Warehousing Corporation. It was completed and handed over to the Afghan Ministry of Agriculture in April 2006.
32. 'Terrorist Attacks and Threats on Indians in Afghanistan Since 2003', South Asia Terrorism Portal (SATP), Institute for Conflict Management (ICM), 2018, at https://www.satp.org/satporgtp/countries/india/database/afganistanindianattack.htm (Accessed 17 June 2023).
33. 'India and Afghanistan: A Development Partnership', External Publicity Division, Ministry of External Affairs, Government of India, 2009, at https://mea.gov.in/Uploads/

PublicationDocs/176_india-and-afghanistan-a-development-partnership.pdf (Accessed 20 April 2023).

34. *Annual Report: 2020–21*, Policy Planning and Research Division, Ministry of External Affairs, Government of India, 25 February 2021, p. 163, at https://mea.gov.in/Uploads/PublicationDocs/33569_MEA_annual_Report.pdf (Accessed 26 April 2023).
35. *Annual Report: 2018–19*, Policy Planning and Research Division, Ministry of External Affairs, Government of India, p. 34, at https://mea.gov.in/Uploads/Publication Docs/31719_MEA_AR18_19.pdf (Accessed 26 April 2023).
36. A MoU on mutual cooperation between the FSI, now SSIFS, of the Indian Ministry of External Affairs and the Institute of Diplomacy of the Afghan Ministry of Foreign Affairs was signed on 1 September 2004. It was signed during Afghan Foreign Minister Abdullah Abdullah's official visit to New Delhi from 31 August to 3 September 2004.
37. '8th Special Course for Diplomats from Afghanistan', *Videsh Sewa*, Vol. XI, July–September 2021, p. 4, at https://ssifs.mea.gov.in/?pdf13504?000 (Accessed 28 April 2023).
38. 'Visitors to SSIFS', *Videsh Sewa*, Vol. XI, July–September 2021, p. 8, at https://ssifs.mea.gov.in/?pdf13504?000 (Accessed 28 April 2023).
39. 'Joint Statement on the 2nd Strategic Partnership Council Meeting between India and Afghanistan, New Delhi (September 11, 2017)', Ministry of External Affairs, Government of India, 11 September 2017, at https://mea.gov.in/bilateral-documents.htm?dtl/28936/Joint_Statement_on_the_2nd_Strategic_Partnership_Council_Meeting_between_India_and_Afghanistan_New_Delhi_September_11_2017 (Accessed 7 May 2023).
40. The first cargo flight from Kabul to Delhi was received on 19 June 2017 by Indian External Affairs Minister Sushma Swaraj in the presence of Afghan Ambassador Shaida Mohammad Abdali. It was flagged off from Kabul by President Ashraf Ghani. Subsequently, the first cargo flight from Kandahar to Delhi arrived on 24 June 2017. See 'Establishment of Air Freight Corridor', Ministry of External Affairs, Press Information Bureau, Government of India, 26 July 2017, at https://pib.gov.in/PressReleasePage.aspx?PRID=1497231 (Accessed 18 May 2023).
41. 'Statement by Ambassador T.S. Tirumurti, Permanent Representative of India to the United Nations', Arria Formula Meeting on Afghanistan at the UN Security Council, Permanent Mission of India to the UN, New York, 20 November 2020, at https://pminewyork.gov.in/IndiaatUNSC?id=NDEwNg,, (Accessed 1 April 2023); 'EAM's Remarks at Afghanistan 2020 Conference on 24 November 2020', Ministry of External Affairs, Government of India, 24 November 2020, at https://mea.gov.in/Speeches-Statements.htm?dtl/33235/EAMs_Remarks_at_Afghanistan_2020_Conference_on_24_November_2020 (Accessed 1 December 2020).
42. Shankar Shinde, 'Report on Dry Run Study: Chabahar Agreement with TIR Intermodal', Ministry of External Affairs, Government of India and Federation of Freight Forwarders' Associations in India (FFFAI), 2021, p. 8.
43. The IPGL, a joint venture company formed by Jawaharlal Nehru Port Trust and Kandla Port Trust (renamed Deendayal Port Trust w.e.f. 25 September 2017), is a wholly owned subsidiary of Sagarmala Development Company Limited (SDCL) under the Ministry of Ports, Shipping and Waterways, GoI. IPGL was incorporated on 22 January 2015 under the Indian Companies Act, 2013, as per directions of the ministry, for development of port projects overseas. The ministry has presently assigned IPGL the task of equipping and operating container/multi-purpose terminals at Chabahar.
44. Lok Sabha, 'Status of Chabahar Project', Starred Q No 189, Statement by Minister of External Affairs Dr Subrahmanyam Jaishankar, 10 December 2021, p. 2, at https://sansad.in/getFile/loksabhaquestions/annex/177/AS189.pdf?source=pqals (Accessed 12 October 2024).

45. 'Agreement on the Establishment of an International Transport and Transit Corridor among the Governments of the Republic of India, the Islamic Republic of Afghanistan and the Islamic Republic of Iran (Chabahar Agreement)', Ministry of External Affairs, Government of India, 23 May 2016, at https://mea.gov.in/Portal/LegalTreatiesDoc/016P2941.pdf (Accessed 6 May 2023).The agreement came into effect in July 2018.
46. 'Joint Statement of the First Meeting of the India–Central Asia Joint Working Group (JWG) on Chabahar', Ministry of External Affairs, Government of India, 14 April 2023, at https://www.mea.gov.in/bilateral-documents.htm?dtl/36488/joint+statement+of+the+first+meeting+of+the+indiacentral+asia+joint+working+group+jwg+on+chabahar (Accessed 4 May 2023).
47. The first Indian shipment via Chabahar Port to Afghanistan was flagged off through a joint video conference by Indian External Affairs Minister Sushma Swaraj and Afghan Foreign Minister Salahuddin Rabbani. See 'Flag Off of the First Consignment of Wheat Assistance to Afghanistan through Chabahar Port', Ministry of External Affairs, Government of India, 29 October 2017, at https://www.mea.gov.in/press-releases.htm?dtl/29062/flag+off+of+the+first+consignment+of+wheat+assistance+to+afghanistan+through+chabahar+port (Accessed 20 May 2023); and *Annual Report: 2017–18*, Ministry of Shipping, Government of India, p. 9, at https://shipmin.gov.in/sites/default/files/2017-18%20English.pdf (Accessed 9 December 2023).
48. 'India's First Shipment Arrives in Afghanistan via Chabahar', *Tolo News*, 11 November 2017, at https://tolonews.com/business/india%E2%80%99s-first-shipment-arrives-afghanistan-chabahar (Accessed 30 November 2023).
49. 'Afghanistan Sends First Exports to India via Iran's Chabahar Port', RFE/RL Radio Azadi, 24 February 2019, at https://www.rferl.org/a/afghanistan-first-exports-india-chabahar-iran/29787862.html (Accessed 25 October 2023).
50. Lok Sabha, 'Unstarred Question No. 513: Status of Chabahar Project', Answer by Minister of State V. Muraleedharan, Ministry of External Affairs, Government of India, 20 November 2019, at https://sansad.in/getFile/loksabhaquestions/annex/172/AU513.pdf?source=pqals (Accessed 1 December 2023).
51. 'India–Afghanistan Bilateral Brief', Ministry of External Affairs, Government of India, August 2020, p. 3, at https://www.mea.gov.in/Portal/ForeignRelation/Kabul_2020.pdf (Accessed 30 November 2023).
52. *Annual Report: 2022–23*, Policy Planning and Research Division, Ministry of External Affairs, Government of India, 23 February 2023, p. 101, at https://mea.gov.in/Uploads/PublicationDocs/36286_MEA_Annual_Report_2022_English_web.pdf (Accessed 29 May 2023). Also see, 'Second Trilateral Working Group Meeting between India, Iran and Uzbekistan on Joint Use of Chabahar Port', Ministry of External Affairs, Government of India, 14 December 2021, at https://mea.gov.in/press-releases.htm?dtl/34653/Second_Trilateral_Working_Group_Meeting_between_India_Iran_and_Uzbekistan_on_joint_use_of_Chabahar_Port (Accessed 20 May 2023).
53. *Annual Report: 2021–22*, Policy Planning and Research Division, Ministry of External Affairs, Government of India, 24 February 2022, p. 92, at https://mea.gov.in/Uploads/PublicationDocs/33569_MEA_annual_Report.pdf (Accessed 26 April 2023).
54. *Annual Report: 2020–21*, Policy Planning and Research Division, Ministry of External Affairs, Government of India, 25 February 2021, pp. 82–83, at https://mea.gov.in/Uploads/PublicationDocs/33569_MEA_annual_Report.pdf (Accessed 26 April 2023).
55. 'India–Iran Joint Statement during Visit of the President of Iran to India (February 17, 2018)', Ministry of External Affairs, Government of India, 17 February 2018, at https://www.mea.gov.in/bilateral-documents.htm?dtl/29495/IndiaIran_Joint_Statement_during_Visit_of_the_President_of_Iran_to_India_February_17_2018 (Accessed 4 May 2023).

56. The INSTC basically envisages the movement of goods from Mumbai (India) to Shahid Beheshti Port–Chabahar (Iran) by sea, from Chabahar to Bandar-e-Anzali (an Iranian port on the Caspian Sea) by road, then from Bandar-e-Anzali to Astrakhan (a Caspian port in the Russian Federation) by ship across the Caspian Sea, and thereafter from Astrakhan to other regions of the Russian Federation and further into Europe by Russian railways. See 'Workshop Conducted on "Linking Chabahar Port with INSTC"', Ministry of Ports, Shipping and Waterways, Government of India, 19 January 2023, at https://pib.gov.in/PressReleasePage.aspx?PRID=1892221 (Accessed 4 May 2023).
57. 'Address by External Affairs Minister on "Chabahar Day" at the Maritime India Summit 2021', Ministry of External Affairs, Government of India, 4 March 2021, at https://www.mea.gov.in/Speeches-Statements.htm?dtl/33584/Address_by_External_Affairs_Minister_on_Chabahar_Day_at_the_Maritime_India_Summit_2021 (Accessed 4 May 2023).
58. *Annual Report: 2020–21*, Policy Planning and Research Division, Ministry of External Affairs, Government of India, 25 February 2021, p. 31, at https://mea.gov.in/Uploads/PublicationDocs/33569_MEA_annual_Report.pdf (Accessed 29 May 2023).
59. 'India–Afghanistan Bilateral Brief', Ministry of External Affairs, Government of India, August 2020, p. 6, at https://www.mea.gov.in/Portal/ForeignRelation/Kabul_2020.pdf (Accessed 30 November 2023).
60. Mahnoor Hayat, Mohammad Uzair, Rafay Ali Syed et al., 'Status of COVID-19 Vaccination Around South Asia', *Human Vaccines & Immunotherapeutics*, Vol. 18, Issue 1, 2022, at https://www.tandfonline.com/doi/full/10.1080/21645515.2021.2016010 (Accessed 10 December 2023).
61. 'India Supplies Next Batch of Humanitarian Assistance to Afghanistan', Ministry of External Affairs, Government of India, 1 January 2022, at https://mea.gov.in/press-releases.htm?dtl/34737/India_supplies_next_batch_of_humanitarian_assistance_to_Afghanistan (Accessed 15 May 2023). Also see 'Vaccine Supply', Ministry of External Affairs, Government of India, as on 15 June 2023, at https://www.mea.gov.in/vaccine-supply.htm (Accessed 10 December 2023).
62. 'EAM's Remarks at Afghanistan 2020 Conference on 24 November 2020', Ministry of External Affairs, Government of India, 24 November 2020, at https://mea.gov.in/Speeches-Statements.htm?dtl/33235/EAMs_Remarks_at_Afghanistan_2020_Conference_on_24_November_2020 (Accessed 1 December 2020).
63. *Annual Report: 2022–2023*, Policy Planning and Research Division, Ministry of External Affairs, Government of India, p. 221, at https://mea.gov.in/Uploads/PublicationDocs/36286_MEA_Annual_Report_2022_English_web.pdf (Accessed 22 May 2023).
64. 'EAM's Remarks at Afghanistan 2020 Conference on 24 November 2020', no. 62.
65. External Affairs Minister's Remarks at the United Nations High-Level Meeting on the Humanitarian Situation in Afghanistan 2021', Ministry of External Affairs, Government of India, 13 September 2021, at https://www.mea.gov.in/Speeches-Statements.htm?dtl/34253/External+Affairs+Ministers+remarks+at+the+United+Nations+HighLevel+Meeting+on+the+Humanitarian+Situation+in+Afghanistan+2021 (Accessed 18 September 2021).
66. Sachin Parashar, 'Afghanistan in Food Crisis, India Plans to Send 50,000MT of Wheat', *The Times of India*, 19 October 2021, at https://timesofindia.indiatimes.com/india/afghanistan-in-food-crisis-india-plans-to-send-50000mt-of-wheat/articleshow/87121362.cms (Accessed 17 August 2023).
67. 'Finally, Pakistan Allowed Transmission of 50,000-ton Wheat India's Aid to Afghanistan Through His County', *Bakhtar News Agency*, 23 January 2022, at https://bakhtarnews.af/en/finally-pakistan-allowed-transmission-of-50000-ton-wheat-indias-aid-to-afghanistan-through-his-county/ (Accessed 23 April 2023).

68. 'The Delhi Regional Security Dialogue on Afghanistan (November 10, 2021)', Ministry of External Affairs, Government of India, 8 November 2021, at https://www.mea.gov.in/press-releases.htm?dtl/34489/The_Delhi_Regional_Security_Dialogue_on_Afghanistan_November_10_2021 (Accessed 9 November 2021).
69. 'Delhi Declaration on Afghanistan', Ministry of External Affairs, Government of India, 10 November 2021, at https://mea.gov.in/bilateral-documents.htm?dtl/34491/Delhi_Declaration_on_Afghanistan (Accessed 11 November 2021).
70. 'India's Humanitarian Assistance to Afghanistan', Ministry of External Affairs, Government of India, 2 June 2022, at https://www.mea.gov.in/press-releases.htm?dtl/35381/Indias+humanitarian+assistance+to+Afghanistan (Accessed 2 June 2022).
71. Ibid.
72. 'FM Muttaqi Meets J.P Singh of India', *Bakhtar News Agency*, 2 June 2022, at https://bakhtarnews.af/en/fm-muttaqi-meets-j-p-singh-of-india/ (Accessed 9 May 2023).
73. 'India Important Stakeholder in Afghanistan, Nothing Can Change It: NSA Ajit Doval in Dushanbe', *News 18*, 27 May 2022, at https://www.news18.com/news/india/india-important-stakeholder-in-afghanistan-nothing-canchange-it-nsa-ajit-doval-in-dushanbe-exclusive-5258209.htm (Accessed 2 June 2023); DD News, 'The NSA's of Tajikistan, India, Russia, Kazakhstan, Uzbekistan, Iran, Kyrgyzstan and China Met in Dushanbe', Twitter (now X) Post, 27 May 2022, 10:30 AM, at https://twitter.com/DDNewslive/status/1530051279967629312 (Accessed 2 June 2023).
74. 'Earthquake Relief Assistance for the People of Afghanistan', Ministry of External Affairs, Government of India, 24 June 2022, at https://mea.gov.in/press-releases.htm?dtl/35440/Earthquake_Relief_Assistance_for_the_people_of_Afghanistan (Accessed 15 April 2023).
75. 'Deployment of a Technical Team in Embassy of India, Kabul', Ministry of External Affairs, Government of India, 23 June 2022, at https://www.mea.gov.in/press-releases.htm?dtl/35437/Deployment_of_a_technical_team_in_Embassy_of_India_Kabul (Accessed 24 June 2022).
76. Amina Hakimi, 'Air Corridor Between Delhi and Kabul to Resume Soon: MoCI, *Tolo News*, 31 October 2022, at, https://tolonews.com/index.php/business-180542 (2 November 2022); Dipanjan Roy Chaudhury, 'India "Agrees to Back" Afghanistan Banking Sector with Technical Support', *The Economic Times*, 31 October 2022, at https://economictimes.indiatimes.com/news/india/india-agrees-to-back-afghanistan-banking-sector-with-technical-support/articleshow/95188131.cms?from=mdr (Accessed 10 March 2023); 'India to Provide Technical Support to DAB', *Afghanistan Times*, 26 October 2022, at https://www.afghanistantimes.af/india-to-provide-technical-support-to-dab/ (Accessed 10 March 2023).
77. Nazir Shinwari, 'India to Resume Projects in Afghanistan: MUDH', *Tolo News*, 29 November 2022, at https://tolonews.com/index.php/business-180968 (Accessed 30 November 2022); and 'India May Restart 20 Projects in Afghanistan: Taliban', ANI, 30 November 2022, at https://www.aninews.in/news/world/asia/india-may-restart-20-projects-in-afghanistan-taliban20221130233301/ (Accessed 5 October 2024).
78. 'Indian Urged to Invest in Urban Sector', *Pajhwok Afghan News*, 29 November 2022, at https://pajhwok.com/2022/11/29/indian-urged-to-invest-in-urban-sector/ (Accessed 26 May 2023).
79. '18 Persons from Afghanistan Took Part in MEA Course: IIM-Kozhikode', *The Hindu*, 14 March 2023, at https://www.thehindu.com/news/national/kerala/18-from-afghanistan-took-part-in-mea-course-iim-kozhikode/article66619629.ece (Accessed 16 March 2023).
80. 'Immersing with Indian Thoughts, an India Immersion Program for Cross Sectoral Foreign Delegates', 14–17 March 2023, at https://www.itecgoi.in/view_course_details?salt4=9ca4e930bd4726 (Accessed 15 March 2023).

81. 'IEA – Foreign Minister's Speech at the "Afghanistan's Regional Cooperation Initiative" Conference', Al Emarah, 29 January 2024, at https://www.alemarahenglish.af/iea-foreign-ministers-speech-at-the-afghanistans-regional-cooperation-initiative-conference/ (Accessed 23 April 2024).
82. '"Afghanistan's Regional Cooperation Initiative" Meeting Held in Kabul', Al Emarah, 29 January 2024, at https://www.alemarahenglish.af/afghanistans-regional-cooperation-initiative-meeting-held-in-kabul/ (Accessed 23 April 2024).
83. 'Transcript of Weekly Media Briefing by the Official Spokesperson (March 08, 2024)', Ministry of External Affairs, Government of India, 9 March 2024, at https://www.mea.gov.in/media-briefings.htm?dtl/37694/Transcript_of_Weekly_Media_Briefing_by_the_Official_Spokesperson_March_08_2024 (Accessed 9 March 2024).
84. 'Today, the Special Representative of the Republic of India for Afghanistan, J.P. Singh Called on IEA-Foreign Minister Mawlawi Amir Khan Muttaqi', Ministry of Foreign Affairs, Afghanistan, 7 March 2024, at https://mfa.gov.af/en/16546 (Accessed 8 March 2024).
85. 'Mullah Abdul Ghani Baradar Akhund, Afghanistan's Deputy Prime Minister for Economic Affairs, Conducted an Official Visit to Chabahar Port in Iran on November 9th', Deputy Prime Minister for Economic Affairs, Afghanistan, 9 November 2023, at https://dpmea.gov.af/News14 (Accessed 8 October 2024).
86. Neeraj Bagga, 'ICP Attari Records Highest Ever Import in 2023–24 FY', *The Tribune*, 1 April 2024, at https://www.tribuneindia.com/news/amritsar/icp-attari-records-highest-ever-import-in-2023-24-fy-606485/ (Accessed 19 October 2024).
87. 'First Ever Onion Exports to India Begin from Kunar', Al Emarah, 7 July 2024, at https://www.alemarahenglish.af/first-ever-onion-exports-to-india-begins-from-kunar/ (Accessed 9 July 2024); 'Apricot and Cherry Exports to India Begin From Wardak', Al Emarah, 15 July 2024, at https://www.alemarahenglish.af/apricot-and-cherry-exports-to-india-begin-from-wardak/ (Accessed 7 September 2024).
88. Parthasarathi Biswas, 'Afghan Economy in Tatters, Relations on Hold, Delhi and Kabul Trade via Dubai', *The Indian Express*, 20 May 2022, at https://indianexpress.com/article/india/afghan-economy-in-tatters-relations-on-hold-delhi-and-kabul-trade-via-dubai-7926769/ (Accessed 28 May 2023).
89. *Annual Report: 2024–25*, Policy Planning and Research Division, Ministry of External Affairs, Government of India, 26 June 2025, p. 10, at https://www.mea.gov.in/Images/CPV/140725MEAAnnualReport2024English.pdf (Accessed 25 July 2025); 'Foreign Secretary's Meeting with the Acting Foreign Minister of Afghanistan', Ministry of External Affairs, Government of India, 8 January 2025, at https://www.mea.gov.in/press-releases.htm?dtl/38898/Foreign+Secretarys+meeting+with+the+Acting+Foreign+Minister+of+Afghanistan (Accessed 8 January 2025).
90. 'Afghanistan Receives Life-Saving Vaccines from India to Fight Rabies, Tetanus, Hepatitis B, and Influenza', Ministry of Public Health, Afghanistan, 23 April 2025, at https://www.moph.gov.af/index.php/en/afghanistan-receives-life-saving-vaccines-india-fight-rabies-tetanus-hepatitis-b-and-influenza (Accessed 25 April 2025); 'India Donates Nearly Five Tonnes of Vaccines to Afghanistan', *Afghanistan International*, 23 April 2025, at https://www.afintl.com/en/202504232388 (Accessed 25 April 2025).
91. Ministry of Refugees and Repatriation Affairs of Afghanistan, X (formerly Twitter), 18 May 2025, 9:12 PM, at https://x.com/MoRRAfg/status/1924128528490012901 (Accessed 19 May 2025).
92. Fidel Rahmati, 'India Donates 11,000 Vaccine Doses to Support Afghanistan's Healthcare System', *The Khaama Press*, 30 May 2025, at https://www.khaama.com/india-donates-11000-vaccine-doses-to-support-afghanistans-healthcare-system/ (Accessed 2 June 2025).
93. 'Scholarships for Afghan Nationals for Online Courses for A.Y 2023–24', ICCR, Ministry of External Affairs, Government of India, 25 August 2023, at https://iccr.gov.in/scholar

ships-afghan-nationals-online-courses-ay-2023-24 (Accessed 18 September 2023). The online courses will be conducted under e-VidyaBharati (e-VB), a tele-education network project launched by External Affairs Minister S. Jaishankar in October 2019 and implemented January 2020 onwards, through the iLearn tele-education portal. See 'Guidelines for Awarding Tele-Education Scholarships to Afghan Students', e-VidyaBharati (e-VB) Network Project, Online Higher Education, ICCR, at https://www.ilearn.gov.in/static/static/pics/Afghan_Guidelines.pdf (Accessed 18 September 2023).

94. *Annual Report 2024–25*, Policy Planning and Research Division, Ministry of External Affairs, Government of India, 26 June 2025, p. 32, at https://www.mea.gov.in/Images/CPV/140725MEAAnnualReport2024English.pdf (Accessed 25 July 2025). For ICCR online scholarship slots for Afghan nationals for AY 2024–25, see 'Scholarship Manual: Academic Year 2024–25', ICCR, January 2024, p. 9, at https://a2ascholarships.iccr.gov.in/assets/site/downloads/ICCR_UserManual.pdf (Accessed 12 October 2024).
95. 'Visa for Afghanistan', Bureau of Immigration, Ministry of Home Affairs, Government of India, updated 29 April 2025, at https://indianvisaonline.gov.in/avisa/index.html (Accessed 27 May 2025).
96. 'Indian SPR on Afghanistan Calls on IEA-Foreign Minister', Ministry of Foreign Affairs, Afghanistan, 6 November 2024, at https://mfa.gov.af/en/32994 (Accessed 12 November 2024).
97. 'Islamic Emirate Appoints New Consul General to Mumbai', Al Emarah, 12 November 2024, at https://www.alemarahenglish.af/islamic-emirate-appoints-new-consul-general-to-mumbai/ (Accessed 15 November 2024).
98. Aroon Deep, 'India Hosts South Asian Nations, Including Afghanistan, For Telecom Regulation Event', *The Hindu*, 11 November 2024, at https://www.thehindu.com/news/national/india-hosts-south-asian-nations-including-afghanistan-for-telecom-regulation-event/article68854890.ece (Accessed 15 November 2025).
99. 'Foreign Secretary's Meeting with the Acting Foreign Minister of Afghanistan', Ministry of External Affairs, Government of India, 8 January 2025, at https://www.mea.gov.in/press-releases.htm?dtl/38898/Foreign+Secretarys+meeting+with+the+Acting+Foreign+Minister+of+Afghanistan (Accessed 8 January 2025).
100. 'Foreign Secretary of India Meets IEA-Foreign Minister', Ministry of Foreign Affairs, Afghanistan, 9 January 2025, at https://mfa.gov.af/en/40979 (Accessed 10 January 2025).
101. 'Indian Special Envoy Calls on IEA-Foreign Minister', Ministry of Foreign Affairs, Afghanistan, 28 April 2025, at https://mfa.gov.af/en/18613 (Accessed 29 April 2025).

# Index